FAMILIAR QUOTATIONS

FAMILIAR QUOTATIONS

JOHN BARTLETT

BEING AN ATTEMPT TO TRACE TO THEIR
SOURCE PASSAGES AND PHRASES IN
COMMON USE

AUTHOR'S EDITION

LONDON
GEORGE ROUTLEDGE & SONS, LTD.
BROADWAY HOUSE, CARTER LANE, E.C.

Printed in Great Britain by Butler & Tanner Ltd., Frome and London

NOTE

THE Compiler of this Collection of Familiar Quotations thinks it desirable to say, in introducing the work to the favour of the public, that it is not easy to determine in all cases the degree of familiarity that may belong to phrases and sentences which present themselves for admission ; for what is familiar to one class of readers may be quite new to another.

Many maxims of the most famous writers of our language, and number-less curious and happy turns from orators and poets, have knocked at the door, and it was hard to deny them admission. But to insert these simply on their own merits, without assurance that the general reader would readily recognize them as old friends, was beside the purpose of this Collection.

Still, it has been thought better to incur the risk of erring on the side of fulness.

The great number of Quotations contained in the book has created the necessity for a very copious Index, the largest perhaps ever given in a similar Collection.

It is hoped that the lovers of this agreeable subsidiary literature may find the present Collection satisfy their expectations, not merely in the variety, but in the scrupulous accuracy, of the Quotations cited.

LIST OF AUTHORS

LIST OF AUTHORS.

vi

A*

FAMILIAR QUOTATIONS

GEOFFREY CHAUCER. 1328—1400.

CANTERBURY TALES.

Ed. Tyrwhitt.

WHANNE that April with his shoures sote
The droughte of March hath perced to the rote.

Prologue. Line 1.

And smale foules maken melodie,
That slepen alle night with open eye,
So priketh hem nature in hir corages;
Than longen folk to gon on pilgrimages.

Line 9.

And of his port as meke as is a mayde.

Line 69.

He was a veray parfit gentil knight.

Line 72.

He coude songes make, and wel endite.

Line 95.

Ful wel she sange the service devine,
Entuned in hire nose ful swetely;
And Frenche she spake ful fayre and fetisly.
After the scole of Stratford atte bowe,
For Frenche of Paris was to hire unknowe.

Line 122.

A Clerk ther was of Oxenforde also.

Line 287.

For him was lever han at his beddes hed
A twenty bokes, clothed in black or red,
Of Aristotle, and his philosophie,
Than robes riche, or fidel, or sautrie.
But all be that he was a philosophre,
Yet hadde he but litel gold in cofre.

Line 295.

And gladly wolde he lerne, and gladly teche.

Line 310.

Nowher so besy a man as he ther n' as,
And yet he semed besier than he was.

Line 323.

His studie was but litel on the Bible.

Line 440.

For gold in phisike is a cordial;
Therefore he loved gold in special.

Line 445.

Wide was his parish, and houses fer asonder.   *Line* 493.

This noble ensample to his shepe he yaf,
That first he wrought, and afterwards he taught.   *Line* 498.

But Cristes lore, and his apostles twelve,
He taught, but first he folwed it himselve.   *Line* 529.

And yet he had a thomb of gold parde.[1]   *Line* 565.

Who so shall telle a tale after a man,
He moste reherse, as neighe as ever he can,
Everich word, if it be in his charge,
All speke he never so rudely and so large;
Or elles he moste tellen his tale untrewe,
Or feinen thinges, or finden wordes newe.   *Line* 733.

For May wol have no slogardie a-night.
The seson priketh every gentil herte,
And maketh him out of his slepe to sterte.
                    The Knightes Tale.   *Line* 1044.

Up rose the sonne, and up rose Emelie.   *Ibid.*   *Line* 2275.

To maken vertue of necessite.   *Ibid.*   *Line* 3044.

And brought of mighty ale a large quart.
                    The Milleres Tale.   *Line* 3497.

Yet in our ashen cold is fire yreken.
                    The Reves Prologue.   *Line* 3880.

So was hire joly whistle wel ywette.   *The Reves Tale.*   4153.

And for to see, and eek for to be seye.[2]
                    The Wif of Bathes Prologue.   *Line* 6134.

Loke who that is most vertuous alway,
Prive and apert, and most entendeth ay
To do the gentil dedes that he can,
And take him for the gretest gentilman.
                    The Wif of Bathes Tale.   *Line* 6695.

That he is gentil that doth gentil dedis.   *Line* 6752.

This flour of wifly patience.
                    The Clerkes Tale.   *Pars* v. *Line* 8797.

Fie on possession,
But if a man be vertuous withal.
                    The Frankeleines Prologue.   *Line* 10998.

---

[1] In allusion to the proverb, "Every honest miller has a golden thumb."
[2] Spectatum veniunt, veniunt spectentur ut ipsae.

Ovid, *Art of Love*, I. 99.

CANTERBURY TALES—*continued.*]

Mordre wol out, that see we day by day.
> *The Nonnes Preestes Tale. Line* 15058.

The firste vertue, sone, if thou wilt lere,
Is to restreine, and kepen wel thy tonge.
> *The Manciples Tale. Line* 17281.

For of fortunes sharpe adversite,
The worst kind of infortune is this,
A man that hath been in prosperite,
And it remember, whan it passed is.
> *Troilus and Creseide. Book* iii. *Line* 1625.

One eare it heard, at the other out it went.
> *Ibid. Book* iv. *Line* 435.

The lyfe so short, the craft so long to lerne,
Th' assay so hard, so sharpe the conquering.
> *The Assembly of Foules. Line* 1.

For out of the old fieldes, as men saithe,
Cometh al this new corne fro yere to yere,
And out of old bookes, in good faithe,
Cometh al this new science that men lere.   *Ibid. Line* 22.

Nature, the vicar of the almightie Lord.   *Ibid. Line* 379.

Of all the floures in the mede,
Than love I most these floures white and rede,
Soch that men callen daisies in our toun.
> *The Legend of Good Women. Line* 41.

That well by reason men it call may
The daisie, or els the eye of the day,
The emprise, and floure of floures all.   *Ibid. Line* 184.

—□—

THOMAS À KEMPIS. 1380—1471.

Man proposes, but God disposes.[1]
> *Imitation of Christ. Book* i. *Ch.* 19.

And when he is out of sight, quickly also is he out of mind.
> *Ibid. Book* i. *Ch.* 23.

Of two evils, the less is always to be chosen.
> *Ibid. Book* iii. *Ch.* 12.

---

[1] This expression is of much greater antiquity; it appears in the *Chronicle of Battel Abbey*, page 27 (Lower's Translation), and in *Piers Ploughman's Vision*, line 13,994.

A man's heart deviseth his way; but the Lord directeth his steps. *Proverbs* xvi. 9.

FRANCIS RABELAIS. 1495—1553.

I am just going to leap into the dark.[1]	*Motteux's Life.*
To return to our wethers.[2]	*Book* i. *Ch.* i. *note* 2.
I drink no more than a sponge.	*Ibid.* *Ch.* 5.
Appetite comes with eating, says Angeston.	*Ibid.*

By robbing Peter he paid Paul, ... and hoped to catch larks if ever the heavens should fall.   *Book* i. *Ch.* 11.

I'll go his halves.   *Book* iv. *Ch.* 23.

The Devil was sick, the Devil a monk would be;
The Devil was well, the Devil a monk was he.   *Book* iv. *Ch.* 24.

—□—

THOMAS TUSSER. 1523—1580.

FIVE HUNDRED POINTS OF GOOD HUSBANDRY.

Time tries the troth in everything.   *The Author's Epistle. Ch.* 1.

God sendeth and giveth, both mouth and the meat.
     Good Husbandry Lessons.

The stone that is rolling can gather no moss.   *Ibid.*

Better late than never.[3]   *An Habitation Enforced.*

At Christmas play, and make good cheer,
For Christmas comes but once a year.
     The Farmer's Daily Diet.

Except wind stands as never it stood,
It is an ill wind turns none to good.[3]
     A Description of the Properties of Winds.

All's fish they get
That cometh to net.   *February's Abstract.*

Such mistress, such Nan.
Such master, such man.[4]   *April's Abstract.*

---

[1] Je m'en vay chercher un grand peut-estre.
[2] *Revenons à nos moutons*, a proverb taken from the old French farce of *Pierre Patelin* (ed. 1762, p. 90).
[3] See Proverbs, *post.*
[4] On the authority of M. Cimber, of the Bibliothèque Royale, we owe this proverb to Chevalier Bayard,
     Tel maître, tel valet.

'T is merry in hall
Where beards wag all.[1]   *August's Abstract.*

Look ere thou leap, see ere thou ~o.[2]   *Of Wiving and Thriving.*

Dry sun, dry wind,
Safe bind, safe find.   *Washing.*

—□—

SIR EDWARD COKE.   1549—1634.

The gladsome light of jurisprudence.   *First Institute.*

For a man's house is his castle, *et domus sua cuique tutissimum refugium.*[3]   *Third Institute. Page* 162.

The house of every one is to him as his castle and fortress, as well for his defence against injury and violence, as for his repose.

Semayne's Case, 5 *Rep.* 91.

They (corporations) cannot commit treason, nor be outlawed nor excommunicate, for they have no souls.

Case of Sutton's Hospital, 10 *Rep.* 32.

—□—

MIGUEL DE CERVANTES.   1547—1616.

He had a face like a benediction.   *Don Quixote.   Part* i. *Book* ii. *Ch.* 4.

Every one is the son of his own works.   *Ibid.   Book* iv. *Ch.* 20.

I would do what I pleased, and doing what I pleased, I should have my will, and having my will, I should be contented; and when one is contented, there is no more to be desired; and when there is no more to be desired, there is an end of it.   *Ibid.   Ch.* 23.

Every one is as God made him, and oftentimes a great deal worse.

Part ii. *Ch.* 4.

Now blessings light on him that first invented sleep! it covers a man all over, thoughts and all, like a cloak; it is meat for the hungry, drink for the thirsty, heat for the cold, and cold for the hot.   *Part* ii. *Ch.* 6.

Don't put too fine a point to your wit for fear it should get blunted.

The Little Gypsy.   (La Gitanilla.)

My heart is wax to be moulded as she pleases, but enduring as marble to retain.[4]   *Ibid.*

---

[1] Merry swithe it is in halle,
When the beards waveth alle.
Adam Davie, 1312, *Life of Alexander.*

[2] See Proverbs, *post.*
[3] From the *Pandects, Lib.* ii. *tit.* iv. *De in Jus vocando.*
[4] Cf. Byron, *post.*

BISHOP STILL (JOHN). 1543—1607.

I cannot eat but little meat,
  My stomach is not good;
But sure I think that I can drink
  With him that wears a hood.

                Gammer Gurton's Needle.   *Act* ii.[1]

Back and side go bare, go bare,
  Both foot and hand go cold;
But, belly, God send thee good ale enough,
  Whether it be new or old.   *Ibid.*

—□—

EDMUND SPENSER. 1533—1599.

FAERIE QUEENE.

A gentle knight was pricking on the plaine.

                        Book i. *Canto* i. *St.* 1.

The noblest mind the best contentment has.

                        Book i. *Canto* i. *St.* 35.

A bold bad man.   *Book* i. *Canto* i. *St.* 37.

              Her angels face,
As the great eye of heaven, shyned bright,
And made a sunshine in the shady place.   *Book* i. *Canto* iii. *St.* 4.

Ay me, how many perils doe enfold
The righteous man, to make him daily fall.

                    Book i. *Canto* viii. *St.* 1.

Entire affection hateth nicer hands.   *Book* i. *Canto* viii. *St.* 40.

That darksome cave they enter, where they find
That cursed man, low sitting on the ground,
Musing full sadly in his sullein mind.   *Book* i. *Canto* ix. *St.* 35.

No daintie flowre or herbe that growes on grownd,
No arborett with painted blossoms drest
And smelling sweete, but there it might be fownd
To bud out faire, and throwe her sweete smels al arownd.

                    Book ii. *Canto* vi. *St.* 12.

And is there care in Heaven?   *Book* ii. *Canto* viii. *St.* 1.
Eftsoones they heard a most melodious sound.

                    Book ii. *Canto* xii. *St.* 70.

---

[1] Stated by Mr. Dyce to be from a MS. in his possession, and of older date than *Gammer Gurton's Needle.* — Skelton, *Works,* ed. Dyce, i. vii.—x., *n.*

FAERIE QUEENE—*continued.*]

Through thick and thin, both over bank and bush,
In hopes her to attain by hook or crook.

Book iii. *Canto* i. *St.* 17.

Her berth was of the wombe of morning dew,[1]
And her conception of the joyous prime.

Book iii. *Canto* vi. *St.* 3.

Be bolde, Be bolde, and everywhere, Be bold.

Book iii. *Canto* xi. *St.* 54.

Dan Chaucer, well of English undefyled,
On Fame's eternall beadroll worthie to be fyled.

Book iv. *Canto* ii. *St.* 32.

Who will not mercie unto others show,
How can he mercy ever hope to have?   *Book* vi. *Canto* i. *St.* 42.

What more felicitie can fall to creature
Than to enjoy delight with libertie,
And to be lord of all the workes of Nature,
To raine in th' aire from earth to highest skie,
To feed on flowres and weeds of glorious feature.

The Fate of the Butterfly.   Line 209.

I was promised on a time
To have reason for my rhyme;
From that time unto this season,
I received nor rhyme nor reason.

Lines on his promised Pension.[2]

For of the soul the body form doth take,
For soul is form, and doth the body make.

Hymn in Honour of Beauty.   Line 132.

A sweet attractive kinde of grace,
A full assurance given by lookes,
Continuall comfort in a face
The lineaments of gospel-books.

Elegiac on a Friend's Passion for his Astrophill.[3]

Full little knowest thou that hast not tride,
What hell it is in suing long to bide;
To loose good dayes that might be better spent,
To wast long nights in pensive discontent;

---

[1] The dew of thy birth is of the womb of the morning. *Psalm* cx. 3.
[2] This tradition is confirmed by an entry in Manningham's nearly contemporaneous Diary, May 4, 1602.
[3] This piece was printed in *The Phœnix Nest*, 4to, 1593, where it is anonymous. Todd has shown that it was written by Mathew Roydon.

To speed to-day, to be put back to-morrow;
To feed on hope, to pine with feare and sorrow.
.   .   .   .   .   .
To fret thy soule with crosses and with cares;
To eate thy heart through comfortlesse dispaires;
To fawne, to crowche, to waite, to ride, to ronne,
To spend, to give, to want, to be undonne.
                    Mother Hubberd's Tale.   Line 895.

———□———

SIR WALTER RALEIGH. 1552—1618.

If all the world and love were young,
And truth in every shepherd's tongue,
These pretty pleasures might me move
To live with thee, and be thy love.
          The Nymph's Reply to the Passionate Shepherd.

Silence in love bewrays more woe
     Than words, though ne'er so witty;
A beggar that is dumb, you know,
     May challenge double pity.
          Passions are likened best to Floods and Streams.

Methought I saw the grave where Laura lay.
                    Verses to Edmund Spenser.

O eloquent, just and mightie Death! whom none could advise, thou
hast perswaded; what none hath dared, thou hast done; and whom all
the world hath flattered, thou only hast cast out of the world and despised:
thou hast drawne together all the farre stretchéd greatnesse, all the pride,
crueltie and ambition of men, and covered it all over with these two narrow
words, *Hic jacet!*   *Historie of the World, Book* v. *Pt.* 1, *ad fin.*

Fain would I climb but that I fear to fall.
Written on a pane of glass, in Queen Elizabeth's presence.[1]

———□——

SIR PHILIP SIDNEY. 1554—1586.

Sweet food of sweetly uttered knowledge.
                    The Defence of Poesy.

He cometh unto you with a tale which holdeth children from play, and
old men from the chimney-corner.   *Ibid.*

I never heard the old song of Percy and Douglass, that I found not my
heart moved more than with a trumpet.   *Ibid.*

---

[1] Her reply was,—
          If thy heart fail thee, why then climb at all.

High erected thoughts seated in the heart of courtesy.   *Arcadia. Book* i.

They are never alone that are accompanied with noble thoughts.   *Ibid.*

My dear, my better half.   *Ibid. Book* iii.

> Have I caught my heavenly jewel.[1]
> > *Astrophel and Stella.   Second Song.*

—▢—

LORD BROOKE. 1554—1628.

O wearisome condition of humanity !
> *Mustapha.   Act* v. Sc. 4.

And out of mind as soon as out of sight.[2]   *Sonnet* lvi.

—▢—

CHRISTOPHER MARLOWE. 1565—1593.

WORKS (*Ed. Dyce*, 1862).

Who ever loved that loved not at first sight ?[3]
> *Hero and Leander.*

> Come live with me, and be my love,
> And we will all the pleasures prove
> That hills and valleys, dales and fields,
> Woods or steepy mountains, yields.
> > *The Passionate Shepherd to his Love.*

> By shallow rivers, to whose falls
> Melodious birds sing madrigals.   *Ibid.*

> And I will make thee beds of roses,
> And a thousand fragrant posies.   *Ibid.*

> > When all the world dissolves,
> And every creature shall be purified,
> All places shall be hell that are not heaven.   *Faustus.*

> Was this the face that launch'd a thousand ships,
> And burnt the topless towers of Ilium ?
> Sweet Helen, make me immortal with a kiss.
> Her lips suck forth my soul : see, where it flies !   *Ibid.*

> O, thou art fairer than the evening air,
> Clad in the beauty of a thousand stars.   *Ibid.*

---

[1] Quoted by Shakespeare, *Merry Wives of Windsor, Act* iii. Sc. 3.
[2] Cf. Kempis, *Imitation of Christ, Book* i. Ch. 23.
[3] Quoted by Shakespeare, *As You Like It, Act* iii. Sc. 5.

Faustus—*continued.*]

> Cut is the branch that might have grown full straight,
> And burnèd is Apollo's laurel bough,[1]
> That sometimes grew within this learnèd man.   *Ibid.*

> Infinite riches in a little room.   *The Jew of Malta.*   *Act* i.

> Excess of wealth is cause of covetousness.   *Ibid.*   *Act* i.

Now will I shew myself to have more of the serpent than the dove; that is, more knave than fool.   *Ibid.*   *Act* ii.

> Love me little, love me long.[2]   *Ibid.*   *Act* iv.

—□—

RICHARD HOOKER.   1553—1600.

Of Law there can be no less acknowledged, than that her seat is the bosom of God, her voice the harmony of the world : all things in heaven and earth do her homage, the very least as feeling her care, and the greatest as not exempted from her power.   *Ecclesiastical Polity.*   *Book* i.

That to live by one man's will became the cause of all men's misery.
                                            Ibid.   *Book* i.

—□—

WILLIAM SHAKESPEARE.   1564—1616.

THE TEMPEST.

> I, thus neglecting worldly ends, all dedicated
> To closeness, and the bettering of my mind.   *Act* i. *Sc.* 2.

> Like one,
> Who having, unto truth, by telling of it,
> Made such a sinner of his memory,
> To credit his own lie.   *Act* i. *Sc.* 2.

> My library
> Was dukedom large enough.   *Act* i. *Sc.* 2.

> From the still-vex'd Bermoothes.   *Act* i. *Sc.* 2.

> I will be correspondent to command,
> And do my spriting [3] gently.   *Act* i. *Sc.* 2.

> Come unto these yellow sands,
>   And then take hands :
> Court'sied when you have, and kiss'd—
>   The wild waves whist.   *Act* i. *Sc.* 2.

---

[1] **O,** withered is the garland of the war,
      The soldier's pole is fallen.
                Shakespeare *Antony and Cleopatra, Act* iv. *Sc.* 13.
[2] See Herrick, p. 95.
[3] 'spiriting,' Cambridge ed.

TEMPEST—*continued.*]

Full fathom five thy father lies;
   Of his bones are coral made;
Those are pearls that were his eyes :
   Nothing of him that doth fade,
But doth suffer a sea-change
Into something rich and strange.   *Act* i. *Sc.* 2.

The fringed curtains of thine eye advance.   *Act* i. *Sc.* 2.

There 's nothing ill can dwell in such a temple :
If the ill spirit have so fair a house,
Good things will strive to dwell with 't.   *Act* i. *Sc.* 2.

A very ancient and fish-like smell.   *Act* ii. *Sc.* 2.

Misery acquaints a man with strange bedfellows.

                                   Act ii. *Sc.* 2.

Fer. Here 's my hand.
Mir. And mine, with my heart in 't.   *Act* iii. *Sc.* 1.

He that dies pays all debts.   *Act* iii. *Sc.* 2.

Deeper than e'er plummet sounded.   *Act* iii. *Sc.* 3.

Our revels now are ended. These our actors,
As I foretold you, were all spirits, and
Are melted into air, into thin air :
And, like the baseless fabric of this vision,
The cloud-capp'd towers, the gorgeous palaces,
The solemn temples, the great globe itself,
Yea, all which it inherit, shall dissolve,
And, like this insubstantial pageant faded,
Leave not a rack [1] behind. We are such stuff
As dreams are made on ; and our little life
Is rounded with a sleep. [2]   *Act* iv. *Sc.* 1.

With foreheads villanous low.   *Act* iv. *Sc.* 1.

Deeper than did ever plummet sound,
I 'll drown my book.   *Act* v. *Sc.* 1.

   Where the bee sucks, there suck I ;
   In a cowslip's bell I lie.   *Act* v. *Sc.* 1.

---

[1] 'wreck,' Dyce.
[2] This passage probably owes its origin to the following lines in Lord Stirling's *Tragedie of Darius*, 1604 :—
   Those golden pallaces, those gorgeous halles,
     With fourniture superfluouslie faire;
   Those statelie courts, those sky encountring walles,
     Evanish all like vapours in the aire.

THE TWO GENTLEMEN OF VERONA.

Home-keeping youth have ever homely wits.   *Act* i. *Sc.* 1.

I have no other but a woman's reason : I think him so, because I think
him so.   *Act* i. *Sc.* 2.

O, how this spring of love resembleth
The uncertain glory of an April day !   *Act* i. *Sc.* 3.

And I as rich in having such a jewel
As twenty seas, if all their sand were pearl,
The water nectar, and the rocks pure gold.   *Act* ii. *Sc.* 4.

He makes sweet music with th' enamel'd stones,
Giving a gentle kiss to every sedge
He overtaketh in his pilgrimage.   *Act* ii. *Sc.* 7.

That man that hath a tongue, I say, is no man,
If with his tongue he cannot win a woman.   *Act* iii. *Sc.* 1.

Except I be by Sylvia in the night,
There is no music in the nightingale.   *Act* iii. *Sc.* 1.

A man I am, cross'd with adversity.   *Act* iv. *Sc.* 1.

Is she not passing fair?   *Act* iv. *Sc.* 4.[1]

How use doth breed a habit in a man !   *Act* v. *Sc.* 4.

THE MERRY WIVES OF WINDSOR.

I will make a Star-chamber matter of it.   *Act* i. *Sc.* 1.

All his successors, gone before him, have done 't; and all his ancestors,
that come after him, may.   *Act* i. *Sc.* 1.

It is a familiar beast to man, and signifies love.   *Act* i. *Sc.* 1.

Mine host of the Garter.   *Act* i. *Sc.* 1.

I had rather than forty shillings I had my book of songs and sonnets
here.   *Act* i. *Sc.* 1.

If there be no great love in the beginning, yet heaven may decrease it
upon better acquaintance, when we are married, and have more occasion
to know one another : I hope upon familiarity will grow more contempt.
                                                          Act i. *Sc.* 1.

Convey, the wise it call.   Steal? foh! a fico for the phrase !
                                                          Act i. *Sc.* 3.

Tester I 'll have in pouch, when thou shalt lack,
Base Phrygian Turk !   *Act* i. *Sc.* 3.

The humour of it.   *Act* i. *Sc.* 3.

Here will be an old abusing of . . . . the king's English. *Act* i. *Sc.* 4.

We burn daylight.   *Act* ii. *Sc.* 1.

---

[1] *Act* iv. *Sc.* 2, Dyce.

MERRY WIVES OF WINDSOR—*continued.*]

Faith, thou hast some crotchets in thy head now.   *Act* ii. *Sc.* 1.

Why, then the world 's mine oyster,
Which I with sword will open.   *Act* ii. *Sc.* 2.

This is the short and the long of it.   *Act* ii. *Sc.* 2.

Unless experience be a jewel.   *Act* ii. *Sc.* 2.

I cannot tell what the dickens his name is.   *Act* iii. *Sc.* 2.

What a taking was he in when your husband asked who was in the
basket !   *Act* iii. *Sc.* 3.

O, what a world of vile ill-favour'd faults
Looks handsome in three hundred pounds a year !   *Act* iii. *Sc.* 4.

I have a kind of alacrity in sinking.   *Act* iii. *Sc.* 5.

As good luck would have it.   *Act* iii. *Sc.* 5.

The rankest compound of villanous smell that ever offended nostril.
   Act iii. *Sc.* 5.

A man of my kidney.   *Act* iii. *Sc.* 5.

Think of that, Master Brook.   *Act* iii. *Sc.* 5.

In his old lunes again.   *Act* iv. *Sc.* 2.

They say, there is divinity in odd numbers, either in nativity, chance, or
death.   *Act* v. *Sc.* 1.

MEASURE FOR MEASURE.

Thyself and thy belongings
Are not thine own so proper, as to waste
Thyself upon thy virtues, they on thee.
Heaven doth with us as we with torches do,
Not light them for themselves; for if our virtues
Did not go forth of us, 't were all alike
As if we had them not. Spirits are not finely touch'd,
But to fine issues; nor Nature never lends
The smallest scruple of her excellence,
But, like a thrifty goddess, she determines
Herself the glory of a creditor—
Both thanks and use.   *Act* i. *Sc.* 1.

He was ever precise in promise-keeping.   *Act* i. *Sc.* 2.

I hold you as a thing enskied, and sainted.   *Act* i. *Sc.* 5.[1]

Our doubts are traitors,
And make us lose the good we oft might win,
By fearing to attempt.   *Act* i. *Sc.* 5.[1]

---

[1] *Act* i. *Sc.* 5, White, Singer, Knight. *Act* i. *Sc.* 4, Cambridge Dyce, Staunton.

MEASURE FOR MEASURE—*continued.*]

The jury, passing on the prisoner's life,
May in the sworn twelve have a thief or two
Guiltier than him they try.   *Act* ii. *Sc.* 1.

This will last out a night in Russia,
When nights are longest there.   *Act* ii. *Sc.* 1.

Condemn the fault, and not the actor of it !   *Act* ii. *Sc.* 2

No ceremony that to great ones 'longs,
Not the king's crown, nor the deputed sword,
The marshal's truncheon, nor the judge's robe,
Become them with one half so good a grace
As mercy does.   *Act* ii. *Sc.* 2.

Why, all the souls that were were forfeit once ;
And he that might the vantage best have took
Found out the remedy.   *Act* ii. *Sc.* 2.

          O ! it is excellent
To have a giant's strength ; but it is tyrannous
To use it like a giant.   *Act* ii. *Sc.* 2.

              But man, proud man,
Drest in a little brief authority,
Most ignorant of what he 's most assur'd,—
His glassy essence,—like an angry ape,
Plays such fantastic tricks before high Heaven,
As make the angels weep.   *Act* ii. *Sc.* 2

That in the captain 's but a choleric word,
Which in the soldier is flat blasphemy.   *Act* ii. *Sc.* 2.

          Our compell'd sins
Stand more for number than for accompt.   *Act* ii. *Sc.* 4.

The miserable have no other medicine,
But only hope.   *Act* iii. *Sc.* 1.

Servile to all the skyey influences.   *Act* iii. *Sc.* 1.

Palsied eld.   *Act* iii. *Sc.* 1.

The sense of death is most in apprehension,
And the poor beetle, that we tread upon,
In corporal sufferance finds a pang as great
As when a giant dies.   *Act* iii. *Sc.* 1.

Ay, but to die, and go we know not where ;
To lie in cold obstruction, and to rot ;
This sensible warm motion to become
A kneaded clod ; and the delighted spirit
To bathe in fiery floods, or to reside

MEASURE FOR MEASURE—*continued.*]

In thrilling regions of thick-ribbed ice;
To be imprison'd in the viewless winds
And blown with restless violence round about
The pendent world.   *Act* iii. *Sc.* **1.**

The weariest and most loathed worldly life,
That age, ache, penury, and imprisonment
Can lay on nature, is a paradise
To what we fear of death.   *Act* iii. *Sc.* **1.**

Virtue is bold, and goodness never fearful.   *Act* iii. *Sc.* **1.**

Take, O, take those lips away,
   That so sweetly were forsworn;
And those eyes, the break of day,
   Lights that do mislead the morn;
But my kisses bring again, bring again,
Seals of love, but seal'd in vain, seal'd in vain.[1]
     Act iv. *Sc.* **1.**

Every true man's apparel fits your thief.   *Act* iv. *Sc.* **2.**

   'Gainst the tooth of time,
And razure of oblivion.   *Act* v. *Sc.* **1.**

      My business in this state
Made me a looker-on here in Vienna.   *Act* v. *Sc.* **1.**

They say, best men are moulded out of faults.   *Act* v. *Sc.* **1.**

What's mine is yours, and what is yours is mine.   *Act* v. *Sc.* **1.**

THE COMEDY OF ERRORS.

The pleasing punishment that women bear.   *Act* i. *Sc.* **1.**

A wretched soul, bruised with adversity.   *Act* ii. *Sc.* **1.**

One Pinch, a hungry lean-fac'd villain,
A mere anatomy.   *Act* v. *Sc.* **1.**

A needy, hollow-ey'd, sharp-looking wretch,
A living dead man.   *Act* v. *Sc.* **1.**

---

[1] This song occurs in Act v. Sc. 2, of Beaumont and Fletcher's *Bloody Brother*, with the following additional stanza:—
   Hide, O, hide those hills of snow,
     Which thy frozen bosom bears,
   On whose tops the pinks that grow
     Are of those that April wears!
   But first set my poor heart free,
   Bound in those icy chains by thee.

MUCH ADO ABOUT NOTHING.

He hath indeed better bettered expectation.   *Act* i. *Sc.* 1.

A very valiant trencher-man.   *Act* i. *Sc.* 1.

A skirmish of wit between them.   *Act* i. *Sc.* 1.

The gentleman is not in your books.   *Act* i. *Sc.* 1.

Benedick the married man.   *Act* i. *Sc.* 1.

As merry as the day is long.   *Act* ii. *Sc.* 1.

    Friendship is constant in all other things,
    Save in the office and affairs of love:
    Therefore, all hearts in love use their own tongues:
    Let every eye negotiate for itself,
    And trust no agent.   *Act* ii. *Sc.* 1.

Silence is the perfectest herald of joy: I were but little happy, if I could
say how much.   *Act* ii. *Sc.* 1.

    Sigh no more, ladies, sigh no more,
      Men were deceivers ever;
    One foot in sea and one on shore;
      To one thing constant never.   *Act* ii. *Sc.* 3.

Sits the wind in that corner?   *Act* ii. *Sc.* 3.

Shall quips, and sentences, and these paper-bullets of the brain, awe a
man from the career of his humour? No; the world must be peopled.
When I said I would die a bachelor, I did not think I should live till I
were married.   *Act* ii. *Sc.* 3.

Some Cupid kills with arrows, some with traps.   *Act* iii. *Sc.* 1.

Every one can master a grief, but he that has it.   *Act* iii. *Sc.* 2.

Are you good men and true?   *Act* iii. *Sc.* 3.

To be a well-favoured man is the gift of fortune, but to write and read
comes by nature.   *Act* iii. *Sc.* 3.

Is most tolerable, and not to be endured.   *Act* iii. *Sc.* 3.

The fashion wears out more apparel than the man.   *Act* iii. *Sc.* 3.

Comparisons are odorous.[1]   *Act* iii. *Sc.* 5.

A good old man, sir; he will be talking: as they say, when the age is
in, the wit is out.   *Act* iii. *Sc.* 5.

O, what men dare do! what men may do! what men daily do, not
knowing what they do!   *Act* iv. *Sc.* 1.

---

[1] This expression is to be found also in Burton's *Anatomy of Melancholy*,
Part 3, *Sect.* 3, *Mem.* 1, *Sub.* 2; in Herbert's *Jacula Prudentum*, p. 350
(Pickering's ed. *Vol.* 1); and in Heywood's *A Woman Killed with Kind-
ness*, *Act* i. *Sc.* 1.

MUCH ADO ABOUT NOTHING—*continued.*]

I have mark'd
A thousand blushing apparitions
To start into her face; a thousand innocent shames,
In angel whiteness, bear away those blushes.   *Act* iv. *Sc.* 1.

For it so falls out,
That what we have we prize not to the worth,
Whiles we enjoy it, but being lack'd and lost,
Why, then we rack the value; then we find
The virtue, that possession would not show us,
Whiles it was ours.   *Act* iv. *Sc.* 1.

Th' idea of her life shall sweetly creep
Into his study of imagination.   *Act* iv. *Sc.* 1.

Into the eye and prospect of his soul.   *Act* iv. *Sc.* 1.

Flat burglary as ever was committed.   *Act* iv. *Sc.* 2.

O that he were here to write me down, an ass!   *Act* iv. *Sc.* 2.

A fellow that hath had losses; and one that hath two gowns, and everything handsome about him.   *Act* iv. *Sc.* 2.

Patch grief with proverbs.   *Act* v. *Sc.* 1.

'T is all men's office to speak patience
To those that wring under the load of sorrow,
But no man's virtue, nor sufficiency,
To be so moral when he shall endure
The like himself.   *Act* v. *Sc.* 1.

For there was never yet philosopher
That could endure the toothache patiently.   *Act* v. *Sc.* 1.

Some of us will smart for it.   *Act* v. *Sc.* 1.

I was not born under a rhyming planet.   *Act* v. *Sc.* 2.

Done to death by slanderous tongues.   *Act* v. *Sc.* 3.

LOVE'S LABOUR 'S LOST.

Light, seeking light, doth light of light beguile.   *Act* i. *Sc.* 1.

Small have continual plodders ever won,
  Save base authority from others' books.
These earthly godfathers of heaven's lights,
  That give a name to every fixed star,
Have no more profit of their shining nights
  Than those that walk, and wot not what they are.
      Act i. *Sc.* 1.

And men sit down to that nourishment which is called supper.
      Act i. *Sc.* 1.

LOVE'S LABOUR'S LOST—*continued.*]

That unlettered, small-knowing soul.   *Act* i. *Sc.* 1.

A child of our grandmother Eve, a female; or, for thy more sweet understanding, a woman.   *Act* i. *Sc.* 1.

The world was very guilty of such a ballad some three ages since; but, I think, now 't is not to be found.   *Act* i. *Sc.* 2.

The rational hind Costard.   *Act* i. *Sc.* 2.

Devise, wit! write, pen! for I am for whole volumes in folio.

                                        Act i. *Sc.* 2.

            A merrier man,
Within the limit of becoming mirth,
I never spent an hour's talk withal.   *Act* ii. *Sc.* 1.

Delivers in such apt and gracious words,
That aged ears play truant at his tales,
And younger hearings are quite ravished,
So sweet and voluble is his discourse.   *Act* ii. *Sc.* 1.

By my penny of observation.   *Act* iii. *Sc.* 1.

The boy hath sold him a bargain, a goose, that 's flat.
                                          Act iii. *Sc.* 1.

A very beadle to a humorous sigh.   *Act* iii. *Sc.* 1.

This senior-junior, giant-dwarf, Dan Cupid;
Regent of love-rhymes, lord of folded arms,
Th' anointed sovereign of sighs and groans,
Liege of all loiterers and malcontents.   *Act* iii. *Sc.* 1.

He hath never fed of the dainties that are bred in a book.   *Act* iv. *Sc.* 2.

Dictynna, good-man Dull.   *Act* iv. *Sc.* 2.

These are begot in the ventricle of memory, nourish'd in the womb of *pia mater*, and delivered upon the mellowing of occasion.   *Act* iv. *Sc.* 2.

        For where is any author in the world
Teaches such beauty as a woman's eye?
Learning is but an adjunct to ourself.   *Act* iv. *Sc.* 3.

It adds a precious seeing to the eye.   *Act* iv. *Sc.* 3.

From women's eyes this doctrine I derive:
They sparkle still the right Promethean fire;
They are the books, the arts, the Academes,
That show, contain, and nourish all the world.   *Act* iv. *Sc.* 3.

             As sweet, and musical,
As bright Apollo's lute, strung with his hair;
And when Love speaks, the voice of all the gods
Makes Heaven drowsy with the harmony.   *Act* iv. *Sc.* 3.

LOVE'S LABOUR'S LOST—*continued.*]

He draweth out the thread of his verbosity finer than the staple of his argument. *Act* v. *Sc.* 1.

Priscian a little scratch'd; 't will serve. *Act* v. *Sc.* 1.

They have been at a great feast of languages, and stolen the scraps.
Act v. *Sc.* 1.

In the posteriors of this day, which the rude multitude call the afternoon.
Act v. *Sc.* 1.

> They have measur'd many a mile,
> To tread a measure with you on this grass. *Act* v. *Sc.* 2.

> A jest's prosperity lies in the ear
> Of him that hears it, never in the tongue
> Of him that makes it. *Act* v. *Sc.* 2.

> When daisies pied, and violets blue,
> And lady-smocks all silver white,
> And cuckoo-buds of yellow hue,
> Do paint the meadows with delight. *Act* v. *Sc.* 2.

A MIDSUMMER NIGHT'S DREAM.

> But earthlier happy[1] is the rose distill'd,
> Than that which, withering on the virgin thorn,
> Grows, lives, and dies, in single blessedness. *Act* i. *Sc.* 1.

> Brief as the lightning in the collied night,
> That, in a spleen, unfolds both heaven and earth,
> And ere a man hath power to say, "Behold!"
> The jaws of darkness do devour it up. *Act* i. *Sc.* 1.

> For aught that ever I could read,
> Could ever hear by tale or history,
> The course of true love never did run smooth.[2] *Act* i. *Sc.* 1.

> Love looks not with the eyes, but with the mind,
> And therefore is wing'd Cupid painted blind. *Act* i. *Sc.* 1.

Masters, spread yourselves. *Act* i. *Sc.* 2.

This is Ercles' vein. *Act* i. *Sc.* 2.

I will roar you as gently as any sucking dove: I will roar you, an't were any nightingale. *Act* i. *Sc.* 2.

---

[1] 'earthlier happy,' White, Cambridge, Dyce.
   'earthly happier,' Singer, Staunton, Knight.
[2] The same sentiment, in very different language, has been expressed by Milton in *Paradise Lost ; Book* 10, *line* 896, and following lines.

MIDSUMMER NIGHT'S DREAM—*continued.*]

A proper man, as one shall see in a summer's day.   *Act* i. *Sc.* 2.

And certain stars shot madly from their spheres,
To hear the sea-maid's music.   *Act* ii. *Sc.* 1.[1]

In maiden meditation, fancy free.   *Act* ii. *Sc.* 1.[1]

I 'll put a girdle round about the Earth [2]
In forty minutes.   *Act* ii. *Sc.* 1.[1]

My heart
Is true as steel.   *Act* ii. *Sc.* 1.[1]

I know a bank whereon the wild thyme blows,
Where ox-lips and the nodding violet grows.   *Act* ii. *Sc.* 1.[1]

A lion among ladies is a most dreadful thing.   *Act* iii. *Sc.* 1.

Bless thee, Bottom ! bless thee ! thou art translated.   *Act* iii. *Sc.* 1.

So we grew together,
Like to a double cherry, seeming parted.   *Act* iii. *Sc.* 2.

Two lovely berries moulded on one stem.   *Act* iii. *Sc.* 2.

I have an exposition of sleep come upon me.   *Act* iv. *Sc.* 1.

The lunatic, the lover, and the poet
Are of imagination all compact.   *Act* v. *Sc.* 1.

The lover, all as frantic,
Sees Helen's beauty in a brow of Egypt :
The poet's eye, in a fine frenzy rolling,
Doth glance from heaven to earth, from earth to heaven;
And, as imagination bodies forth
The forms of things unknown, the poet's pen
Turns them to shapes, and gives to airy nothing
A local habitation and a name.   *Act* v. *Sc.* 1

That is the true beginning of our end.   *Act* v. *Sc.* 1

The best in this kind are but shadows.   *Act* v. *Sc.* 1.

The iron tongue of midnight hath told twelve.   *Act* v. *Sc.* 1.

---

[1] *Act* ii. *Sc.* 1, White, Cambridge, Dyce, Staunton. *Act* ii. *Sc.* 2, Singer, Knight.

[2] This expression is also to be found in Champman's *Bussy d'Ambois*, *Act* i. *Sc.* 1 (1607).

THE MERCHANT OF VENICE.

Now, by two-headed Janus,
Nature hath fram'd strange fellows in her time. *Act* i. *Sc.* 1.

Though Nestor swear the jest be laughable. *Act* i. *Sc.* 1.

You have too much respect upon the world:
They lose it, that do buy it with much care. *Act* i. *Sc.* 1.

I hold the world but as the world, Gratiano;
A stage, where every man must play a part,
And mine a sad one. *Act* i. *Sc.* 1.

Why should a man, whose blood is warm within,
Sit like his grandsire cut in alabaster? *Act* i. *Sc.* 1.

There are a sort men, whose visages
Do cream and mantle, like a standing pond. *Act* i. *Sc.* 1.

I am Sir Oracle,
And, when I ope my lips, let no dog bark! *Act* i. *Sc.* 1.

Gratiano speaks an infinite deal of nothing, more than any man in all Venice. His reasons are as two grains of wheat hid in two bushels of chaff: you shall seek all day ere you find them; and when you have them, they are not worth the search. *Act* i. *Sc.* 1.

They are as sick, that surfeit with too much, as they that starve with nothing. *Act* i. *Sc.* 2.

God made him, and therefore let him pass for a man. *Act* i. *Sc.* 2.

Ships are but boards, sailors but men; there be land-rats and water-rats, land-thieves and water-thieves. *Act* i. *Sc.* 3.

I will feed fat the ancient grudge I bear him. *Act* i. *Sc.* 3.

Even there where merchants most do congregate. *Act* i. *Sc.* 3.

The Devil can cite Scripture for his purpose. *Act* i. *Sc.* 3.

A goodly apple rotten at the heart.
O, what a goodly outside falsehood hath! *Act* i. *Sc.* 3.

Many a time and oft,
In the Rialto, you have rated me. *Act* i. *Sc.* 3.

For sufferance is the badge of all our tribe. *Act* i. *Sc.* 3.

In a bondman's key,
With 'bated breath, and whisp'ring humbleness. *Act* i. *Sc.* 3.

It is a wise father that knows his own child. *Act* ii. *Sc.* 2.

MERCHANT OF **VENICE**—*continued.*]

And the vile squeaking of the wry-neck'd fife.   *Act* ii. *Sc.* 5.

All things that are,
Are with more spirit chased than enjoy'd.   *Act* ii. *Sc.* 6.[1]

I am a Jew.   Hath not a Jew eyes? hath not a Jew hands, organs,
dimensions, senses, affections, passions?   *Act* iii. *Sc.* 1.

In law, what plea so tainted and corrupt,
But, being season'd with a gracious voice,
Obscures the show of evil?   *Act* iii. *Sc.* 2.

Thus when I shun Scylla, your father, I fall into Charybdis, your
mother.[2]   *Act* iii. *Sc.* 5.

Let it serve for table-talk.   *Act* iii. *Sc.* 5.

What! wouldst thou have a serpent sting thee twice?
                              Act iv. *Sc.* 1.

The quality of mercy is not strain'd;
It droppeth as the gentle rain from heaven
Upon the place beneath : it is twice bless'd ;
It blesseth him that gives, and him that takes :
'T is mightiest in the mightiest : it becomes
The throned monarch better than his crown:
His sceptre shows the force of temporal power,
The attribute to awe and majesty,
Wherein doth sit the dread and fear of kings;
But mercy is above this sceptred sway;
It is enthroned in the hearts of kings,
It is an attribute to God himself,
And earthly power doth then show likest God's,
When mercy seasons justice.   Therefore, Jew,
Though justice be thy plea, consider this,—
That in the course of justice none of us
Should see salvation : we do pray for mercy,
And that same prayer doth teach us all to render
The deeds of mercy.   *Act* iv. *Sc.* 1.

A Daniel come to judgment!   *Act* iv. *Sc.* 1.

'T is not in the bond.   *Act* iv. *Sc.* 1.

A second Daniel, a Daniel, Jew!
Now, infidel, I have thee on the hip.   *Act* iv. *Sc.* 1.

I thank thee, Jew, for teaching me that word.   *Act* iv. *Sc.* 1.

---

1 *Act* ii. *Sc.* 5, Dyce.
2 Incidis in Scyllam cupiens vitare Charybdim.   Philippe Gaultier (about
the 13th century), *Alexandreis, Book* v, *line* 301.

MERCHANT OF VENICE—*continued.*]

You take my house when you do take the prop
That doth sustain my house; you take my life
When you do take the means whereby I live. *Act* iv. *Sc.* 1.

He is well paid that is well satisfied. *Act* iv. *Sc.* 1

How sweet the moonlight sleeps upon this bank!
Act v. *Sc.* 1.

Look, how the floor of Heaven
Is thick inlaid with patines of bright gold;
There's not the smallest orb which thou behold'st
But in his motion like an angel sings,
Still quiring to the young-eyed cherubins:
Such harmony is in immortal souls;
But, whilst this muddy vesture of decay
Doth grossly close it in, we cannot hear it. *Act* v. *Sc.* 1.

I am never merry when I hear sweet music. *Act* v. *Sc.* 1.

The man that hath no music in himself,
Nor is not mov'd with concord of sweet sounds,
Is fit for treasons, stratagems, and spoils:
The motions of his spirit are dull as night,
And his affections dark as Erebus.
Let no such man be trusted. *Act* v. *Sc.* 1.

How far that little candle throws his beams!
So shines a good deed in a naughty world. *Act* v. *Sc.* 1.

AS YOU LIKE IT.

Well said: that was laid on with a trowel. *Act* i. *Sc.* 2.

My pride fell with my fortunes. *Act* i. *Sc.* 2.

Cel. Not a word?
Ros. Not one to throw at a dog. *Act* i. *Sc.* 3.

O how full of briars is this working-day world! *Act* i. *Sc.* 3.

We'll have a swashing and a martial outside. *Act* i. *Sc.* 3.

Sweet are the uses of adversity,
Which, like the toad, ugly and venomous,
Wears yet a precious jewel in his head;
And this our life, exempt from public haunt,
Finds tongues in trees, books in the running brooks,
Sermons in stones, and good in everything. *Act* ii. *Sc.* 1

The big round tears
Cours'd one another down his innocent nose
In piteous chase. *Act* ii. *Sc.* 1.

B

" Poor deer," quoth he, "thou mak'st a testament
As worldlings do, giving thy sum of more
To that which had too much."   *Act* ii. *Sc.* 1.

Sweep on, you fat and greasy citizens.   *Act* ii. *Sc.* 1.

   And He that doth the ravens feed,
Yea, providently caters for the sparrow,
Be comfort to my age !   *Act* ii. *Sc.* 3.

For in my youth I never did apply
Hot and rebellious liquors in my blood.   *Act* ii. *Sc.* 3.

Therefore my age is as a lusty winter,
Frosty, but kindly.   *Act* ii. *Sc.* 3.

O good old man ! how well in thee appears
The constant service of the antique world,
When service sweat for duty, not for meed !
Thou art not for the fashion of these times,
Where none will sweat, but for promotion.   *Act* ii. *Sc.* 3.

And rail'd on Lady Fortune in good terms,
In good set terms.   *Act* ii. *Sc.* 7.

And then he drew a dial from his poke,
And, looking on it with lack-lustre eye,
Says, very wisely, " It is ten o'clock :
Thus we may see," quoth he, "how the world wags."

            Act ii. *Sc.* 7.

And so, from hour to hour, we ripe and ripe,
And then, from hour to hour, we rot and rot,
And thereby hangs a tale.   *Act* ii. *Sc.* 7.

My lungs began to crow like chanticleer.   *Act* ii. *Sc.* 7.

Motley 's the only wear.   *Act* ii. *Sc.* 7.

   If ladies be but young and fair,
They have the gift to know it : and in his brain,
Which is as dry as the remainder biscuit
After a voyage, he hath strange places cramm'd
With observation, the which he vents
In mangled forms.   *Act* ii. *Sc.* 7.

   I must have liberty
Withal, as large a charter as the wind,
To blow on whom I please.   *Act* ii. *Sc.* 7.

The why is plain as way to parish church.   *Act* ii. *Sc.* 7.

As You Like It—*continued.*]

            All the world 's a stage—
And all the men and women merely players:
They have their exits and their entrances;
And one man in his time plays many parts,—
His Acts being seven ages. At first, the Infant,
Mewling and puking in the nurse's arms.
Then the whining School-boy, with his satchel
And shining morning face, creeping like snail
Unwillingly to school. And then the Lover,
Sighing like furnace, with a woful ballad
Made to his mistress' eyebrow. Then a Soldier,
Full of strange oaths, and bearded like the pard;
Jealous in honour, sudden and quick in quarrel,
Seeking the bubble Reputation
Even in the cannon's mouth. And then the Justice,
In fair round belly with good capon lin'd,
With eyes severe and beard of formal cut,
Full of wise saws and modern instances,—
And so he plays his part. The sixth age shifts
Into the lean and slipper'd Pantaloon,
With spectacle on nose and pouch on side;
His youthful hose well sav'd, a world too wide
For his shrunk shank; and his big manly voice,
Turning again toward childish treble, pipes
And whistles in his sound. Last scene of all,
That ends this strange eventful history,
Is second childishness and mere oblivion;
Sans teeth, sans eyes, sans taste, sans—everything.

Act ii. *Sc.* 7.[1]

    Blow, blow, thou winter wind,
    Thou art not so unkind
      As man's ingratitude.   *Act* ii. *Sc.* 7.

The fair, the chaste, and unexpressive she.   *Act* iii. *Sc.* 2.

Hast any philosophy in thee, shepherd?   *Act* iii. *Sc.* 2.

O wonderful, wonderful, and most wonderful wonderful! and yet again
wonderful, and after that out of all whooping.   *Act* iii. *Sc.* 2.

Every one fault seeming monstrous, till his fellow-fault came to match it.
        Act iii. *Sc.* 2.

Neither rhyme nor reason can express how much.[2]   *Act* iii. *Sc.* 2.

---

[1] "Totus mundus agit histrionem" is said to have been the motto over
the Globe Theatre.
[2] See Proverbs, *post.*

As You Like It—*continued.*]

Truly, I would the gods had made thee poetical.   *Act* iii. *Sc.* 3.

> Down on your knees,
> And thank Heaven, fasting, for a good man's love.

Act iii. *Sc.* 5.

It is a melancholy of mine own, compounded of many simples, extracted from many objects, and, indeed, the sundry contemplation of my travels, in which my often rumination wraps me in a most humorous sadness.

Act iv. *Sc.* 1.

I had rather have a fool to make me merry, than experience to make me sad.   *Act* iv. *Sc.* 1.

Very good orators, when they are out, they will spit.   *Act* iv. *Sc.* 1.

Men have died from time to time, and worms have eaten them, but not for love.   *Act* iv. *Sc.* 1.

Men are April when they woo, December when they wed.

Act iv. *Sc.* 1.

> Pacing through the forest,
> Chewing the food[1] of sweet and bitter fancy.   *Act* iv. *Sc.* 3.

No sooner met, but they looked; no sooner looked, but they loved; no sooner loved, but they sighed; no sooner sighed, but they asked one another the reason.   *Act* v. *Sc.* 2.

How bitter a thing it is to look into happiness through another man's eyes!   *Act* v. *Sc.* 2.

An ill-favoured thing, sir, but mine own.   *Act* v. *Sc.* 4.

The Retort Courteous. . . . . Lie Circumstantial, and the Lie Direct.

Act v. *Sc.* 4.

Your *If* is the only peacemaker; much virtue in *If*.   *Act* v. *Sc.* 4.

Good wine needs no bush.   *Epilogue.*

THE TAMING OF THE SHREW

> As Stephen Sly, and old John Naps of Greece,
> And Peter Turf, and Henry Pimpernell;
> And twenty more such names and men as these,
> Which never were, nor no man ever saw.   *Induction*, *Sc.* 2.

> No profit grows where is no pleasure ta'en;
> In brief, sir, study what you most affect.   *Act* i. *Sc.* 1.

There's small choice in rotten apples.   *Act* i. *Sc.* 1.

---

[1] 'cud,' Dyce, Staunton.

The Taming of the Shrew—*continued.*]

Tush! tush! fear boys with bugs.	*Act* i. *Sc.* 2.
And do as adversaries do in law,—	
Strive mightily, but eat and drink as friends.	*Act* i. *Sc.* 2.
And thereby hangs a tale.[1]	*Act* iv. *Sc.* 1.
My cake is dough.	*Act* v. *Sc.* 1.
Intolerable, not to be endured.	*Act* v. *Sc.* 2.
A woman mov'd is like a fountain troubled,	
Muddy, ill-seeming, thick, bereft of beauty.	*Act* v. *Sc.* 2.
Such duty as the subject owes the prince,	
Even such a woman oweth to her husband.	*Act* v. *Sc.* 2.

ALL 'S WELL THAT ENDS WELL.

It were all one	
That I should love a bright particular star,	
And think to wed it.	*Act* i. *Sc.* 1.
The hind that would be mated by the lion	
Must die for love.	*Act* i. *Sc.* 1.
Our remedies oft in ourselves do lie,	
Which we ascribe to Heaven.	*Act* i. *Sc.* 1.
He must needs go that the Devil drives.	*Act* i. *Sc.* 3.
My friends were poor but honest.	*Act* i. *Sc.* 3.
Oft expectation fails, and most oft there	
Where most it promises.	*Act* ii. *Sc.* 1.
I will show myself highly fed, and lowly taught.	*Act* ii. *Sc.* 2.
From lowest place when virtuous things proceed,	
The place is dignified by th' doer's deed.	*Act* ii. *Sc.* 3.
The web of our life is of a mingled yarn, good and ill together.	
	Act iv. *Sc.* 3.
Whose words all ears took captive.	*Act* v. *Sc.* 3.
Praising what is lost	
Makes the remembrance dear.	*Act* v. *Sc.* 3.
The inaudible and noiseless foot of Time.	*Act* v. *Sc.* 3.
All impediments in fancy's course	
Are motives of more fancy.	*Act* v. *Sc.* 3.

---

[1] Othello, Act iii. Sc. 1.   Merry Wives of Windsor, Act i. Sc. 4.   As You Like It, Act ii. Sc. 7.

TWELFTH NIGHT.

If music be the food of love, play on;
Give me excess of it, that, surfeiting,
The appetite may sicken, and so die.
That strain again; it had a dying fall:
O, it came o'er my ear like the sweet south,
That breathes upon a bank of violets,
Stealing and giving odour.   *Act* i. *Sc.* 1.

I am sure care's an enemy to life.   *Act* i. *Sc.* 3.

'T is beauty truly blent, whose red and white
Nature's own sweet and cunning hand laid on.   *Act* i. *Sc.* 5.

Journeys end in lovers' meeting
Every wise man's son doth know.   *Act* ii. *Sc.* 3.

He does it with a better grace, but I do it more natural.   *Act* ii. *Sc.* 3.

Sir To. Dost thou think, because thou art virtuous, there shall be no more cakes and ale?
Clo. Yes, by Saint Anne; and ginger shall be hot i' the mouth too.
                       Act ii. *Sc.* 3.

Let still the woman take
An elder than herself : so wears she to him,
So sways she level in her husband's heart,
For, boy, however we do praise ourselves,
Our fancies are more giddy and unfirm,
More longing, wavering, sooner lost and won,
Than women's are.   *Act* ii. *Sc.* 4.

And dallies with the innocence of love,
Like the old age.   *Act* ii. *Sc.* 4.

She never told her love;
But let concealment, like a worm i' the bud,
Feed on her damask cheek : she pined in thought;
And, with a green and yellow melancholy,
She sat, like Patience on a monument,
Smiling at grief.   *Act* ii. *Sc.* 4.

I am all the daughters of my father's house,
And all the brothers too.   *Act* ii. *Sc.* 4.

An you had any eye behind you, you might see more detraction at your heels than fortune before you.   *Act* ii. *Sc.* 5.

Some are born great, some achieve greatness, and some have greatness thrust upon them.   *Act* ii. *Sc.* 5.

O, what a deal of scorn looks beautiful
In the contempt and anger of his lip!   *Act* iii. *Sc.* 1.

TWELFTH NIGHT—*continued.*]

Love sought is good, but given unsought is better.   *Act* iii. *Sc.* 1.

Let there be gall enough in thy ink; though thou write with a goose-pen, no matter.   *Act* iii. *Sc.* 2.

Why, this is very Midsummer madness.   *Act* iii. *Sc.* 4.

Still you keep o' the windy side of the law.   *Act* iii. *Sc.* 4.

An I thought he had been valiant, and so cunning in fence, I 'd have seen him damned ere I 'd have challenged him.   *Act* iii. *Sc.* 4.[1]

Clo.   What is the opinion of Pythagoras concerning wild-fowl?
Mal.   That the soul of our grandam might haply inhabit a bird.
Clo.   What thinkest thou of his opinion?
Mal.   I think nobly of the soul, and no way approve his opinion.
   Act iv. *Sc.* 2.

Thus the whirligig of Time brings in his revenges.   *Act* v. *Sc.* 1.

THE WINTER'S TALE.

A snapper-up of unconsidered trifles.   *Act* iv. *Sc.* 2.

> A merry heart goes all the day,
>   Your sad tires in a mile-a.   *Act* iv. *Sc.* 2.

>   Daffodils,
> That come before the swallow dares, and take
> The winds of March with beauty; violets, dim,
> But sweeter than the lids of Juno's eyes,
> Or Cytherea's breath.   *Act* iv. *Sc.* 3.[2]

>   When you do dance, I wish you
> A wave o' th' sea, that you might ever do
> Nothing but that.   *Act* iv. *Sc.* 3.[2]

KING JOHN.

Lord of thy presence, and no land beside.   *Act* i. *Sc.* 1.

And if his name be George, I 'll call him Peter;
For new-made honour doth forget men's names.   *Act* i. *Sc.* 1.

For he is but a bastard to the time,
That doth not smack of observation.   *Act* i. *Sc.* 1.

Sweet, sweet, sweet poison for the age's tooth.   *Act* i. *Sc.* 1.

For courage mounteth with occasion.   *Act* ii. *Sc.* 1.

----

[1] *Sc.* 5, Dyce.   [2] *Sc.* 4, Cambridge ed.

KING JOHN—*continued.*]

I would that I were low laid in my grave;
I am not worth this coil that 's made for me. *Act* ii. *Sc.* 1.

St. George, that swinged the dragon, and e'er since
Sits on his horseback at mine hostess' door. *Act* ii. *Sc.* 1.

Talks as familiarly of roaring lions,
As maids of thirteen do of puppy-dogs! *Act* ii. *Sc.* 2.[1]

Here I and sorrows sit;
Here is my throne; bid kings come bow to it. *Act* iii. *Sc.* 1.[2]

Thou slave, thou wretch, thou coward;
Thou little valiant, great in villany!
Thou ever strong upon the stronger side!
Thou Fortune's champion, that dost never fight
But when her humorous ladyship is by
To teach thee safety! *Act* iii. *Sc.* 1.

Thou wear a lion's hide! doff it for shame,
And hang a calf's-skin on those recreant limbs. *Act* iii. *Sc.* 1

Grief fills the room up of my absent child,
Lies in his bed, walks up and down with me;
Puts on his pretty looks, repeats his words,
Remembers me of all his gracious parts,
Stuffs out his vacant garments with his form. *Act* iii. *Sc.* 4.

Life is as tedious as a twice-told tale,
Vexing the dull ear of a drowsy man. *Act* iii. *Sc.* 4.

When Fortune means to men most good,
She looks upon them with a threatening eye. *Act* iii. *Sc.* 4.

And he that stands upon a slippery place
Makes nice of no vile hold to stay him up. *Act* iii. *Sc.* 4.

How now, foolish rheum! *Act* iv. *Sc.* 1.

To gild refined gold, to paint the lily,
To throw a perfume on the violet,
To smooth the ice, or add another hue
Unto the rainbow, or with taper-light
To seek the beauteous eye of heaven to garnish,
Is wasteful and ridiculous excess. *Act* iv. *Sc.* 2.

And, oftentimes, excusing of a fault
Doth make the fault the worse by the excuse. *Act* iv. *Sc.* 2.

1 *Sc.* 2, Singer, Staunton, Knight. *Sc.* 1, White, Dyce, Cambridge.
2 *Act* ii. *Sc.* 2, White.

King John—*continued.*]

I saw a smith stand with his hammer, thus,
The whilst his iron did on the anvil cool,
With open mouth swallowing a tailor's news. *Act* iv. *Sc.* 2.

Another lean, unwash'd artificer. *Act* iv. *Sc.* 2.

How oft the sight of means to do ill deeds
Makes ill deeds done ! *Act* iv. *Sc.* 2.

Mocking the air with colours idly spread. *Act* v. *Sc.* 1.

This England never did, nor never shall,
Lie at the proud foot of a conqueror. *Act* v. *Sc.* 7.

Come the three corners of the world in arms,
And we shall shock them. Nought shall make us rue,
If England to itself do rest but true. *Act* v. *Sc.* 7.

KING RICHARD II.

All places that the eye of heaven visits
Are to a wise man ports and happy havens *Act* i. *Sc.* 3.

O, who can hold a fire in his hand
By thinking on the frosty Caucasus?
Or cloy the hungry edge of appetite
By bare imagination of a feast ?
Or wallow naked in December snow,
By thinking on fantastic Summer's heat.
O, no ! the apprehension of the good
Gives but the greater feeling to the worse. *Act* i. *Sc.* 3.

This royal throne of kings, this sceptred isle,
This earth of majesty, this seat of Mars,
This other Eden, demi-paradise ;
This fortress, built by Nature for herself,
Against infection and the hand of war ;
This happy breed of men, this little world,
This precious stone set in the silver sea,
Which serves it in the office of a wall,
Or as a moat defensive to a house,
Against the envy of less happier lands ;
This blessed plot, this earth, this realm, this England.
Act ii. *Sc.* 1.

The ripest fruit first falls. *Act* ii. *Sc.* 1.

Evermore thanks, the exchequer of the poor. *Act* ii. *Sc.* 3.

Not all the water in the rough rude sea
Can wash the balm from an anointed king *Act* iii. *Sc.* 2.

King Richard II.—*continued*.]

Let 's talk of graves, of worms, and epitaphs.   *Act* iii. *Sc.* 2.

And nothing can we call our own but death,
And that small model of the barren earth
Which serves as paste and cover to our bones.
For heaven's sake, let us sit upon the ground,
And tell sad stories of the death of kings.   *Act* iii. *Sc.* 2.

He is come to ope
The purple testament of bleeding war.   *Act* iii. *Sc.* 3.

And my large kingdom for a little grave,
A little little grave, an obscure grave.   *Act* iii. *Sc.* 3.

Gave
His body to that pleasant country's earth,
And his pure soul unto his captain, Christ,
Under whose colours he had fought so long.   *Act* iv. *Sc.* 1.

A mockery king of snow.   *Act* iv. *Sc.* 1.

As in a theatre, the eyes of men,
After a well-graced actor leaves the stage,
Are idly bent on him that enters next,
Thinking his prattle to be tedious.   *Act* v. *Sc.* 2.

———

KING HENRY IV., PART I.

In those holy fields,
Over whose acres walk'd those blessed feet
Which fourteen hundred years ago were nail'd,
For our advantage, on the bitter cross.   *Act* i. *Sc.* 1.

Diana's foresters, gentlemen of the shade, minions of the moon.
  Act i. *Sc.* 2.

Old father antic the law.   *Act* i. *Sc.* 2

Thou hast damnable iteration.   *Act* i. *Sc.* 2.

And now am I, if a man should speak truly, little better than one of the
wicked.   *Act* i. *Sc.* 2.

'T is my vocation, Hal ; 't is no sin for a man to labour in his vocation.
  Act i. *Sc.* 2.

He will give the Devil his due.   *Act* i. *Sc.* 2.

There 's neither honesty, manhood, nor good fellowship in thee.
  Act i. *Sc.* 2.

KING HENRY IV., PART I.—*continued.*]

    If all the year were playing holidays,
    To sport would be as tedious as to work.   *Act* i. *Sc.* 2.

    Fresh as a bridegroom; and his chin, new reap'd,
    Show'd like a stubble-land at harvest-home;
    He was perfumed like a milliner,
    And 'twixt his finger and his thumb he held
    A pouncet-box, which ever and anon
    He gave his nose, and took 't away again.   *Act* i. *Sc.* 3.

    And as the soldiers bore dead bodies by,
    He call'd them untaught knaves, unmannerly,
    To bring a slovenly unhandsome corse
    Betwixt the wind and his nobility.   *Act* i. *Sc.* 3.

    And telling me, the sovereign'st thing on earth
    Was parmaceti for an inward bruise;
    And that it was great pity, so it was,
    This villanous saltpetre should be digg'd
    Out of the bowels of the harmless earth,
    Which many a good tall fellow had destroy'd
    So cowardly; and, but for these vile guns,
    He would himself have been a soldier.   *Act* i. *St* 3.

            The blood more stirs
    To rouse a lion than to start a hare!   *Act* i. *Sc.* 3

    By Heaven, methinks, it were an easy leap,
    To pluck bright honour from the pale-fac'd moon,
    Or dive into the bottom of the deep,
    Where fathom-line could never touch the ground,
    And pluck up drowned honour by the locks.   *Act* i. *Sc.* 3.

I know a trick worth two of that.   *Act* ii. *Sc.* 1.

If the rascal have not given me medicines to make me love him, I 'll be
hanged.   *Act* ii. *Sc.* 2.

It would be argument for a week, laughter for a month, and a good jest
forever.   *Act* ii. *Sc.* 2.

            Falstaff sweats to death,
    And lards the lean earth as he walks along.   *Act* ii. *Sc.* 2.

Out of this nettle, danger, we pluck this flower, safety.   *Act* ii. *Sc.* 3.

Brain him with his lady's fan.   *Act* ii. *Sc.* 3.

A Corinthian, a lad of mettle, a good boy.   *Act* ii. *Sc.* 4.

A plague of all cowards, I say.   *Act* ii. *Sc.* 4.

Call you that backing of your friends? A plague upon such backing!
   Act ii. *Sc.* 4.

King Henry IV., Part I.—*continued*.]

I am a Jew else, an Ebrew Jew.   *Act* ii. *Sc.* 4.

Thou knowest my old ward : here I lay, and thus I bore my point.
Four rogues in buckram let drive at me.   *Act* ii. *Sc.* 4.

Three misbegotten knaves in Kendal green.   *Act* ii. *Sc.* 4.

Give you a reason on compulsion ! If reasons were as plenty as blackberries, I would give no man a reason upon compulsion. *Act* ii. *Sc.* 4.

Mark now, how a plain tale shall put you down.   *Act* ii. *Sc.* 4.

I was a coward on instinct.   *Act* ii. *Sc.* 4.

No more of that, Hal, an thou lovest me !   *Act* ii. *Sc.* 4.

A plague of sighing and grief ! it blows a man up like a bladder.
                                                        Act ii. *Sc.* 4.

In King Cambyses' vein.   *Act* ii. *Sc.* 4.

Banish plump Jack, and banish all the world.   *Act* ii. *Sc.* 4.

O monstrous ! but one half-pennyworth of bread to this intolerable deal
of sack !   *Act* ii. *Sc.* 4.

          Diseased nature oftentimes breaks forth
          In strange eruptions.   *Act* iii. *Sc.* 1.

          I am not in the roll of common men.   *Act* iii. *Sc.* 1.

              Glen. I can call spirits from the vasty deep.
              Hot. Why, so can I, or so can any man ;
          But will they come when you do call for them ? *Act* iii. *Sc.* 1.

          O, while you live, tell truth, and shame the Devil.
                                                        Act iii. *Sc.* 1.

          I had rather be a kitten and cry mew,
          Than one of these same metre ballad-mongers. *Act* iii. *Sc.* 1.

          But, in the way of bargain, mark ye me,
          I 'll cavil on the ninth part of a hair.   *Act* iii. *Sc.* 1.

          A good mouth-filling oath.   *Act* iii. *Sc.* 1.

          A fellow of no mark nor likelihood.   *Act* iii. *Sc.* 2.

          To loathe the taste of sweetness, whereof a little
          More than a little is by much too much.   *Act* iii. *Sc.* 2.

An I have not forgotten what the inside of a church is made of, I am a
pepper-corn.   *Act* iii. *Sc.* 3.

Shall I not take mine ease in mine inn ?   *Act* iii. *Sc.* 3.

Rob me the exchequer.   *Act* iii. *Sc.* 3.

This sickness doth infect
The very life-blood of our enterprise. *Act* iv. *Sc.* 1.

That daff'd the world aside,
And bid it pass. *Act* iv. *Sc.* 1.

I saw young Harry, with his beaver on,
His cuisses on his thighs, gallantly arm'd,
Rise from the ground like feather'd Mercury,
And vaulted with such ease into his seat,
As if an angel dropp'd down from the clouds,
To turn and wind a fiery Pegasus,
And witch the world with noble horsemanship. *Act* iv. *Sc.* 1.

The cankers of a calm world and a long peace. *Act* iv. *Sc.* 2.

A mad fellow met me on the way, and told me I had unloaded all the
gibbets, and pressed the dead bodies. No eye hath seen such scarecrows.
I'll not march through Coventry with them, that's flat: nay, and the villains
march wide betwixt the legs, as if they had gyves on; for, indeed, I had
the most of them out of prison. There's but a shirt and a half in all my
company; and the half-shirt is two napkins, tacked together and thrown
over the shoulders like a herald's coat without sleeves. *Act* iv. *Sc.* 2.

Food for powder, food for powder; they'll fill a pit as well as better.
Act iv. *Sc.* 2.

I would it were bedtime, Hal, and all well. *Act* v. *Sc.* 1.

Honour pricks me on. Yea, but how if honour prick me off when I
come on? how then? Can honour set to a leg? No. Or an arm? No.
Or take away the grief of a wound? No. Honour hath no skill in
surgery, then? No. What is honour? A word. What is that word,
honour? Air. A trim reckoning. Who hath it? He that died o' Wed-
nesday. Doth he feel it? No. Doth he hear it? No. Is it insensible,
then? Yea, to the dead. But will it not live with the living? No. Why?
Detraction will not suffer it: therefore, I'll none of it: honour is a mere
scutcheon, and so ends my catechism. *Act* v. *Sc.* 1.

Two stars keep not their motion in one sphere. *Act* v. *Sc.* 4.

I could have better spared a better man. *Act* v. *Sc.* 4.

The better part of valour is discretion. *Act* v. *Sc.* 4.

Lord, lord, how this world is given to lying! I grant you I was down
and out of breath, and so was he; but we rose both at an instant, and
fought a long hour by Shrewsbury clock. *Act* v. *Sc.* 4.

Purge, and leave sack, and live cleanly. *Act* v. *Sc.* 4

KING HENRY IV., PART II.

Even such a man, so faint, so spiritless,
So dull, so dead in look, so woe-begone,
Drew Priam's curtain in the dead of night,
And would have told him, half his Troy was burn'd.

Act i. *Sc.* 1.

Yet the first bringer of unwelcome news
Hath but a losing office; and his tongue
Sounds ever after as a sullen bell,
Remember'd knolling a departed friend.   *Act* i. *Sc.* 1.

I am not only witty in myself, but the cause that wit is in other men.

Act i. *Sc.* 2.

Some smack of age in you, some relish of the saltness of time.

Act i. *Sc.* 2.

We that are in the vaward of our youth.   *Act* i. *Sc.* 2.

For my voice, I have lost it with hollaing and singing of anthems.

Act i. *Sc.* 2.

If I do, fillip me with a three-man beetle.   *Act* i. *Sc.* 2.

I 'll tickle your catastrophe.   *Act* ii. *Sc.* 1.

He hath eaten me out of house and home.   *Act* ii. *Sc.* 1.

Thus we play the fools with the time, and the spirits of the wise sit in the clouds and mock us.   *Act* ii. *Sc.* 2.

He was, indeed, the glass
Wherein the noble youth did dress themselves.   *Act* ii. *Sc.* 3.

Sleep ! O gentle sleep !
Nature's soft nurse, how have I frighted thee,
That thou no more wilt weigh my eyelids down,
And steep my senses in forgetfulness ?   *Act* iii. *Sc.* 1.

With all appliances and means to boot.   *Act* iii. *Sc.* 1.

Uneasy lies the head that wears a crown.   *Act* iii. *Sc.* 1.

Death, as the Psalmist saith, is certain to all : all shall die. How a good yoke of bullocks at Stamford fair ?   *Act* iii. *Sc.* 2.

Accommodated : that is, when a man is, as they say, accommodated ; or when a man is—being—whereby—he may be thought to be accommodated ; which is an excellent thing.   *Act* iii. *Sc.* 2.

Let that suffice, most forcible Feeble.   *Act* iii. *Sc.* 2.

We have heard the chimes at midnight.   *Act* iii. *Sc.* 2.

Like a man made after supper of a cheese-paring : when he was naked, he was, for all the world, like a forked radish, with a head fantastically carved upon it with a knife.   *Act* iii. *Sc.* 2.

He hath a tear for pity, and a hand
Open as day for melting charity.   *Act* iv. *Sc.* 4.

Thy wish was father, Harry, to that thought.   *Act* iv. *Sc.* 4.

A joint of mutton, and any pretty little tiny kickshaws, tell William cook.   *Act* v. *Sc.* 1.

A foutra for the world and worldlings base !
I speak of Africa and golden joys.   *Act* v. *Sc.* 3.

Under which king, Bezonian ? speak, or die.   *Act* v. *Sc.* 3.

KING HENRY V.

O for a muse of fire, that would ascend
The brightest heaven of invention !   *Chorus.*

Consideration, like an angel, came
And whipp'd th' offending Adam out of him.   *Act* i. *Sc.* 1.

Turn him to any cause of policy,
The Gordian knot of it he will unloose,
Familiar as his garter : that, when he speaks,
The air, a charter'd libertine, is still.   *Act* i. *Sc.* 1.

I dare not fight ; but I will wink, and hold out my iron.   *Act* ii. *Sc.* 1.

Base is the slave that pays.   *Act* ii. *Sc.* 1.

His nose was as sharp as a pen, and 'a babbled of green fields.
                    Act ii. *Sc.* 3.

Self-love, my liege, is not so vile a sin
As self-neglecting.   *Act* ii. *Sc.* 4.

Once more unto the breach, dear friends, once more,
Or close the wall up with our English dead !
In peace there 's nothing so becomes a man
As modest stillness and humility ;
But when the blast of war blows in our ears,
Then imitate the action of the tiger :
Stiffen the sinews, summon up the blood.   *Act* iii. *Sc.* 1.

And sheath'd their swords for lack of argument.   *Act* iii. *Sc.* 1.

King Henry V.—*continued.*]

> I see you stand like greyhounds in the slips,
> Straining upon the start.   *Act* iii. *Sc.* 1.

> I thought upon one pair of English legs
> Did march three Frenchmen.   *Act* iii. *Sc.* 6.

You may as well say, that 's a valiant flea that dare eat his breakfast on the lip of a lion.   *Act* iii. *Sc.* 7.[1]

> The hum of either army stilly sounds,
> That the fix'd sentinels almost receive
> The secret whispers of each other's watch.
> Fire answers fire ; and through their paly flames
> Each battle sees the other's umbered face.
> Steed threatens steed, in high and boastful neighs
> Piercing the night's dull ear ; and from the tents,
> The armourers, accomplishing the knights,
> With busy hammers closing rivets up,
> Give dreadful note of preparation.   *Act* iv. *Chorus.*

> There is some soul of goodness in things evil,
> Would men observingly distil it out.   *Act* iv. *Sc.* 1.

Every subject's duty is the king's ; but every subject's soul is his own.
                                                   Act iv. *Sc.* 1.

That 's a perilous shot out of an elder gun.   *Act* iv. *Sc.* 1.

> Gets him to rest, cramm'd with distressful bread.   *Act* iv. *Sc.* 1.
> This day is call'd the feast of Crispian :
> He that outlives this day, and comes safe home,
> Will stand a tiptoe when this day is named,
> And rouse him at the name of Crispian.   *Act* iv. *Sc.* 3.

>   Then shall our names,
> Familiar in their mouths[2] as household words,—
> Harry the King, Bedford and Exeter,
> Warwick and Talbot, Salisbury and Gloster,—
> Be in their flowing cups freshly remember'd.   *Act* iv. *Sc.* 3.

In the universal 'orld, or in France, or in England.   *Act* iv. *Sc.* 8.

There is occasions and causes why and wherefore in all things.
                                                   Act v. *Sc.* 1.

If he be not fellow with the best king, thou shalt find the best king of good fellows.   *Act* v. *Sc.* 2.

Act iii. *Sc.* 6, Dyce.
[2] 'in his mouth,' White, Cambridge, Knight.

KING HENRY VI., PART I.

Hung be the heavens with black. *Act* i. *Sc.* 1.

Between two hawks, which flies the higher pitch,
Between two dogs, which hath the deeper mouth,
Between two horses, which doth bear him best,
Between two girls, which hath the merriest eye,
I have, perhaps, some shallow spirit of judgment;
But in these nice sharp quillets of the law,
Good faith, I am no wiser than a daw. *Act* ii. *Sc.* 4.

She 's beautiful, and therefore to be woo'd;
She is a woman, therefore to be won.[1] *Act* v. *Sc.* 3.

KING HENRY VI., PART II.

Could I come near your beauty with my nails,
I 'd set my ten commandments[2] in your face. *Act* i. *Sc.* 3.

Smooth runs the water where the brook is deep. *Act* iii. *Sc.* 1.

What stronger breastplate than a heart untainted?
Thrice is he arm'd that hath his quarrel just;
And he but naked, though lock'd up in steel,
Whose conscience with injustice is corrupted.[3] *Act* iii. *Sc.* 2.

He dies, and makes no sign. *Act* iii. *Sc.* 3.

There shall be, in England, seven half-penny loaves sold for a penny: the three-hooped pot shall have ten hoops; and I will make it felony to drink small beer. *Act* iv. *Sc.* 2.

Is not this a lamentable thing, that of the skin of an innocent lamb should be made parchment? that parchment, being scribbled o'er, should undo a man? *Act* iv. *Sc.* 2.

Sir, he made a chimney in my father's house, and the bricks are alive at this day to testify it. *Act* iv. *Sc.* 2.

Thou hast most traitorously corrupted the youth of the realm in erecting a grammar-school: and whereas, before, our forefathers had no other books but the score and the tally, thou hast caused printing to be used; and, contrary to the King, his crown, and dignity, thou hast built a paper-mill. *Act* iv. *Sc.* 7.

---

[1] See also *Titus Andronicus, Act* ii. *Sc.* 1.
[2] See Proverbs, *post.*
[3] I 'm armed with more than complete steel,
The justice of my quarrel. *Lust's Dominion.*

KING HENRY VI., PART III.

How sweet a thing it is to wear a crown,
Within whose circuit is Elysium,
And all that poets feign of bliss and joy.   *Act* i. *Sc.* 2.

And many strokes, though with a little axe,
Hew down and fell the hardest-timber'd oak.   *Act* ii. *Sc.* 1.

The smallest worm will turn, being trodden on.   *Act* ii. *Sc.* 2.

  Things ill got had ever bad success,
And happy always was it for that son
Whose father, for his hoarding, went to hell?   *Act* ii. *Sc.* 2.

A little fire is quickly trodden out,
Which, being suffered, rivers cannot quench.   *Act* iv. *Sc.* 8.

Suspicion always haunts the guilty mind :
The thief doth fear each bush an officer.   *Act* v. *Sc.* 6.

KING RICHARD III.

Now is the winter of our discontent
Made glorious summer by this sun of York,
And all the clouds that lower'd upon our house
In the deep bosom of the ocean buried.
Now are our brows bound with victorious wreaths;
Our bruised arms hung up for monuments;
Our stern alarums chang'd to merry meetings,
Our dreadful marches to delightful measures.
Grim-visaged war hath smooth'd his wrinkled front.   *Act* i. *Sc.* 1.

I, that am curtail'd of this fair proportion,
Cheated of feature by dissembling nature,
Deform'd, unfinish'd, sent before my time
Into this breathing world, scarce half made up,
And that so lamely and unfashionable
That dogs bark at me as I halt by them,—
Why, I, in this weak piping time of peace,
Have no delight to pass away the time.   *Act* i. *Sc.* 1.

To leave this keen encounter of our wits.   *Act* i. *Sc.* 2.

Was ever woman in this humour woo'd?
Was ever woman in this humour won?   *Act* i. *Sc.* 2.

Framed in the prodigality of nature.   *Act* i. *Sc.* 2.

King Richard III.—*continued.*]

And thus I clothe my naked villany
With old odd ends, stol'n out of[1] holy writ,
And seem a saint, when most I play the Devil.   *Act* i. *Sc.* 3.

O, I have pass'd a miserable night,
So full of fearful dreams, of ugly sights,
That, as I am a Christian faithful man,
I would not spend another such a night,
Though 't were to buy a world of happy days.   *Act* i. *Sc.* 4.

O Lord, methought, what pain it was to drown !
What dreadful noise of water in mine ears !
What sights of ugly death within mine eyes !
Methought I saw a thousand fearful wracks ;
A thousand men that fishes gnaw'd upon ;
Wedges of gold, great anchors, heaps of pearl,
Inestimable stones, unvalued jewels,
All scattered in the bottom of the sea :
Some lay in dead men's skulls ; and in those holes
Where eyes did once inhabit, there were crept,
As 't were in scorn of eyes, reflecting gems.   *Act* i. *Sc.* 4.

So wise so young, they say, do ne'er live long.   *Act* iii. *Sc.* 1.

Off with his head ![2]   *Act* iii. *Sc.* 4.

Lives like a drunken sailor on a mast ;
Ready with every nod to tumble down.   *Act* iii. *Sc.* 4.

Even in the afternoon of her best days.   *Act* iii. *Sc.* 7.

Thou troublest me : I am not in the vein.   *Act* iv. *Sc.* 2.

Their lips were four red roses on a stalk.   *Act* iv. *Sc.* 3.

The sons of Edward sleep in Abraham's bosom.   *Act* iv. *Sc.* 3.

Let not the heavens hear these tell-tale women
Rail on the Lord's anointed.   *Act* iv. *Sc.* 4.

Tetchy and wayward.   *Act* iv. *Sc.* 4.

An honest tale speeds best, being plainly told.   *Act* iv. *Sc.* 4.

Thus far into the bowels of the land
Have we march'd on without impediment.   *Act* v. *Sc.* 2.

True hope is swift, and flies with swallow's wings ;
Kings it makes gods, and meaner creatures kings.
    Act v. *Sc.* 2.

---

[1] ' stol'n forth,' White, Knight.   [2] Cf. Cibber, p. 146.

KING RICHARD III.—*continued.*]

The king's name is a tower of strength.[1]	*Act* v. *Sc.* 3.
O, coward conscience, how dost thou afflict me !	*Act* v. *Sc.* 3.

My conscience hath a thousand several tongues,
And every tongue brings in a several tale,
And every tale condemns me for a villain.　　　*Act* v. *Sc.* 3.

　　By the apostle Paul, shadows to-night
Have struck more terror to the soul of Richard
Than can the substance of ten thousand soldiers.　*Act* v. *Sc.* 3.

　　　　　　　The self-same heaven
That frowns on me looks sadly upon him.　　*Act* v. *Sc.* 3.

A thing devised by the enemy.[2]　　　　　*Act* v. *Sc.* 3.

A horse ! a horse !　My kingdom for a horse !　*Act* v. *Sc.* 4.

　　　　I have set my life upon a cast,
And I will stand the hazard of the die.
I think there be six Richmonds in the field.　*Act* v. *Sc.* 4.

KING HENRY VIII.

Order gave each thing view.	*Act* i. *Sc.* 1.
This bold bad man.[3]	*Act* ii. *Sc.* 2.

　　　　　　　Verily
I swear, 't is better to be lowly born,
And range with humble livers in content,
Than to be perk'd up in a glist'ring grief,
And wear a golden sorrow.　　　　　　*Act* ii. *Sc.* 3.

　　　　And then to breakfast, with
What appetite you have.　　　　　　*Act* iii. *Sc.* 2.

I have touch'd the highest point of all my greatness,
And from that full meridian of my glory,
I haste now to my setting : I shall fall
Like a bright exhalation in the evening,
And no man see me more.　　　　　*Act* iii. *Sc.* 2.

Press not a falling man too far.　　　　*Act* iii. *Sc.* 2.

---

[1] The name of the Lord is a strong tower.　*Prov.* xviii. 10.
[2] Cf. Cibber, p. 147.
[3] Cf. Spenser, *Faerie Queene, Book* i. *Ch.* i. *St.* 37, and Massinger,
A New Way to Pay Old Debts, Act iv. *Sc.* 2.

KING HENRY VIII.—*continued.*]

> Farewell, a long farewell, to all my greatness !
> This is the state of man : to-day he puts forth
> The tender leaves of hope, to-morrow blossoms,
> And bears his blushing honours thick upon him :
> The third day, comes a frost, a killing frost.   *Act* iii. *Sc.* 2.

> Vain pomp, and glory of this world, I hate ye ;
> I feel my heart new open'd.   O, how wretched
> Is that poor man, that hangs on princes' favours !
> There is betwixt that smile we would aspire to,
> That sweet aspect of princes and their ruin,
> More pangs and fears than wars or women have ;
> And when he falls, he falls like Lucifer,
> Never to hope again.   *Act* iii. *Sc.* 2.

> And sleep in dull, cold marble.   *Act* iii. *Sc.* 2.

> Say, Wolsey, that once trod the ways of glory,
> And sounded all the depths and shoals of honour.   *Act* iii. *Sc.* 2.

>   I charge thee, fling away ambition :
> By that sin fell the angels.   *Act* iii. *Sc.* 2.

> Love thyself last : cherish those hearts that hate thee,
> Corruption wins not more than honesty.
> Still in thy right hand carry gentle peace,
> To silence envious tongues : be just, and fear not.
> Let all the ends thou aim'st at be thy country's,
> Thy God's, and truth's.   *Act* iii. *Sc.* 2.

> Had I but serv'd my God with half the zeal
> I serv'd my king, he would not in mine age
> Have left me naked to mine enemies.   *Act* iii. *Sc.* 2.

> An old man, broken with the storms of state,
> Is come to lay his weary bones among ye ;
> Give him a little earth for charity !   *Act* iv. *Sc.* 2.

> He gave his honours to the world again,
> His blessed part to Heaven, and slept in peace.   *Act* iv. *Sc.* 2.

> So may he rest: his faults lie gently on him.   *Act* iv. *Sc.* 2.

>   He was a man
> Of an unbounded stomach.   *Act* iv. *Sc.* 2.

> Men's evil manners live in brass ; their virtues
> We write in water.[1]   *Act* iv. *Sc.* 2.

---

[1] For men use, if they have an evil tourne, to write it in marble : and whoso doth us a good tourne we write it in duste.   Sir Thomas More, *Richard III.*

> L'injure se grave en metal
> Et le bienfait s'escrit en l'onde.
>   Jean Bertaut (1570—1611), *Carey's French Poets.*

KING HENRY VIII.—*continued.*]

He was a scholar, and a ripe and good one;
Exceeding wise, fair spoken, and persuading :
Lofty, and sour, to them that lov'd him not ;
But to those men that sought him, sweet as Summer.

Act iv. *Sc.* 2.

After my death I wish no other herald,
No other speaker of my living actions,
To keep mine honour from corruption,
But such an honest chronicler as Griffith.

Act iv. *Sc.* 2.

To dance attendance on their lordships' pleasures.

Act v. *Sc.* 2.

'T is a cruelty,
To load a falling man.

Act v. *Sc.* 2.

TROILUS AND CRESSIDA.

I have had my labour for my travail.

Act i. *Sc.* 1.

The baby figure of the giant mass
Of things to come.

Act i. *Sc.* 3.

Welcome ever smiles,
And farewell goes out sighing.

Act iii. *Sc.* 3.

One touch of nature makes the whole world kin.

Act iii. *Sc.* 3.

And give to dust, that is a little gilt,
More laud than gilt o'er-dusted.

Act iii. *Sc.* 3.

And, like a dew-drop from the lion's mane,
Be shook to air.

Act iii. *Sc.* 3.

The end crowns all.

Act iv. *Sc.* 5.

CORIOLANUS.

I thank you for your voices, thank you,—
Your most sweet voices.

Act ii. *Sc.* 3.

Hear you this Triton of the minnows ?

Act iii. *Sc.* 1.

His nature is too noble for the world :
He would not flatter Neptune for his trident,
Or Jove for his power to thunder.

Act iii. *Sc.* 1.

Serv. Where dwellest thou ?
Cor. Under the canopy.

Act iv. *Sc.* 5.

A name unmusical to the Volscians' ears,
And harsh in sound to thine.

Act iv. *Sc.* 5.

CORIOLANUS—*continued.*]

> Chaste as the icicle,
> That 's curded by the frost from purest snow,
> And hangs on Dian's temple.   *Act* v. *Sc.* 3.

> If you have writ your annals true, 't is there,
> That, like an eagle in a dove-cote, I
> Flutter'd your Volscians in Corioli :
> Alone I did it.—Boy ! [1]   *Act* v. *Sc.* 6.

TITUS ANDRONICUS.

Sweet mercy is nobility's true badge.   *Act* i. *Sc.* 2.

> She is a woman, therefore may be woo'd;
> She is a woman, therefore may be won;
> She is Lavinia, therefore must be lov'd.
> What, man ! more water glideth by the mill
> Than wots the miller of ; and easy it is
> Of a cut loaf to steal a shive.   *Act* ii. *Sc.* 1.

ROMEO AND JULIET.

The weakest goes to the wall.   *Act* i. *Sc.* 1.

Gregory, remember thy swashing blow.   *Act* i. *Sc.* 1.

> An hour before the worshipp'd sun
> Peer'd forth the golden window of the east.   *Act* i. *Sc.* 1.

> As is the bud bit with an envious worm,
> Ere he can spread his sweet leaves to the air,
> Or dedicate his beauty to the sun.   *Act* i. *Sc.* 1.

Saint-seducing gold.   *Act* i. *Sc.* 1.

> He that is stricken blind, cannot forget
> The precious treasure of his eyesight lost.   *Act* i. *Sc.* 1.

> One fire burns out another's burning,
> One pain is lessen'd by another's anguish.   *Act* i. *Sc.* 2.

> That book in many's eyes doth share the glory,
> That in gold clasps locks in the golden story.   *Act* i. *Sc.* 3.

For I am proverb'd with a grandsire phrase.   *Act* i. *Sc.* 4.

> O, then, I see, Queen Mab hath been with you.
> She is the fairies' midwife; and she comes
> In shape no bigger than an agate-stone
> On the fore-finger of an alderman,
> Drawn with a team of little atomies
> Over men's noses as they lie asleep.   *Act* i. *Sc.* 4.

---

[1] *Act* v. *Sc.* 5, Singer, Knight.

ROMEO AND JULIET—*continued.*]

True, I talk of dreams,
Which are the children of an idle brain,
Begot of nothing but vain fantasy.   *Act* i. *Sc.* 4.

For you and I are past our dancing days.   *Act* i. *Sc.* 5.

Her beauty hangs upon the cheek of night
Like a rich jewel in an Ethiop's ear.   *Act* i. *Sc.* 5.

Too early seen unknown, and known too late!   *Act* i. *Sc.* 5.

When King Cophetua lov'd the beggar maid.   *Act* ii. *Sc.* 1.

He jests at scars, that never felt a wound.   *Act* ii. *Sc.* 2.[1]

See, how she leans her cheek upon her hand!
O, that I were a glove upon that hand,
That I might touch that cheek!   *Act* ii. *Sc.* 2.[1]

O Romeo, Romeo! wherefore art thou Romeo?   *Act* ii. *Sc.* 2.[1]

What's in a name? that which we call a rose,
By any other name would smell as sweet.   *Act* ii. *Sc.* 2.[1]

For stony limits cannot hold love out.   *Act* ii. *Sc.* 2.

Alack! there lies more peril in thine eye,
Than twenty of their swords.   *Act* ii. *Sc.* 2.[1]

At lovers' perjuries,[2]
They say, Jove laughs.   *Act* ii. *Sc.* 2.[1]

Rom. Lady, by yonder blessed moon I swear,
That tips with silver all these fruit-tree tops,—
Jul. O, swear not by the moon, the inconstant moon
That monthly changes in her circled orb,
Lest that thy love prove likewise variable.   *Act* ii. *Sc.* 2.[1]

The god of my idolatry.   *Act* ii. *Sc.* 2.[1]

This bud of love, by Summer's ripening breath,
May prove a beauteous flower when next we meet.
                                                         Act ii. *Sc.* 2.[1]

How silver-sweet sound lovers' tongues by night,
Like softest music to attending ears!   *Act* ii. *Sc.* 2.[1]

Good night, good night: parting is such sweet sorrow,
That I shall say good night till it be morrow.   *Act* ii. *Sc.* 2.[1]

---

[1] *Act* ii. *Sc.* 1, White.
[2] Perjuria ridet amantum Jupiter-   Tibullus, *Lib.* iii. *El.* 7, *Line* 17.

ROMEO AND JULIET—*continued.*]

For nought so vile that on the earth doth live,
But to the earth some special good doth give;
Nor aught so good, but, strain'd from that fair use,
Revolts from true birth, stumbling on abuse :
Virtue itself turns vice, being misapplied,
And vice sometime's by action dignified.   *Act* ii. *Sc.* 3.

Care keeps his watch in every old man's eye.   *Act* ii. *Sc.* 3.

Thy old groans ring yet in my ancient ears.   *Act* ii. *Sc.* 3.

Stabbed with a white wench's black eye.   *Act* ii. *Sc.* 4.

O flesh, flesh, how art thou fishified !   *Act* ii. *Sc.* 4.

I am the very pink of courtesy.   *Act* ii. *Sc.* 4.

My man's as true as steel.[1]   *Act* ii. *Sc.* 4.

Here comes the lady.—O, so light a foot
Will ne'er wear out the everlasting flint.   *Act* ii. *Sc.* 6.

Rom. Courage, man; the hurt cannot be much.
Mer. No, 't is not so deep as a well, nor so wide as a church-door; but
't is enough.   *Act* iii. *Sc.* 1.

A plague o' both your houses !   *Act* iii. *Sc.* 1.

    When he shall die,
Take him and cut him out in little stars,
And he will make the face of heaven so fine,
That all the world will be in love with night,
And pay no worship to the garish sun.   *Act* iii. *Sc.* 2.

Beautiful tyrant ! fiend angelical !   *Act* iii. *Sc.* 2.

Was ever book containing such vile matter
So fairly bound ?   O, that deceit should dwell
In such a gorgeous palace !   *Act* iii. *Sc.* 2.

    They may seize
On the white wonder of dear Juliet's hand,
And steal immortal blessing from her lips ;
Who, even in pure and vestal modesty,
Still blush, as thinking their own kisses sin.   *Act* iii. *Sc.* 3.

Adversity's sweet milk, philosophy.   *Act* iii. *Sc.* 3.

Night's candles are burnt out, and jocund day
Stands tiptoe on the misty mountain-tops.   *Act* iii. *Sc.* 5.

Straining harsh discords, and unpleasing sharps.   *Act* iii. *Sc.* 5.

Villain and he are many miles asunder.   *Act* iii. *Sc.* 5.

---

[1] 'true as steel,' Chaucer, *Troilus and Creseide, Book* v.   Shakespeare,
Troilus and Cressida, Act iii. *Sc.* 2.

ROMEO AND JULIET—*continued.*]

Not stepping o'er the bounds of modesty.	*Act* iv. *Sc.* **2.**
My bosom's lord sits lightly in his throne.	*Act* v. *Sc.* **1.**
I do remember an apothecary,— And hereabouts he dwells.	*Act* v. *Sc.* **1.**
Sharp misery had worn him to the bones.	*Act* v. *Sc.* **1.**
A beggarly account of empty boxes.	*Act* v. *Sc.* **1.**

Ap. My poverty, but not my will, consents.
Rom. I pay thy poverty, and not thy will. *Act* v. *Sc.* **1.**

One writ with me in sour misfortune's book !	*Act* v. *Sc.* **3.**
A feasting presence full of light.	*Act* v. *Sc.* **3.**

Beauty's ensign yet
Is crimson in thy lips, and in thy cheeks,
And death's pale flag is not advanced there. *Act* v. *Sc.* **3.**

Eyes, look your last :
Arms, take your last embrace ! *Act* v. *Sc.* **3.**

TIMON OF ATHENS.

But flies an eagle flight, bold, and forth on, Leaving no tract behind.	*Act* i. *Sc.* **1.**
We have seen better days.	*Act* iv. *Sc.* **2.**
Are not within the leaf of pity writ.	*Act* iv. *Sc.* **3.**

I 'll example you with thievery :
The sun 's a thief, and with his great attraction
Robs the vast sea : the moon 's an arrant thief,
And her pale fire she snatches from the sun :
The sea 's a thief, whose liquid surge resolves
The moon into salt tears : the earth 's a thief,
That feeds and breeds by a composture stolen
From general excrement : each thing 's a thief. *Act* iv. *Sc.* **3.**

JULIUS CÆSAR.

As proper men as ever trod upon neat's leather.	*Act* i. *Sc.* **1.**
Beware the Ides of March !	*Act* i. *Sc.* **2.**

Well, honour is the subject of my story.
I cannot tell what you and other men
Think of this life ; but for my single self
I had as lief not be, as live to be
In awe of such a thing as I myself. *Act* i. *Sc.* **2.**

JULIUS CÆSAR—*continued.*]

      Dar'st thou, Cassius, now
Leap in with me into this angry flood,
And swim to yonder point ?—Upon the word,
Accoutred as I was, I plunged in,
And bade him follow.   *Act* i. *Sc.* 2.

Help me, Cassius, or I sink !   *Act* i. *Sc.* 2.

      Ye gods, it doth amaze me,
A man of such a feeble temper should
So get the start of the majestic world,
And bear the palm alone.   *Act* i. *Sc.* 2.

Why, man, he doth bestride the narrow world
Like a Colossus ; and we petty men
Walk under his huge legs, and peep about
To find ourselves dishonourable graves.
Men at some time are masters of their fates ;
The fault, dear Brutus, is not in our stars,
But in ourselves, that we are underlings.   *Act* i. *Sc.* 2.

      Conjure with them,
Brutus will start a spirit as soon as *Cæsar.*
Now, in the names of all the gods at once,
Upon what meat doth this our Cæsar feed,
That he is grown so great ? Age, thou art sham'd !
Rome, thou hast lost the breed of noble bloods.   *Act* i. *Sc.* 2.

Let me have men about me, that are fat ;
Sleek-headed men, and such as sleep o' nights ;
Yond' Cassius has a lean and hungry look ;
He thinks too much : such men are dangerous.   *Act* i. *Sc.* 2.

Seldom he smiles, and smiles in such a sort,
As if he mock'd himself, and scorn'd his spirit,
That could be mov'd to smile at anything.   *Act* i. *Sc.* 2.

But, for mine own part, it was Greek to me.   *Act* i. *Sc.* 2.

      Lowliness is young ambition's ladder,
Whereto the climber-upward turns his face ;
But when he once attains the upmost[1] round,
He then unto the ladder turns his back,
Looks in the clouds, scorning the base degrees
By which he did ascend.   *Act* ii. *Sc.* 1.

Between the acting of a dreadful thing,
And the first motion, all the interim is
Like a phantasma, or a hideous dream :

---

     [1] 'utmost,' Singer, Knight.

JULIUS CÆSAR—*continued.*]

The Genius, and the mortal instruments,
Are then in council; and the state of man,
Like to a little kingdom, suffers then
The nature of an insurrection.   *Act* ii. *Sc.* 1.

But, when I tell him, he hates flatterers,
He says, he does, being then most flattered.   *Act* ii. *Sc.* 1.

You are my true and honourable wife;
As dear to me as are the ruddy drops
That visit my sad heart.   *Act* ii. *Sc.* 1.

Fierce fiery warriors fought upon the clouds,
In ranks and squadrons, and right form of war,
Which drizzled blood upon the Capitol.   *Act* ii. *Sc.* 2.

When beggars die there are no comets seen;
The heavens themselves blaze forth the death of princes.
                                                  Act ii. *Sc.* 2.

Cowards die many times before their deaths;
The valiant never taste of death but once.   *Act* ii. *Sc.* 2.

But I am constant as the northern star,
Of whose true-fix'd and resting quality,
There is no fellow in the firmament.   *Act* iii. *Sc.* 1.

The choice and master spirits of this age.   *Act* iii. *Sc.* 1.

Though last, not least, in love.[1]   *Act* iii. *Sc.* 1.

O, pardon me, thou bleeding piece of earth,
That I am meek and gentle with these butchers !
Thou art the ruins of the noblest man
That ever lived in the tide of times.   *Act* iii. *Sc.* 1.

Cry " Havock !" and let slip the dogs of war.   *Act* iii. *Sc.* 1.

Romans, countrymen, and lovers ! hear me for my cause; and be silent
that you may hear.   *Act* iii. *Sc.* 2.

Not that I loved Cæsar less, but that I loved Rome more. *Act* iii. *Sc.* 2.

Who is here so base, that would be a bondman ? If any, speak; for him
have I offended.   I pause for a reply.   *Act* iii. *Sc.* 2.

Friends, Romans, countrymen, lend me your ears :
I come to bury Cæsar, not to praise him.
The evil that men do lives after them,
The good is oft interred with their bones.   *Act* iii. *Sc.* 2.

For Brutus is an honourable man;
So are they all, all honourable men.   *Act* iii. *Sc.* 2.

---

[1] See King Lear, *Act* ii. *Sc.* 1.

When that the poor have cried, Cæsar hath wept :
Ambition should be made of sterner stuff. *Act* iii. *Sc.* 2.

O judgment ! thou art fled to brutish beasts,
And men have lost their reason ! *Act* iii. *Sc.* 2.

But yesterday, the word of Cæsar might
Have stood against the world : now lies he there,
And none so poor to do him reverence. *Act* iii. *Sc.* 2.

If you have tears, prepare to shed them now. *Act* iii. *Sc.* 2.

See what a rent the envious Casca made. *Act* iii. *Sc.* 2.

This was the most unkindest cut of all. *Act* iii. *Sc.* 2.

           Great Cæsar fell.
O, what a fall was there, my countrymen ! *Act* iii. *Sc.* 2.

I come not, friends, to steal away your hearts :
I am no orator, as Brutus is.
. . . . . . I only speak right on. *Act* iii. *Sc.* 2.

           Put a tongue
In every wound of Cæsar, that should move
The stones of Rome to rise and mutiny. *Act* iii. *Sc.* 2.

When love begins to sicken and decay,
It useth an enforced ceremony.
There are no tricks in plain and simple faith. *Act* iv. *Sc.* 2.

           You yourself
Are much condemn'd to have an itching palm. *Act* iv. *Sc.* 3.

The foremost man of all this world. *Act* iv. *Sc.* 3

I had rather be a dog, and bay the moon,
Than such a Roman. *Act* iv. *Sc.* 3.

There is no terror, Cassius, in your threats ;
For I am arm'd so strong in honesty,
That they pass by me as the idle wind,
Which I respect not. *Act* iv. *Sc.* 3.

When Marcus Brutus grows so covetous,
To lock such rascal counters from his friends,
Be ready, gods, with all your thunderbolts,
Dash him to pieces ! *Act* iv. *Sc.* 3.

A friend should bear his friend's infirmities,
But Brutus makes mine greater than they are. *Act* iv. *Sc.* 3.

There is a tide in the affairs of men,
Which, taken at the flood, leads on to fortune ;
Omitted, all the voyage of their life
Is bound in shallows, and in miseries. *Act* iv. *Sc.* 3.

Julius Cæsar—*continued.*]

For ever, and for ever, farewell, Cassius.
If we do meet again, why, we shall smile;
If not, why, then this parting was well made.   *Act* v. *Sc.* 1.

The last of all the Romans, fare thee well !   *Act* v. *Sc.* 3.

This was the noblest Roman of them all.   *Act* v. *Sc.* 5.

His life was gentle; and the elements
So mix'd in him, that Nature might stand up
And say to all the world, "This was a man !"   *Act* v. *Sc.* 5.

MACBETH.

1 *Witch.*   When shall we three meet again,
              In thunder, lightning, or in rain?
2 *Witch.*   When the hurly-burly 's done,
              When the battle 's lost and won.   *Act* i. *Sc.* 1.

Fair is foul, and foul is fair.   *Act* i. *Sc.* 1.

Sleep shall, neither night nor day,
Hang upon his penthouse lid.   *Act* i. *Sc.* 3.

          What are these,
So wither'd, and so wild in their attire;
That look not like the inhabitants o' the earth,
And yet are on 't?   *Act* i. *Sc.* 3.

If you can look into the seeds of time,
And say which grain will grow, and which will not.
          Act i. *Sc.* 3.

Stands not within the prospect of belief.   *Act* i. *Sc.* 3.

The earth hath bubbles, as the water has,
And these are of them.   *Act* i. *Sc.* 3.

          The insane root
That takes the reason prisoner.   *Act* i. *Sc.* 3.

And oftentimes, to win us to our harm,
The instruments of darkness tell us truths;
Win us with honest trifles, to betray us
In deepest consequence.   *Act* i. *Sc.* 3.

          Two truths are told,
As happy prologues to the swelling act
Of the imperial theme.   *Act* i. *Sc.* 3.

And make my seated heart knock at my ribs.   *Act* i. *Sc.* 3.

          Present fears
Are less than horrible imaginings.   *Act* i. *Sc.* 3

MACBETH—*continued.*]

Nothing is
But what is not.   *Act* i. *Sc.* 4.

Come what come may,
Time and the hour runs through the roughest day.   *Act* i. *Sc.* 3.

Nothing in his life
Became him like the leaving it; he died,
As one that had been studied in his death,
To throw away the dearest thing he owed,
As 't were a careless trifle.   *Act* i. *Sc.* 4.

There 's no art
To find the mind's construction in the face.   *Act* i. *Sc* 4.

Yet do I fear thy nature :
It is too full o' the milk of human kindness. *Act* i. *Sc.* 5.

What thou wouldst highly,
That wouldst thou holily ; wouldst not play false,
And yet wouldst wrongly win.   *Act* i. *Sc.* 5.

That no compunctious visitings of nature
Shake my fell purpose.   *Act* i. *Sc.* 5.

Your face, my Thane, is as a book, where men
May read strange matters.   *Act* i. *Sc.* 5.

This castle hath a pleasant seat : the air
Nimbly and sweetly recommends itself
Unto our gentle senses.   *Act* i. *Sc.* 6.

The heaven's breath
Smells wooingly here.   *Act* i. *Sc.* 6.

Coigne of vantage.   *Act* i. *Sc.* 6.

If it were done, when 't is done, then 't were well
It were done quickly : if the assassination
Could trammel up the consequence, and catch
With his surcease, success ; that but this blow
Might be the be-all and the end-all here,
But here, upon this bank and shoal of time,—
We 'd jump the life to come.   *Act* i. *Sc.* 7.

We but teach
Bloody instructions, which, being taught, return
To plague the inventor.   This even-handed justice
Commends the ingredients of our poison'd chalice
To our own lips.   *Act* i. *Sc.* 7.

MACBETH—*continued.*]

                 Besides, this Duncan
Hath borne his faculties so meek, hath been
So clear in his great office, that his virtues
Will plead like angels, trumpet-tongued, against
The deep damnation of his taking-off;
And pity, like a naked new-born babe,
Striding the blast, or Heaven's cherubin, hors'd
Upon the sightless couriers of the air.   *Act* i. *Sc.* 7.

                 I have no spur
To prick the sides of my intent; but only
Vaulting ambition, which o'er-leaps itself,
And falls on the other.   *Act* i. *Sc.* 7.

                 I have bought
Golden opinions from all sorts of people.   *Act* i. *Sc.* 7.

Letting *I dare not* wait upon *I would*,
Like the poor cat i' the adage.   *Act* i. *Sc.* 7.

I dare do all that may become a man;
Who dares do more, is none.   *Act* i. *Sc.* 7.

            Nor time, nor place,
Did then adhere.   *Act* i. *Sc.* 7.

    Macb.   If we should fail,—
    Lady M.   We fail!
But screw your courage to the sticking-place,
And we'll not fail.   *Act* i. *Sc.* 7.

Memory, the warder of the brain.   *Act* i. *Sc.* 7.

         There's husbandry in heaven;
Their candles are all out.   *Act* ii. *Sc.* 1.

         Shut up
In measureless content.   *Act* ii. *Sc.* 1.

Is this a dagger which I see before me,
The handle toward my hand? Come, let me clutch thee:
I have thee not, and yet I see thee still.
Art thou not, fatal vision, sensible
To feeling, as to sight? or art thou but
A dagger of the mind, a false creation,
Proceeding from the heat-oppressed brain?   *Act* ii. *Sc.* 1.

Thou marshall'st me the way that I was going.   *Act* ii. *Sc.* 1.

        Thou sure and firm-set earth,
Hear not my steps, which way they walk, for fear
Thy very stones prate of my whereabout.   *Act* ii. *Sc.* 1.

MACBETH—*continued.*]

      Hear it not, Duncan ; for it is a knell
      That summons thee to Heaven or to Hell !   *Act* ii. *Sc.* 1.

      It was the owl that shrieked, the fatal bellman
      Which gives the stern'st good night.   *Act* ii. *Sc.* 1.[1]

             The attempt, and not the deed,
      Confounds us.   *Act* ii. *Sc.* 1.[1]

      I had most need of blessing, and " Amen "
      Stuck in my throat.   *Act* ii. *Sc.* 1.[1]

      Methought, I heard a voice cry, " Sleep no more !
      Macbeth does murder sleep," the innocent sleep ;
      Sleep, that knits up the ravell'd sleave of care,
      The death of each day's life, sore labour's bath,
      Balm of hurt minds, great nature's second course,
      Chief nourisher in life's feast.   *Act* ii. *Sc.* 1.[1]

      Infirm of purpose !   *Act* ii. *Sc.* 1.[1]

             My hand will rather
      The multitudinous seas incarnadine,
      Making the green—one red.   *Act* ii. *Sc.* 1.[1]

      The labour we delight in physics pain.   *Act* ii. *Sc.* 1.[2]

      Confusion now hath made his master-piece.
      Most sacrilegious murder hath broke ope
      The Lord's anointed temple, and stole thence
      The life o' the building.   *Act* ii. *Sc.* 1.[2]

      The wine of life is drawn, and the mere lees
      Is left this vault to brag of.   *Act* ii. *Sc.* 1.[2]

      A falcon, towering in her pride of place,
      Was by a mousing owl hawk'd at, and killed.   *Act* ii. *Sc.* 2.[3]

      Upon my head they plac'd a fruitless crown,
      And put a barren sceptre in my gripe,
      Thence to be wrench'd with an unlineal hand,
      No son of mine succeeding.   *Act* iii. *Sc.* 1.

      Mur.   We are men, my liege.
      Mac.   Ay, in the catalogue ye go for men.   *Act* iii. *Sc* 1.

             Things without all remedy,
      Should be without regard: what 's done is done.   *Act* iii. *Sc.* 2.

---

[1] *Act* ii. *Sc.* 1, White, Dyce, Staunton.   *Act* ii. *Sc.* 2, Cambridge, Singer, Knight.
[2] *Act* ii. *Sc.* 1, White, Dyce.   *Act* ii. *Sc.* 2, Staunton.   *Act* ii. *Sc.* 3, Cambridge, Singer, Knight.
[3] *Act* ii. *Sc.* 2, White, Dyce.   *Act* ii. *Sc.* 3, Staunton.   *Act* ii. *Sc.* 4. Cambridge, Singer, Knight.

c

MACBETH – *continued.*]

We have scotch'd the snake, not kill'd it.   *Act* iii. *Sc.* 2.

            Better be with the dead,
Whom we to gain our peace have sent to peace,
Than on the torture of the mind to lie
In restless ecstasy.   Duncan is in his grave;
After life's fitful fever, he sleeps well;
Treason has done his worst : nor steel, nor poison,
Malice domestic, foreign levy, nothing,
Can touch him further !   *Act* iii. *Sc.* 2.

In them Nature's copy 's not eterne.   *Act* iii. *Sc.* 2.

A deed of dreadful note.   *Act* iii. *Sc.* 2.

Now spurs the lated traveller apace,
To gain the timely inn.   *Act* iii. *Sc.* 3.

But now, I am cabin'd, cribb'd, confin'd, bound in
To saucy doubts and fears.   *Act* iii. *Sc.* 4.

Now, good digestion wait on appetite,
And health on both !   *Act* iii. *Sc.* 4.

Thou canst not say I did it : never shake
Thy gory locks at me.   *Act* iii. *Sc.* 4.

          The times have been,
That, when the brains were out, the man would die,
And there an end ; but now they rise again,
With twenty mortal murders on their crowns,
And push us from our stools.   *Act* iii. *Sc.* 4.

Thou hast no speculation in those eyes,
Which thou dost glare with !   *Act* iii. *Sc.* 4.

         What man dare, I dare
Approach thou like the rugged Russian bear,
The arm'd rhinoceros, or the Hyrcan tiger;
Take any shape but that, and my firm nerves
Shall never tremble.   *Act* iii. *Sc.* 4.

        Hence, horrible shadow !
Unreal mockery, hence !   *Act* iii. *Sc.* 4.

You have displac'd the mirth, broke the good meeting,
With most admir'd disorder.   *Act* iii. *Sc.* 4.

        Can such things be,
And overcome us like a summer's cloud,
Without our special wonder?   *Act* iii. *Sc.* 4.

Stand not upon the order of your going,
But go at once.   *Act* iii. *Sc.* 4.

MACBETH—*continued.*]

Double, double toil and trouble.	*Act* iv. *Sc.* 1.
Eye of newt, and toe of frog.	*Act* iv. *Sc.* 1.
Black spirits and white, Red spirits and gray, Mingle, mingle, mingle, You that mingle may.[1]	*Act* iv. *Sc.* 1.
By the pricking of my thumbs, Something wicked this way comes: Open, locks, whoever knocks.	*Act* iv. *Sc.* 1.
How now, you secret, black, and midnight hags?	*Act* iv. *Sc.* 1.
A deed without a name.	*Act* iv. *Sc.* 1.
I 'll make assurance double sure, And take a bond of Fate.	*Act* iv. *Sc.* 1.
Show his eyes, and grieve his heart ; Come like shadows, so depart.	*Act* iv. *Sc.* 1.
What ! will the line stretch out to the crack of doom ?	*Act* iv. *Sc.* 1.
The weird sisters.	*Act* iv. *Sc.* 1.
The flighty purpose never is o'ertook, Unless the deed go with it.	*Act* iv. *Sc.* 1.
When our actions do not, Our fears do make us traitors.	*Act* iv. *Sc.* 2.
Angels are bright still, though the brightest fell.	*Act* iv. *Sc.* 3.
Stands Scotland where it did?	*Act* iv. *Sc.* 3.
Give sorrow words ; the grief that does not speak Whispers the o'er-fraught heart, and bids it break.	*Act* iv. *Sc.* 3.
What, all my pretty chickens, and their dam, At one fell swoop?	*Act* iv. *Sc.* 3.
I cannot but remember such things were, That were most precious to me.	*Act* iv. *Sc.* 3.
O, I could play the woman with mine eyes, And braggart with my tongue !	*Act* iv. *Sc.* 3.
Out, damned spot ! out, I say !	*Act* v. *Sc.* 1.
Fie, my lord, fie ! a soldier, and afeard?	*Act* v. *Sc.* 1.

* This song is found entire in "The Witch," by Thomas Middleton, *Act* v. *Sc.* 2, (*Works*, ed. Dyce,) iii. 328, and is there called *A charme Song about a Vessel.*

MACBETH—*continued.*]

All the perfumes of Arabia will not sweeten this little hand.

Act v. *Sc.* 1.

My way of life[1]
Is fall'n into the sear, the yellow leaf;
And that which should accompany old age,
As honour, love, obedience, troops of friends,
I must not look to have; but, in their stead,
Curses, not loud, but deep, mouth-honour, breath,
Which the poor heart would fain deny, and dare not.

Act v *Sc.* 3.

Doct.   Not so sick, my lord,
As she is troubled with thick-coming fancies,
That keep her from her rest.
Macb.   Cure her of that :
Canst thou not minister to a mind diseas'd,
Pluck from the memory a rooted sorrow,
Raze out the written troubles of the brain,
And with some sweet oblivious antidote
Cleanse the stuff'd bosom of that perilous stuff,
Which weighs upon the heart?
Doct.   Therein the patient
Must minister to himself.
Macb. Throw physic to the dogs; I 'll none of it.

Act v. *Sc.* 3.

I would applaud thee to the very echo,
That should applaud again.

Act v. *Sc.* 3.

Hang out our banners on the outward walls;
The cry is still, *They come.* Our castle's strength
Will laugh a siege to scorn.

Act v. *Sc.* 5.

And my fell of hair
Would at a dismal treatise rouse, and stir,
As life were in 't.   I have supp'd full with horrors.

Act v. *Sc.* 5

To-morrow, and to-morrow, and to-morrow,
Creeps in this petty pace from day to day,
To the last syllable of recorded time;
And all our yesterdays have lighted fools
The way to dusty death.   Out, out, brief candle !
Life 's but a walking shadow; a poor player,
That struts and frets his hour upon the stage,
And then is heard no more : it is a tale
Told by an idiot, full of sound and fury,
Signifying nothing.

Act v. *Sc.* 5.

---

[1] Johnson would read, 'May of life.'

MACBETH—*continued.*]

To doubt the equivocation of the fiend,
That lies like truth : *Fear not, till Birnam wood*
Do come to Dunsinane.   *Act* v. *Sc.* 5.

      Blow, wind ! come, wrack !
At least we 'll die with harness on our back.   *Act* v. *Sc.* 5.

I bear a charmed life.   *Act* v. *Sc.* 7.[1]

And be these juggling fiends no more believ'd,
That palter with us in a double sense ;
That keep the word of promise to our ear,
And break it to our hope.   *Act* v. *Sc.* 7.[1]

Live to be the show and gaze o' the time.   *Act* v. *Sc.* 7.[1]

     Lay on, Macduff;
And damn'd be him that first cries, " Hold, enough !"
                                             Act v. *Sc.* 7.[1]

HAMLET.

For this relief much thanks.   *Act* i. *Sc.* 1.

But in the gross and scope of mine opinion,
This bodes some strange eruption to our State. *Act* i. *Sc.* 1.

Does not divide the Sunday from the week.   *Act* i. *Sc.* 1.

Doth make the night joint-labourer with the day. *Act* i. *Sc.* 1.

In the most high and palmy state of Rome,
A little ere the mightiest Julius fell,
The graves stood tenantless, and the sheeted dead
Did squeak and gibber in the Roman streets. *Act* i. *Sc.* 1.

And then it started, like a guilty thing
Upon a fearful summons.   *Act* i. *Sc.* 1.

Whether in sea or fire, in earth or air,
The extravagant and erring spirit hies
To his confine.   *Act* i. *Sc.* 1.

Some say, that ever 'gainst that season comes
Wherein our Saviour's birth is celebrated,
The bird of dawning singeth all night long :
And then, they say, no spirit dare stir[2] abroad;
The nights are wholesome; then no planets strike,
No fairy takes, nor witch hath power to charm,
So hallow'd and so gracious is the time.   *Act* i. *Sc.* 1.

---

[1] *Act* v. *Sc.* 7, White, Singer, Knight. *Act* v. *Sc.* 8, Cambridge, Dyce, Staunton.
[2] ' can walk,' White, Knight.

HAMLET *—continued.*]

The morn, in russet mantle clad,	
Walks o'er the dew of yon high eastern hill.	*Act* i. *Sc.* 1.
With one auspicious, and one dropping eye,	
With mirth in funeral, and with dirge in marriage,	
In equal scale weighing delight and dole.	*Act* i. *Sc.* 2.
The head is not more native to the heart.	*Act* i. *Sc.* 2.
A little more than kin, and less than kind.	*Act* i. *Sc.* 2.
Seems, madam ! nay, it is; I know not seems.	*Act* i. *Sc.* 2.
But I have that within, which passeth show;	
These but the trappings and the suits of woe.	*Act* i. *Sc.* 2.
O, that this too, too solid flesh would melt,	
Thaw, and resolve itself into a dew;	
Or that the Everlasting had not fix'd	
His canon 'gainst self-slaughter. O God ! **O God !**	
How weary, stale, flat, and unprofitable	
Seem to me all the uses of this world !	*Act* i. *Sc.* 2.
That it should come to this !	*Act* i. *Sc.* 2.
Hyperion to a satyr : so loving to my mother,	
That he might not beteem the winds of heaven	
Visit her face too roughly.	*Act* i. *Sc.* 2.
Why, she would hang on him,	
As if increase of appetite had grown	
By what it fed on.	*Act* i. *Sc.* 2.
Frailty, thy name is woman !	*Act* i. *Sc.* 2.
A little month.	*Act* i. *Sc.* 2.
Like Niobe, all tears.	*Act* i. *Sc.* 2.
A beast, that wants discourse of reason.	*Act* i. *Sc.* 2.
My father's brother, but no more like my father,	
Than I to Hercules.	*Act* i. *Sc.* 2.
It is not, nor it cannot come to, good.	*Act* i. *Sc.* 2.
Thrift, thrift, Horatio ! the funeral bak'd meats	
Did coldly furnish forth the marriage tables.	*Act* i. *Sc.* 2.
In my mind's eye, Horatio.	*Act* i. *Sc.* 2.
He was a man, take him for all in all,	
I shall not look upon his like again.	*Act* i. *Sc.* 2.
Season your admiration for a while.	*Act* i. *Sc.* 2.
In the dead vast and middle of the night.	*Act* i. *Sc.* 2.
Armed at all points.	*Act* i. *Sc.* 2.

HAMLET—*continued.*]

A countenance more
In sorrow than in anger.   *Act* i. *Sc.* 2.

While one with moderate haste might tell a hundred.
                                            Act i. *Sc.* 2.

It was, as I have seen it in his life,
A sable silvered.   *Act* i. *Sc.* 2.

Give it an understanding, but no tongue.   *Act* i. *Sc.* 2.

Foul deeds will rise,
Though all the earth o'erwhelm them, to men's eyes.
                                            Act i. *Sc.* 2.

The chariest maid is prodigal enough,
If she unmask her beauty to the moon.   *Act* i. *Sc.* 3.

The canker galls the infants of the spring,
Too oft before their buttons be disclosed;
And in the morn and liquid dew of youth
Contagious blastments are most imminent.   *Act* i. *Sc.* 3.

Do not, as some ungracious pastors do,
Show me the steep and thorny way to Heaven,
Whilst, like a puff'd and reckless libertine,
Himself the primrose path of dalliance treads,
And recks not his own rede.   *Act* i. *Sc.* 3.

Give thy thoughts no tongue.   *Act* i. *Sc.* 3.

Be thou familiar, but by no means vulgar:
The friends thou hast, and their adoption tried,
Grapple them to thy soul with hoops [1] of steel. *Act* i. *Sc.* 3.

Beware
Of entrance to a quarrel; but, being in,
Bear 't that the opposed may beware of thee.
Give every man thine ear, but few thy voice;
Take each man's censure, but reserve thy judgment.
Costly thy habit as thy purse can buy,
But not express'd in fancy; rich, not gaudy:
For the apparel oft proclaims the man.   *Act* i. *Sc.* 3.

Neither a borrower nor a lender be,
For loan oft loses both itself and friend;
And borrowing dulls the edge of husbandry.
This above all,—to thine own self be true;
And it must follow, as the night the day,
Thou canst not then be false to any man.   *Act* i. *Sc.* 3.

---

[1] 'hooks,' Singer.

HAMLET—*continued.*]

Springes to catch woodcocks.	*Act* 1. *Sc.* 3.
Be somewhat scanter of your maiden presence.	*Act* i. *Sc.* 3.

Ham. The air bites shrewdly; it is very cold.
Hor. It is a nipping and an eager air.   *Act* i. *Sc.* 4

But to my mind,—though I am native here,
And to the manner born,—it is a custom
More honour'd in the breach, than the observance   *Act* i. *Sc.* 4.

Angels and ministers of grace, defend us !   *Act* i. *Sc.* 4

Be thou a spirit of health, or goblin damn'd,
Bring with thee airs from heaven or blasts from hell,
Be thy intents wicked or charitable,
Thou com'st in such a questionable shape,
That I will speak to thee.   *Act* i. *Sc.* 4.

Let me not burst in ignorance; but tell,
Why thy canoniz'd bones hearsed in death,
Have burst their cerements ? why the sepulchre,
Wherein we saw thee quietly inurn'd,
Hath oped his ponderous and marble jaws,
To cast thee up again ? What may this mean,
That thou, dead corse, again, in complete steel
Revisit'st thus the glimpses of the moon,
Making night hideous; and we fools of nature,
So horridly to shake our disposition
With thoughts beyond the reaches of our souls ?   *Act* i. *Sc.* 4

I do not set my life at a pin's fee.   *Act* i. *Sc.* 4.

          My fate cries out,
And makes each petty artery in this body
As hardy as the Nemean lion's nerve.   *Act* i. *Sc.* 4.

        Unhand me, gentlemen,
By Heaven, I'll make a ghost of him that lets me.   *Act* i. *Sc.* 4

Something is rotten in the state of Denmark.   *Act* i. *Sc.* 4.

      I am thy father's spirit :
Doom'd for a certain term to walk the night,
And for the day confin'd to fast in fires,[1]
Till the foul crimes, done in my days of nature,
Are burnt and purged away.   But that I am forbid
To tell the secrets of my prison-house,
I could a tale unfold, whose lightest word

---

[1] 'to lasting fires,' Singer.

HAMLET—*continued.*]

Would harrow up thy soul, freeze thy young blood,
Make thy two eyes, like stars, start from their spheres,
Thy knotted and combined locks to part,
And each particular hair to stand on end,
Like quills upon the fretful porcupine :
But this eternal blazon must not be
To ears of flesh and blood.   List, list, O list !   *Act* i. *Sc.* 5.

And duller shouldst thou be than the fat weed
That rots itself[1] in ease on Lethe wharf.   *Act* i. *Sc.* 5.
          O my prophetic soul !
Mine uncle !   *Act* i. *Sc.* 5.

O Hamlet, what a falling-off was there !   *Act* i. *Sc.* 5.

But soft : methinks I scent the morning air :
Brief let me be.   Sleeping within mine orchard,
My custom always in the afternoon.   *Act* i. *Sc.* 5.

Cut off even in the blossoms of my sin,
Unhousel'd, disappointed, unanel'd ;
No reckoning made, but sent to my account
With all my imperfections on my head.   *Act* i. *Sc.* 5.

          Leave her to Heaven,
And to those thorns that in her bosom lodge,
To prick and sting her.   .   .   .   .   .
The glow-worm shows the matin to be near,
And 'gins to pale his uneffectual fire.   *Act* i. *Sc.* 5.

          While memory holds a seat
In this distracted globe.   Remember thee ?
Yea, from the table of my memory
I 'll wipe away all trivial fond records.   *Act* i. *Sc.* 5.

Within the book and volume of my brain.   *Act* i. *Sc.* 5.

My tables, my tables,—meet it is, I set it down,
That one may smile, and smile, and be a villain ;
At least, I am sure it may be so in Denmark.   *Act* i. *Sc.* 5.

There needs no ghost, my lord, come from the grave
To tell us this.   *Act* i. *Sc.* 5.

There are more things in heaven and earth, Horatio,
Than are dreamt of in your[2] philosophy.   *Act* i. *Sc.* 5.

Rest, rest, perturbed spirit !   *Act* i. *Sc.* 5.

The time is out of joint ; O cursed spite !
That ever I was born to set it right.   *Act* i. *Sc.* 5.

----

[1] 'roots itself,' White, Dyce, Cambridge.
[2] 'our,' White, Dyce, Knight.

c*

HAMLET—*continued*.]

The flash and outbreak of a fiery mind;
A savageness in unreclaimed blood.   *Act* ii. *Sc.* 1.

This is the very ecstasy of love.   *Act* ii. *Sc.* 1.

Brevity is the soul of wit.   *Act* ii. *Sc.* 2.

More matter, with less art.   *Act* ii. *Sc.* 2.

That he is mad, 't is true : 't is true 't is pity,
And pity 't is 't is true.   *Act* ii. *Sc.* 2.

    Find out the cause of this effect ;
Or rather say, the cause of this defect,
For this effect defective comes by cause.   *Act* ii. *Sc.* 2.

    Doubt thou the stars are fire,
      Doubt that the sun doth move ;
    Doubt truth to be a liar,
      But never doubt I love.   *Act* ii. *Sc.* 2.

Still harping on my daughter.   *Act* ii. *Sc.* 2.

Pol. What do you read, my lord?
Ham. Words, words, words.   *Act* ii. *Sc.* 2.

They have a plentiful lack of wit.   *Act* ii. *Sc.* 2.

Though this be madness, yet there's method in 't.   *Act* ii. *Sc.* 2.

On Fortune's cap we are not the very button.   *Act* ii. *Sc.* 2.

There is nothing either good or bad, but thinking makes it so.
                        Act ii. *Sc.* 2.

Beggar that I am, I am even poor in thanks.   *Act* ii. *Sc.* 2.

This goodly frame, the earth, seems to me a sterile promontory; this most excellent canopy, the air, look you, this brave o'erhanging firmament, this majestical roof fretted with golden fire, why, it appears no other thing to me, than a foul and pestilent congregation of vapours. What a piece of work is a man! How noble in reason! how infinite in faculties! in form and moving, how express and admirable! in action, how like an angel! in apprehension, how like a god!   *Act* ii. *Sc.* 2.

Man delights not me; no, nor woman neither.   *Act* ii. *Sc.* 2.

I know a hawk from a hand-saw.   *Act* ii. *Sc.* 2.

Come, give us a taste of your quality.   *Act* ii. *Sc.* 2.

The play, I remember, pleased not the million; 'twas caviare to the general.   *Act* ii. *Sc.* 2.

They are the abstracts and brief chronicles of the time.   *Act* ii. *Sc.* 2.

Use every man after his desert, and who should 'scape whipping?
                        Act ii. *Sc.* 2.

HAMLET—*continued.*]

What's Hecuba to him, or he to Hecuba,
That he should weep for her?   *Act* ii. *Sc.* 2.

For murder, though it have no tongue, will speak
With most miraculous organ.[1]   *Act* ii. *Sc.* 2.

        The Devil hath power
To assume a pleasing shape.   *Act* ii. *Sc.* 2.

        The play's the thing
Wherein I'll catch the conscience of the King. *Act* ii. *Sc.* 2.

        With devotion's visage,
And pious action, we do sugar o'er
The Devil himself.   *Act* iii. *Sc.* 1.

  To be, or not to be; that is the question:—
Whether 't is nobler in the mind to suffer
The slings and arrows of outrageous fortune;
Or to take arms against a sea of troubles,
And by opposing end them? To die: to sleep,—
No more: and, by a sleep, to say we end
The heartache, and the thousand natural shocks
That flesh is heir to,—'t is a consummation
Devoutly to be wish'd. To die,—to sleep:—
To sleep! perchance, to dream: ay, there's the rub;
For in that sleep of death what dreams may come,
When we have shuffled off this mortal coil,
Must give us pause. There's the respect
That makes calamity of so long life:
For who would bear the whips and scorns of time,
The oppressor's wrong, the proud man's contumely,
The pangs of despis'd love, the law's delay,
The insolence of office, and the spurns
That patient merit of the unworthy takes,
When he himself might his quietus make
With a bare bodkin? Who would fardels[2] bear,
To grunt and sweat under a weary life,
But that the dread of something after death,—
The undiscover'd country, from whose bourn
No traveller returns,—puzzles the will,
And makes us rather bear those ills we have,
Than fly to others that we know not of?
Thus conscience does make cowards of us all;
And thus the native hue of resolution

[1] Cf. Chaucer, *The Nonnes Preestes Tale, Line* 15058.
[2] 'Who would these fardels,' White, Knight.

HAMLET—*continued*.]

> Is sicklied o'er with the pale cast of thought;
> And enterprises of great pith and moment,
> With this regard their currents turn awry,
> And lose the name of action.   *Act* iii. *Sc.* **1.**

> > Nymph, in thy orisons
> Be all my sins remember'd.   *Act* iii. *Sc.* 1.

> Rich gifts wax poor when givers prove unkind.   *Act* iii. *Sc.* 1.

Be thou as chaste as ice, as pure as snow, thou shalt not escape calumny.
> > > > > > > > > > *Act* iii. *Sc.* 1.

> O, what a noble mind is here o'erthrown!
> The courtier's, scholar's, soldier's eye, tongue, sword.
> > > > > > > > > > *Act* iii. *Sc.* **1.**

> The glass of fashion, and the mould of form,
> The observed of all observers!   *Act* iii. *Sc.* **1.**

> Now see that noble and most sovereign reason,
> Like sweet bells jangled, out of tune and harsh. *Act* iii. *Sc.* 1.

Nor do not saw the air too much with your hand, thus; but use **all** gently.   *Act* iii. *Sc.* 2.

Tear a passion to tatters, to very rags, to split the ears of the ground-lings.   *Act* iii. *Sc.* 2.

It out-herods Herod.   *Act* iii. *Sc.* 2.

Suit the action to the word, the word to the action, with this special observance, that you o'erstep not the modesty of nature.   *Act* iii. *Sc.* 2.

To hold, as 't were, the mirror up to nature.   *Act* iii. *Sc.* 2.

Though it make the unskilful laugh, cannot but make the judicious grieve.   *Act* iii. *Sc.* 2.

Not to speak it profanely.   *Act* iii. *Sc.* 2.

I have thought some of Nature's journeymen had made men, and not made them well, they imitated humanity so abominably.   *Act* iii. *Sc.* 2.

O, reform it altogether.   *Act* iii. *Sc.* 2.

> Horatio, thou art e'en as just a man
> As e'er my conversation coped withal.   *Act* iii. *Sc.* 2.

> No; let the candied tongue lick absurd pomp;
> And crook the pregnant hinges of the knee,
> Where thrift may follow fawning.   *Act* iii. *Sc.* **2.**

> A man, that Fortune's buffets and rewards
> Hast ta'en with equal thanks.   *Act* iii. *Sc.* 2.

HAMLET—*continued.*]

> They are not a pipe for Fortune's finger
> To sound what stop she please.   Give me that man
> That is not passion's slave, and I will wear him
> In my heart's core, aye, in my heart of heart,
> As I do thee.   Something too much of this.   *Act* iii. *Sc.* 2.

> And my imaginations are as foul
> As Vulcan's stithy.   *Act* iii. *Sc.* 2.

> Here's metal more attractive.   *Act* iii. *Sc.* 2.

Nay, then let the Devil wear black, for I 'll have a suit of sables.
                                                  Act iii. *Sc.* 2.

For, O, for, O, the hobby-horse is forgot.[1]   *Act* iii. *Sc.* 2.

This is miching *mallecho;* it means mischief   *Act* iii. *Sc.* 2.

Ham. Is this a prologue, or the posy of a ring?
Oph. T is brief, my lord.
Ham. As woman's love.   *Act* iii. *Sc.* 2.

The lady doth protest[2] too much, methinks.   *Act* iii. *Sc.* 2.

Let the galled jade wince, our withers are unwrung. *Act* iii. *Sc.* 2.

> Why, let the strucken deer go weep,
>   The hart ungalled play;
> For some must watch, while some must sleep;
>   Thus runs the world away.   *Act* iii. *Sc.* 2.

> 'T is as easy as lying.   *Act* iii. *Sc.* 2.

> It will discourse most eloquent music.   *Act* iii. *Sc.* 2.

> Pluck out the heart of my mystery.   *Act* iii. *Sc.* 2.

Ham. Do you see yonder cloud that 's almost in shape of a camel?[3]
Pol. By the mass, and 't is like a camel, indeed.
Ham. Methinks it is like a weasel.
Pol. It is back'd like a weasel.
Ham. Or, like a whale?
Pol. Very like a whale.   *Act* iii. *Sc.* 2.

> They fool me to the top of my bent.   *Act* iii. *Sc.* 2.

> 'T is now the very witching time of night,
> When churchyards yawn, and Hell itself breathes out
> Contagion to this world.   *Act* iii. *S* 2

> I will speak daggers to her, but use none   *Act* iii. *Sc.* 2.

---

[1] See *Love's Labour's Lost, Act* iii. *Sc.* 1.
[2] 'protests too much,' White, Knight.
[3] 'in shape like a camel'; so the folios.

HAMLET—*continued.*]

O, my offence is rank, it smells to heaven;
It hath the primal eldest curse upon 't,
A brother's murder   *Act* iii. *Sc.* 3.

　　　　　Help, angels ! make assay :
Bow, stubborn knees; and, heart, with strings of steel,
Be soft as sinews of the new-born babe.   *Act* iii. *Sc.* 3.

　　　　　About some act,
That has no relish of salvation in 't.   *Act* iii. *Sc.* 3.

Dead, for a ducat, dead.   *Act* iii. *Sc.* 4

And let me wring your heart : for so I shall,
if it be made of penetrable stuff.   *Act* iii. *Sc.* 4

False as dicers' oaths.   *Act* iii. *Sc.* 4.

Look here, upon this picture, and on this ;
The counterfeit presentment of two brothers.
See, what a grace was seated on this brow :
Hyperion's curls ; the front of Jove himself ;
An eye like Mars, to threaten and command ;
A station like the herald Mercury,
New-lighted on a heaven-kissing hill ;
A combination, and a form, indeed,
Where every god did seem to set his seal,
To give the world assurance of a man.   *Act* iii. *Sc.* 4.

　　　　　At your age,
The hey-day in the blood is tame, it 's humhle.   *Act* iii. *Sc.* 4.

O shame ! where is thy blush ?   *Act* iii. *Sc.* 4.

A cutpurse of the empire and the rule,
That from a shelf the precious diadem stole,
And put it in his pocket !   *Act* iii. *Sc.* 4.

A king of shreds and patches.   *Act* iii. *Sc.* 4.

This is the very coinage of your brain.   *Act* iii. *Sc.* 4.

　　　　　Bring me to the test,
And I the matter will re-word, which madness
Would gamble from.　Mother, for love of grace,
Lay not that flattering unction to your soul.   *Act* iii. *Sc.* 4.

Assume a virtue, if you have it not.   *Act* iii. *Sc.* 4.

I must be cruel, only to be kind :
Thus bad begins, and worse remains behind.   *Act* iii. *Sc.* 4.

For 't is the sport to have the engineer
Hoist with his own petar.   *Act* iii. *Sc.* 4.

HAMLET—*continued.*]

<blockquote>
Diseases, desperate grown,
By desperate appliance are relieved,
Or not at all.   *Act* iv. *Sc.* 3.
</blockquote>

A man may fish with the worm that hath eat of a king; and eat of the fish that hath fed of that worm.   *Act* iv. *Sc.* 3.

<blockquote>
Sure, He that made us with such large discourse,
Looking before and after, gave us not
That capability and godlike reason,
To fust in us unus'd.   *Act* iv. *Sc.* 4.
</blockquote>

<blockquote>
Greatly to find quarrel in a straw,
When honour 's at the stake.   *Act* iv. *Sc.* 4.
</blockquote>

<blockquote>
So full of artless jealousy is guilt,
It spills itself in fearing to be spilt.   *Act* iv. *Sc.* 5.
</blockquote>

We know what we are, but know not what we may be.   *Act* iv. *Sc.* 5.

<blockquote>
When sorrows come, they come not single spies,
But in battalions.   *Act* iv. *Sc.* 5.
</blockquote>

<blockquote>
There 's such divinity doth hedge a king,
That treason can but peep to what it would.   *Act* iv. *Sc.* 5.
</blockquote>

There 's rosemary, that 's for remembrance ; . . . . and there is pansies, that 's for thoughts.   *Act* iv. *Sc.* 5.

<blockquote>
A very riband in the cap of youth.   *Act* iv. *Sc.* 7.
</blockquote>

<blockquote>
One woe doth tread upon another's heel
So fast they follow.   *Act* iv. *Sc.* 7.
</blockquote>

Cudgel thy brains no more about it.   *Act* v. *Sc.* 1.

Has this fellow no feeling of his business?   *Act* v. *Sc.* 1.

The hand of little employment hath the daintier sense.   *Act* v. *Sc.* 1.

One, that was a woman, sir ; but, rest her soul, she 's dead.   *Act* v. *Sc.* 1.

How absolute the knave is ! we must speak by the card, or equivocation will undo us.   *Act* v. *Sc.* 1.

The age is grown so picked, that the toe of the peasant comes so near the heel of the courtier, he galls his kibe.   *Act* v. *Sc.* 1.

Alas, poor Yorick ! I knew him, Horatio : a fellow of infinite jest, of most excellent fancy.   *Act* v. *Sc.* 1.

Where be your gibes now? your gambols? your songs? your flashes of merriment, that were wont to set the table on a roar?   *Act* v. *Sc.* 1.

Now get you to my lady's chamber and tell her, let her paint an inch thick, to this favour she must come.   *Act* v. *Sc.* 1.

HAMLET—*continued.*]

To what base uses we may return, Horatio !   Why may not imagination trace the noble dust of Alexander, till he find it stopping a bung-hole ?

Act v. *Sc.* 1.

Imperious Cæsar, dead, and turn'd to clay,
Might stop a hole to keep the wind away.   *Act* v. *Sc.* 1.

           Lay her i' the earth ;
And from her fair and unpolluted flesh,
May violets spring.[1]   *Act* v. *Sc.* 1.

Sweets to the sweet : farewell.   *Act* v. *Sc.* 1.

I thought thy bride-bed to have deck'd, sweet maid,
And not t' have strewed thy grave.   *Act* v. *Sc.* 1.

For though I am not splenetive and rash,
Yet have I in me something dangerous.   *Act* v. *Sc.* 1.

           Nay, and thou 'lt mouth,
I 'll rant as well as thou.   *Act* v. *Sc.* 1.

Let Hercules himself do what he may,
The cat will mew, and dog will have his day.   *Act* v. *Sc.* 1.

There 's a divinity that shapes our ends,
Rough-hew them how we will.   *Act* v. *Sc.* 2.

Into a towering passion.   *Act* v. *Sc.* 2.

The phrase would be more german to the matter, if we could carry a cannon by our sides.   *Act* v. *Sc.* 2.

There is a special providence in the fall of a sparrow.

Act v. *Sc.* 2.

I have shot mine arrow o'er the house,
And hurt my brother.   *Act* v. *Sc.* 2.

A hit, a very palpable hit.   *Act* v. *Sc.* 2.

Report me and my cause aright.   *Act* v. *Sc.* 2.

          This fell sergeant, death,
Is strict in his arrest.   *Act* v. *Sc.* 2.

---

[1] Cf. Tennyson, *In Memoriam*, xviii.

KING LEAR.

How sharper than a serpent's tooth it is
To have a thankless child !   *Act* i. *Sc.* 4.

Striving to better, oft we mar what 's well.   *Act* i. *Sc.* 4.

> Down, thou climbing sorrow !
Thy element 's below.   *Act* ii. *Sc.* 4.

O, let not women's weapons, water-drops,
Stain my man's cheeks.   *Act* ii. *Sc.* 4.

Blow, winds, and crack your cheeks ! rage ! blow !
                                                      Act iii. *Sc.* 2.

I tax not you, you elements, with unkindness.   *Act* iii. *Sc.* 2.

A poor, infirm, weak, and despis'd old man.   *Act* iii. *Sc.* 2.

> Tremble, thou wretch,
That hast within thee undivulged crimes,
Unwhipp'd of justice.   *Act* iii. *Sc.* 2.

> I am a man
More sinn'd against than sinning.   *Act* iii. *Sc.* 2.

O, that way madness lies; let me shun that.   *Act* iii. *Sc.* 4.

Poor naked wretches, wheresoe'er you are,
That bide the pelting of this pitiless storm,
How shall your houseless heads and unfed sides,
Your loop'd and window'd raggedness, defend you
From seasons such as these ?   *Act* iii. *Sc.* 4.

> Take physic, pomp ;
Expose thyself to feel what wretches feel.   *Act* iii. *Sc.* 4.

Out-paramoured the Turk.   *Act* iii. *Sc.* 4.

'T is a naughty night to swim in.   *Act* iii. *Sc.* 4.

The green mantle of the standing pool.   *Act* iii. *Sc.* 4.

But mice, and rats, and such small deer,
Have been Tom's food for seven long year.   *Act* iii. *Sc.* 4.

The prince of darkness is a gentleman.   *Act* iii. *Sc.* 4

I 'll talk a word with this same learned Theban.   *Act* iii. *Sc.* 4.

> Fie, foh, and fum,
I smell the blood of a British man.   *Act* iii. *Sc.* 4.

> The little dogs and all,
Tray, Blanch, and Sweet-heart, see, they bark at me.
                                                      Act iii. *Sc.* 6.

KING LEAR—*continued.*]

Mastiff, greyhound, mongrel, grim,
Hound, or spaniel, brach, or lym;
Or bobtail tike, or trundle-tail.   *Act* iii. *Sc.* 6.

Patience and sorrow strove,
Who should express her goodliest.   *Act* iv. *Sc.* 3.

Half-way down
Hangs one that gathers samphire; dreadful trade!
Methinks he seems no bigger than his head.
The fishermen that walk upon the beach
Appear like mice.   *Act* iv. *Sc.* 6.

Ay, every inch a king.   *Act* iv. *Sc.* 6.

Give me an ounce of civet, good apothecary, to sweeten my imagination.
                                                     Act iv. *Sc.* 6.

Through tatter'd clothes small vices do appear;
Robes and furr'd gowns hide all.   *Act* iv. *Sc.* 6.

Mine enemy's dog,
Though he had bit me, should have stood that night
Against my fire.   *Act* iv. *Sc.* 7.

The gods are just, and of our pleasant vices
Make instruments to plague us.[1]   *Act* v. *Sc.* 3.

Her voice was ever soft,
Gentle, and low,—an excellent thing in woman.   *Act* v. *Sc.* 3.

Vex not his ghost : O, let him pass : he hates him,
That would upon the rack of this tough world
Stretch him out longer.   *Act* v. *Sc.* 3.

OTHELLO.

That never set a squadron in the field,
Nor the division of a battle knows.   *Act* i. *Sc.* 1.

The bookish theoric.   *Act* i. *Sc.* 1.

Whip me such honest knaves.   *Act* i. *Sc.* 1.

But I will wear my heart upon my sleeve
For daws to peck at.   *Act* i. *Sc.* 1.

The wealthy curled darlings of our nation.   *Act* i. *Sc.* 2.

---

[1] ' scourge us,' Singer.

OTHELLO—*continued.*]

Most potent, grave, and reverend seigniors,
My very noble and approv'd good masters,
That I have ta'en away this old man's daughter,
It is most true ; true, I have married her :
The very head and front of my offending
Hath this extent, no more.   Rude am I in my speech,
And little bless'd with the soft phrase of peace ;
For since these arms of mine had seven years' pith,
Till now some nine moons wasted, they have us'd
Their dearest action in the tented field ;
And little of this great world can I speak,
More than pertains to feats of broil and battle ;
And, therefore, little shall I grace my cause
In speaking for myself.   Yet, by your gracious patience,
I will a round unvarnish'd tale deliver
Of my whole course of love.   *Act* i. *Sc.* 3.

Her father lov'd me ; oft invited me ;
Still question'd me the story of my life,
From year to year, the battles, sieges, fortunes,
That I have pass'd.
I ran it through, even from my boyish days,
To the very moment that he bade me tell it :
Wherein I spake of most disastrous chances,
Of moving accidents by flood and field ;
Of hair-breadth 'scapes i' the imminent deadly breach ;
Of being taken by the insolent foe,
And sold to slavery ; of my redemption thence,
And portance in my travel's history :
Wherein of antres vast, and deserts idle,
Rough quarries, rocks and hills whose heads touch heaven,
It was my hint to speak,—such was the process.   *Act* i. *Sc.* 3.

The Anthropophagi, and men whose heads
Do grow beneath their shoulders.   This to hear,[1]
Would Desdemona seriously incline.   *Act* i. *Sc.* 3.

And often did beguile her of her tears,
When I did speak of some distressful stroke
That my youth suffer'd.   My story being done,
She gave me for my pains a world of sighs :
She swore,—in faith, 't was strange, 't was passing strange ;
'T was pitiful, 't was wondrous pitiful :
She wish'd she had not heard it ; yet she wish'd
That Heaven had made her such a man : she thank'd me ;

---

[1] ' these things to hear,' Singer, Knight.

OTHELLO—*continued.*]

And bade me, if I had a friend that loved her,
I should but teach him how to tell my story,
And that would woo her.   Upon this hint I spake;
She loved me for the dangers I had passed,
And I loved her that she did pity them.
This only is the witchcraft I have used.   *Act* i. *Sc.* 3.

I do perceive here a divided duty.   *Act* i. *Se.* 3.

The robb'd that smiles, steals something from the thief.
     Act i. *Sc.* 3

The tyrant custom, most grave senators,
Hath made the flinty and steel couch of war
My thrice-driven bed of down.   *Act* i. *Sc.* 3.

I saw Othello's visage in his mind.   *Act.* i. *Sc.* 3.

Put money in thy purse.   *Act* i. *Sc.* 3.

The food that to him now is as luscious as locusts, shall be to him
shortly as bitter as coloquintida.   *Act* i. *Sc.* 3.

Framed to make women false.   *Act* i. *Sc.* 3.

One that excels the quirks of blazoning pens.   *Act* ii. *Sc.* 1.

For I am nothing, if not critical.   *Act* ii. *Sc.* 1.

I am not merry; but I do beguile
The thing I am, by seeming otherwise.   *Act.* ii. *Sc.* 1.

She was a wight,—if ever such wight were,—
   Des. To do what?
   Iago. To suckle fools, and chronicle small beer.
   Des. O, most lame and impotent conclusion!   *Act* ii. *Sc.* 1.

Egregiously an ass.   *Act* ii. *Se.* 1.

Potations pottle deep.   *Act* ii. *Sc.* 3.

King Stephen was a worthy peer,
   His breeches cost him but a crown;
He held them sixpence all too dear,
   With that he called the tailor, lown.[1]   *Act* ii. *Sc.* 3.

Silence that dreadful bell! it frights the isle
From her propriety.   *Act* ii. *Sc.* 3.

Your name is great
In mouths of wisest censure.   *Act* ii. *Sc.* 3.

---

[1] Though these lines are from an old ballad given in *Percy's Reliques*
they are much altered by Shakespeare, and it is his version we sing in
the nursery.

OTHELLO—*continued.*]

Cassio, I love thee;
But never more be officer of mine. *Act* ii. *Sc.* 3.

Iago. What, are you hurt, lieutenant?
Cas. Ay, past all surgery. *Act* ii. *Sc.* 3.

Reputation, reputation, reputation! O, I have lost my reputation! I have lost the immortal part, sir, of myself, and what remains is bestial.
Act ii. *Sc.* 3.

O thou invisible spirit of wine, if thou hast no name to be known by, let us call thee devil! *Act* ii. *Sc.* 3.

O that men should put an enemy in their mouths, to steal away their brains! *Act* ii. *Sc.* 3.

Cas. Every inordinate cup is unbless'd, and the ingredient is a devil.
Iago. Come, come; good wine is a good familiar creature, if it be well used. *Act* ii. *Sc.* 3.

Excellent wretch! Perdition catch my soul,
But I do love thee! and when I love thee not,
Chaos is come again.[1] *Act* iii. *Sc.* 3.

Speak to me as to thy thinkings,
As thou dost ruminate; and give thy worst of thoughts
The worst of words. *Act* iii. *Sc.* 3.

Good name, in man and woman, dear my lord,
Is the immediate jewel of their souls.
Who steals my purse, steals trash; 't is something, nothing;
'T was mine, 't is his, and has been slave to thousands;
But he that filches from me my good name,
Robs me of that which not enriches him,
And makes me poor indeed. *Act* iii. *Sc.* 3.

O, beware, my lord, of jealousy;
It is the green-eyed monster which doth mock
The meat it feeds on. *Act* iii. *Sc.* 3.

But, O, what damned minutes tells he o'er,
Who dotes, yet doubts; suspects, yet strongly[2] loves!
Act iii. *Sc.* 3.

Poor and content is rich, and rich enough. *Act* iii. *Sc* 3.

To be once in doubt,
Is once to be resolved. *Act* iii. *Sc.* 3.

If I do prove her haggard,
Though that her jesses were my dear heart-strings,
I 'd whistle her off, and let her down the wind,
To prey at fortune. *Act* iii. *Sc.* 3.

[1] For he being dead, with him is beauty slain,
And, beauty dead, black chaos comes again.—*Venus and Adonis.*
[2] 'fondly,' White, Knight. 'soundly,' Staunton.

Othello—*continued.*]

I am declined
Into the vale of years. *Act* iii. *Sc.* 3.

That we can call these delicate creatures ours,
And not their appetites ! *Act* iii. *Sc.* 3.

Trifles, light as air,
Are to the jealous confirmations strong
As proofs of holy writ. *Act* iii. *Sc.* 3.

Not poppy, nor mandragora,
Nor all the drowsy syrups of the world,
Shall ever medicine thee to that sweet sleep
Which thou ow'dst yesterday. *Act* iii. *Sc.* 3.

He that is robb'd, not wanting what is stolen,
Let him not know 't, and he 's not robb'd at all. *Act* iii. *Sc.* 3.

O, now, for ever,
Farewell the tranquil mind ! farewell content !
Farewell the plumed troop, and the big wars,
That make ambition virtue ! O, farewell !
Farewell the neighing steed, and the shrill trump,
The spirit-stirring drum, th' ear-piercing fife,
The royal banner, and all quality,
Pride, pomp, and circumstance of glorious war !
And, O you mortal engines, whose rude throats
The immortal Jove's dread clamours counterfeit,
Farewell ! Othello's occupation 's gone ! *Act* iii. *Sc.* 3.

Be sure of it : give me the ocular proof. *Act* iii. *Sc.* 3.

No hinge, nor loop,
To hang a doubt on. *Act* iii. *Sc.* 3.

On horror's head horrors accumulate. *Act* iii. *Sc.* 3.

But this denoted a foregone conclusion. *Act* iii. *Sc.* 3.

Swell, bosom, with thy fraught,
For 't is of aspics' tongues ! *Act* iii. *Sc.* 3.

They 'augh that win. *Act* iv. *Sc.* 1.

But yet the pity of it, Iago ! O, Iago, the pity of it, Iago !
Act iv. *Sc.* 1.

Steep'd me in poverty to the very lips. *Act* iv. *Sc.* 2.

But, alas ! to make me
A fixed figure, for the time of scorn
To point his slow unmoving finger [1] at. *Act* iv. *Sc.* 2.

---

[1] ' slow and moving finger,' Knight, Staunton.

OTHELLO—*continued.*]

O Heaven! that such companions thou'dst unfold,
And put in every honest hand a whip,
To lash the rascals naked through the world.   *Act* iv. *Sc.* 2.

'T is neither here nor there.   *Act* iv. *Sc.* 3,

He hath a daily beauty in his life.   *Act* v. *Sc.* 1.

              This is the night
That either makes me, or fordoes me quite.   *Act* v. *Sc.* 1.

Put out the light, and then—put out the light.   *Act* v. *Sc.* 2.

One entire and perfect chrysolite.   *Act* v. *Sc.* 2.

I have done the State some service, and they know it;
No more of that.   I pray you, in your letters,
When you shall these unlucky deeds relate,
Speak of me as I am; nothing extenuate,
Nor set down aught in malice: then, must you speak
Of one that lov'd, not wisely, but too well:
Of one not easily jealous, but, being wrought,
Perplex'd in the extreme; of one, whose hand,
Like the base Indian, threw a pearl away,
Richer than all his tribe; of one, whose subdu'd eyes,
Albeit unused to the melting mood,
Drop tears as fast as the Arabian trees
Their med'cinable gum.   *Act* v. *Sc.* 2.

ANTONY AND CLEOPATRA.

There's beggary in the love that can be reckon'd.   *Act* i. *Sc.* 1.

           My salad days,
When I was green in judgment.   *Act* i. *Sc.* 5.

          For her own person,
It beggared all description.   *Act* ii. *Sc.* 2.

Age cannot wither her, nor custom stale
Her infinite variety.   *Act* ii. *Sc.* 2.

Come, thou monarch of the vine,
Plumpy Bacchus, with pink eyne.   *Act* ii. *Sc.* 7.

Who does i' the wars more than his captain can,
Becomes his captain's captain; and ambition,
The soldier's virtue, rather makes choice of loss,
Than gain which darkens him.   *Act* iii. *Sc.* 1.

ANTONY AND CLEOPATRA—*continued.*]

                    He wears the rose
Of youth upon him.   *Act* iii. *Sc.* **11.**

This morning, like the spirit of a youth
That means to be of note, begins betimes   *Act* iv. *Sc.* **4.**

Sometime, we see a cloud that 's dragonish,
A vapour, sometime, like a bear, or lion,
A tower'd citadel, a pendant rock.   *Act* iv. *Sc.* 12.

That which is now a horse, even with a thought,
The rack dislimns, and makes it indistinct.   *Act* iv. *Sc.* 12.

Let 's do it after the high Roman fashion.   *Act* iv. *Sc.* 13.

                    Mechanic slaves
With greasy aprons, rules, and hammers.   *Act* v. *Sc.* **2.**

CYMBELINE.

Hark, hark! the lark at heaven's gate sings,[1]
    And Phœbus 'gins arise,
His steeds to water at those springs
    On chalic'd flowers that lies;
And winking Mary-buds begin
    To ope their golden eyes.   *Act* ii. *Sc.* **3.**

Some griefs are med'cinable.   *Act* iii. *Sc.* **3.**

Prouder than rustling in unpaid-for silk.   *Act* iii. *Sc.* **3.**

                    No, 'tis slander,
Whose edge is sharper than the sword; whose tongue
Outvenoms all the worms of Nile.   *Act* iii. *Sc.* 4

                    Weariness
Can snore upon the flint, when resty sloth,
Finds the down pillow hard.   *Act* iii. *Sc.* **6.**

Golden lads and girls all must,
As chimney-sweepers, come to dust.   *Act* iv. *Sc.* **2.**

---

[1] None but the lark so shrill and clear!
Now at Heaven's gate she claps her wings,
The morn not waking till she sings.

            John Lylye, *Alexander and Campaspe, Act* v. *Sc.* **1.**

PERICLES.

3 Fish. Master, I marvel how the fishes live in the sea.
1 Fish. Why, as men do a-land : the great ones eat up the little ones.
Act ii. *Sc.* 1.

POEMS.

Bid me discourse, I will enchant thine ear.
Venus and Adonis.   Line 145.

For greatest scandal waits on greatest state.
Lucrece.   Line 1006.

Crabbed age and youth
Cannot live together.   *The Passionate Pilgrim*, viii.

Have you not heard it said full oft,
A woman's nay doth stand for naught ?   *Ibid.* xiv.

As it fell upon a day
In the merry month of May.[1]   *Ibid.* xv.

She in thee
Calls back the lovely April of her prime.   *Sonnet* iii.

And stretched metre of an antique song.   *Sonnet* xvii.

But thy eternal summer shall not fade.   *Sonnet* xviii.

The painful warrior, famoused for fight,
After a thousand victories once foil'd,
Is from the books of honour razed quite,
And all the rest forgot for which he toil'd.   *Sonnet* xxv

When to the sessions of sweet silent thought
I summon up remembrance of things past.   *Sonnet* xxx.

Like stones of worth, they thinly placed are,
Or captain jewels in the carcanet.   *Sonnet* lii.

And art made tongue-tied by authority.   *Sonnet* lxvi

And simple truth miscall'd simplicity,
And captive good attending captain ill.   *Ibid.*

The ornament of beauty is suspect,
A crow that flies in heaven's sweetest air.   *Sonnet* lxx.

Do not drop in for an after-loss.
Ah, do not, when my heart hath scap'd this sorrow,
Come in the rearward of a conquered woe ;
Give not a windy night a rainy morrow,
To linger out a purpos'd overthrow.   *Sonnet* xc.

---

[1] See Barnfield, p. 84.

POEMS—*continued.*]

> When proud-pied April, dress'd in all his trim,
> Hath put a spirit of youth in everything.   *Sonnet* xcviii.

> And beauty, making beautiful old rhyme.   *Sonnet* cvi.

>   My nature is subdu'd
> To what it works in, like the dyer's hand.   *Sonnet* cxi.

> Let me not to the marriage of true minds
> Admit impediments : love is not love
> Which alters when it alteration finds.   *Sonnet* cxvi.

> That full star that ushers in the even.   *Sonnet* cxxxii.

> O father, what a hell of witchcraft lies
> In the small orb of one particular tear !

> *A Lover's Complaint, St.* xlii.

——□——

FRANCIS BACON. 1561—1626.

WORKS (*Ed. Spedding and Ellis*).

Come home to men's business and bosoms.

Dedication to the Essays. Ed. 1625.

No pleasure is comparable to the standing upon the vantage-ground of truth.   *Essay* i. *Of Truth.*

A little philosophy inclineth a man's mind to atheism, but depth in philosophy bringeth men's minds about to religion.   *Essay* xvi. *Atheism.*

He that hath wife and children hath given hostages to fortune ; for they are impediments to great enterprises, either of virtue or mischief.

Essay viii. *Of Marriage and Single Life.*

Princes are like to heavenly bodies, which cause good or evil times, and which have much veneration, but no rest.[1]   *Essay* xix. *Empire.*

Some books are to be tasted, others to be swallowed, and some few to be chewed and digested.   *Essay* l. *Of Studies.*

Reading maketh a full man, conference a ready man, and writing an exact man.   *Ibid.*

Histories make men wise; poets, witty; the mathematics, subtile; natural philosophy, deep; moral, grave; logic and rhetoric, able to contend.   *Ibid.*

---

[1] Cf. Shelley, *Hellas.*

I hold every man a debtor to his profession; from the which as men of course do seek to receive countenance and profit, so ought they of duty to endeavour themselves by way of amends to be a help and ornament thereunto.   *Maxims of the Law. Preface.*

Knowledge is power.—*Nam et ipsa scientia potestas est.*[1]
                                                                       Meditationes Sacræ. De Hæresibus.

When you wander, as you often delight to do, you wander indeed, and give never such satisfaction as the curious time requires. This is not caused by any natural defect, but first for want of election, when you, having a large and fruitful mind, should not so much labour what to speak, as to find what to leave unspoken. Rich soils are often to be weeded.
                                                                       Letter of Expostulation to Coke.

My Lord St. Albans said that nature did never put her precious jewels into a garret four stories high, and therefore that exceeding tall men had ever very empty heads.[2]   *Apothegm, No.* 17.

"Antiquitas sæculi juventus mundi." These times are the ancient times, when the world is ancient, and not those which we account ancient *ordine retrogrado*, by a computation backward from ourselves.[3]
                                                                       Advancement of Learning. Book i. (1605).

It [Poesy] was ever thought to have some participation of divineness, because it doth raise and erect the mind, by submitting the shews of things to the desires of the mind.   *Ibid. Book* ii.

---

[1] A wise man is strong; yea, a man of knowledge increaseth strength.— *Prov.* xxiv. 5.

[2] Cf. Fuller, p. 125.

[3] As in the little, so in the great world, reason will tell you that old age or antiquity is to be accounted by the farther distance from the beginning and the nearer approach to the end. The times wherein we now live being in propriety of speech the most ancient since the world's creation.—George Hakewill, *An Apologie or Declaration of the Power and Providence of God in the Government of the World.* London, 1627.

For as old age is that period of life most remote from infancy, who does not see that old age in this universal man ought not to be sought in the times nearest his birth, but in those most remote from it?—Pascal, *Preface to the Treatise on Vacuum.*

                    We are Ancients of the earth,
                    And in the morning of the times.
                                    Tennyson, *The Day Dream.* (*L'Envoi.*)

It is worthy of remark that a thought which is often quoted from Francis Bacon occurs in [Giordano] Bruno's *Cena di Cenere*, published in 1584; I mean the notion that the later times are more aged than the earlier.— Whewell, *Philos. of the Inductive Sciences, Vol.* ii. *p.* 198, London, 1847.

ADVANCEMENT OF LEARNING—*continued.*]

The sun, which passeth through pollutions and itself remains as pure as before.'   *Ibid.   Book* ii.

For my name and memory, I leave it to men's charitable speeches, to foreign nations, and to the next ages.   *From his Will.*

—□—

RICHARD ALLISON.

There is a garden in her face,
   Where roses and white lilies grow ;
A heavenly paradise is that place,
   Wherein all pleasant fruits do grow :
There cherries grow that none may buy
Till cherry ripe themselves do cry.
      From *An Howres Recreation in Musike,* 1606.

Those cherries fairly do enclose
   Of orient pearl a double row,
Which, when her lovely laughter shows,
   They look like rosebuds fill'd with snow.   *Ibid.*

—□—

GEORGE PEELE. 1552—1598.

His golden locks time hath to silver turned ;
   O time too swift ! O swiftness never ceasing !
His youth 'gainst time and age hath ever spurned,
   But spurn'd in vaine; youth waneth by encreasing.
      Sonnet ad fin.   Polyhymnia.

His helmet now shall make a hive for bees,
   And lovers' songs be turn'd to holy psalms ;
A man at arms must now serve on his knees,
   And feed on prayers, which are old age's alms.   *Ibid.*

---

[1] The sun, though it passes through dirty places, yet remains as pure as before.—*Adv. of Learning,* ed. Dewey.
  Spiritalis enim virtus sacramenti ita est ut lux : etsi per immundos transeat, non inquinatur.—St. Augustine, *Works, Vol.* 3, *In Johannis Evang., Cap.* 1. *Tr.* v. § 15.
  The sun reflecting upon the mud of strands and shores is unpolluted in his beam.—Taylor, *Holy Living, Ch.* i. *Sect.* 3.
  Truth is as impossible to be soiled by any outward touch as the sunbeam —Milton. *The Doctrine and Discipline of Divorce.*

My merry, merry, merry roundelay
    Concludes with Cupid's curse :
They that do change old love for new,
    Pray gods, they change for worse !

Cupid's Curse,
From the *Arraignment of Paris.*

———□———

JOHN HEYWOOD. ——1565.

The loss of wealth is loss of dirt,
As sages in all times assert ;
The happy man's without a shirt.   *Be Merry Friends.*

Let the world slide, let the world go :
A fig for care, and a fig for woe !
If I can't pay, why I can owe,
And death makes equal the high and low.   *Ibid.*

———□———

SIR HENRY WOTTON. 1568—1639.

How happy is he born or taught,
That serveth not another's will ;
Whose armour is his honest thought,
And simple truth his utmost skill !

The Character of a Happy Life.

And entertains the harmless day
With a religious book or friend.   *Ibid.*

Lord of himself, though not of lands ;
And having nothing, yet hath all.   *Ibid.*

You meaner beauties of the night,
That poorly satisfy our eyes
More by your number than your light,
You common people of the skies ;
What are you when the moon[1] shall rise ?

To his Mistress, the Queen of Bohemia.

I am but a gatherer and disposer of other men's stuff.

Preface to the Elements of Architecture.

Hanging was the worst use man could be put to.

The Disparity between Buckingham and Essex.

---

[1] "sun" in *Reliquiæ Wottorianæ,* Eds. 1651, 1672, 1685.

Wotton—*continued.*]

An ambassador is an honest man sent to lie abroad for the common-wealth.[1]

The itch of disputing will prove the scab of churches.[2]

A Panegyric to King Charles.

—□—

SIR JOHN HARRINGTON.   1561—1612.

Treason doth never prosper, what 's the reason?
Why if it prosper, none dare call it treason.[3]

Epigrams.   Book iv. *Ep.* 5.

—□—

SAMUEL DANIEL.   1562—1619.

Unless above himself he can
Erect himself, how poor a thing is man!

To the Countess of Cumberland.   Stanza 12.

—□—

MICHAEL DRAYTON.   1563—1631.

For that fine madness still he did retain,
Which rightly should possess a poet's brain.

(Of Marlowe.)   *To Henry Reynolds, of Poets and Poesy.*

—□—

RICHARD BARNFIELD.   (*Born circa* 1570.)

As it fell upon a day
In the merry month of May,
Sitting in a pleasant shade
Which a grove of myrtles made.

Address to the Nightingale.

---

[1] In a letter to Velserus, 1612, Wotton says, "This merry definition of an Ambassador I had chanced to set down at my friend's Mr. Christopher Fleckamore, in his Album."

[2] In his will, he directed the stone over his grave to be thus inscribed :—

Hic jacet hujus sententiæ primus author :
DISPUTANDI PRURITUS ECCLESIARUM SCABIES.
Nomen alias quære.

Walton's *Life of Wotton.*

[3] Prosperum ac felix scelus
Virtus vocatur.

Seneca, *Herc. Furens,* 2, 250.

This song, often attributed to Shakespeare, is now confidently assigned to Barnfield; it is found in his collection of Poems in *Divers Humours,* published in 1598.

DR. JOHN DONNE. 1573—1631.

He was the Word, that spake it;
He took the bread and brake it;
And what that Word did make it,
I do believe and take it.

Divine Poems. On the Sacrament.

We understood
Her by her sight; her pure and eloquent blood
Spoke in her cheeks, and so distinctly wrought,
That one might almost say her body thought.

Funeral Elegies. On the Death of Mistress Drury.

She and comparisons are odious.[1]

Elegy 8. The Comparison.

——□——

BEN JONSON. 1574—1637.

Drink to me only with thine eyes,
 And I will pledge with mine;
Or leave a kiss but in the cup,
 And I'll not look for wine.[2]   *The Forest. To Celia.*

Still to be neat, still to be drest
As you were going to a feast.[3]

The Silent Woman. Act i. Sc. 1.

Give me a look, give me a face,
That makes simplicity a grace.
Robes loosely flowing, hair as free;
Such sweet neglect more taketh me,
Than all th' adulteries of art;
They strike mine eyes, but not my heart.   *Ibid.*

In small proportion we just beauties see,
And in short measures life may perfect be.

Good Life, Long Life.

Underneath this stone doth lie
As much beauty as could die;
Which in life did harbour give
To more virtue than doth live.   *Epitaph on Elizabeth.*

---

[1] Cf. Burton, *Anatomy of Melancholy*, Pt. iii. Sc. 3. Mem. 1. Subs. 2. Herbert, *Jacula Prudentum.*

[2] Ἐμοὶ δὲ μόνοις πρόπινε τοῖς ὄμμασιν. . . . . . Εἰ δὲ βούλει, τοῖς χείλεσι προσφέρουσα, πλήρου φιλημάτων τὸ ἔκπωμα, καὶ οὕτως δίδου. Philostratus, *Letter* xxiv.

[2] A true translation from Bonnefonius.

Underneath this sable hearse
Lies the subject of all verse,
Sidney's sister, Pembroke's mother.
Death! ere thou hast slain another,
Learn'd and fair and good as she,
Time shall throw a dart at thee.

Epitaph on the Countess of Pembroke.[1]

Soul of the age!
The applause! delight! the wonder of our stage!
My Shakespeare rise! I will not lodge thee by
Chaucer, or Spenser, or bid Beaumont lie
A little further, to make thee a room.[2]

To the Memory of Shakespea: e.

Small Latin, and less Greek.   *Ibid.*

He was not of an age, but for all time.   *Ibid.*

Sweet swan of Avon!   *Ibid.*

Get money; still get money, boy;
No matter by what means.[3]

Every Man in his Humour   Act ii. *Sc.* 3.

—▢—

CYRIL TOURNEUR.

A drunkard clasp his teeth, and not undo 'em,
To suffer wet damnation to run through 'em.

The Revenger's Tragedy.   Act iii. *Sc.* 1.

—▢—

BISHOP HALL.   1574—1656.

Moderation is the silken string running through the pearl chain of all
virtues.   *Christian Moderation.   Introduc.*

Death borders upon our birth, and our cradle stands in the grave.[4]

Epistles.   Dec. iii. *Ep.* 2.

---

[1] In a manuscript collection of Browne's poems preserved amongst the
Lansdowne MSS., in the British Museum, this epitaph is ascribed to
Browne (1590—1645).
[2] Cf. Basse, p. 125.
[3] Cf. Pope, *Horace, Book* i. *Ep.* 1, *Line* 103.
[4] Cf. Young, *Night Thoughts, N.* 5, *Line* 719.

PHILIP MASSINGER.   1584—1640.

Some undone widow sits upon mine arm,
And takes away the use of it ; and my sword,
Glued to my scabbard with wronged orphans' tears,
Will not be drawn.

A New Way to pay Old Debts.   Act v. *Sc.* 1.

This many-headed monster.[1]

The Roman Actor.   Act iii. *Sc.* 2

Grim death.[2]

Ibid.   Act iv. *Sc.* 2.

—□—

SIR THOMAS OVERBURY.   1581—1613.

In part to blame is she,

Which natn without consent bin only tride :
He comes to neere that comes to be denide.[3]

A Wife.   St. 36

—□—

JOHN FLETCHER.   1576—1625.

Man is his own star, and the soul that can
Render an honest and a perfect man
Commands all light, all influence, all fate.
Nothing to him falls early, or too late.
Our acts our angels are, or good or ill,
Our fatal shadows that walk by us still.

Upon an " Honest Man's Fortune."

All things that are

Made for our general uses are at war,—
Even we among ourselves.   *Ibid.*

Man is his own star, and that soul that can
Be honest is the only perfect man.   *Ibid.*

And he that will to bed go sober,
Falls with the leaf still in October.[4]

Rollo, Duke of Normandy.   Act ii. *Sc.* 3

---

[1] Cf. Pope, *Satires, Book* ii. *Ep.* 1, *Line* 304.
[2] Cf. Milton, *Par. Lost, Book* ii. *Line* 804.
[3] Cf. Montague, *post.*
- The following well-known catch, or glee, is formed on this song :—
  He who goes to bed, and goes to bed sober,
  Falls as the leaves do, and dies in October ;
  But he who goes to bed, and goes to bed mellow,
  Lives as he ought to do, and dies an honest fellow.

D

ROLLO, DUKE OF NORMANDY—*continued.*⟩

   Three merry boys, and three merry boys,
    And three merry boys are we,
   As ever did sing in a hempen string
    Under the gallows-tree. *Ibid. Act.* iii. *Sc.* 2.

   Hence, all you vain delights,
   As short as are the nights
    Wherein you spend your folly !
   There 's naught in this life sweet,
   If man were wise to see 't,
    But only melancholy;
    O sweetest Melancholy !
       The Nice Valour. Act iii. *Sc.* 3.

   Fountain heads and pathless groves,
   Places which pale passion loves!   *Ibid.*

   Weep no more, nor sigh, nor groan,
   Sorrow calls no time that 's gone :
   Violets plucked, the sweetest rain
   Makes not fresh nor grow again.[1]
     The Queen of Corinth. Act iii. *Sc.* 2.

—◻—

FRANCIS BEAUMONT. 1586—1616.

    What things have we seen
Done at the Mermaid ! heard words that have been
So nimble and so full of subtile flame,
As if that every one from whence they came
Had meant to put his whole wit in a jest,
And resolved to live a fool the rest
Of his dull life.   *Letter to Ben Jonson.*

—◻—

BEAUMONT AND FLETCHER.

A soul as white as heaven. *The Maid's Tragedy. Act* iv. *Sc.* 1.

There is a method in man's wickedness,
It grows up by degrees.[2] *A King and no King. Act* v. *Sc.* 4.

---

[1] Weep no more, lady, weep no more,
  Thy sorrow is in vain ;
For violets plucked the sweetest showers
  Will ne'er make grow again.
    Percy's Reliques, The Friar of Orders Gray.

[2] **Nemo** repente venit turpissimus.—*Juvenal,* ii. 83.

Calamity is man's true touchstone.[1]
> *Four Plays in One. The Triumph of Honour.* **Sc. 1.**

The fit 's upon me now !
Come quickly, gentle lady :
The fit 's upon me now !
> *Wit without Money.* *Act* v. *Sc.* 5.

Of all the paths lead to a woman's love
Pity 's the straightest.[2] *The Knight of Malta.* *Act* i. *Sc.* 1.

What 's one man's poison, signor,
Is another's meat or drink. *Love's Cure.* *Act* iii. *Sc.* 2.

Nothing can cover his high fame, but Heaven;
No pyramids set off his memories,
But the eternal substance of his greatness ;
To which I leave him. *The False One.* *Act* ii. *Sc.* 1.

Primrose, first-born child of Ver,
Merry spring-time's harbinger.
> *The Two Noble Kinsmen.* *Act* i. *Sc.* 1.

O great corrector of enormous times,
Shaker of o'er-rank states, thou grand decider
Of dusty and old titles, that healest with blood
The earth when it is sick, and curest the world
O' the plurisy of people. *Ibid.* *Act* v. *Sc.* 1.

—▯—

RICHARD TARLTON.   — —1588.

The King of France, with forty thousand men,
Went up a hill, and so came down agen.
> *From the Pigges Corantoe,* 1642

—▯—

THOMAS CAREW. 1589—1639.

He that loves a rosy cheek,
  Or a coral lip admires,
Or from star-like eyes doth seek
  Fuel to maintain his fires;
As old Time makes these decay,
So his flames must waste away. *Disdain Returned.*

Then fly betimes, for only they
Conquer Love, that run away. *Conquest by Flight.*

---

[1] Ignis aurum probat, miseria fortes viros.—Seneca, *De Prov.* v 9.
[2] Cf. Southerne, *post.*

GEORGE WITHER. 1588—1667.

Shall I, wasting in despair,
   Die because a woman 's fair?
Or make pale my cheeks with care,
   'Cause another's rosy are?
Be she fairer than the day,
   Or the flow'ry meads in May,
     If she be not so to me,
    What care I how fair she be?

The Shepherd's Resolution.

Jack shall pipe, and Gill shall dance.   *Poem on Christmas.*

Hang sorrow ! care will kill a cat,
And therefore let 's be merry.   *Ibid.*

Though I am young, I scorn to flit
On the wings of borrowed wit.   *The Shepherd's Hunting.*

And I oft have heard defended
Little said is soonest mended.   *Ibid.*

——□——

THOMAS HOBBES. 1588—1679.

For words are wise men's counters, they do but reckon by them; but
they are the money of fools.   *The Leviathan. Part* i. *Ch.* 4.

And the life of man solitary, poor, nasty, brutish, and short.

Ibid. Ch. 13.

——□——

JOHN SELDEN. 1584—1654.

Equity is a roguish thing : for law we have a measure, know what to
trust to; equity is according to the conscience of him that is Chancellor,
and as that is larger or narrower, so is equity. 'T is all one as if they
should make the standard for the measure we call a foot a Chancellor's
foot; what an uncertain measure would this be?   One Chancellor has
a long foot, another a short foot, a third an indifferent foot. 'T is the
same in the Chancellor's conscience.   *Table Talk. Equity.*

Old friends are best.   King James used to call for his old shoes; they
were easiest for his feet.   *Friends.*

Commonly we say a judgment falls upon a man for something in him
we cannot abide.   *Judgments.*

No man is the wiser for his learning . . . . wit and wisdom are born
with a man.   *Learning.*

Take a straw and throw it up into the air, you may see by that which way the wind is. *Libels.*

Thou little thinkest what a little foolery governs the world.[1] *Pope.*

Syllables govern the world. *Power.*

——□——

IZAAK WALTON. 1593—1683.
THE COMPLETE ANGLER.

Of which, if thou be a severe, sour-complexioned man, then I here disallow thee to be a competent judge. *The Author's Preface.*

I am, Sir, a Brother of the Angle. *Part i. Ch 1.*

Angling is somewhat like Poetry, men are to be born so.
Part i. Ch. 1.

Old-fashioned poetry, but choicely good. *Part i. Ch. 4.*

We may say of angling as Dr. Boteler[2] said of strawberries : " Doubtless God could have made a better berry, but doubtless God never did " : and so, if I might be judge, God never did make a more calm, quiet, innocent recreation than angling. *Part i. Ch. 5.*

Thus use your frog : put your hook, I mean the arming wire, through his mouth, and out at his gills, and then with a fine needle and silk sew the upper part of his leg with only one stitch to the arming wire of your hook, or tie the frog's leg above the upper joint to the armed wire; and in so doing use him as though you loved him. *Part i. Ch. 8.*

This dish of meat is too good for any but anglers, or very honest men.
Part i. Ch. 8.

All that are lovers of virtue, ... be quiet, and go a-Angling.
Part i. Ch. 21.

——□——

FRANCIS QUARLES. 1592—1644.

Sweet Phosphor, bring the day
Whose conquering ray
May chase these fogs;
  Sweet Phosphor, bring the day !
Sweet Phosphor, bring the day ;
Light will repay
The wrongs of night;
  Sweet Phosphor, bring the day !
Emblems, Book i. **14.**

---

[1] Behold, my son, with how little wisdom the world is governed. Oxenstiern (1583—1654).
[2] William Butler, styled by Dr. Fuller in his *Worthies* (Suffolk) the " Æsculapius of the Age."

Be wisely worldly, be not worldly wise.   *Ibid.   Book* ii. **2.**

This house is to be let for life or years ;
Her rent is sorrow, and her income tears ;
Cupid 't has long stood void; her bills make known,
She must be dearly let, or let alone.   *Ibid.   Book* ii. **10**, *Ep.* **10.**

The slender debt to nature 's quickly paid,
Discharged, perchance, with greater ease than made.
                                        Ibid.   Book ii. **13.**

The next way home 's the farthest way about.
                                        Ibid.   Book iv. **2**, *Ep.* **2.**

——□——

GEORGE   HERBERT.   1593—1632.

Sweet day, so cool, so calm, so bright,
The bridal of the earth and sky.   *Virtue*

Sweet Spring, full of sweet days and roses,
A box where sweets compacted lie.   *Ibid.*

Only a sweet and virtuous soul,
Like seasoned timber, never gives.   *Ibid.*

                        Like summer friends,
Flies of estate and sunnenshine.   *The Answer.*

            A servant with this clause
                Makes drudgery divine ;
            Who sweeps a room as for thy laws
                Makes that and the action fine.   *The Elixir.*

A verse may find him who a sermon flies,
And turn delight into a sacrifice.   *The Church Porch.*

Dare to be true, nothing can need a lie;
A fault which needs it most grows two thereby.[1]   *Ibid.*

The worst speak something good; if all want sense,
God takes a text, and preacheth Pa-ti-ence.   *Ibid.*

Bibles laid open, millions of surprises.   *Sin.*

            Man is one world, and hath
Another to attend him.   *Man.*

If goodness lead him not, yet weariness
    May toss him to my breast.   *The Pulley.*

Wouldst thou both eat thy cake and have it ?   *The Size.*

---

[1] Cf. Watts, *post.*

Do well and right, and let the world sink.[1]   *Country Parson.   Ch.* 29.

His bark is worse than his bite.

After death the doctor.

Hell is full of good meanings and wishes.

No sooner is a temple built to God, but the devil builds a chapel hard by.

Comparisons are odious.

God's mill grinds slow but sure.

It is a poor sport that is not worth the candle.

To a close-shorn sheep, God gives wind by measure.

Help thyself, and God will help thee.   *Jacula Prudentum.*

MARTYN PARKER.

Ye gentlemen of England
  That live at home at ease,
Ah! little do you think upon
  The dangers of the seas.

SIR JOHN SUCKLING.   1609—164x.

Her feet beneath her petticoat
Like little mice stole in and out,
  As if they feared the light;
But O, she dances such a way!
No sun upon an Easter-day
  Is half so fine a sight.   *Ballad upon a Wedding.*

Her lips were red, and one was thin,
Compared with that was next her chin;
  Some bee had stung it newly.   *Ibid.*

Why so pale and wan, fond lover?
  Prithee, why so pale?
Will, when looking well can't move her,
  Looking ill prevail?
  Prithee, why so pale?   *Song.*

'T is expectation makes a blessing dear;
Heaven were not heaven, if we knew what it were.
  Against Fruition.

---

[1] Ruat cœlum, fiat voluntas tua.—Sir T. Browne, *Relig. Med. P.* 2, *Sec.* xi.

She is pretty to walk with,
    And witty to talk with,
    And pleasant, too, to think on.   *Brennoralt. Act* ii.

Her face is like the milky way i' the sky,
A meeting of gentle lights without a name.   *Ibid.   Act* iii.

The prince of darkness is a gentleman.[1]   *The Goblins.*

—□—

ROBERT HERRICK.   1591—1674.

Some asked me where the Rubies grew,
    And nothing I did say;
But with my finger pointed to
    The lips of Julia.
            The Rock of Rubies, and the Quarrie of Pearls.

Some asked how Pearls did grow, and where?
    Then spoke I to my Girl,
To part her lips, and showed them there
    The quarelets of Pearl.   *Ibid.*

Her pretty feet, like snails, did creep
    A little out, and then,[2]
As if they played at bo-peep,
    Did soon draw in again.   *On Her Feet.*

Gather ye rose-buds while ye may,
    Old Time is still a-flying,
And this same flower, that smiles to-day,
    To-morrow will be dying.[3]
            To the Virgins to make much of Time

Her eyes the glow-worm lend thee,
The shooting-stars attend thee;
    And the elves also,
    Whose little eyes glow
Like the sparks of fire, befriend thee.
            Night Piece to Juila

Cherry ripe, ripe, ripe, I cry,
Full and fair ones,—come and buy;
If so be you ask me where
They do grow, I answer, there,
Where my Julia's lips do smile,
There's the land, or cherry-isle.   *Cherry Ripe.*

---

[1] Shakespeare, *King Lear, Act iii. Sc. 4.*
[2] Cf. Suckling, p. 93.
[3] Let us crown ourselves with rose buds, before they be withered.—
Wisdom of Solomon, ii. 8.

Fall on me like a silent dew,
  Or like those maiden showers,
Which, by the peep of day, do strew
  A baptism o'er the flowers.
                    To Music, to becalm his Fever.

Fair daffadills, we weep to see
  You haste away so soon :
As yet the early rising sun
  Has not attained his noon.   *To Daffadills.*

A sweet disorder in the dress
Kindles in clothes a wantonness.   *Delight in Disorder.*

A winning wave, deserving note,
In the tempestuous petticoat,—
A careless shoe-string, in whose tie
I see a wild civility,—
Do more bewitch me, than when art
Is too precise in every part.   *Ibid.*

Thus woe succeeds a woe, as wave a wave. *Sorrows Succeed.*

You say to me-wards your affection's strong ;
Pray love me little, so you love me long.[1]
                    Love me little, love me long.

Attempt the end, and never stand to doubt ;
Nothing 's so hard but search will find it out.[2]
                                Seek and Find.

———□———

JAMES SHIRLEY. 1596—1666.

The glories of our blood and state
  Are shadows, not substantial things ;
There is no armour against fate ;
  Death lays his icy hands on kings.
          Contention of Ajax and Ulysses, Sc. iii.

Only the actions of the just[3]
Smell sweet and blossom in the dust.[4]   *Ibid.*

Death calls ye to the crowd of common men.
                    The Last Conqueror.   Stanza 1.

---

[1] Love me little, love me long.—Marlowe, *The Jew of Malta, Act* iv.
Sc. 5.
[2] Nil tam difficile est quin quærendo investigari possit.—Terence, *Heau-
ton Timorumenos,* iv. 2, 8.
          [3] The sweet remembrance of the just
            Shall flourish when he sleeps in dust.
                    Psalm xci. 4.   *Common Prayer.*
[4] 'their dust.' Works, ed. Dyce, *Vol.* vi.

  D*

JOHN KEPLER. 1571—1630.

It may well wait a century for a reader, as God has waited six thousand years for an observer.   From *Brewster's Martyrs of Science, p.* 197.

———□———

RICHARD LOVELACE. 1618—1658.

Oh ! could you view the melody
   Of every grace,
   And music of her face,[1]
You 'd drop a tear;
   Seeing more harmony
   In her bright eye,
Than now you hear.   *Orpheus to Beasts.*

I could not love thee, dear, so much,
   Loved I not honour more.
          To Lucasta, on going to the Wars.

When flowing cups pass swiftly round
   With no allaying Thames.[2]
         To Althea from Prison, ii.

Fishes, that tipple in the deep,
   Know no such liberty.   *Ibid.*

Stone walls do not a prison make,
   Nor iron bars a cage;
Minds innocent and quiet take
   That for an hermitage;
If I have freedom in my love,
   And in my soul am free,
Angels alone that soar above
   Enjoy such liberty.   *Ibid.* iv.

———□———

JOHN WEBSTER. ——1638.

'T is just like a summer bird-cage in a garden ; the birds that are without despair to get in, and the birds that are within despair and are in a consumption, for fear they shall never get out.[3]
         The White Devil. Act i. *Sc.* 2.

---

[1] There is music in the beauty, and the silent note which Cupid strikes, far sweeter than the sound of an instrument.—Sir Thomas Browne, *Relig. Med. Part* 2.
   Cf. Byron, *Bride of Abydos, Canto* i. *St.* 6.
[2] A cup of hot wine with not a drop of allaying Tyber in 't.—Shakespeare, *Coriolanus, Act* ii. *Sc.* 1.
[3] Le mariage est comme une forteresse assiégée ; ceux qui sont dehors

THE WHITE DEVIL—*continued.*]

> Call for the robin-redbreast and the wren,
> Since o'er shady groves they hover,
> And with leaves and flowers did cover
> The friendless bodies of unburied men.　　*Ibid. Act* i. *Sc.* 2.

> Glories, like glow-worms, afar off shine bright,
> But look'd to near have neither heat nor light.
> 　　　　　　　　　　　　*Ibid.　Act* iv. *Sc.* 4.

—□—

RICHARD CRASHAW.　*Circa* 1616—1650.

The conscious water saw its God and blushed.[1]
　　　　　　　Translation of Epigram on John ii.

> Whoe'er she be,
> That not impossible she,
> That shall command my heart and me.
> 　　　　　　*Wishes to his Supposed Mistress.*

> Where'er she lie,
> Locked up from mortal eye,
> In shady leaves of destiny.　　　　　　　*Ibid.*

> Days that need borrow
> No part of their good morrow,
> From a fore-spent night of sorrow.　　　*Ibid.*

> Life that dares send
> A challenge to his end,
> And when it comes, say, Welcome, friend !　*Ibid.*

> Sydneian showers
> Of sweet discourse, whose powers
> Can crown old Winter's head with flowers.　*Ibid.*

---

veulent y entrer, et ceux qui sont dedans veulent en sortir.—Un proverbe Arabe.　Quitard, *Etudes sur les Proverbes Français, p.* 102.

It happens as with cages : the birds without despair to get in, and those within despair of getting out.—Montaigne, *Essays, Ch.* v. *Vol.* iii.

> Wedlock, indeed, hath oft compared been
> To public feasts, where meet a public rout,
> Where they that are without would fain go in,
> And they that are within would fain go out.
> 　　　Sir John Davis, *Contention betwixt a Wife, a
> 　　　Widow, and a Maid.* (From Davison's
> 　　　*Poetical Rhapsody,* Lond. 1826.)

Is not marriage an open question, when it is alleged, from the beginning of the world, that such as are in the institution wish to get out, and such as are out wish to get in ?—Emerson, *Representative Men : Montaigne.*

[1] Nympha pudica Deum vidit, et erubuit.
　　　　Epig. Sacra.　Aquæ in vinum versæ, p. 299.

A happy soul, that all the way
To heaven hath a summer's day.
                    In Praise of Lessius's Rule of Health.

The modest front of this small floor,
Believe me, reader, can say more
Than many a braver marble can,—
"Here lies a truly honest man !"   *Epitaph upon Mr. Ashton.*

—☐—

THOMAS HEYWOOD. ——1649.

The world 's a theatre, the earth a stage
Which God and nature do with actors fill.
                         Apology for Actors.   1612.

Seven cities warr'd for Homer being dead ;
Who living had no roofe to shrowd his head.[1]
       The Hierarchie of the blessed Angells.   Lond. 1635, *p.* 207.

—☐— *

SIR JOHN DENHAM. 1615—1668.

Though with those streams he no resemblance hold,
Whose foam is amber and their gravel gold ;
His genuine and less guilty wealth t' explore,
Search out his bottom, but survey his shore.
                         Cooper's Hill, Line 165.

O, could I flow like thee, and make thy stream
My great example, as it is my theme !
Though deep, yet clear ; though gentle, yet not dull ;
Strong without rage ; without o'erflowing full.   *Line* 189.

Actions of the last age are like almanacs of the last year.
                         The Sophy.   A Tragedy.

But whither am I strayed ?   I need not raise
Trophies to thee from other men's dispraise ;
Nor is thy fame on lesser ruins built ;
Nor needs thy juster title the foul guilt
Of Eastern kings, who, to secure their reign,
Must have their brothers, sons, and kindred slain.[2]
                         On Mr. John Fletcher's Works.

---

[1] Seven wealthy towns contend for Homer dead,
  Through which the living Homer begged his bread.   *Anon.*
[2] Poets are sultans, if they had their will;
  For every author would his brother kill.
            Orrery, " in one of his Prologues," says Johnson.
  Should such a man, too fond to rule alone,
  Bear like the Turk, no brother near the throne.
                    Pope, *Prologue to the Satires, Line* 197.

THOMAS DEKKER. ——1641.

And though mine arm should conquer twenty worlds,
There 's a lean fellow beats all conquerors.   *Old Fortunatus.*

The best of men
That e'er wore earth about him was a sufferer ;
A soft, meek, patient, humble, tranquil spirit.
The first true gentleman that ever breathed.[1]
                    The Honest Whore. Part i. *Act* i. *Sc.* 12.

We are ne'er like angels till our passion dies.
                    Ibid. Part ii. *Act* i. *Sc.* 2.

To add to golden numbers, golden numbers.
                    Patient Grissell. Act i. *Sc.* 1.

Honest labour bears a lovely face.   *Ibid.*

——□——

ABRAHAM COWLEY. 1618—1667.

What shall I do to be for ever known,
And make the age to come my own?   *The Motto.*

His time is for ever, everywhere his place.
                    Friendship in Absence.

We spent them not in toys, in lusts, or wine ;
     But search of deep philosophy,
         Wit, eloquence, and poetry ;
Arts which I loved, for they, my friend, were thine.
                    On the Death of Mr. William Harvey.

His *faith*, perhaps, in some nice tenets might
Be wrong; his *life*, I 'm sure, was in the right.[2]
                    On the Death of Crashaw.

We grieved, we sighed, we wept : we never blushed before.
          Discourse concerning the Government of Oliver Cromwell.

The thirsty earth soaks up the rain,
And drinks and gapes for drink again ;
The plants suck in the earth, and are
With constant drinking fresh and fair.
                    From Anacreon. Drinking.

                    Why
Should every creature drink but I ?
Why, man of morals, tell me why?   *Ibid.*

---

1 Of the offspring of the gentilman Jafeth, come Habraham, Moyses, Aron, and the profettys; and also the Kyng of the right lyne of Mary, of whom that gentilman Jhesus was borne.—Juliana Berners, *Heraldic Blazonry.*
2 Cf. Pope, *Essay on Man, Ep.* iii. *Line* 306.

> Th' adorning thee with so much art
>> Is but a barb'rous skill;
> 'T is like the poisoning of a dart,
>> Too apt before to kill.   *The Waiting Maid.*

Nothing is there to come, and nothing past,
But an eternal now does always last.[1]   *Davideis. Vol.* i. *Book* 1.

The monster London . . . .

Let but thy wicked men from out thee go,
And all the fools that crowd thee so,
Even thou, who dost thy millions boast,
A village less than Islington will grow,
A solitude almost.   *Of Solitude.*

God the first garden made, and the first city Cain.[2]
                     The Garden.   *Essay* v.

Hence ye profane, I hate ye all,
Both the great vulgar and the small.   *Horace. Book* iii. *Ode* 1.

—□—

SIR WILLIAM DAVENANT.   1605—1668.

Th' assembled souls of all that men held wise.
            Gondibert. Book ii. *Canto* v. *St.* 37.

—□—

EDMUND WALLER.   1605—1687.

The soul's dark cottage, battered and decayed,[3]
Lets in new light thro' chinks that time has made.
Stronger by weakness, wiser men become,
As they draw near to their eternal home.
            Verses upon his Divine Poesy.

Under the tropic is our language spoke,
And part of Flanders hath received our yoke.
            Upon the Death of the Lord Protector.

A narrow compass! and yet there
Dwelt all that 's good, and all that 's fair :
Give me but what this riband bound,
Take all the rest the sun goes round.   *On a Girdle.*

---

[1] One of our poets (which is it?) speaks of an *everlasting now.*—Southey, *The Doctor, p.* 63.

[2] Cf. Cowper, *post.*

[3] Drawing near her death, she sent most pious thoughts as harbingers to heaven; and her soul saw a glimpse of happiness through the chinks of her sickness-broken body.—Fuller, *The Holy and the Profane State, Book* i. *Ch.* ii.

How small a part of time they share
That are so wondrous sweet and fair !   *Go, lovely rose.*

That eagle's fate and mine are one,
  Which, on the shaft that made him die,
Espied a feather of his own,
  Wherewith he wont to soar so high.[1]
                    To a Lady singing a Song of his Composing.

The yielding marble of her snowy breast.
                    On a Lady passing through a Crowd of People.

Illustrious acts high raptures do infuse,
And every conqueror creates a muse.   *Panegyric on Cromwell.*

For all we know
Of what the blessed do above
Is, that they sing and that they love.
                    While I listen to thy voice.

Poets lose half the praise they should have got,
Could it be known what they discreetly blot.
                    Upon Roscommon's Trans. of Horace, De Arte Poetica.

Could we forbear dispute, and practise love,
We should agree as angels do above.   *Divine Love.   Canto* iii.

——□——

MARQUIS OF MONTROSE. 1612—1650.

He either fears his fate too much,
  Or his deserts are small,
That dares not put it to the touch
  To gain or lose it all.   *My Dear and only Love.*[2]

I 'll make thee glorious by my pen,
  And famous by my sword.   *Ibid.*

——□——

JOHN MILTON. 1608—1674.

PARADISE LOST.

Of Man's first disobedience and the fruit
Of that forbidden tree, whose mortal taste
Brought death into the world and all our woe.   *Book* i. *Line* 1.

---

[1] Cf. Byron, *post.*
[2] From Napier's *Mem. of Montrose, Vol.* i. *App.* xxxiv.
            That puts it not unto the touch,
              To win or lose it all.
        From Napier's *Montrose and the Covenanters, Vol.* ii. *p.* 566.

      Or if Sion hill
Delight thee more, and Siloa's brook, that flowed
Fast by the oracle of God.   *Book* i. *Line* 10.

Things unattempted yet in prose or rhyme. *Book* i. *Line* 16.

      What in me is dark
Illumine, what is low raise and support;
That to the height of this great argument
I may assert eternal Providence,
And justify the ways of God to men. *Book* i. *Line* 22.

As far as Angel's ken.   *Book* i. *Line* 59.

      Yet from those flames
No light, but rather darkness visible. *Book* i. *Line* 62.

      Where peace
And rest can never dwell, hope never comes,
That comes to all.   *Book* i. *Line* 65.

     What though the field be lost?
All is not lost; th' unconquerable will,
And study of revenge, immortal hate,
And courage never to submit or yield. *Book* i. *Line* 105.

     To be weak is miserable,
Doing or suffering.   *Book* i. *Line* 157.

And out of good still to find means of evil. *Book* i. *Line* 165.

      Farewell happy fields,
Where joy for ever dwells: hail, horrors; hail.
          Book i. *Line* 249.

A mind not to be changed by place or time.
The mind is its own place, and in itself
Can make a heaven of hell, a hell of heaven.
          Book i. *Line* 253.

Here we may reign secure, and in my choice
To reign is worth ambition, though in hell:
Better to reign in hell, than serve in heaven. *Book* i. *Line* 261.

       Heard so oft
In worst extremes, and on the perilous edge
Of battle.   *Book* i. *Line* 275.

His spear, to equal which the tallest pine,
Hewn on Norwegian hills, to be the mast
Of some great ammiral, were but a wand,
He walk'd with to support uneasy steps
Over the burning marle.   *Book* i. *Line* 292.

Thick as autumnal leaves that strow the brooks
In Vallombrosa, where th' Etrurian shades
High over-arch'd imbower.   *Book* i. *Line* 302.

Awake, arise, or be for ever fallen!	*Book* i.	*Line* 330.

Spirits when they please

Can either sex assume, or both.	*Book* i.	*Line* 423.
Execute their airy purposes.	*Book* i.	*Line* 430.

When night
Darkens the streets, then wander forth the sons

Of Belial, flown with insolence and wine.	*Book* i.	*Line* 500.

Th' imperial ensign, which, full high advanc'd,

Shone like a meteor, streaming to the wind.	*Book* i.	*Line* 536.

Sonorous metal blowing martial sounds:
At which the universal host up sent
A shout that tore hell's concave, and beyond

Frighted the reign of Chaos and old Night.	*Book* i.	*Line* 540.

In perfect phalanx, to the Dorian mood

Of flutes and soft recorders.	*Book* i.	*Line* 550.

His form had yet not lost
All her original brightness, nor appear'd
Less than archangel ruined, and th' excess

Of glory obscured.	*Book* i.	*Line* 591.

In dim eclipse, disastrous twilight sheds
On half the nations, and with fear of change

Perplexes monarchs.	*Book* i.	*Line* 597.

Thrice he assayed, and thrice in spite of scorn

Tears, such as angels weep, burst forth.	*Book* i.	*Line* 619.

Who overcomes

By force, hath overcome but half his foe.	*Book* i.	*Line* 648

Mammon, the least erected spirit that fell
From heaven; for ev'n in heaven his looks and thoughts
Were always downward bent, admiring more
The riches of heaven's pavement, trodden gold,
Than aught divine or holy else enjoy'd

In vision beatific.	*Book* i.	*Line* 679.

Let none admire
That riches grow in hell: that soil may best

Deserve the precious bane.	*Book* i.	*Line* 690.

Anon out of the earth a fabric huge

Rose, like an exhalation.	*Book* i.	*Line* 710.

From morn
To noon he fell, from noon to dewy eve,
A summer's day; and with the setting sun

Dropt from the zenith like a falling star.	*Book* i.	*Line* 745.

PARADISE LOST—*continued.*]

     Faëry elves,
Whose midnight revels, by a forest-side,
Or fountain, some belated peasant sees,
Or dreams he sees, while overhead the moon
Sits arbitress.   *Book* i. *Line* 781.

High on a throne of royal state, which far
Outshone the wealth of Ormus and of Ind,
Or where the gorgeous East with richest hand
Showers on her kings barbaric pearl and gold,
Satan exalted sat, by merit rais'd
To that bad eminence.   *Book* ii. *Line* 1.

Surer to prosper than prosperity
Could have assured us.   *Book* ii. *Line* 39.

   The strongest and the fiercest spirit
That fought in heaven, now fiercer by despair.
          Book ii. *Line* 44.

   Rather than be less,
Cared not to be at all.   *Book* ii. *Line* 47.

My sentence is for open war. *Book* ii. *Line* 51.

That in our proper motion we ascend
Up to our native seat : descent and fall
To us is adverse.   *Book* ii. *Line* 75.

    When the scourge
Inexorable, and the torturing hour
Calls us to penance.   *Book* ii. *Line* 90.

Which, if not victory, is yet revenge. *Book* ii. *Line* 105.

But all was false and hollow; though his tongue
Dropped manna, and could make the worse appear
The better reason, to perplex and dash
Maturest counsels.   *Book* ii. *Line* 112.
    Th' ethereal mould
Incapable of stain would soon expel
Her mischief, and purge off the baser fire,
Victorious. Thus repuls'd, our final hope
Is flat despair.   *Book* ii. *Line* 139.
    For who would lose,
Though full of pain, this intellectual being,
Those thoughts that wander through eternity,
To perish rather, swallowed up and lost
In the wide womb of uncreated night? *Book* ii. *Line* 146.

His red right hand.   *Book* ii. *Line* 175.

---

i Rubente dextera.—Horace, *Od.* i. ii. 2.

Unrespited, unpitied, unreprieved. *Book* ii. *Line* 185.

The never-ending flight
Of future days. *Book* ii. *Line* 221.

Our torments also may in length of time
Become our elements. *Book* ii. *Line* 270.

With grave
Aspect he rose, and in his rising seemed
A pillar of state; deep on his front engraven
Deliberation sat, and public care;
And princely counsel in his face yet shone,
Majestic though in ruin. Sage he stood,
With Atlantean shoulders, fit to bear
The weight of mightiest monarchies; his look
Drew audience and attention still as night
Or summer's noontide air. *Book* ii. *Line* 300.

The palpable obscure. *Book* ii. *Line* 406.

Long is the way
And hard, that out of hell leads up to light.
Book ii. *Line* 432.

Their rising all at once was as the sound
Of thunder heard remote. *Book* ii. *Line* 476.

The lowering element
Scowls o'er the darken'd landscape. *Book* ii. *Line* 490.

Oh, shame to men! devil with devil damn'd
Firm concord holds, men only disagree
Of creatures rational. *Book* ii. *Line* 496.

In discourse more sweet,
For eloquence the soul, song charms the sense,
Others apart sat on a hill retired,
In thoughts more elevate, and reason'd high
Of providence, foreknowledge, will, and fate,
Fixed fate, free will, foreknowledge absolute;
And found no end, in wand'ring mazes lost.
Book ii. *Line* 555.

Vain wisdom all, and false philosophy. *Book* ii. *Line* 565.

Arm the obdured breast
With stubborn patience as with triple steel. *Book* ii. *Line* 568.

A gulf profound as that Serbonian bog,
Betwixt Damiata and Mount Casius old,
Where armies whole have sunk: the parching air
Burns frore, and cold performs th' effect of fire.

PARADISE LOST—*continued.*]

Thither by harpy-footed Furies hal'd
At certain revolutions all the damn'd
Are brought; and feel by turns the bitter change
Of fierce extremes, extremes by change more fierce,
From beds of raging fire to starve in ice
Their soft ethereal warmth, and there to pine
Immovable, infix'd, and frozen round,
Periods of time; thence hurried back to fire.   *Book* ii. *Line* 592.

O'er many a frozen, many a fiery Alp,
Rocks, caves, lakes, fens, bogs, dens, and shades of death.
                                                    Book ii.   *Line* 620.

Gorgons, and Hydras, and Chimæras dire.   *Book* ii.   *Line* 628.

                The other shape—
If shape it might be call'd that shape had none
Distinguishable in member, joint, or limb,
Or substance might be call'd that shadow seem'd,
For each seem'd either—black it stood as night,
Fierce as ten furies, terrible as hell,
And shook a dreadful dart.   *Book* ii.   *Line* 665.

Whence and what art thou, execrable shape?
                                        Book ii.   *Line* 681.

            Back to thy punishment,
False fugitive, and to thy speed add wings.   *Book* ii.   *Line* 699.

So spake the grisly terror.   *Book* ii.   *Line* 704.

Incens'd with indignation Satan stood
Unterrified, and like a comet burn'd,
That fires the length of Ophiucus huge
In th' arctic sky, and from his horrid hair
Shakes pestilence and war.   *Book* ii.   *Line* 707.

            Their fatal hands
No second stroke intend.   *Book* ii.   *Line* 712.

                Hell
Grew darker at their frown.   *Book* ii.   *Line* 710.

        I fled, and cried out DEATH !
Hell trembled at the hideous name, and sigh'd
From all her caves, and back resounded DEATH.
                                        Book ii.   *Line* 787.

Before mine eyes in opposition sits
Grim Death, my son and foe.   *Book* ii.   *Line* 803.

                Death
Grinned horrible a ghastly smile, to hear
His famine should be filled.   *Book* ii.   *Line* 845.

PARADISE LOST—*continued*.]

On a sudden open fly
With impetuous recoil and jarring sound
Th' infernal doors, and on their hinges grate
Harsh thunder.   *Book* ii.   *Line* 879.

Where eldest Night
And Chaos, ancestors of Nature, hold
Eternal anarchy amidst the noise
Of endless wars, and by confusion stand :
For hot, cold, moist, and dry, four champions fierce,
Strive here for mastery.   *Book* ii.   *Line* 894.

Into this wild abyss,
The womb of Nature and perhaps her grave.
                                                  Book ii.   *Line* 910.

O'er bog or steep, through strait, rough, dense, or rare,
With head, hands, wings, or feet, pursues his way,
And swims, or sinks, or wades, or creeps, or flies.
                                                  Book ii.   *Line* 948.

With ruin upon ruin, rout on rout,
Confusion worse confounded.   *Book* ii.   *Line* 995.

So he with difficulty and labour hard
Mov'd on, with difficulty and labour he.   *Book* ii.   *Line* 1021.

And fast by, hanging in a golden chain
This pendent world, in bigness as a star
Of smallest magnitude close by the moon.   *Book* ii.   *Line* 1051.

Hail, holy light ! offspring of heaven first-born.
                                                  Book iii.   *Line* 1.

The rising world of waters dark and deep.   *Book* iii.   *Line* 11.

Thoughts, that voluntary move
Harmonious numbers.   *Book* iii.   *Line* 37.

Thus with the year
Seasons return ; but not to me returns
Day, or the sweet approach of even or morn,
Or sight of vernal bloom, or summer's rose,
Or flock, or herds, or human face divine ;
But cloud instead, and ever-during dark
Surrounds me, from the cheerful ways of men
Cut off, and for the book of knowledge fair
Presented with a universal blank
Of nature's works to me expung'd and ras'd,
And wisdom at one entrance quite shut out.   *Book* iii.   *Line* 48.

Sufficient to have stood, though free to fall.   *Book* iii.   *Line* 99.

Dark with excessive bright.   *Book* iii.   *Line* 380.

Eremites and friars,
White, black, and gray, with all their trumpery.

                              Book iii.   *Line* 474.

                 Since called
The Paradise of Fools, to few unknown.   *Book* iii.   *Line* 495.

And oft, though wisdom wake, suspicion sleeps
At wisdom's gate, and to simplicity
Resigns her charge, while goodness thinks no ill
Where no ill seems.   *Book* iii.   *Line* 686.

The hell within him.   *Book* iv.   *Line* 20.

        Now conscience wakes despair
That slumber'd, wakes the bitter memory
Of what he was, what is, and what must be.   *Book* iv.   *Line* 23.

        At whose sight all the stars
Hide their diminish'd heads.   *Book* iv.   *Line* 34.

        A grateful mind
By owing owes not, but still pays, at once
Indebted and discharg'd.   *Book* iv.   *Line* 55.

        Which way shall I fly
Infinite wrath, and infinite despair?
Which way I fly is hell; myself am hell;
And, in the lowest deep, a lower deep,
Still threat'ning to devour me, opens wide,
To which the hell I suffer seems a heaven. *Book* iv.   *Line* 73.

Such joy ambition finds.   *Book* iv.   *Line* 92.

So farewell hope, and with hope farewell fear,
Farewell remorse : all good to me is lost.
Evil, be thou my good.   *Book* iv.   *Line* 108.

That practis'd falsehood under saintly shew,
Deep malice to conceal couch'd with revenge.

                              Book iv.   *Line* 122.

Sabean odours from the spicy shore
Of Arabie the blest.   *Book* iv.   *Line* 162.

        And on the Tree of Life
The middle tree and highest there that grew,
Sat like a cormorant.   *Book* iv.   *Line* 194.

A heaven on earth.   *Book* iv.   *Line* 208.

Flowers of all hue, and without thorn the rose.

                              Book iv.   *Line* 256.

For contemplation he and valour form'd,
For softness she and sweet attractive grace ;
He for God only, she for God in him.
His fair large front and eye sublime declar'd

Absolute rule ; and hyacinthine locks
Round from his parted forelock manly hung
Clust'ring, but not beneath his shoulders broad.

Book iv. *Line* 297.

Implied
Subjection, but requir'd with gentle sway,
And by her yielded, by him best receiv'd,
Yielded with coy submission, modest pride,
And sweet, reluctant, amorous delay.   *Book* iv. *Line* 307.

Adam the goodliest man of men since born
His sons, the fairest of her daughters Eve. *Book* iv. *Line* 323.

And with necessity,
The tyrant's plea, excus'd his devilish deeds.

Book iv. *Line* 393.

As Jupiter
On Juno smiles, when he impregns the clouds
That shed May flowers.   *Book* iv. *Line* 499.

Imparadis'd in one another's arms.   *Book* iv. *Line* 505.

Now came still evening on, and twilight gray
Had in her sober livery all things clad ;
Silence accompany'd ; for beast and bird,
They to their grassy couch, these to their nests,
Were slunk, all but the wakeful nightingale ;
She all night long her amorous descant sung ;
Silence was pleas'd : now glow'd the firmament
With living sapphires ; Hesperus, that led
The starry host, rode brightest, till the moon,
Rising in clouded majesty, at length
Apparent queen unveil'd her peerless light,
And o'er the dark her silver mantle threw. *Book* iv. *Line* 598.

The timely dew of sleep.   *Book* iv. *Line* 614.

With thee conversing I forget all time ;
All seasons and their change, all please alike.
Sweet is the breath of morn, her rising sweet,
With charm of earliest birds ; pleasant the sun,
When first on this delightful land he spreads
His orient beams, on herb, tree, fruit, and flower,
Glist'ring with dew ; fragrant the fertile earth
After soft showers ; and sweet the coming on
Of grateful evening mild ; then silent night
With this her solemn bird and this fair moon,
And these the gems of heaven, her starry train :
But neither breath of morn when she ascends

PARADISE LOST—*continued.*]

With charm of earliest birds, nor rising sun
On this delightful land, nor herb, fruit, flower,
Glist'ring with dew, nor fragrance after showers,
Nor grateful evening mild, nor silent night
With this her solemn bird, nor walk by moon,
Or glitt'ring starlight, without thee is sweet. *Book* iv. *Line* 639.

Millions of spiritual creatures walk the earth
Unseen, both when we wake, and when we sleep.
Book iv.   *Line* 677.

            Eas'd the putting off
These troublesome disguises which we wear.
Book iv.   *Line* 739.

Hail wedded love, mysterious law, true source
Of human offspring. *Book* iv.   *Line* 750.

Squat like a toad, close at the ear of Eve. *Book* iv.   *Line* 800.

Him thus intent Ithuriel with his spear
Touch'd lightly; for no falsehood can endure
Touch of celestial temper. *Book* iv.   *Line* 810.

Not to know me argues yourselves unknown,
The lowest of your throng. *Book* iv.   *Line* 830.

            Abash'd the devil stood,
And felt how awful goodness is, and saw
Virtue in her shape how lovely. *Book* iv.   *Line* 846.

All hell broke loose. *Book* iv.   *Line* 918.

Like Teneriff or Atlas unremov'd. *Book* iv.   *Line* 987.

            The starry cope
Of heaven. *Book* iv.   *Line* 992

            Fled
Murmuring, and with him fled the shades of night.
Book v.   *Line* 1014.

Now morn, her rosy steps in th' eastern clime
Advancing, sow'd the earth with orient pearl,
When Adam wak'd, so custom'd, for his sleep
Was aery-light, from pure digestion bred. *Book* v.   *Line* 3.

Hung over her enamour'd, and beheld
Beauty, which, whether waking or asleep,
Shot forth peculiar graces. *Book* v.   *Line* 13.

            My latest found,
Heaven's last best gift, my ever new delight. *Book* v.   *Line* 18.

            Good, the more
Communicated, more abundant grows. *Book* v.   *Line* 71.

These are thy glorious works, Parent of good!
Book v. *Line* 153.

Fairest of stars, last in the train of night,
If better thou belong not to the dawn. *Book* v. *Line* 166.

A wilderness of sweets. *Book* v. *Line* 294.

Another morn
Risen on mid-noon. *Book* v. *Line* 310.

So saying, with despatchful looks in haste
She turns, on hospitable thoughts intent. *Book* v. *Line* 331.

Nor jealousy
Was understood, the injur'd lover's hell. *Book* v. *Line* 449.

The bright consummate flower. *Book* v. *Line* 481.

Thrones, dominations, princedoms, virtues, powers.
Book v. *Line* 601.

They eat, they drink, and in communion sweet
Quaff immortality and joy. *Book* v. *Line* 637.

Satan; so call him now, his former name
Is heard no more in heaven. *Book* v. *Line* 658.

Midnight brought on the dusky hour
Friendliest to sleep and silence. *Book* v. *Line* 667.

Innumerable as the stars of night,
Or stars of morning, dew-drops, which the sun
Impearls on every leaf and every flower. *Book* v. *Line* 745.

So spake the seraph Abdiel, faithful found
Among the faithless, faithful only he. *Book* v. *Line* 896.

Morn,
Wak'd by the circling hours, with rosy hand
Unbarr'd the gates of light. *Book* vi. *Line* 2.

Servant of God, well done. *Book* vi. *Line* 29.

Arms on armour clashing bray'd
Horrible discord, and the madding wheels
Of brazen chariots rag'd; dire was the noise
Of conflict. *Book* vi. *Line* 209.

Far off his coming shone. *Book* vi. *Line* 768.

More safe I sing with mortal voice, unchang'd
To hoarse or mute, though fall'n on evil days,
On evil days though fall'n, and evil tongues.
Book vii. *Line* 24.

Still govern thou my song,
Urania, and fit audience find, though few. *Book* vii. *Line* 30.

                    Heaven open'd wide
Her ever-during gates, harmonious sound
On golden hinges moving.   *Book* vii.   *Line* 205.

Hither, as to their fountain, other stars
Repairing, in their golden urns draw light. *Book* vii.   *Line* 364.

                 Now half appear'd
The tawny lion, pawing to get free
His hinder parts.   *Book* vii.   *Line* 463.
                   Indued
With sanctity of reason.   *Book* vii.   *Line* 507.

The Angel ended, and in Adam's ear
So charming left his voice, that he awhile
Thought him still speaking, still stood fix'd to hear.
                             Book viii.   *Line* 1.

And grace that won who saw to wish her stay.
                             Book viii.   *Line* 43.

And, touch'd by her fair tendance, gladlier grew.
                             Book viii.   *Line* 47.

With centric and eccentric scribbled o'er,
Cycle and epicycle, orb in orb.   *Book* viii.   *Line* 83.

                 To know
That which before us lies in daily life,
Is the prime wisdom.   *Book* viii.   *Line* 192.

Liquid lapse of murmuring streams.   *Book* viii.   *Line* 263.

And feel that I am happier than I know. *Book* viii.   *Line* 282.

Grace was in all her steps, heaven in her eye,
In every gesture dignity and love.   *Book* viii.   *Line* 488.

Her virtue and the conscience of her worth,
That would be wooed, and not unsought be won.
                             Book viii.   *Line* 502.

              She what was honour knew,
And with obsequious majesty approv'd
My pleaded reason. To the nuptial bower
I led her, blushing like the morn : all heaven,
And happy constellations on that hour
Shed their selectest influence ; the earth
Gave sign of gratulation, and each hill ;
Joyous the birds ; fresh gales and gentle airs
Whisper'd it to the woods, and from their wings
Flung rose, flung odours from the spicy shrub.
                             Book viii.   *Line* 508.

PARADISE LOST—*continued.*]

              So well to know
Her own, that what she wills to do or say
Seems wisest, virtuousest, discreetest, best.

                             Book viii.   *Line* 548.

Accuse not Nature, she hath done her part ;
Do thou but thine.   *Book* viii.   *Line* 561.

              Those graceful acts,
Those thousand decencies, that daily flow
From all her words and actions.   *Book* viii.   *Line* 600.

To whom the angel with a smile that glow'd
Celestial rosy red, love's proper hue.   *Book* viii.   *Line* 618.

My unpremeditated verse.   *Book* ix.   *Line* 23.

Pleas'd me, long choosing and beginning late.

                             Book ix.   *Line* 26.

        Unless an age too late, or cold
Climate, or years, damp my intended wing. *Book* ix.   *Line* 44.

        Revenge, at first though sweet,
Bitter ere long back on itself recoils.   *Book* ix.   *Line* 171.

        The work under our labour grows,
Luxurious by restraint.   *Book* ix.   *Line* 208.

        Smiles from reason flow,
To brute deny'd, and are of love the food. *Book* ix.   *Line* 239.

For solitude sometimes is best society,
And short retirement urges sweet return.   *Book* ix.   *Line* 249.

At shut of evening flowers.   *Book* ix.   *Line* 278.

As one who long in populous city pent,
Where houses thick and sewers annoy the air.

                             Book ix.   *Line* 445.

So glozed the tempter.   *Book* ix.   *Line* 549.

        Hope elevates, and joy
Brightens his crest.   *Book* ix.   *Line* 633.

        Left that command
Sole daughter of his voice.[1]   *Book* ix.   *Line* 652.

Earth felt the wound ; and Nature from her seat,
Sighing through all her works, gave signs of woe,
That all was lost.   *Book* ix.   *Line* 782.

        In her face excuse
Came prologue, and apology too prompt. *Book* ix.   *Line* 853.

---

[1] Cf. Wordsworth, *Ode to Duty*, post.

PARADISE LOST—*continued.*]

A pillar'd shade

High overarch'd, and echoing walks between.

Book ix.   *Line* 1106.

Yet I shall temper so

Justice with mercy, as may illustrate most
Them fully satisfy'd, and thee appease.   *Book* x.   *Line* 77.

So scented the grim Feature, and upturn'd
His nostril wide into the murky air,
Sagacious of his quarry from so far.   *Book* x.   *Line* 279.

How gladly would I meet

Mortality my sentence, and be earth
Insensible! how glad would lay me down
As in my mother's lap!   *Book* x.   *Line* 775.

Must I thus leave thee, Paradise? thus leave
Thee, native soil, these happy walks and shades?
Book xi.   *Line* 269.

Then purged with euphrasy and rue

The visual nerve, for he had much to see.   *Book* xi.   *Line* 414.

Moping melancholy,

And moon-struck madness.   *Book* xi.   *Line* 485.

And over them triumphant Death his dart
Shook, but delay'd to strike, though oft invok'd.
Line 491.

So mayst thou live, till like ripe fruit thou drop
Into thy mother's lap.   *Book* xi.   *Line* 535.

Nor love thy life, nor hate; but what thou liv'st
Live well; how long or short permit to heaven.[1]
Book xi.   *Line* 553.

A bevy of fair women.   *Book* xi.   *Line* 582.

Some natural tears they dropp'd, but wip'd them soon;
The world was all before them, where to choose
Their place of rest, and Providence their guide.
They, hand in hand, with wand'ring steps and slow,
Through Eden took their solitary way.   *Book* xii.   *Line* 645.

PARADISE REGAINED.

Beauty stands

In the admiration only of weak minds
Led captive.   *Book* ii.   *Line* 220.

Rocks whereon greatest men have oftest wreck'd.
Book ii.   *Line* 228.

---

[1] Summum nec metuas diem, nec optes.—Martial, *lib.* x. 47; 14.

PARADISE REGAINED—*continued.*]

Of whom to be disprais'd were no small praise.
Book iii.   *Line* 56.

Elephants endors'd with towers.   *Book* iii.   *Line* 329.

Syene, and where the shadow both way falls,
Meroe, Nilotic isle.   *Book* iv.   *Line* 70.

Dusk faces with white silken turbans wreath'd.
Book iv.   *Line* 76.

> The childhood shows the man
As morning shows the day.[1]   *Book* iv.   *Line* 220.

Athens, the eye of Greece, mother of arts
And eloquence.   *Book* iv.   *Line* 240.

> The olive grove of Academe,
Plato's retirement, where the Attic bird
Trills her thick-warbled notes the summer long.
Book iv.   *Line* 244.

Thence to the famous orators repair,
Those ancient, whose resistless eloquence
Wielded at will that fierce democratie,
Shook the arsenal, and fulmin'd over Greece,
To Macedon, and Artaxerxes' throne.   *Book* iv.   *Line* 267.

Socrates . . . .
Whom well inspir'd the oracle pronounc'd
Wisest of men.   *Book* iv.   *Line* 274.

Deep vers'd in books, and shallow in himself.
Book iv.   *Line* 327.

As children gath'ring pebbles on the shore.[2]   *Book* iv.   *Line* 330.

> Till morning fair
Came forth with pilgrim steps in amice gray.
Book iv.   *Line* 426.

SAMSON AGONISTES.

O dark, dark, dark, amid the blaze of noon!   *Line* 80.

The sun to me is dark
And silent as the moon,
When she deserts the night
Hid in her vacant interlunar cave.   *Line* 86.

Ran on embattled armies clad in iron.   *Line* 129.

> Just are the ways of God,
And justifiable to men ;
Unless there be who think not God at all.   *Line* 293.

What boots it at one gate to make defence,
And at another to let in the foe?   *Line* 560.

---

[1] Cf. Wordsworth, *post.*   [2] Cf. Newton, p. 140.

SAMSON AGONISTES—*continued.*]

But who is this? what thing of sea or land?
Female of sex it seems,
That so bedeck'd, ornate, and gay,
Comes this way sailing
Like a stately ship
Of Tarsus, bound for th' isles
Of Javan or Gadire,
With all her bravery on, and tackle trim,
Sails fill'd, and streamers waving,
Courted by all the winds that hold them play,
An amber scent of odorous perfume
Her harbinger.   *Line* 710.

He 's gone, and who knows how he may report
Thy words by adding fuel to the flame?   *Line* 1350.

For evil news rides post, while good news baits.   *Line* 1538.

And as an evening dragon came,
Assailant on the perched roosts
And nests in order rang'd
Of tame villatic fowl.   *Line* 1692.

Nothing is here for tears, nothing to wail
Or knock the breast, no weakness, no contempt,
Dispraise or blame, nothing but well and fair,
And what may quiet us in a death so noble.   *Line* 1721.

COMUS.

Above the smoke and stir of this dim spot
Which men call Earth.   *Line* 5.

                          That golden key
That opes the palace of eternity.   *Line* 13.

The nodding horror of whose shady brows.   *Line* 38.

The star that bids the shepherd fold.   *Line* 93.
Midnight shout and revelry,
Tipsy dance and jollity.   *Line* 103.

Ere the blabbing eastern scout,
The nice morn, on the Indian steep
From her cabin'd loop-hole peep.   *Line* 138.

              When the gray-hooded Even,
Like a sad votarist in palmer's weed,
Rose from the hindmost wheels of Phœbus' wain.   *Line* 188.

              A thousand fantasies
Begin to throng into my memory,
Of calling shapes, and beckoning shadows dire,
And airy tongues, that syllable men's names
On sands, and shores, and desert wildernesses.   *Line* 205.

Comus—*continued.*]

O welcome pure-ey'd Faith, white-handed Hope,
Thou hovering angel, girt with golden wings !   *Line* 213.

Was I deceived, or did a sable cloud
Turn forth her silver lining on the night ?   *Line* 221.

Can any mortal mixture of earth's mould
Breathe such divine enchanting ravishment ?   *Line* 244.

How sweetly did they float upon the wings
Of silence, through the empty-vaulted night,
At every fall smoothing the raven down
Of darkness till it smiled.   *Line* 249.

Who, as they sung, would take the prison'd soul
And lap it in Elysium.   *Line* 256.

Such sober certainty of waking bliss.   *Line* 263.

I took it for a faery vision
Of some gay creatures of the element,
That in the colours of the rainbow live
And play i' th' plighted clouds.   *Line* 298.

It were a journey like the path to heaven,
To help you find them.   *Line* 303.

With thy long-levell'd rule of streaming light.   *Line* 340.

Virtue could see to do what virtue would
By her own radiant light, though sun and moon
Were in the flat sea sunk.   *Line* 373.

He that has light within his own clear breast
May sit in the centre and enjoy bright day;
But he that hides a dark soul and foul thoughts
Benighted walks under the midday sun.   *Line* 381.

                    The unsunn'd heaps
Of miser's treasure.   *Line* 398.

'T is chastity, my Brother, chastity :
She that has that is clad in complete steel.   *Line* 420.

Some say no evil thing that walks by night
In fog or fire, by lake or moorish fen,
Blue meagre hag, or stubborn unlaid ghost
That breaks his magic chains at curfew time,
No goblin, or swart faery of the mine,
Hath hurtful power o'er true virginity.   *Line* 432.

So dear to heaven is saintly chastity,
That, when a soul is found sincerely so,
A thousand liveried angels lacky her,
Driving far off each thing of sin and guilt.   *Line* 453.

Comus—*continued*.]

How charming is divine philosophy !
Not harsh and crabbed, as dull fools suppose;
But musical as is Apollo's lute,[1]
And a perpetual feast of nectar'd sweets,
Where no crude surfeit reigns.   *Line* 476.

Fill'd the air with barbarous dissonance.   *Line* 550.

        I was all ear,
And took in strains that might create a soul
Under the ribs of death.   *Line* 560.
          If this fail,
The pillar'd firmament is rottenness,
And earth's base built on stubble.   *Line* 597.

The leaf was darkish, and had prickles on it,
But in another country, as he said, -
Bore a bright golden flower, but not in this soil :
Unknown, and like esteem'd, and the dull swain
Treads on it daily with his clouted shoon.   *Line* 631.

Enter'd the very lime-twigs of his spells,
And yet came off.   *Line* 646.

And live like Nature's bastards, not her sons.   *Line* 727.

It is for homely features to keep home,
They had their name thence.   *Line* 748.

What need a vermeil-tinctur'd lip for that,
Love-darting eyes, or tresses like the morn ?   *Line* 752.

         Swinish gluttony
Ne'er looks to heaven amidst his gorgeous feast,
But with besotted base ingratitude
Crams, and blasphemes his feeder.   *Line* 777.

Enjoy your dear wit, and gay rhetoric,
That hath so well been taught her dazzling fence. *Line* 790.

         His rod revers'd,
And backward mutters of dissevering power.   *Line* 816.

Sabrina fair,
   Listen where thou art sitting
Under the glassy, cool, translucent wave,
   In twisted braids of lilies knitting
The loose train of thy amber-dropping hair.   *Line* 859.

But now my task is smoothly done,
I can fly, or I can run.   *Line* 1012.

Or, if Virtue feeble were,
Heaven itself would stoop to her.   *Line* 1022.

---

[1] As sweet and musical
As bright Apollo's lute.   *Love's Labour's Lost.*   *Act* iv. *Sc.* 3.

LYCIDAS.

i come to pluck your berries harsh and crude,
And with forc'd fingers rude,
Shatter your leaves before the mellowing year.   *Line 3.*

           He knew
Himself to sing, and build the lofty rhyme.   *Line 10.*

Without the meed of some melodious tear.   *Line 14.*

Under the opening eyelids of the morn.   *Line 26.*

The gadding vine.   *Line 40*

And strictly meditate the thankless Muse.   *Line 66.*

To sport with Amaryllis in the shade,
Or with the tangles of Neæra's hair.   *Line 68.*

Fame is the spur that the clear spirit doth raise,[1]
(That last infirmity of noble mind)
To scorn delights, and live laborious days;
But the fair guerdon when we hope to find,
And think to burst out into sudden blaze,
Comes the blind Fury with the abhorred shears,
And slits the thin-spun life.   *Line 70.*

Fame is no plant that grows on mortal soil.   *Line 78.*

It was that fatal and perfidious bark,
Built in the eclipse and rigg'd with curses dark.   *Line 100.*

The pilot of the Galilean lake.   *Line 109.*

Throw hither all your quaint enamell'd eyes,
That on the green turf suck the honied showers,
And purple all the ground with vernal flowers.
Bring the rathe primrose that forsaken dies,
The tufted crow-toe, and pale jessamine,
The white pink, and the pansy freak'd with jet,
The glowing violet,
The musk-rose, and the well-attir'd wood-bine,
With cowslips wan that hang the pensive head,
And every flower that sad embroidery wears.   *Line 139.*

So sinks the day-star in the ocean-bed,
And yet anon repairs his drooping head,
And tricks his beams, and with new-spangled ore
Flames in the forehead of the morning sky.   *Line 168.*

To-morrow to fresh woods and pastures new.   *Line 193.*

---

[1] Erant quibus appetentior famæ videretur, quando etiam sapientibus cupido gloriæ novissima exuitur.—Tacitus, *Histor.* iv. 6.

E

ARCADES.

Under the shady roof
Of branching elm star-proof.   *Line* 88.

L' ALLEGRO.

Haste thee, Nymph, and bring with thee
Jest, and youthful jollity,
Quips, and cranks, and wanton wiles,
Nods, and becks, and wreathed smiles.   *Line* 25.

Sport, that wrinkled Care derides,
And Laughter holding both his sides.
Come, and trip it as you go,
On the light fantastic toe.   *Line* 31.

And every shepherd tells his tale
Under the hawthorn in the dale.   *Line* 67.

Meadows trim with daisies pied,
Shallow brooks, and rivers wide;
Towers and battlements it sees
Bosom'd high in tufted trees,
Where perhaps some beauty lies,
The cynosure of neighbouring eyes.   *Line* 75.

Herbs, and other country messes,
Which the neat-handed Phillis dresses.   *Line* 85.

To many a youth, and many a maid,
Dancing in the chequer'd shade.   *Line* 95.

Then to the spicy nut-brown ale.   *Line* 100.

Tower'd cities please us then,
And the busy hum of men.   *Line* 117.

       Ladies, whose bright eyes
Rain influence, and judge the prize.   *Line* 121.

Such sights as youthful poets dream
On summer eves by haunted stream.
Then to the well-trod stage anon,
If Jonson's learned soek be on,
Or sweetest Shakespeare, Fancy's child,
Warble his native wood-notes wild.   *Line* 129.

And ever, against eating cares
Lap me in soft Lydian airs,
Married to immortal verse,
Such as the meeting soul may pierce,
In notes, with many a winding bout
Of linked sweetness long drawn out.   *Line* 135.

L' ALLEGRO—*continued.*]

> Untwisting all the chains that tie
> The hidden soul of harmony.

Line 143

IL PENSEROSO.

> The gay motes that people the sunbeams.

Line 8

> And looks commercing with the skies,
> Thy rapt soul sitting in thine eyes.

Line 39.

> And join with thee calm Peace and Quiet,
> Spare Fast, that oft with gods doth diet.

Line 45.

> And add to these retired Leisure,
> That in trim gardens takes his pleasure.

Line 49.

> Sweet bird, that shunn'st the noise of folly,
> Most musical, most melancholy!

Line 61.

> To behold the wandering moon,
> Riding near her highest noon,
> Like one that had been led astray
> Through the heaven's wide pathless way;
> And oft, as if her head she bow'd,
> Stooping through a fleecy cloud.

Line 67.

> Where glowing embers through the room
> 'Teach light to counterfeit a gloom.

Line 79.

> Save the cricket on the hearth.

Line 82.

> Sometime let gorgeous Tragedy
> In sceptred pall come sweeping by,
> Presenting Thebes, or Pelops' line,
> Or the tale of Troy divine.

Line 97.

> Or bid the soul of Orpheus sing
> Such notes as, warbled to the string.
> Drew iron tears down Pluto's cheek.

Line 105.

> Or call up him that left half told
> The story of Cambuscan bold.

Line 109.

> Where more is meant than meets the ear

Line 120.

> Ending on the rustling leaves,
> With minute drops from off the eaves.

Line 129.

> And storied windows richly dight,
> Casting a dim religious light.

Line 159.

> Till old experience do attain
> To something like prophetic strain.

Line 173.

> Nor war or battle's sound
> Was heard the world around.

Hymn on Christ's Nativity. *Line* 53.

IL PENSEROSO—*continued.*]

Time will run back, and fetch the age of gold.	*Line* 135.
Swinges the scaly horror of his folded tail.	*Line* 172.

The oracles are dumb,
No voice or hideous hum
Runs thro' the arched roof in words deceiving.
Apollo from his shrine
Can no more divine,
With hollow shriek the steep of Delphos leaving.
No nightly trance, or breathed spell
Inspires the pale-ey'd priest from the prophetic cell.   *Line* 178.

From haunted spring, and dale
Edg'd with poplar pale,
The parting genius is with sighing sent.   *Line* 184.

Peor and Baälim
Forsake their temples dim.   *Line* 197.

Under a star-y-pointing pyramid.
Dear son of memory, great heir of fame.
             Epitaph on Shakespeare. *Line* 4.

And so sepulchred in such pomp dost lie,
'That kings for such a tomb would wish to die.   *Line* 15.

SONNETS.

Thy liquid notes that close the eye of day.   *To the Nightingale.*

As ever in my great task-master's eye.
      On his being arrived to the Age of Twenty-Three.

The great Emathian conqueror bid spare
The house of Pindarus, when temple and tower
Went to the ground.
        When the Assault was intended to the City.

That old man eloquent.   *To the Lady Margaret Ley.*

That would have made Quintilian stare and gasp.
      *On the Detraction which followed upon my Writing
              Certain Treatises.*

License they mean when they cry liberty.   *On the Same.*

      Peace hath her victories
No less renown'd than war.   *To the Lord General Cromwell.*

      Thousands at His bidding speed,
And post o'er land and ocean without rest;
They also serve who only stand and wait.   *On his Blindness.*

In mirth, that after no repenting draws.   *To Cyriac Skinner.*

SONNETS—*continued.*]

> For other things mild Heav'n a time ordains.
> And disapproves that care, though wise in show,
>   That with superfluous burden loads the day,
> And, when God sends a cheerful hour, refrains.   *Ibid.*

>   Yet I argue not
> Against Heaven's hand or will, nor bate a jot
> Of heart or hope; but still bear up and steer
> Right onward.   *To the Same.*

> Of which all Europe rings from side to side.   *Ibid.*

> But O, as to embrace me she inclin'd,
> I wak'd, she fled, and day brought back my night.
>   *On his Deceased Wife.*

>   Have hung
> My dank and dropping weeds
> To the stern god of sea.
>   *Translation of Horace.   Book* i. *Ode* 5.

Truth is as impossible to be soiled by any outward touch as the sunbeam.
    The Doctrine and Discipline of Divorce.

A poet soaring in the high reason of his fancies, with his garland and singing robes about him.   *The Reason of Church Government.   Book* ii.

By labour and intent study (which I take to be my portion in this life), joined with the strong propensity of nature, I might perhaps leave something so written to after times, as they should not willingly let it die.   *Ibid.*

Beholding the bright countenance of truth in the quiet and still air of delightful studies.   *Ibid.*

He who would not be frustrate of his hope to write well hereafter in laudable things ought himself to be a true poem.
                          Apology for Smectymnuus.

Litigious terms, fat contentions, and flowing fees.
                          Tractate of Education.

I shall detain you no longer in the demonstration of what we should not do, but strait conduct ye to a hillside, where I will point ye out the right path of a virtuous and noble education; laborious indeed at the first ascent, but else so smooth, so green, so full of goodly prospect, and melodious sounds on every side, that the harp of Orpheus was not more charming.   *Ibid.*

In those vernal seasons of the year, when the air is calm and pleasant, it were an injury and sullenness against Nature not to go out and see her riches, and partake in her rejoicing with heaven and earth.   *Ibid.*

Tractate of Education—*continued.*]

Enflamed with the study of learning and the admiration of virtue; stirred up with high hopes of living to be brave men and worthy patriots, dear to God, and famous to all ages. *Ibid.*

As good almost kill a man as kill a good book; who kills a man kills a reasonable creature, God's image; but he who destroys a good book kills reason itself. *Areopagitica.*

A good book is the precious life-blood of a master-spirit embalmed and treasured up on purpose to a life beyond life. *Ibid.*

I cannot praise a fugitive and cloistered virtue, unexercised and unbreathed, that never sallies out and seeks her adversary. *Ibid.*

Methinks I see in my mind a noble and puissant nation rousing herself like a strong man after sleep, and shaking her invincible locks; methinks I see her as an eagle mewing her mighty youth, and kindling her undazzled eyes at the full midday beam. *Ibid.*

Who ever knew truth put to the worse, in a free and open encounter? *Ibid.*

By this time, like one who had set out on his way by night, and travelled through a region of smooth and idle dreams, our history now arrives on the confines, where daylight and truth meet us with a clear dawn, representing to our view, though at far distance, true colours and shapes.
History of England. Book i. *ad fin.*

Men of most renowned virtue have sometimes by transgressing most truly kept the law. *Tetrarchordon.*

For such kind of borrowing as this, if it be not bettered by the borrower, among good authors is accounted Plagiarè.
Iconoclastes, xxiv. *ad fin.*

—□—

THOMAS FULLER. 1608—1661.

THE HOLY AND THE PROFANE STATE.

Ed. Nichols, 1841.

Drawing near her death, she sent most pious thoughts as harbingers to heaven; and her soul saw a glimpse of happiness through the chinks of her sickness-broken body.[1] *The Life of Monica.*

But our captain counts the image of God, nevertheless his image, cut in ebony as if done in ivory. *The Good Sea-Captain.*

The lion is not so fierce as painted.[2] *Of Expecting Preferment.*

Their heads sometimes so little, that there is no room for wit; sometimes so long, that there is no wit for so much room. *Of Natural Fools.*

---

[1] Cf. Waller, p. 100.
[2] The lion is not so fierce as they paint him.—Herbert, *Jacula Prudentum.*

The Pyramids themselves, doting with age, have forgotten the names of their founders.
Of Tombs.

Learning hath gained most by those books by which the printers have lost.
Of Books.

They that marry ancient people, merely in expectation to bury them, hang themselves, in hope that one will come and cut the halter.
Of Marriage.

To smell to a turf of fresh earth is wholesome for the body; no less are thoughts of mortality cordial to the soul.
The Court Lady.

Often the cockloft is empty, in those whom Nature hath built many stories high.[1]
Andronicus. Ad. fin. 1.

—◻—

FRANCIS DUC DE ROCHEFOUCAULD. 1613—1680.

Philosophy triumphs easily over past, and over future evils, but present evils triumph over philosophy.[2]
Maxim 23.

Hypocrisy is a sort of homage that vice pays to virtue.
Maxim 227.

In the adversity of our best friends we often find something which does not displease us.[3]
Maxim 245.

—◻—

WILLIAM BASSE. 1613—1648.

Renowned Spenser, lie a thought more nigh
To learned Chaucer, and rare Beaumont lie
A little nearer Spenser, to make room
For Shakespeare in your threefold, fourfold tomb.[4]
On Shakespeare.

—◻—

HENRY VAUGHAN. 1621—1695.

I see them walking in an air of glory
Whose light doth trample on my days;
My days which are at best but dull and hoary,
Mere glimmering and decays.
They are all gone.

---

[1] My Lord St. Albans said that wise nature did never put her precious jewels into a garret four stories high, and therefore that exceeding tall men had ever very empty heads.—Bacon, *Apothegm, No.* 17.

[2] This same philosophy is a good horse in the stable, but an arrant jade on a journey.—Goldsmith, *The Good-Natured Man, Act* i.

[3] I am convinced that we have a degree of delight and that no small one in the real misfortunes and pains of others.—Burke, *The Sublime and Beautiful. Pt.* 1, *Sec.* 14, 15.   [4] I will not lodge thee by
Chaucer, or Spenser, or bid Beaumont lie
A little further, to make thee a room.
Jonson, *To the Memory of Shakespeare.*

THEY ARE ALL GONE—*continued.*]

  Dear beauteous death, the jewel of the just.   *Ibid.*

  And yet, as angels in some brighter dreams
  Call to the soul when man doth sleep,
  So some strange thoughts transcend our wonted themes,
  And into glory peep.   *Ibid.*

—□—

SAMUEL BUTLER. 1600—1680.
HUDIBRAS.

And pulpit, drum ecclesiastick,
Was beat with fist instead of a stick.   *Part* i. *Canto* i. *Line* 11.

We grant, altho' he had much wit,
He was very shy of using it.   *Part* i. *Canto* i. *Line* 45.

Beside, 't is known he could speak Greek
As naturally as pigs squeak ;
That Latin was no more difficile
Than to a blackbird 't is to whistle.   *Part* i. *Canto* i. *Line* 51.

He could distinguish, and divide
A hair, 'twixt south and south-west side. *Part* i. *Canto* i. *Line* 67.

For rhetoric, he could not ope
His mouth, but out there flew a trope. *Part* i. *Canto* i. *Line* 81.

For all a rhetorician's rules
Teach nothing but to name his tools.   *Part* i. *Canto* i. *Line* 89.

For he, by geometric scale,
Could take the size of pots of ale.   *Part* i. *Canto* i. *Line* 121.

And wisely tell what hour o' th' day
The clock does strike, by Algebra.   *Part* i. *Canto* i. *Line* 125.

Whatever sceptic could inquire for,
For every why he had a wherefore.   *Part* i. *Canto* i. *Line* 131.

Where entity and quiddity,
The ghosts of defunct bodies fly.   *Part* i. *Canto* i. *Line* 145.

He knew what 's what, and that 's as high [1]
As metaphysic wit can fly.   *Part* i. *Canto* i. *Line* 149.

Such as take lodgings in a head
That 's to be let unfurnished. [2]   *Part* i. *Canto* i. *Line* 161.

'T was Presbyterian true blue.   *Part* i. *Canto* i. *Line* 191.

---

[1] He said he knew what was what. — Skelton, *Why come ye not to Courte ? Line* 1106.

[2] Often the cockloft is empty in those whom Nature hath built many stories high.—Fuller, *Holy and Profane State.* Andronicus, *Ad. fin.* 1.

HUDIBRAS—*continued.*]

And prove their doctrine orthodox,
By apostolic blows and knocks. *Part* i. *Canto* i. *Line* 199.

Compound for sins they are inclined to,
By damning those they have no mind to.
Part i. *Canto* i. *Line* 215.

The trenchant blade, Toledo trusty,
For want of fighting was grown rusty,
And ate into itself for lack
Of somebody to hew and hack. *Part* i. *Canto* i. *Line* 359.

For rhyme the rudder is of verses,
With which, like ships, they steer their courses.
Part i. *Canto* i. *Line* 463.

And force them, though it were in spite
Of Nature, and their stars, to write. *Part* i. *Canto* i. *Line* 647.

Quoth Hudibras, "I smell a rat;[1]
Ralpho, thou dost prevaricate." *Part* i. *Canto* i. *Line* 821.

Or shear swine, all cry and no wool.[2] *Part* i. *Canto* i. *Line* 852.

With many a stiff thwack, many a bang,
Hard crab-tree and old iron rang. *Part* i. *Canto* ii. *Line* 831.

Ay me! what perils do environ
The man that meddles with cold iron.[3] *Part* i. *Canto* iii. *Line* 1.

Nor do I know what is become
Of him, more than the Pope of Rome. *Part* i. *Canto* iii. *Line* 263.

                He had got a hurt
C' th' inside of a deadlier sort. *Part* i. *Canto* iii. *Line* 309.

For those that run away, and fly,
Take place at least o' th' enemy.[4] *Part* i. *Canto* iii. *Line* 609.

I am not now in fortune's power;
He that is down can fall no lower.[5] *Part* i. *Canto* iii. *Line* 877.

Cheer'd up himself with ends of verse,
And sayings of philosophers. *Part* i. *Canto* iii. *Line* 1011.

If he that in the field is slain
Be in the bed of honour lain,
He that is beaten may be said
To lie in honour's truckle-bed. *Part* i. *Canto* iii. *Line* 1047.

---

[1] See *Proverbs, post.*
[2] And so his Highness schal have thereof, but as had the man that scheryd his Hogge, *moche Crye and no Wull.*—Fortescue (1395—1485), *Treatise on Absolute and Limited Monarchy, Ch.* x.
[3] Ay me, how many perils do enfold
            The righteous man, to make him daily fall.
                    Spenser, *Faerie Queene, Book* i. *Canto* 8. *St.* 1.
[4] See *Appendix, post: He that fights and runs away.*   [5] Cf. Bunyan, p. 137.

E*

HUDIBRAS—*continued.*]

  When pious frauds and holy shifts
  Are dispensations and gifts.   *Part* i. *Canto* iii. *Line* 1145.

    Friend Ralph, thou hast
  Outrun the constable at last.   *Part* i. *Canto* iii. *Line* 1367.

  Some force whole regions, in despite
  O' geography, to change their site;
  Make former times shake hands with latter,
  And that which was before, come after;
  But those that write in rhyme still make
  The one verse for the other's sake;
  For one for sense, and one for rhyme,
  I think 's sufficient at one time.   *Part* ii. *Canto* i. *Line* 23.

  Some have been beaten till they know
  What wood a cudgel 's of by th' blow;
  Some kick'd until they can feel whether
  A shoe be Spanish or neat's leather.   *Part* ii. *Canto* i. *Line* 221.

  Quoth she, I 've heard old cunning stagers
  Say, fools for arguments use wagers.   *Part* ii. *Canto* i. *Line* 297.

  For what is worth in anything,
  But so much money as 't will bring?   *Part* ii. *Canto* i. *Line* 465.

  Love is a boy by poets styl'd;
  Then spare the rod and spoil the child.[1] *Part* ii. *Canto* i. *Line* 843.

  The sun had long since in the lap
  Of Thetis taken out his nap,
  And, like a lobster boiled, the morn
  From black to red began to turn.   *Part* ii. *Canto* ii. *Line* 29.

  Have always been at daggers-drawing,
  And one another clapper-clawing.   *Part* ii. *Canto* ii. *Line* 79.

  For truth is precious and divine,
  Too rich a pearl for carnal swine.   *Part* ii. *Canto* ii. *Line* 257.

  He that imposes an oath makes it,
  Not he that for convenience takes it:
  Then how can any man be said
  To break an oath he never made?   *Part* ii. *Canto* ii. *Line* 377.

    As the ancients
  Say wisely, Have a care o' th' main chance,[2]
  And look before you ere you leap;[2]
  For as you sow, y' are like to reap.[3] *Part* ii. *Canto* ii. *Line* 501.

---

[1] He that spareth his rod hateth his son.—*Proverbs*, ch. xiii. 24.
[2] See Proverbs, *post.*
[3] Whatsoever a man soweth that shall he also reap.—*Galatians*, ch. vi. 7.
 Cf. Tusser, *ante*, p. 4.

HUDIBRAS—*continued.*]

Doubtless the pleasure is as great
Of being cheated, as to cheat.
                              Part ii. *Canto* iii. *Line* 1.

He made an instrument to know
If the moon shine at full or no.
                              Part ii. *Canto* iii. *Line* 261.

Each window like a pill'ry appears,
With heads thrust thro' nailed by the ears.
                              Part ii. *Canto* iii. *Line* 391.

To swallow gudgeons ere they 're catched,
And count their chickens ere they 're hatched.
                              Part ii. *Canto* iii. *Line* 923.

There 's but the twinkling of a star
Between a man of peace and war.
                              Part ii. *Canto* iii. *Line* 957.

As quick as lightning in the breech,
Just in the place where honour 's lodged,
As wise philosophers have judged;
Because a kick in that place more
Hurts honour, than deep wounds before.
                              Part ii. *Canto* iii. *Line* 1067.

As men of inward light are wont
To turn their optics in upon 't.
                              Part iii. *Canto* i. *Line* 481.

Still amorous, and fond, and billing,
Like Philip and Mary on a shilling.
                              Part iii. *Canto* i. *Line* 687.

What makes all doctrines plain and clear?
About two hundred pounds a year.
And that which was proved true before,
Prove false again? Two hundred more.
                              Part iii. *Canto* i. *Line* 1277.

'Cause grace and virtue are within
Prohibited degrees of kin;
And therefore no true saint allows
They should be suffer'd to espouse.
                              Part iii. *Canto* i. *Line* 1293.

Nick Machiavel had ne'er a trick,
Though he gave his name to our old Nick.
                              Part iii. *Canto* i. *Line* 1313.

With crosses, relics, crucifixes,
Beads, pictures, rosaries, and pixes;
The tools of working out Salvation
By mere mechanic operation.
                              Part iii. *Canto* i. *Line* 1495.

True as the dial to the sun,
Although it be not shin'd upon.
                              Part iii. *Canto* ii. *Line* 175.

For those that fly may fight again,
Which he can never do that 's slain.[1] *Part* iii. *Canto* iii. *Line* 243.

[1] See Appendix. *post: He that fights and runs away.*

HUDIBRAS—*continued.*]

He that complies against his will
Is of his own opinion still.   *Part* iii. *Canto* iii. *Line* 547.

With books and money plac'd for show,
Like nest-eggs to make clients lay,
And for his false opinion pay.   *Part* iii. *Canto* iii. *Line* 624.

——□——

ANDREW MARVELL. 1620—1678.

And all the way, to guide their chime,
With falling oars they kept the time.   *Bermudas.*

In busy companies of men.   *The Garden.* (Translated.)
Annihilating all that 's made
To a green thought in a green shade.   *Ibid.*

The world in all doth but two nations bear,
The good, the bad, and these mixed everywhere.
                                        The Loyal Scot.

The inglorious arts of peace.
                    Upon Cromwell's return from Ireland.

He nothing common did, or mean,
Upon that memorable scene.   *Ibid.*

So much one man can do,
That does both act and know.   *Ibid.*

——□——

JOHN DRYDEN. 1631—1701.
ALEXANDER'S FEAST.

None but the brave deserves the fair.   *Line* 15.

With ravish'd ears
The monarch hears,
Assumes the god,
Affects to nod,
And seems to shake the spheres.   *Line* 37.

Bacchus, ever fair and young.   *Line* 54.

    Rich the treasure,
    Sweet the pleasure,
Sweet is pleasure after pain.   *Line* 58.

Sooth'd with the sound, the king grew vain;
Fought all his battles o'er again;
And thrice he routed all his foes; and thrice he slew the slain.
                                        Line 66.

Fallen, fallen, fallen, fallen,
Fallen from his high estate,
    And weltering in his blood;

ALEXANDER'S FEAST—*continued.*]

> Deserted, at his utmost need,
> By those his former bounty fed;
> On the bare earth expos'd he lies,
> With not a friend to close his eyes.   *Line 77*
>
> For pity melts the mind to love.   *Line 96.*
>
> Softly sweet, in Lydian measures,
> Soon he sooth'd his soul to pleasures.
> War, he sung, is toil and trouble;
> Honour, but an empty bubble;
> Never ending, still beginning,
> Fighting still, and still destroying.
> If all the world be worth the winning,
> Think, O think it worth enjoying:
> Lovely Thais sits beside thee,
> Take the good the gods provide thee.   *Line 97.*
>
> Sigh'd and look'd, and sigh'd again.   *Line 120*
>
> And, like another Helen, fir'd another Troy.   *Line 154.*
>
> Could swell the soul to rage, or kindle soft desire.   *Line 160.*
>
> He rais'd a mortal to the skies,
> She drew an angel down.   *Line 169.*

ABSALOM AND ACHITOPHEL.

> Whate'er he did was done with so much ease,
> In him alone 't was natural to please.   *Part* i. *Line 27.*
>
> A fiery soul, which, working out its way,
> Fretted the pygmy-body to decay,
> And o'er-inform'd the tenement of clay.[1]   *Part* i. *Line 156.*
>
> Great wits are sure to madness near allied,
> And thin partitions do their bounds divide.[2]   *Part* i. *Line 163.*
>
> And all to leave what with his toil he won,
> To that unfeather'd two-legg'd thing, a son.   *Part* i. *Line 169.*
>
> Resolv'd to ruin or to rule the state.   *Part* i. *Line 174.*
>
> And heaven had wanted one immortal song.
> But wild ambition loves to slide, not stand,
> And Fortune's ice prefers to Virtue's land.[3]   *Part* i. *Line 197.*

---

[1] He was one of a lean body and visage, as if his eager soul, biting for anger at the clog of his body, desired to fret a passage through it.—Fuller, *Holy and Profane State. Life of Duke d'Alva.*

[2] Cf. Pope, *Essay on Man, Ep.* 1, *Line* 226.

[3] Greatnesse on goodnesse loves to slide, not stand,
And leaves, for Fortune's ice, Vertue's ferme land.
From *Knolles's History* (under a portrait of Mustapha I.).

ABSALOM AND ACHITOPHEL—*continued.*]

The people's prayer, the glad diviner's theme,
The young men's vision, and the old men's dream![1]
                                    Part i. *Line* 238.

Behold him setting in his western skies,
The shadows lengthening as the vapours rise.[2] *Part* i. *Line* 268.

Than a successive title, long and dark,
Drawn from the mouldy rolls of Noah's ark.   *Part* i. *Line* 301.

Not only hating David, but the king.   *Part* i. *Line* 512.

Who think too little, and who talk too much. *Part* i. *Line* 534.

A man so various, that he seem'd to be
Not one, but all mankind's epitome;
Stiff in opinions, always in the wrong,
Was everything by starts, and nothing long.
But in the course of one revolving moon,
Was chymist, fiddler, statesman, and buffoon.[3] *Part* i. *Line* 545.

So over-violent, or over-civil,
That every man with him was God or Devil.   *Part* i. *Line* 557.

His tribe were God Almighty's gentlemen.   *Part* i. *Line* 645.

Him of the western dome, whose weighty sense
Flows in fit words and heavenly eloquence.   *Part* i. *Line* 868.

Beware the fury of a patient man.[4]   *Part* i. *Line* 1005.

Made still a blundering kind of melody;
Spurr'd boldly on, and dash'd through thick and thin,
Through sense and nonsense, never out nor in.
                                    Part ii. *Line* 413.
For every inch that is not fool is rogue.   *Part* ii. *Line* 463

CYMON AND IPHIGENIA.

He trudged along, unknowing what he sought,
And whistled as he went, for want of thought.   *Line* 84.

The fool of nature stood with stupid eyes,
And gaping mouth, that testified surprise.   *Line* 107.

She hugged the offender, and forgave the offence.
Sex to the last.[5]   *Line* 367.

---

[1] Your old men shall dream dreams, your young men shall see visions.—
Joel ii. 28.
[2] Cf. Young, *Night Thoughts*, v. 661.
[3] Grammaticus, rhetor, geometres, pictor, aliptes,
Augur, schœnobates, medicus, magus, omnia novit.
                            Juvenal, *Sat.* iii. *Line* 76.
[4] Furor fit læsa sæpius patientia.—Publius Syrus.
[5] Cf. Pope, *Eloisa to Abelard, Line* 192.

CYMON AND IPHIGENIA—*continued.*]

> And raw in fields the rude militia swarms;
> Mouths without hands : maintained at vast expense,
> In peace a charge, in war a weak defence;
> Stout once a month they march, a blustering band,
> And ever, but in times of need, at hand. *Line* 400.

> Of seeming arms to make a short essay,
> Then hasten to be drunk, the business of the day. *Line* 407

> Better to hunt in fields for health unbought,
> Than fee the doctor for a nauseous draught.
> The wise for cure on exercise depend ;
> God never made his work for man to mend.
> *Epistle* xiii. *Line* 92.

> And threatening France, plac'd like a painted Jove,
> Kept idle thunder in his lifted hand.
> *Annus Mirabilis. Stanza* 39.

> Men met each other with erected look,
> The steps were higher that they took,
> Friends to congratulate their friends made haste;
> And long-inveterate foes saluted as they pass'd.
> *Threnodia Augustalis. Line* 124.

> For truth has such a face and such a mien,
> As to be lov'd needs only to be seen.[1]
> *The Hind and Panther. Line* 33.

> And kind as kings upon their coronation day. *Ibid. Line* 271.

> But Shadwell never deviates into sense. *Mac Flecknoe. Line* 20.

> And torture one poor word ten thousand ways. *Ibid. Line* 208.

> Fool, not to know that love endures no tie,
> And Jove but laughs at lovers' perjury.[2]
> *Palamon and Arcite. Book* ii. *Line* 758.

> For Art may err, but Nature cannot miss.
> *The Cock and Fox. Line* 452.

> And that one hunting, which the Devil design'd
> For one fair female, lost him half the kind.
> *Theodore and Honoria.*

> Three Poets, in three distant ages born,
> Greece, Italy, and England did adorn;

---

[1] Cf. Pope, *Essay on Man, Ep.* ii. *Line* 217.
[2] Perjuria ridet amantum
Jupiter.
Tibullus, *Lib.* iii. *El.* 7, *Line* 17.
This proverb Dryden repeats in *Amphitryon, Act* i. *Sc.* 2.

The first in loftiness of thought surpass'd,
The next in majesty, in both the last.
The force of Nature could no further go;
To make a third, she join'd the former two.[1]

Under Mr. Milton's Picture.

A very merry, dancing, drinking,
Laughing, quaffing, and unthinking time.

The Secular Masque. Line 40.

Thus all below is strength, and all above is grace.

Epistle to Congreve. Line 19.

Be kind to my remains; and O defend,
Against your judgment, your departed friend !   *Ibid. Line* 72.

Happy who in his verse can gently steer,
From grave to light; from pleasant to severe.[2]

The Art of Poetry. Canto i. *Line* 75.

Since heaven's eternal year is thine.

Elegy on Mrs. Killegrew. Line 15.

Her wit was more than man, her innocence a child.[3]

Ibid. Line 70.

Above any Greek or Roman name.[4]

Upon the Death of Lord Hastings. Line 76.

He was exhal'd; his great Creator drew
His spirit, as the sun the morning dew.[5]

On the Death of a very Young Gentleman.

From harmony, from heavenly harmony,
This universal frame began :
From harmony to harmony
Through all the compass of the notes it ran,
The diapason closing full in Man.

A Song for St. Cecilia's Day. Line 11.

Happy the man, and happy he alone,
He who can call to-day his own :
He who, secure within, can say,
To-morrow, do thy worst, for I have liv'd to-day.

Imitation of Horace. Book i. *Ode* 29. *Line* 65.

Not heaven itself upon the past has power;
But what has been, has been, and I have had my hour.

Ibid. Line 71.

---

[1] Græcia Mæonidam, jactet sibi Roma Maronem,
   Anglia Miltonum jactat utrique parem.
Selvaggi, *Ad Joannem Miltonum.*
[2] Cf. Pope, *Essay on Man, Ep.* iv. *Line* 379.
[3] Cf. Pope, *Epitaph on Gay.*
[4] Cf. Pope, *Satires and Epistles, Book* ii. *Ep.* i. *Line* 26.
[5] Cf. Young, *Night Thoughts,* v. *Line* 600.

IMITATION OF HORACE—*continued.*]

I can enjoy her while she 's kind;
But when she dances in the wind,
And shakes the wings, and will not stay,
I puff the prostitute away.   *Ibid.   Line* 81.

And virtue, though in rags, will keep me warm.   *Ibid.   Line* 87.

Arms and the man I sing, who, forced by fate
And haughty Juno's unrelenting hate.   *Virgil.   Æneid,* 1.

Ill habits gather by unseen degrees,
As brooks make rivers, rivers run to seas.
                    Ovid.   Metamorphoses.   Book xv.   *Line* 155.

She knows her man, and when you rant and swear,
Can draw you to her with a single hair.[1]
                    Persius.   Satire v.   *Line* 246.

Look round the habitable world, how few
Know their own good, or, knowing it, pursue !
                    Juvenal.   Satire x.

Thespis, the first professor of our art,
At country wakes sung ballads from a cart.
                    Prologue to Lee's Sophonisba.

Errors like straws upon the surface flow;
He who would search for pearls must dive below.
                    All for Love.   Prologue.

Men are but children of a larger growth.   *Ibid.   Act* iv. *Sc.* 1.

Your ignorance is the mother of your devotion to me.
                    The Maiden Queen.   Act i. *Sc.* 2.

But Shakespeare's magic could not copied be;
Within that circle none durst walk but he.
                    The Tempest.   Prologue.

I am as free as nature first made man,
Ere the base laws of servitude began,
When wild in woods the noble savage ran.
                    The Conquest of Granada.   Part i. *Act* i. *Sc.* 1.

Forgiveness to the injured does belong;
But they ne'er pardon who have done the wrong.[2]
                    Ibid.   Part ii. *Act* i. *Sc.* 2.

What precious drops are those,
Which silently each other's track pursue,
Bright as young diamonds in their infant dew?
                    Ibid.   Part ii. *Act* iii. *Sc.* 1.

---

[1] Cf. Pope, *The Rape of the Lock, Canto* ii. *Line* 27.
[2] Quos læserunt et oderunt.—Seneca, *De Ira, Lib.* ii. *cap.* xxxiii.
Proprium humani ingenii est odisse quem læseris.—Tacitus, *Agrivo.*
42, 4.
The offender never pardons.—Herbert, *Jacula Prudentum.*

When I consider life, 't is all a cheat.
Yet, fooled with hope, men favour the deceit;
Trust on, and think to-morrow will repay :
To-morrow 's falser than the former day;
Lies worse; and while it says, "We shall be blest
With some new joys," cuts off what we possest.
Strange cozenage! none would live past years again,
Yet all hope pleasure in what yet remain;
And from the dregs of life think to receive
What the first sprightly running could not give.
Aureng-zebe.   Act iv. *Sc.* 1.

All delays are dangerous in war.[1]   *Tyrannic Love.   Act* i. *Sc.* 1.

Pains of love be sweeter far
Than all other pleasures are.   *Ibid.   Act* iv. *Sc.* 1.

    His hair just grizzled
As in a green old age.   *Œdipus.   Act* iii. *Sc.* 1.

Of no distemper, of no blast he died,
But fell like autumn fruit that mellowed long;
Even wondered at, because he dropt no sooner.
Fate seemed to wind him up for fourscore years;
Yet freshly ran he on ten winters more :
Till, like a clock worn out with eating time,
The wheels of weary life at last stood still.   *Ibid.   Act* iv. *Sc.* 1.

She, though in full-blown flower of glorious beauty,
Grows cold, even in the summer of her age.
Ibid.   Act iv. *Sc.* 1.

    There is a pleasure sure
In being mad which none but madmen know.[2]
The Spanish Friar.   Act ii. *Sc.* 1.

This is the porcelain clay of humankind.[3]
Don Sebastian.   Act i. *Sc.* 1.

I have a soul that, like an ample shield,
Can take in all, and verge enough for more.[4]   *Ibid.   Act* i. *Sc.* 1.

A knock-down argument : 't is but a word and a blow.
Amphitryon.   Act i. *Sc.* 1.

The true Amphitryon.   *Ibid.   Act* iv. *Sc.* 1.

The spectacles of books.   *Essay on Dramatic Poetry.*

---

[1] Delays have dangerous ends.—Shakespeare, *King Henry VI.   Part* i.
Act III. *Sc.* 2.
[2] Cf. Cowper, *post.*   [3] Cf. Byron, *Don Juan, Canto* iv. *St.* xx.
[4] Cf. Gray, *post.*

STEPHEN HARVEY.

And there 's a lust in man no charm can tame
Of loudly publishing our neighbour's shame;
On eagles' wings immortal scandals fly,
While virtuous actions are but born and die.

Juvenal. Satire ix.[1]

——□——

JOHN BUNYAN. 1628—1688.

And so I penned
It down, until at last it came to be,
For length and breadth, the bigness which you see.

Apology for His Book.

Some said, "John, print it," others said, "Not so,"
Some said, "It might do good," others said, "No."

Ibid.

The name of the slough was Despond. *Pilgrim's Progress. Part* i.

It beareth the name of Vanity Fair, because the town where 't is kept is
lighter than vanity. *Ibid. Part* i.

Some things are of that nature as to make
One's fancy chuckle, while his heart doth ache.

*The Author's Way of sending forth his
Second Part of the Pilgrim.*

He that is down needs fear no fall.[2] *Ibid. Part* ii

——□——

RICHARD BAXTER. 1615—1691.

I preached as never sure to preach again,
And as a dying man to dying men.

Love breathing Thanks and Praise.

——□——

EARL OF ROSCOMMON. 1633—1684.

Remember Milo's end,
Wedged in that timber which he strove to rend.

Essay on Translated Verse. Line 87.

Choose an author as you choose a friend. *Ibid. Line* 96.

Immodest words admit of no defence,
For want of decency is want of sense. *Ibid. Line* 113.

The multitude is always in the wrong. *Ibid. Line* 184.

My God, my Father, and my Friend,
Do not forsake me at my end. *Translation of Dies Iræ.*

---

[1] From Anderson's *British Poets, Vol.* xii. *p.* 697.
[2] He that is down can fall no lower.—Butler, *Hudibras, Part* i. **Canto**
iii. *Line* 877.

ROGER L'ESTRANGE.   1616—1740.

Though this may be play to you,
'T is death to us.
Fables from Several Authors.   Fable 398.

—□—

JOHN TILLOTSON.   1630—1694.

If God were not a necessary Being of himself, he might almost seem to
be made for the use and benefit of men.[1]   *Sermon* 93, *1712.*

—□—

MATTHEW HENRY.   1662—1714.

To their own second and sober thoughts.[2]
Exposition, Job vi. 29.   (London, 1710.)

—□—

SIR JOHN POWELL.   —1713.

Let us consider the reason of the case.   For nothing is law that is not
reason.[3]   *Coggs* vs. *Bernard,* 2 *Ld. Raym.* 911.

—□—

RICHARD RUMBOLD.   —1685.

I never could believe that Providence had sent a few men into the world,
ready booted and spurred to ride, and millions ready saddled and bridled
to be ridden.   *When on the Scaffold* (1685).   Macaulay, *Hist. of England.*

—□—

EARL OF ROCHESTER.   1647—1680.

Angels listen when she speaks :
   She 's my delight, all mankind's wonder;
But my jealous heart would break,
   Should we live one day asunder.   *Song.*

Here lies our sovereign lord the king,
   Whose word no man relies on ;
He never says a foolish thing,
   Nor ever does a wise one.
Written on the Bedchamber Door of Charles II.

And ever since the conquest have been fools.
Artemisia in the Town to Chloe in the Country.

---

[1] Si Dieu n'existait pas, il faudroit l'inventer.—Voltaire, *A l'Auteur du
livre des trois imposteurs, Epit.* cxi.

[2] I consider biennial elections as a security that the sober, second thought
of the people shall be law.—Fisher Ames, *Speech on Biennial Elections,*
1788.

[3] Reason is the life of the law; nay, the common law itself is nothing
else but reason. . . . . The law, which is perfection of reason.—Coke,
Institute, Book i. *Fol.* 976.

For pointed satire I would Buckhurst choose,
The best good man with the worst-natured muse.
                    An Allusion to Satire x.   *Horace.   Book* i.

A merry monarch, scandalous and poor.   *On the King.*

—□—

SIR CHARLES SEDLEY. 1639—1701.

When change itself can give no more,
'T is easy to be true.   *Reasons for Constancy.*

—□—

SHEFFIELD, DUKE OF BUCKINGHAMSHIRE. 1649—1720.

Of all those arts in which the wise excel,
Nature's chief masterpiece is writing well.   *Essay on Poetry.*

There 's no such thing in nature, and you 'll draw
A faultless monster which the world ne'er saw.   *Ibid.*

Read Homer once, and you can read no more,
For all books else appear so mean, so poor;
Verse will seem prose; but still persist to read,
And Homer will be all the books you need.   *Ibid.*

—□—

HENRY ALDRICH. 1647—1710.

If on my theme I rightly think,
There are five reasons why men drink:
Good wine, a friend, because I 'm dry,
Or least I should be by and by,
Or any other reason why.[1]   *Biog. Britannica. Vol.* i. *p.* **131.**

—□—

THOMAS OTWAY. 1651—1685.

O woman! lovely woman! nature made thee
To temper man; we had been brutes without you.
Angels are painted fair, to look like you:
There 's in you all that we believe of heaven;
Amazing brightness, purity, and truth,
Eternal joy, and everlasting love.
                    Venice Preserved.   Act i. *Sc.* **1.**

---

[1] These lines are a translation of a Latin epigram (erroneously ascribed to Aldrich in the Biog. Brit.) which Menage and De la Monnoye attribute to Père Sirmond.

> Si bene commemini, causæ sunt quinque bibendi;
> Hospitis adventus; præsens sitis atque futura;
> Et vini bonitas, et quælibet altera causa.
>   *Menagiana, Vol.* i. *p.* **172.**

VENICE PRESERVED—*continued.*]

> Dear as the vital warmth that feeds my life;
> Dear as these eyes, that weep in fondness o'er thee.[1]
>
> *Ibid.*   *Act* i. *Sc.* 1.

> What mighty ills have not been done by woman?
> Who was 't betray'd the Capitol?   A woman!
> Who lost Mark Antony the world?   A woman!
> Who was the cause of a long ten years' war,
> And laid at last old Troy in ashes?   Woman!
> Destructive, damnable, deceitful woman!
>
> *The Orphan.*   *Act* iii. *Sc.* 1.

—□—

ANDREW FLETCHER OF SALTOUN. 1653—1716.

I knew a very wise man that believed that, if a man were permitted to make all the ballads, he need not care who should make the laws of a nation.   *Letter to the Marquis of Montrose, the Earl of Rothes, etc.*

—□—

ISAAC NEWTON. 1642—1727.

I do not know what I may appear to the world, but to myself I seem to have been only like a boy playing on the sea-shore, and diverting myself in now and then finding a smoother pebble, or a prettier shell than ordinary, whilst the great ocean of truth lay all undiscovered before me.[2]

> Brewster's *Memoirs of Newton.*   *Vol.* ii. *Ch.* 27.

—□—

NATHANIEL LEE. 1655—1692.

> Then he will talk—good gods! how he will talk![3]
>
> *Alexander the Great.*   *Act* i. *Sc.* 3.

> When Greeks joined Greeks, then was the tug of war.
>
> *Ibid.*   *Act* iv. *Sc.* 2.

> 'T is beauty calls, and glory shows the way.[4]
>
> *Ibid.*   *Act* iv. *Sc.* 2.

> Man, false man, smiling, destructive man.
>
> *Theodosius.*   *Act* iii. *Sc.* 2

---

[1] Cf. Gray, *The Bard,* Part i. *St.* 3.
[2] Cf. Milton, *Paradise Reg.,* Book iv. *Lines* 327—330.
[3] It would talk,
       Lord! how it talked!
       Beaumont and Fletcher, *The Scornful Lady,* *Act* v. *Sc.* 1.
[4] 'leads the way,' in the stage editions, which contain various interpolations, among them
       " See the conquering hero comes,
       Sound the trumpet, beat the drums."

JOHN NORRIS. 1657—1711.

How fading are the joys we dote upon !
Like apparitions seen and gone ;
But those which soonest take their flight
Are the most exquisite and strong ;
Like angels' visits, short and bright,1
Mortality 's too weak to bear them long. *The Parting.*

—◻—

DR. WALTER POPE. 1630—1714.

May I govern my passion with absolute sway,
And grow wiser and better as my strength wears away.
The Old Man's Wish.

—◻—

THOMAS SOUTHERNE. 1660—1746.

Pity 's akin to love.[2] *Oroonoka. Act* ii. *Sc.* 1.

—◻—

JOHN DENNIS. 1657—1734.

A man who could make so vile a pun would not scruple to pick a pocket.[3]
They will not let my play run ; and yet they steal my thunder.[4]

—◻—

JOHN POMFRET. 1667—1703.

We bear it calmly, though a ponderous woe,
And still adore the hand that gives the blow.[5]
Verses to his Friend under Affliction.

Heaven is not always angry when he strikes,
But most chastises those whom most he likes. *Ibid.*

---

[1] Cf. Campbell, *post.*
[2] *Vio.* I pity you.
  Oli. That 's a degree to Love.
      Shakespeare, *Twelfth Night, Act* iii. *Sc.* 1.
  Of all the paths that lead to woman's love
  Pity 's the straightest.
      Beaumont and Fletcher, *Knight of Malta, Act* i. *Sc.* 1.
[3] This on the authority of *The Gentleman's Magazine, Vol* li. *p.* 324.
[4] Our author, for the advantage of this play [Appius and Virginia], had
invented a new species of thunder, which was approved of by the actors,
and is the very sort that at present is used in the theatre. The tragedy,
however, was coldly received notwithstanding such assistance, and was
acted but a short time. Some nights after, Mr. Dennis being in the pit,
at the representation of Macbeth, heard his own thunder made use of ;
upon which he rose in a violent passion, and exclaimed, with an oath, that
it was his thunder. "See," said he, "how the rascals use me ! They will
not let my play run ; and yet they steal my thunder."—*Biog. Britannica,*
Vol. v. *p.* 103.
[5] Bless the hand that gave the blow.
      Dryden, *The Spanish Friar, Act* ii. *Sc.* 1.

DANIEL DEFOE. 1663—1731.

Wherever God erects a house of prayer,
The Devil always builds a chapel there;[1]
And 't will be found, upon examination,
The latter has the largest congregation.
The True-Born Englishman. Part i. *Line* 1.

Great families of yesterday we show,
And lords, whose parents were the Lord knows who.
Ibid. Lin. ult.

—◻—

RICHARD BENTLEY. 1662—1742.

It is a maxim with me that no man was ever written out of reputation
but by himself.   Monk's *Life of Bentley, p.* 90.

—◻—

TOM BROWN. 1663—1704.

I do not love thee, Doctor Fell,
The reason why I cannot tell;
But this alone I know full well,
I do not love thee, Doctor Fell.[2]

—◻—

MATTHEW PRIOR. 1664—1721.

Be to her virtues very kind;
Be to her faults a little blind.   *An English Padlock.*

Abra was ready ere I call'd her name;
And, though I call'd another, Abra came.
Solomon on the Vanity of the World. Book ii. *Line* 364.

For hope is but the dream of those that wake.[3]
Ibid. Book iii. *Line* 102.

Who breathes, must suffer, and who thinks, must mourn;
And he alone is bless'd who ne'er was born.   *Ibid. Book* iii. *Line* 240.

---

1 See Proverbs, *post.*

2 A slightly different version is found in Brown's Works collected and
pulished after his death.

> Non amo te, Sabidi, nec possum dicere quare;
> Hoc tantum possum dicere, non amo te.—Martial, *Ep.* 1. xxxiii.
>
> Je ne vous aime pas, Hylas;
> Je n'en saurois dire la cause;
> Je sais seulement un chose;
> C'est que je ne vous aime pas.
>   Bussy, *Comte de Rabutin, Epistle* 33, *Book* i.

3 This thought is ascribed to Aristotle by Diogenes Laertius, *Lib.* v. § 18.
Ἐρωτηθεὶς τί ἐστιν ἐλπίς; Ἐγρηγορότος, εἶπεν, ἐνύπνιον.

Menage, in his *Observations upon Laertius,* says that Stobæus (*Serm.* cix.)
ascribes it to Pindar, whilst Ælian (*Var. Hist.* xiii. 29) refers it to Plato:
Ἔλεγεν ὁ Πλάτων, τὰς ἐλπίδας ἐγρηγορότων ἀνθρώπων ὀνείρους εἶναι.

Now fitted the halter, now travers'd the cart,
And often took leave; but was loth to depart.
The Thief and the Cordelier.

Till their own dreams at length deceive 'em,
And, oft repeating, they believe 'em.
Alma. Canto iii. *Line* 13.

And thought the nation ne'er would thrive
Till all the whores were burnt alive. *Paulo Purganti.*

Nobles and heralds, by your leave,
  Here lies what once was Matthew Prior;
The son of Adam and of Eve:
  Can Bourbon or Nassau claim higher?[1] *Epitaph on Himself.*

Odds life! must one swear to the truth of a song?
A Better Answer.

That, if weak women went astray,
Their stars were more in fault than they. *Hans Carvel.*

The end must justify the means. *Ibid.*

That air and harmony of shape express,
Fine by degrees, and beautifully less.[2] *Henry and Emma.*

Our hopes, like tow'ring falcons, aim
  At objects in an airy height;
The little pleasure of the game
  Is from afar to view the flight.[3] *To the Hon. Charles Montague.*

From ignorance our comfort flows,
The only wretched are the wise.[4] *Ibid.*

They never taste who always drink;
They always talk who never think.
Upon a Passage in the Scaligerana.

HENRY CAREY. 1663—1743.

God save our gracious king,
Long live our noble king,
  God save the king. *God save the King.*

---

[1] The following epitaph was written long before the time of Prior:—
    Johnnie Carnegie lais heer.
      Descendit of Adam and Eve,
      Gif ony con gang hieher,
      Ise willing give him leve.
[2] Cf. Pope, *Moral Essays, Epistle* ii. *Line* 43.
    [3] But all the pleasure of the game
      Is afar off to view the flight.
          Variations in a copy printed 1692.
        [4] Cf. Gray, *Eton College, post.*

Aldeborontiphoscophornio !
Where left you Chrononhotonthologos ? *Chronon.   Act* i. *Sc.* 1.

His cogitative faculties immers'd
In cogibundity of cogitation.   *Ibid.   Act* i. *Sc.* 1.

        Let the singing singers
With vocal voices, most vociferous,
In sweet vociferation, out-vociferize
Ev'n sound itself.   *Ibid.   Act* i. *Sc.* 1.

To thee, and gentle Rigdom Funnidos,
Our gratulations flow in streams unbounded. *Ibid. Act* i. *Sc.* 3.

Go call a coach, and let a coach be called,
And let the man who calleth be the caller ;
And in his calling let him nothing call,
But Coach ! Coach ! Coach ! O for a coach, ye gods !
                                           Ibid. Act ii. *Sc.* 4.

     Genteel in personage,
     Conduct, and equipage ;
     Noble by heritage,
     Generous and free. *The Contrivances. Act* i. *Sc.* 2.

What a monstrous tail our cat has got !
                    The Dragon of Wantley.   Act ii. *Sc.* 1.

   Of all the girls that are so smart,
     There 's none like pretty Sally.[1]   *Sally in our Alley.*

   Of all the days that 's in the week
     I dearly love but one day,
   And that 's the day that comes betwixt
     A Saturday and Monday.   *Ibid.*

—□—

SAMUEL GARTH. 1670—1719.

To die is landing on some silent shore,
Where billows never break, nor tempests roar ;
Ere well we feel the friendly stroke, 't is o'er.
                    The Dispensary.[2] *Canto* iii. *Line* 225.

---

   [1] Of all the girls that e'er was seen,
    There 's none so fine as Nelly.
              Swift, *Ballad on Miss Nelly Bennet.*
   [2] Thou hast no faults, or I no faults can spy,
    Thou art all beauty, or all blindness I.
           Christopher Codrington, *On Garth's Dispensary.*

JONATHAN SWIFT. 1667—1745.

I 've often wished that I had clear,
For life, six hundred pounds a year,
A handsome house to lodge a friend,
A river at my garden's end.
Imitation of Horace. Book ii. *Sat. 6.*

So geographers, in Afric maps,[1]
With savage pictures fill their gaps,
And o'er unhabitable downs
Place elephants for want of towns. *Poetry, a Rhapsody.*

Where Young must torture his invention
To flatter knaves, or lose his pension. *Ibid.*

Hobbes clearly proves, that every creature
Lives in a state of war by nature. *Ibid.*

So, naturalists observe, a flea
Has smaller fleas that on him prey;
And these have smaller still to bite 'em:
And so proceed *ad infinitum.* *Ibid.*

Libertas et natale solum;
Fine words! I wonder where you stole 'em.
Verses occasioned by Whitshed's Motto on his Coach.

A college joke to cure the dumps. *Cassimus and Peter.*

'T is an old maxim in the schools,
That flattery 's the food of fools;
Yet now and then your men of wit
Will condescend to take a bit. *Cadenus and Vanessa.*

The two noblest things, which are sweetness and light.
Battle of the Books.

And he gave it for his opinion, that whoever could make two ears of corn, or two blades of grass, to grow upon a spot of ground where only one grew before, would deserve better of mankind, and do more essential service to his country, than the whole race of politicians put together.
Gulliver's Travels. Part ii. *Ch.* vii. *Voyage to Brobdingnag.*

He had been eight years upon a project for extracting sunbeams out of cucumbers, which were to be put in phials hermetically sealed, and let out to warm the air in raw inclement summers.
Ibid. Part iii. *Ch.* v. *Voyage to Laputa.*

Seamen have a custom, when they meet a whale, to fling him out an empty tub by way of amusement, to divert him from laying violent hands upon the ship.[2] *Tale of a Tub, Preface.*

---

[1] As geographers crowd into the edges of their maps parts of the world which they do not know about, adding notes in the margin to the effect that beyond this lies nothing but sandy deserts full of wild beasts and un-approachable bogs.—Plutarch, *Theseus.*

[2] In Sebastian Munster's *Cosmography*, there is a cut of a ship, to which

Bread is the staff of life.   *Tale of a Tub.*

The reason why so few marriages are happy is because young ladies
spend their time in making nets, not in making cages.
                                        Thoughts on Various Subjects.

Censure is the tax a man pays to the public for being eminent.   *Ibid.*

A nice man is a man of nasty ideas.   *Ibid.*

Not die here in a rage like a poisoned rat in a hole.
                            Letter to Bolingbroke, March 21, 1729.

I shall be like that tree, I shall die at the top.   Scott's *Life of Swift.*[1]

——□——

ALAIN RENÉ LE SAGE.   1668—1747.

I wish you all sorts of prosperity with a little more taste.
                                    Gil Blas. Book vii. *Ch.* 4.

——□——

COLLEY CIBBER.   1671—1757.

So mourned the dame of Ephesus her love;
And thus the soldier, armed with resolution,
Told his soft tale, and was a thriving wooer.
                        Richard III. Altered. Act ii. *Sc.* 1.

Now by St. Paul the work goes bravely on.   *Act* iii. *Sc.* 1.

The aspiring youth that fired the Ephesian dome
Outlives in fame the pious fool that raised it.   *Act* iii. *Sc.* 1.

I 've lately had two spiders
Crawling upon my startled hopes.
Now tho' thy friendly hand has brushed 'em from me,
Yet still they crawl offensive to my eyes ;
I would have some kind friend to tread upon 'em.   *Act* iv. *Sc.* 3.

Off with his head ! so much for Buckingham !   *Act* iv. *Sc.* 3.

And the ripe harvest of the new-mown hay
Gives it a sweet and wholesome odour.   *Act* v. *Sc.* 3.

With clink of hammers[2] closing rivets up.   *Act* v. *Sc.* 3.

---

a whale was coming too close for her safety, and of the sailors throwing a tub
to the whale evidently to play with.   This practice is also mentioned in an
old prose translation of the *Ship of Fools.*—Sir James Mackintosh, *Appendix to the Life of Sir Thomas More.*

[1] When the poem of " Cadenus and Vanessa," was the general topic of
conversation some one said, " Surely that Vanessa must be an extraordinary
woman, that could inspire the Dean to write so finely upon her."   Mrs.
Johnson smiled and answered, that " she thought that point not quite so
clear, for it was well known the Dean could write finely upon a broom
stick."—Johnson's *Life of Swift.*

[2] With busy hammers.—Shakespeare, *Henry V., Act* iv. *Chorus.*

RICHARD III.—*continued.*]

    Perish that thought! No, never be it said
    That Fate itself could awe the soul of Richard.
    Hence, babbling dreams; you threaten here in vain;
    Conscience, avaunt, Richard's himself again!
    Hark! the shrill trumpet sounds, to horse, away,
    My soul's in arms, and eager for the fray.   *Ibid.*   *Act* v. *Sc.* 3.

    A weak invention of the enemy.[1]   *Act* v. *Sc.* 3.

—□—

SUSANNAH CENTLIVRE. 1667—1723.

The real Simon Pure. *A Bold Stroke for a Wife.* *Act* v. *Sc.* 8.

—□—

SIR RICHARD STEELE. 1671—1729.

(Lady Elizabeth Hastings.) Though her mien carries much more invitation than command, to behold her is an immediate check to loose behaviour; to love her was a liberal education.[2]   *The Tatler.* *No.* 49.

—□—

JOSEPH ADDISON. 1672—1719.
CATO.

    The dawn is overcast, the morning lowers,
    And heavily in clouds brings on the day,
    The great, the important day, big with the fate
    Of Cato, and of Rome.   *Act* i. *Sc.* 1.

           Thy steady temper, Portius,
    Can look on guilt, rebellion, fraud, and Cæsar,
    In the calm lights of mild philosophy.   *Act* i. *Sc.* 1.

    'T is not in mortals to command success,
    But we'll do more, Sempronius; we'll deserve it. *Act* i. *Sc.* 2.

    Blesses his stars and thinks it luxury.   *Act* i. *Sc.* 4.

    'T is pride, rank pride, and haughtiness of soul;
    I think the Romans call it stoicism.   *Act* i. *Sc.* 4.

    Were you with these, my prince, you'd soon forget
    The pale, unripened beauties of the north.   *Act* i. *Sc.* 4.

    Beauty soon grows familiar to the lover,
    Fades in his eye, and palls upon the sense.
    The virtuous Marcia towers above her sex.   *Act* i. *Sc.* 4.

---

  [1] A thing devised by the enemy.—Shakespeare, *Richard III.*, *Act* v. *Sc.* 3.

  [2] Leigh Hunt incorrectly ascribes this expression to Congreve.

CATO—*continued.*]

My voice is still for war.
Gods ! can a Roman senate long debate
Which of the two to choose, slavery or death ?   *Act* ii. *Sc.* 1.

A day, an hour, of virtuous liberty
Is worth a whole eternity in bondage.   *Act* ii. *Sc.* 1.

The woman that deliberates is lost.   *Act* iv. *Sc.* 1.

When vice prevails, and impious men bear sway,
The post of honour is a private station.   . *Act* iv. *Sc.* 4.

It must be so—Plato, thou reasonest well !—
Else whence this pleasing hope, this fond desire,
This longing after immortality ?
Or whence this secret dread, and inward horror,
Of falling into naught ? Why shrinks the soul
Back on herself, and startles at destruction ?
'T is the divinity that stirs within us ;
'T is heaven itself that points out an hereafter,
And intimates eternity to man.
Eternity ! thou pleasing, dreadful thought !   *Act* v. *Sc.* 1.

I 'm weary of conjectures,—this must end 'em.
Thus am I doubly armed : my death and life,
My bane and antidote, are both before me :
This in a moment brings me to an end ;
But this informs me I shall never die.
The soul, secured in her existence, smiles
At the drawn dagger, and defies its point.
The stars shall fade away, the sun himself
Grow dim with age, and nature sink in years,
But thou shalt flourish in immortal youth,
Unhurt amidst the war of elements,
The wrecks of matter, and the crush of worlds.   *Act* v. *Sc.* 1.

From hence, let fierce contending nations know
What dire effects from civil discord flow.   *Act* v. *Sc.* 4.

Unbounded courage and compassion joined,
Tempering each other in the victor's mind,
Alternately proclaim him good and great,
And make the hero and the man complete.
                        The Campaign.   Line 219.

And, pleased the Almighty's orders to perform,
Rides in the whirlwind and directs the storm.[1] *Ibid.*   *Line* 291

And those that paint them truest praise them most.[2]
                                Ibid.   *Line ult.*

---

[1] This line is frequently ascribed to Pope, as it is found in the *Dunciad*, *Book* iii. *Line* 261.
[2] Cf. Pope, Eloisa to Abelard, *Lin. ult.*

For wheresoe'er I turn my ravished eyes,
Gay gilded scenes and shining prospects rise,
Poetic fields encompass me around.
And still I seem to tread on classic ground.[1]

A Letter from Italy.

The spacious firmament on high,
With all the blue ethereal sky,
And spangled heavens, a shining frame,
Their great Original proclaim. *Ode.*

Soon as the evening shades prevail,
The moon takes up the wondrous tale,
And nightly to the listening earth
Repeats the story of her birth;
While all the stars that round her burn,
And all the planets in their turn,
Confirm the tidings as they roll,
And spread the truth from pole to pole. *Ibid.*

For ever singing, as they shine,
The hand that made us is divine. *Ibid.*

—□—

SIR ROBERT WALPOLE. 1674—1746.

Flowery oratory he despised. He ascribed to the interested views of themselves or their relatives the declarations of pretended patriots, of whom he said, All those men have their price.[2]

From *Coxe's Memoirs of Walpole. Vol.* iv. *p.* 369.

Anything but history, for history must be false. *Walpoliana. No.* 141.

The gratitude of place-expectants is a lively sense of future favours.[3]

—□—

AMBROSE PHILIPS. 1671—1749.

Studious of ease and fond of humble things.

From Holland to a Friend in England.

—□ —

ISAAC WATTS. 1674—1748.

DIVINE SONGS.

Whene'er I take my walks abroad,
How many poor I see!
What shall I render to my God
For all his gifts to me? *Song* iv.

---

[1] Malone states that this was the first time the phrase "classic ground," since so common, was ever used.

[2] The political axiom, *All men have their price,* is commonly ascribed to Walpole.

[3] Hazlitt, in his *Wit and Humour,* says, "This is Walpole's phrase."

A flower, when offered in the bud,
Is no vain sacrifice.   *Song* xii.

And he that does one fault at first,
And lies to hide it, makes it two.[1]   *Song* xv.

Let dogs delight to bark and bite,
For God hath made them so ;
Let bears and lions growl and fight,
For 't is their nature too.   *Song* xvi.

Your little hands were never made
To tear each other's eyes.   *Ibid.*

How doth the little busy bee
Improve each shining hour,
And gather honey all the day,
From every opening flower !   *Song* xx.

For Satan finds some mischief still
For idle hands to do.   *Ibid.*

To God the Father, God the Son,
And God the Spirit, three in one;
Be honour, praise, and glory given,
By all on earth, and all in heaven.
           Glory to the Father and the Son.

Hush, my dear, lie still and slumber !
Holy angels guard thy bed !
Heavenly blessings without number
Gently falling on thy head.   *A Cradle Hymn.*

'T is the voice of the sluggard ; I heard him complain,
"You have waked me too soon, I must slumber again."
                                          The Sluggard.

Hark ! from the tombs a doleful sound.   *A Funeral Thought.*

Strange ! that a harp of thousand strings
Should keep in tune so long.
           Hymns and Spiritual Songs. Book ii. *Hymn* 19.

Were I so tall to reach the pole,
Or grasp the ocean with my span,
I must be measur'd by my soul :
The mind 's the standard of the man.[2]
           Horæ Lyricæ. Book ii. *False Greatness.*

[1] Dare to be true, nothing can need a lie;
   A fault which needs it most grows two thereby.
                              Herbert, *The Church Porch.*
[2] I do not distinguish by the eye, but by the mind, which is the proper judge of the man. — Seneca, *On a Happy Life,* Ch. i.   (L'Estrange's Abstract.)

WILLIAM CONGREVE. 1670—1729.

Music hath charms to soothe the savage breast,
To soften rocks, or bend a knotted oak.
The Mourning Bride.　Act i. *Sc.* 1.

By magic numbers and persuasive sound.　*Ibid.　Act* i. *Sc.* 1.

Heaven has no rage like love to hatred turned,
Nor hell a fury like a woman scorned.　*Ibid.　Act* iii. *Sc.* 8.

For blessings ever wait on virtuous deeds,
And though a late, a sure reward succeeds. *Ibid. Act* v. *Sc.* 12.

If there 's delight in love, 't is when I see
That heart which others bleed for bleed for me.
The Way of the World.　Act iii. *Sc.* 12.

Ferdinand Mendez Pinto was but a type of thee, thou liar of the first
magnitude.　　　　　　　　　　*Love for Love.　Act* ii. *Sc.* 5.

Hannibal was a very pretty fellow in those days.
The Old Bachelor.　Act ii. *Sc.* 2.

Thus grief still treads upon the heels of pleasure;
Married in haste, we may repent at leisure.[1]　*Ibid. Act* v. *Sc.* 1.

Defer not till to-morrow to be wise,
To-morrow's sun to thee may never rise.[2]　　*Letter to Cobham.*

NICHOLAS ROWE. 1673—1718.

As if Misfortune made the throne her seat,
And none could be unhappy but the great.[3]
The Fair Penitent.　Prologue.

Is she not more than painting can express,
Or youthful poets fancy when they love?　*Ibid. Act* iii. *Sc.* 1.

Is this that haughty gallant, gay Lothario?　*Ibid. Act* v. *Sc.* 1.

JOHN PHILIPS. 1676—1708.

My galligaskins, that have long withstood
The winter's fury, and encroaching frosts,
By time subdued, (what will not time subdue!)
A horrid chasm disclosed.　*The Splendid Shilling.　Line* 121.

---

[1] Cf. Shakespeare, *Taming of the Shrew, Act* ii. *Sc.* 2; Quarles,
Enchiridion, Canto 4, xl.
[2] Cf. Young, *Night Thoughts*, i. *Line* 1.
[3] Cf. Young, *The Love of Fame, Satire* i. *Line* 238.

F

BISHOP BERKELEY. 1684—1753.

Westward the course of empire takes its way ; [1]
  The four first acts already past,
A fifth shall close the drama with the day ;
  Time's noblest offspring is the last.
  On the Prospect of Planting Arts and Learning in America.

—▢—

HENRY ST. JOHN, VISCOUNT BOLINGBROKE. 1678—1751.

I have read somewhere or other, in Dionysius of Halicarnassus, I think,
that History is Philosophy teaching by examples.[2]
  On the Study and Use of History. Letter 2.

—▢—

GEORGE FARQUHAR. 1678—1707.

Cos. Pray now, what may be that same bed of honour?
Kite. Oh! a mighty large bed! bigger by half than the great bed at
Ware : ten thousand people may lie in it together, and never feel one
another. *The Recruiting Officer. Act i. Sc. i.*

I believe they talked of me, for they laughed consumedly.
  The Beaux' Stratagem. Act iii. Sc. i.

'T was for the good of my country that I should be abroad.[3]
  Ibid. Act iii. Sc. 2.

Necessity, the mother of invention. *The Twin Rivals. Act i.*

—▢—

THOMAS PARNELL. 1679—1717.

Still an angel appear to each lover beside,
But still be a woman to you. *When thy beauty appears.*

Remote from man, with God he passed the days,
Prayer all his business, all his pleasure praise.
  The Hermit. Line 5.

We call it only pretty Fanny's way.
  An Elegy to an Old Beauty.

Let those love now who never lov'd before,
Let those who always loved now love the more.
  Translation of the Pervigilium Veneris.[4]

---

[1] Westward the *star* of empire takes its way.
  Epigraph to Bancroft's *History of the United States.*
[2] Dionysius of Halicarnassus, *Ars Rhet.* xi. 2 (*p.* 398, *R.*), says :—
Παιδεία ἄρα ἐστὶν ἡ ἔντευξις τῶν ἠθῶν· τοῦτο καὶ Θουκυδίδης ἔοικε λέγειν, περὶ
ἱστορίας λέγων· ὅτι καὶ ἱστορία φιλοσοφία ἐστὶν ἐκ παραδειγμάτων, quoting
Thucydides, I. 22.
[3] Cf. Barrington, *post.*
[4] Written in the time of Julius Cæsar, and by some ascribed to Catullus :—
  Cras amet qui numquam amavit ;
  Quique amavit, cras amet.

JANE BRERETON. 1685—1740.

The picture, placed the busts between,
  Adds to the thought much strength;
Wisdom and Wit are little seen,
  But Folly 's at full length.

> *On Beau Nash's Picture at full length, between the*
> *Busts of Sir Isaac Newton and Mr. Pope.*[1]

—□—

AARON HILL. 1685—1750.

First, then, a woman will, or won 't, depend on 't;
If she will do 't, she will; and there 's an end on 't.
But if she won 't, since safe and sound your trust is,
Fear is affront, and jealousy injustice.[2]   *Epilogue to Zara.*

Tender-handed stroke a nettle,
  And it stings you for your pains;
Grasp it like a man of mettle,
  And it soft as silk remains.

> *Verses written on a Window in Scotland.*

'T is the same with common natures:
  Use 'em kindly, they rebel;
But be rough as nutmeg-graters,
  And the rogues obey you well.   *Ibid.*

—□—

SIR SAMUEL TUKE. ——1673.

He is a fool who thinks by force or skill
To turn the current of a woman's will.

> *Adventures of Five Hours. Act* v. *Sc.* 3.

—□—

EDWARD YOUNG. 1684—1765.
NIGHT THOUGHTS.

Tired Nature's sweet restorer, balmy sleep!   *Night* i. *Line* 1.

Night, sable goddess! from her ebon throne,
In rayless majesty, now stretches forth
Her leaden sceptre o'er a slumbering world.   *Night* i. *Line* 18.

---

1 From Dyce's *Specimens of British Poetesses.* This epigram is generally ascribed to Chesterfield; see Campbell's *Specimens, Note, p.* 521.

2 The following lines are copied from the pillar erected on the mount in the Dane John Field, Canterbury :—*Examiner, May* 31, 1829.
  Where is the man who has the power and skill
  To stem the torrent of a woman's will?
  For if she will, she will, you may depend on 't;
  And if she won't she won't: so there 's an end on 't.

NIGHT T**HOUGHTS**—*continued.*]

Creation sleeps!　'T is as the gen'ral pulse
Of life stood still, and nature made a pause;
An awful pause! prophetic of her end.　　　　*Night* i. *Line* 23.

The bell strikes one.　We take no note of time,
But from its loss.　　　　　　　　　　　　*Night* i. *Line* 55.

Poor pensioner on the bounties of an hour.　*Night* i. *Line* 67.

To waft a feather or to drown a fly.　　　　*Night* i. *Line* 154.

Insatiate archer! could not one suffice?
Thy shaft flew thrice : and thrice my peace was slain;
And thrice, ere thrice yon moon had fill'd her horn.
　　　　　　　　　　　　　　　　　　　Night i. *Line* 212.

Be wise to-day; 't is madness to defer.[1]　*Night* i. *Line* 390.

Procrastination is the thief of time.　　　　*Night* i. *Line* 393.

At thirty, man suspects himself a fool;
Knows it at forty, and reforms his plan.　　*Night* i. *Line* 417.

All men think all men mortal but themselves.　*Night* i. *Line* 424.

He mourns the dead who lives as they desire.　*Night* ii. *Line* 24.

And what its worth, ask death-beds; they can tell.
　　　　　　　　　　　　　　　　　　　Night ii. *Line* 51.
Thy purpose firm is equal to the deed :
Who does the best his circumstance allows,
Does well, acts nobly; angels could no more.　*Night* ii. *Line* 90.

" I 've lost a day"—the prince who nobly cried,
Had been an emperor without his crown.　　*Night* ii. *Line* 99.

Ah! how unjust to nature, and himself,
Is thoughtless, thankless, inconsistent man.　*Night* ii. *Line* 112.

The spirit walks of every day deceased.　　*Night* ii. *Line* 180.

Time flies, death urges, knells call, heaven invites,
Hell threatens.　　　　　　　　　　　　　*Night* ii. *Line* 292.

'T is greatly wise to talk with our past hours,
And ask them what report they bore to heaven.
　　　　　　　　　　　　　　　　　　　Night ii. *Line* 376.
　　　　　　Thoughts shut up want air,
And spoil, like bales unopen'd to the sun.　*Night* ii. *Line* 466.

How blessings brighten as they take their flight!
　　　　　　　　　　　　　　　　　　　Night ii. *Line* 602.

---

[1] Defer not till to-morrow to be wise,
　To-morrow's sun to thee may never rise.
　　　　　　　　Congreve, *Letter to Cobham.*

NIGHT THOUGHTS—*continued.*]

The chamber where the good man meets his fate
Is privileged beyond the common walk
Of virtuous life, quite in the verge of heaven.　　*Night* ii. *Line* 633.

A death-bed's a detector of the heart.　　　　*Night* ii. *Line* 641.

Woes cluster ; rare are solitary woes;
They love a train, they tread each other's heel.[1]　*Night* iii. *Line* 63.

　　　　　　Beautiful as sweet !
And young as beautiful ! and soft as young !
And gay as soft ! and innocent as gay !　　　　*Night* iii. *Line* 81.

Lovely in death the beauteous ruin lay ;
And if in death still lovely, lovelier there ;
Far lovelier ! pity swells the tide of love.　　*Night* iii. *Line* 104.

Heaven's Sovereign saves all beings but himself
That hideous sight, a naked human heart.　　*Night* iii. *Line* 226.

The knell, the shroud, the mattock, and the grave,
The deep damp vault, the darkness, and the worm.
　　　　　　　　　　　　Night iv. *Line* 10.

Man makes a death which nature never made.　*Night* iv. *Line* 15.

Wishing, of all employments, is the worst.　　*Night* iv. *Line* 71.

Man wants but little, nor that little long.[2]　*Night* iv. *Line* 118.

A God all mercy is a God unjust.　　　　　*Night* iv. *Line* 233

'T is impious in a good man to be sad.　　　*Night* iv. *Line* 676.

A Christian is the highest style of man.[3]　　*Night* iv. *Line* 788.

Men may live fools, but fools they cannot die.　*Night* iv. *Line* 843.

By night an atheist half believes a God.　　　*Night* v. *Line* 177.

Early, bright, transient, chaste, as morning dew,
She sparkled, was exhal'd, and went to heaven.[4]　*Night* v. *Line* 600.

We see time's furrows on another's brow,
And death intrench'd, preparing his assault ;
How few themselves in that just mirror see !　*Night* v. *Line* 627.

---

[1] One woe doth tread upon another's heel,—
　So fast they follow.　　Shakespeare, *Hamlet*, *Act* iv. *Sc.* 7.
　Thus woe succeeds a woe, as wave a wave.
　　　　　　　Herrick, *Hesperides, Sorrows Succeed.*
[2] Cf. Goldsmith, *post.*
[3] A Christian is God Almighty's gentleman.—Hare, *Guesses at Truth.*
　His tribe were God Almighty's gentlemen.
　　　　　Dryden, *Absalom and Achitophel*, Pt. i. L. 645.
[4] He was exhal'd ; his great Creator drew
　His spirit, as the sun the morning dew.
　　　　　Dryden, *On the Death of a very Young Gentleman.*

NIGHT THOUGHTS—*continued.*]

Like our shadows,

Our wishes lengthen as our sun declines.[1]   *Night* v. *Line* 661.

While man is growing, life is in decrease;
And cradles rock us nearer to the tomb.
Our birth is nothing but our death begun.[2]   *Night* v. *Line* 717.

That life is long which answers life's great end.
Night v. *Line* 773.

The man of wisdom is the man of years.   *Night* v. *Line* 775.

Death loves a shining mark, a signal blow.   *Night* v. *Line* 1011.

Pygmies are pygmies still, though perched on Alps;
And pyramids are pyramids in vales.
Each man makes his own stature, builds himself:
Virtue alone outbuilds the Pyramids;
Her monuments shall last when Egypt's fall.   *Night* vi. *Line* 309.

And all may do what has by man been done.   *Night* vi. *Line* 606.

The man that blushes is not quite a brute.   *Night* vii. *Line* 496.

Prayer ardent opens heaven.   *Night* viii. *Line* 721.

A man of pleasure is a man of pains.   *Night* viii. *Line* 793.

To frown at pleasure, and to smile in pain.   *Night* viii. *Line* 1045.

Final Ruin fiercely drives

Her ploughshare o'er creation.[3]   *Night* ix. *Line* 167.

'T is elder Scripture, writ by God's own hand:
Scripture authentic! uncorrupt by man.   *Night* ix. *Line* 644.

An undevout astronomer is mad.   *Night* ix. *Line* 771.

The course of nature is the art of God.[4]   *Night* ix. *Line* 1267.

LOVE OF FAME.

The love of praise, howe'er concealed by art,
Reigns more or less, and glows in ev'ry heart.   *Satire* i. *Line* 51.

Some, for renown, on scraps of learning dote,
And think they grow immortal as they quote.   *Satire* i. *Line* 89.

---

[1] Behold him setting in his western skies,
The shadows lengthening as the vapours rise.
Dryden, *Absalom and Achitophel, Line* 268.
[2] Death borders upon our birth, and our cradle stands in the grave.—
Bishop Hall, *Epistles, Dec.* iii. *Epist.* ii.
[3] Cf. Burns, *post.*
[4] In brief, all things are artificial; for Nature is the art of God.—Sir
Thomas Browne. *Relig. Med., Pt.* i. *Sect.* xvi.

LOVE OF FAME—*continued.*]

None think the great unhappy, but the great.[1]
                              Satire i. *Line* 238.

Where nature's end of language is declined,
And men talk only to conceal the mind.[2]   *Satire* ii. *Line* 207.

        Be wise with speed;
A fool at forty is a fool indeed.   *Satire* ii. *Line* 282.

Think naught a trifle, though it small appear;
Small sands the mountain, moments make the year,
And trifles life.   *Satire* vi. *Line* 208.

One to destroy is murder by the law;
And gibbets keep the lifted hand in awe;
To murder thousands takes a specious name,
War's glorious art, and gives immortal fame.
                              Satire vii. *Line* 55.

How commentators each dark passage shun,
And hold their farthing candle to the sun.[3]   *Satire* vii. *Line* 97.

Their feet through faithless leather met the dirt,
And oftener changed their principles than shirt.
                       Epistle to Mr. Pope. Line 277.

Accept a miracle, instead of wit,—
See two dull lines with Stanhope's pencil writ.
    Lines written with the Diamond Pencil of Lord Chesterfield.[4]

Time elaborately thrown away.   *The Last Day. Book* i.

There buds the promise of celestial worth.   *Ibid. Book* iii.

In records that defy the tooth of time.   *The Statesman's Creed.*

Great let me call him, for he conquered me.
                              The Revenge. Act i. *Sc.* 1.

The blood will follow where the knife is driven,
The flesh will quiver where the pincers tear.   *Ibid. Act* v. *Sc.* 1.

Souls made of fire, and children of the sun,
With whom revenge is virtue.   *Ibid. Act* v. *Sc.* 2.

---

[1]   As if Misfortune made the throne her seat,
      And none could be unhappy but the great.
            Rowe, *The Fair Penitent, Prologue.*
[2]   The germ of this thought is found in Jeremy Taylor : Lloyd, South,
Butler, Young, and Goldsmith have repeated it after him ; see Appendix,
Speech given to man to conceal his thoughts.
[3]   But to enlarge or illustrate this power and effects of love is to set a
candle in the sun.—Burton, *Anatomy of Melancholy, Pt.* iii. *Sect.* 2. *Mem.* 1.
Subs. 2.
      I forbear to light a candle to the sun.—Selden, *Preface to Mare Clausum,*
ed. 1635.
      To match the candle with the sun.—Surrey, *A Praise of His Love.*
[4]   From Mitford's *Life of Young.*   See also Spence's *Anecdotes, p.* 378.

BARTON BOOTH. 1681—1733.

True as the needle to the pole,
Or as the dial to the sun.[1]   *Song.*

—□—

ALEXANDER POPE. 1688—1744.

ESSAY ON MAN.

Awake, my St. John ! leave all meaner things
To low ambition, and the pride of kings.
Let us (since life can little more supply
Than just to look about us, and to die)
Expatiate free o'er all this scene of man ;
A mighty maze ! but not without a plan.   *Epistle* i. *Line* 1.

Together let us beat this ample field,
Try what the open, what the covert yield.   *Epistle* i. *Line* 9.

Eye Nature's walks, shoot folly as it flies,
And catch the manners living as they rise ;
Laugh where we must, be candid where we can,
But vindicate the ways of God to man.[2]   *Epistle* i. *Line* 13.

Heaven from all creatures hides the book of Fate.
                                            Epistle i. *Line* 77.

Pleased to the last, he crops the flowery food,
And licks the hand just raised to shed his blood.
                                            Epistle i. *Line* 83.

Who sees with equal eye, as God of all,
A hero perish, or a sparrow fall,
Atoms or systems into ruin hurled,
And now a bubble burst, and now a world.   *Epistle* i. *Line* 87.

Hope springs eternal in the human breast :
Man never is, but always to be blest.
The soul, uneasy, and confin'd from home,
Rests and expatiates in a life to come.
Lo, the poor Indian ! whose untutored mind
Sees God in clouds, or hears him in the wind.
                                            Epistle i. *Line* 95.

Far as the solar walk or milky way.   *Epistle* i. *Line* 102.

But thinks, admitted to that equal sky,
His faithful dog shall bear him company.   *Epistle* i. *Line* 111.

---

[1] True as the dial to the sun,
    Although it be not shin'd upon.
            Butler, *Hudibras, Pt.* iii. *C.* 2, *L.* 175.
[2] And justify the ways of God to men.
            Milton, *Paradise Lost, Book* i. *Line* 26.

ESSAY ON MAN—*continued.*]

In pride, in reasoning pride, our error lies;
All quit their sphere, and rush into the skies.
Pride still is aiming at the blessed abodes,
Men would be angels, angels would be gods.

Epistle i. *Line* 123.

Die of a rose in aromatic pain. *Epistle* i. *Line* 200.

The spider's touch, how exquisitely fine !
Feels at each thread, and lives along the line.[1]

Epistle i. *Line* 217.

What thin partitions sense from thought divide.[2]

Epistle i. *Line* 226.

All are but parts of one stupendous whole,
Whose body Nature is, and God the soul. *Epistle* i. *Line* 267.

Warms in the sun, refreshes in the breeze,
Glows in the stars, and blossoms in the trees.

Epistle i. *Line* 272.

As full, as perfect, in vile man that mourns,
As the rapt seraph that adores and burns :
To Him no high, no low, no great, no small;
He fills, he bounds, connects, and equals all !

Epistle i. *Line* 277.

All nature is but art, unknown to thee;
All chance, direction, which thou canst not see;
All discord, harmony not understood;
All partial evil, universal good;
And spite of pride, in erring reason's spite,
One truth is clear, Whatever is, is right.[3] *Epistle* i. *Line* 289.

---

[1] Much like a subtle spider which doth sit,
In middle of her web, which spreadeth wide;
If aught do touch the utmost thread of it,
She feels it instantly on every side.
    Sir John Davies (1570—1626), *The Immortality of the Soul.*

Our souls sit close and silently within,
And their own web from their own entrails spin;
And when eyes meet far off, our sense is such,
That, spider-like, we feel the tenderest touch.
        Dryden, *Mariage à la Mode, Act* ii. *Sc.* 1.

[1] Great wits are sure to madness near allied,
And thin partitions do their bounds divide.
            Dryden, *ante, p.* 131.

"Nullum magnum ingenium sine mixtura dementiæ fuit." Seneca, *De Tranquillitate Animi,* xvii. 10, quotes this from Aristotle, who gives as one of his *Problemata* (xxx. 1.), Διὰ τί πάντες ὅσοι περιττοὶ γεγόνασιν ἄνδρες ἢ κατὰ φιλοσοφίαν ἢ πολιτικὴν ἢ ποίησιν ἢ τέχνας φαίνονται μελαγχολικοὶ ὄντες.

[3] Whatever is, is in its causes just.
            Dryden, *Œdipus, Act* iii. *Sc.* 1.

F*

ESSAY ON MAN—*continued.*]

Know then thyself, presume not God to scan ;
The proper study of mankind is man.[1]   *Epistle* ii. *Line* 1

Chaos of thought and passion, all confus'd ;
Still by himself abused or disabused ;
Created half to rise, and half to fall ;
Great lord of all things, yet a prey to all ;
Sole judge of truth, in endless error hurl'd ;
The glory, jest, and riddle of the world ![2]   *Epistle* ii. *Line* 13.

Fix'd like a plant, on his peculiar spot,
To draw nutrition, propagate, and rot.   *Epistle* ii. *Line* 63.

On life's vast ocean diversely we sail,
Reason the card, but passion is the gale.   *Epistle* ii. *Line* 107.

And hence one master-passion in the breast,
Like Aaron's serpent, swallows up the rest.   *Epistle* ii. *Line* 131.

The young disease, that must subdue at length,
Grows with his growth, and strengthens with his strength.
                                                Epistle ii.   *Line* 135.

Vice is a monster of so frightful mien,[3]
As, to be hated, needs but to be seen ;
Yet seen too oft, familiar with her face,
We first endure, then pity, then embrace.   *Epistle* ii. *Line* 217.

Virtuous and vicious every man must be,
Few in th' extreme, but all in the degree.   *Epistle* ii. *Line* 231.

Behold the child, by Nature's kindly law,
Pleas'd with a rattle, tickled with a straw :
Some livelier plaything gives his youth delight,
A little louder, but as empty quite ;
Scarfs, garters, gold, amuse his riper stage,
And beads and prayer-books are the toys of age,
Pleas'd with this bauble still, as that before,
Till tir'd he sleeps, and life's poor play is o'er.
                                                Epistle ii. *Line* 275.

Learn of the little nautilus to sail,
Spread the thin oar, and catch the driving gale.
                                                Epistle iii. *Line* 177.

---

[1] La vraye science et le vray étude de l'homme c'est l'homme.—Charron, *De la Sagesse, Lib.* i. *Ch.* i.

[2] Quelle chimère est-ce donc que l'homme ! quelle nouveauté, quel chaos, quel sujet de contradiction ! Juge de toutes choses, imbécile ver de terre, dépositaire du vrai, amas d'incertitude, gloire et rebut de l'univers.—Pascal, *Systèmes des Philosophes*, xxv.

[3] For truth has such a face and such a mien,
As to be lov'd needs only to be seen.
                                Dryden, *The Hind and Panther. Line* 33.

ESSAY ON MAN—*continued.*]

> Th' enormous faith of many made for one.   *Epistle* iii. *Line* 242.

> For forms of government let fools contest;
> Whate'er is best administer'd is best :
> For modes of faith let graceless zealots fight;
> His can't be wrong whose life is in the right.[1]
> > *Epistle* iii. *Line* 303.

> In Faith and Hope the world will disagree,
> But all mankind's concern is charity.   *Epistle* iii. *Line* 307.

> O happiness ! our being's end and aim !
> Good, pleasure, ease, content ! whate'er thy name :
> That something still which prompts th' eternal sigh,
> For which we bear to live, or dare to die.   *Epistle* iv. *Line* 1.

> Order is Heaven's first law.   *Epistle* iv. *Line* 49.

> Reason's whole pleasure, all the joys of sense,
> Lie in three words—health, peace, and competence.
> > *Epistle* iv. *Line* 79.

> The soul's calm sunshine and the heartfelt joy.
> > *Epistle* iv. *Line* 168.

> Honour and shame from no condition rise;
> Act well your part, there all the honour lies.   *Epistle* iv. *Line* 193.

> Worth makes the man, and want of it the fellow;
> The rest is all but leather or prunello.   *Epistle* iv. *Line* 203.

> What can ennoble sots, or slaves, or cowards?
> Alas ! not all the blood of all the Howards.
> > *Epistle* iv. *Line* 215.

> A wit 's a feather, and a chief a rod;
> An honest man 's the noblest work of God.[2]   *Epistle* iv. *Line* 247.

> Plays round the head, but comes not to the heart :
> One self-approving hour whole years outweighs
> Of stupid starers and of loud huzzas :
> And more true joy Marcellus exiled feels
> Than Cæsar with a senate at his heels.   *Epistle* iv. *Line* 254.

---

[1] His faith, perhaps, in some nice tenets might
Be wrong; his life, I 'm sure, was in the right.
> > Cowley, *On the Death of Crashaw.*

[2] Man is his own star, and that soul that can
Be honest is the only perfect man.
> > Fletcher, *Upon an Honest Man's Fortune*

ESSAY ON MAN—*continued.*]

> If parts allure thee, think how Bacon shin'd,
> The wisest, brightest, meanest of mankind !
> Or, ravish'd with the whistling of a name,[1]
> See Cromwell, damn'd to everlasting fame ![2]
> > *Epistle* iv. *Line* 281.

> Know then this truth (enough for man to know),
> "Virtue alone is happiness below."   *Epistle* iv. *Line* 309.

> Slave to no sect, who takes no private road,
> But looks through nature up to nature's God.[3]
> > *Epistle* iv. *Line* 331.

> Form'd by thy converse, happily to steer
> From grave to gay, from lively to severe.[4]   *Epistle* iv. *Line* 379.

> Say, shall my little bark attendant sail,
> Pursue the triumph, and partake the gale?   *Epistle* iv. *Line* 385.

> Thou wert my guide, philosopher, and friend.
> > *Epistle* iv. *Line* 390.

> That virtue only makes our bliss below,
> And all our knowledge is, ourselves to know.
> > *Epistle* iv. *Line* 397.

MORAL ESSAYS.

> To observations which ourselves we make,
> We grow more partial for the observer's sake. *Epistle* i. *Line* 11.

> Like following life through creatures you dissect,
> You lose it in the moment you detect.   *Epistle* i. *Line* 29.

> Half our knowledge we must snatch, not take. *Epistle* i. *Line* 40.

> 'T is from high life high characters are drawn ;
> A saint in crape is twice a saint in lawn.   *Epistle* i. *Line* 135.

> 'T is education forms the common mind :
> Just as the twig is bent the tree's inclined.   *Epistle* i. *Line* 149.

---

[1] Charm'd with the foolish whistling of a name.
> Cowley, *Trans. Georgics, Book* ii. *Line* 458.
[2] May see thee now, though late, redeem thy name,
And glorify what else is damn'd to fame.
> Savage, *Character of Foster.*
:You will find that it is the modest, not the presumptuous inquirer, who makes a real and safe progress in the discovery of divine truths. One follows nature and nature's God—that is, he follows God in his works and in his word.—Bolingbroke, *A Letter to Mr. Pope.*
[4] Happy who in his verse can gently steer,
From grave to light : from pleasant to severe.
> Dryden, *The Art of Poetry, C.* i. *Line* 75.
Heureux qui, dans ses vers, sait d'une voix légère
Passer du grave au doux, du plaisant au sévère.
> Boileau, *L'Art Poétique,* Chant Ier

MORAL ESSAYS—*continued.*]

Manners with fortunes, humours turn with climes,
Tenets with books, and principles with times.[1]

Epistle i. *Line* 172.

Odious! in woollen! 't would a saint provoke,
Were the last words that poor Narcissa spoke.

Epistle i. *Line* 246.

And you, brave Cobham! to the latest breath
Shall feel your ruling passion strong in death.

Epistle i. *Line* 262.

Whether the charmer sinner it, or saint it,
If folly grow romantic, I must paint it. *Epistle* ii. *Line* 15.

Choose a firm cloud before it fall, and in it
Catch, ere she change, the Cynthia of this minute.

Epistle ii. *Line* 19.

Fine by defect, and delicately weak.[2] *Epistle* ii. *Line* 43.

With too much quickness ever to be taught;
With too much thinking to have common thought.

Epistle ii. *Line* 97.

To heirs unknown descends th' unguarded store,
Or wanders, heaven-directed, to the poor. *Epistle* ii. *Line* 149.

Virtue she finds too painful an endeavour,
Content to dwell in decencies forever. *Epistle* ii. *Line* 163.

Men, some to business, some to pleasure take;
But every woman is at heart a rake. *Epistle* ii. *Line* 215.

See how the world its veterans rewards!
A youth of frolics, an old age of cards. *Epistle* ii. *Line* 243.

Oh! bless'd with temper whose unclouded ray
Can make to-morrow cheerful as to-day. *Epistle* ii. *Line* 257.

She who ne'er answers till a husband cools,
Or, if she rules him, never shows she rules. *Epistle* ii. *Line* 261.

And mistress of herself, though china fall. *Epistle* ii. *Line* 268.

Woman 's at best a contradiction still. *Epistle* ii. *Line* 270.

Who shall decide, when doctors disagree,
And soundest casuists doubt, like you and me?

Epistle iii. *Line* 1.

Blest paper-credit! last and best supply!
That lends corruption lighter wings to fly. *Epistle* iii. *Line* 39.

---

[1] Tempora mutantur nos et mutamur in illis. *Borbonius.*
[2] Fine by degrees, and beautifully less.
Prior, Henry and Emma.

MORAL ESSAYS—*continued.*]

But thousands die without or this or that,
Die, and endow a college or a cat. *Epistle* iii. *Line* 95.

The ruling passion, be it what it will,
The ruling passion conquers reason still. *Epistle* iii. *Line* 153.

Extremes in nature equal good produce;
Extremes in man concur to general use. *Epistle* iii. *Line* 161.

Rise, honest muse! and sing The Man of Ross.
Epistle iii. *Line* 250.

Ye little stars! hide your diminish'd rays.[1] *Epistle* iii. *Line* 282.

Who builds a church to God, and not to fame,
Will never mark the marble with his name. *Epistle* iii. *Line* 285.

Where London's column, pointing at the skies,
Like a tall bully, lifts the head and lies. *Epistle* iii. *Line* 339.

Good sense, which only is the gift of Heaven,
And though no science, fairly worth the seven.
Epistle iv. *Line* 43.

To rest, the cushion and soft dean invite,
Who never mentions hell to ears polite.[2] *Epistle* iv. *Line* 149.

Statesman, yet friend to truth! of soul sincere,
In action faithful, and in honour clear;
Who broke no promise, serv'd no private end,
Who gain'd no title, and who lost no friend. *Epistle* v. *Line* 67.

AN ESSAY ON CRITICISM.

'T is with our judgments as our watches, none
Go just alike, yet each believes his own.[3] *Part* i. *Line* 9.

One science only will one genius fit;
So vast is art, so narrow human wit. *Part* i. *Line* 60.

From vulgar bounds with brave disorder part,
And snatch a grace beyond the reach of art. *Part* i. *Line* 154.

---

[1] At whose sight all the stars
Hide their diminished heads.
Milton, *Par. Lost, Book* iv. *Line* 34.

[2] In the reign of Charles II. a certain worthy divine at Whitehall thus addressed himself to the auditory at the conclusion of his sermon :—" In short, if you don't live up to the precepts of the Gospel, but abandon yourselves to your irregular appetites, you must expect to receive your reward in a certain place which 't is not good manners to mention here."— Tom Brown, *Laconics.*

[3] But as when an authentic watch is shown,
Each man winds up and rectifies his own,
So in our very judgments, &c.
Suckling. *Epilogue to Aglaura.*

Pride, the never-failing vice of fools.   *Part* ii. *Line* 4.

A little learning is a dangerous thing ;
Drink deep, or taste not the Pierian spring :
There shallow draughts intoxicate the brain,
And drinking largely sobers us again.[1]   *Part* ii. *Line* 15.

Hills peep o'er hills, and Alps on Alps arise !   *Part* ii. *Line* 32.

Whoever thinks a faultless piece to see,
Thinks what ne'er was, nor is, nor e'er shall be.[2]
    Part ii. *Line* 53.

True wit is nature to advantage dress'd,
What oft was thought, but ne'er so well express'd.
    Part ii. *Line* 97.

Words are like leaves ; and where they most abound,
Much fruit of sense beneath is rarely found.   *Part* ii. *Line* 109.

Such labour'd nothings, in so strange a style,
Amaze th' unlearn'd, and make the learned smile.
    Part ii. *Line* 126.

In words, as fashions, the same rule will hold,
Alike fantastic if too new or old :
Be not the first by whom the new are tried,
Nor yet the last to lay the old aside.   *Part* ii. *Line* 133.

      Some to church repair,
Not for the doctrine, but the music there.   *Part* ii. *Line* 142.

These equal syllables alone require,
Though oft the ear the open vowels tire,
While expletives their feeble aid do join,
And ten low words oft creep in one dull line.   *Part* ii *Line* 144.

A needless Alexandrine ends the song,
That, like a wounded snake, drags its slow length along.[3]
    Part ii. *Line* 158.

---

[1] A little philosophy inclineth man's mind to atheism, but depth in philosophy bringeth men's minds about to religion.—Bacon, *Essays, Of Atheism.*
A little skill in antiquity inclines a man to Popery ; but depth in that study brings him about again to our religion.—Fuller, *Holy State, The True Church Antiquary.*
[2] " High characters," cries one, and he would see
Things that ne'er were, nor are, nor e'er will be.
    Suckling, *Epilogue to The Goblin.*
There 's no such thing in nature, and you 'll draw
A faultless monster, which the world ne'er saw.
    Sheffield, *Essay on Poetry.*
[3] Solvuntur, tardosque trahit sinus ultimus orbes.
    Virgil, *Georgics, Lib.* iii. 424.

ESSAY ON CRITICISM—*continued.*]

True ease in writing comes from art, not chance,
As those move easiest who have learn'd to dance.
'T is not enough no harshness gives offence;
The sound must seem an echo to the sense.
Soft is the strain when zephyr gently blows,
And the smooth stream in smoother numbers flows;
But when loud surges lash the sounding shore,
The hoarse rough verse should like the torrent roar.
When Ajax strives some rock's vast weight to throw,
The line too labours, and the words move slow;
Not so when swift Camilla scours the plain,
Flies o'er th' unbending corn, and skims along the main.

Part ii. *Line* 162.

For fools admire, but men of sense approve. *Part* ii. *Line* 191.

But let a lord once own the happy lines,
How the wit brightens! how the style refines! *Part* ii. *Line* 220.

Envy will merit as its shade pursue,
But, like a shadow, proves the substance true. *Part* ii. *Line* 266.

To err is human, to forgive divine.   *Part* ii. *Line* 325.

All seems infected that th' infected spy,
As all looks yellow to the jaundic'd eye.   *Part* ii. *Line* 358.

And make each day a critic on the last.   *Part* iii. *Line* 12.

Men must be taught as if you taught them not,
And things unknown propos'd as things forgot.

Part iii. *Line* 15.

The bookful blockhead, ignorantly read,
With loads of learned lumber in his head.   *Part* iii. *Line* 53.

        Most authors steal their works, or buy;
Garth did not write his own Dispensary.   *Part* iii. *Line* 59.

For fools rush in where angels fear to tread.[1] *Part* iii. *Line* 66.

Led by the light of the Mæonian star.   *Part* iii. *Line* 89.

Content if hence th' unlearn'd their wants may view,
The learn'd reflect on what before they knew.[2] *Part* iii. *Line* 180.

---

[1] That wrens make prey where eagles dare not perch.
                    Shakespeare, *Richard III.*, *Act* i. *Sc.* 3.
[2] "Indocti discant et ament meminisse periti."
This Latin hexameter, which is commonly ascribed to Horace, appeared
for the first time as an epigraph to President Hénault's *Abrégé Chronolo-
gique*, and in the preface to the third edition of this work, Hénault acknow-
ledges that he had given it as a translation of this couplet.

THE RAPE OF THE LOCK.

What dire offence from amorous causes springs,
What mighty contests rise from trivial things.   *Canto* i. *Line* 1.

And all Arabia breathes from yonder box.   *Canto* i. *Line* 134.

On her white breast a sparkling cross she wore,
Which Jews might kiss, and infidels adore.   *Canto* ii. *Line* 7.

If to her share some female errors fall,
Look on her face, and you'll forget them all. *Canto* ii. *Line* 17.

Fair tresses man's imperial race insnare,
And beauty draws us with a single hair.[1]   *Canto* ii. *Line* 27.

Here thou, great Anna! whom three realms obey,
Dost sometimes counsel take—and sometimes tea.
                                   Canto iii. *Line* 7.

At every word a reputation dies.   *Canto* iii. *Line* 16.

The hungry judges soon the sentence sign,
And wretches hang, that jurymen may dine. *Canto* iii. *Line* 21.

Coffee, which makes the politician wise,
And see through all things with his half-shut eyes.
                                   Canto iii. *Line* 117.

The meeting points the sacred hair dissever
From the fair head, for ever, and for ever! *Canto* iii. *Line* 153.

Sir Plume, of amber snuff-box justly vain,
And the nice conduct of a clouded cane.   *Canto* iv. *Line* 123.

Charms strike the sight, but merit wins the soul.
                                   Canto v. *Line* 34.

EPISTLE TO DR. ARBUTHNOT.
(*Prologue to the Satires.*)

Shut, shut the door, good John! fatigu'd, I said;
Tie up the knocker, say I'm sick, I'm dead.   *Line* 1.

Fire in each eye, and papers in each hand,
They rave, recite, and madden round the land.   *Line* 5.

E'en Sunday shines no sabbath day to me.   *Line* 12.

Is there a parson much bemus'd in beer,
A maudlin poetess, a rhyming peer,
A clerk foredoom'd his father's soul to cross
Who pens a stanza when he should engross?   *Line* 15.

---

[1] She knows her man, and, when you rant and swear,
   Can draw you to her with a single hair.
                         Dryden, *Persius, Satire* i.

Friend to my life, which did not you prolong,
The world had wanted many an idle song.   *Line* 27.

Oblig'd by hunger and request of friends.   *Line* 44.

Fir'd that the house rejects him, "'Sdeath! I'll print it,
And shame the fools."   *Line* 61.

No creature smarts so little as a fool.   *Line* 84.

Destroy his fib, or sophistry—in vain!
The creature's at his dirty work again.   *Line* 91.

As yet a child, nor yet a fool to fame,
I lisp'd in numbers, for the numbers came.   *Line* 127

Pretty! in amber to observe the forms
Of hairs, or straws, or dirt, or grubs, or worms!
The things, we know, are neither rich nor rare,
But wonder how the devil they got there.   *Line* 169.

Means not, but blunders round about a meaning;
And he whose fustian's so sublimely bad,
It is not poetry, but prose run mad.   *Line* 186.

Should such a man, too fond to rule alone,
Bear, like the Turk, no brother near the throne.   *Line* 197.

Damn with faint praise, assent with civil leer,
And without sneering teach the rest to sneer;
Willing to wound, and yet afraid to strike,
Just hint a fault, and hesitate dislike.   *Line* 201.

                By flatterers besieg'd,
And so obliging that he ne'er oblig'd;
Like Cato, give his little senate laws,
And sit attentive to his own applause.   *Line* 207.

Who but must laugh, if such a man there be?
Who would not weep, if Atticus were he?   *Line* 213.

Curst be the verse, how well soe'er it flow,
That tends to make one worthy man my foe.   *Line* 283.

Satire or sense, alas! can Sporus feel?
Who breaks a butterfly upon a wheel?   *Line* 307.

Eternal smiles his emptiness betray,
As shallow streams run dimpling all the way.   *Line* 315.

Wit that can creep, and pride that licks the dust.   *Line* 333.

That not in fancy's maze he wander'd long,
But stoop'd to truth, and moraliz'd his song.   *Line* 340.

EPISTLE TO DR. ARBUTHNOT—*continued.*]

    Me, let the tender office long engage
To rock the cradle of reposing age,
With lenient arts extend a mother's breath,
Make languor smile, and smooth the bed of death;
Explore the thought, explain the asking eye,
And keep awhile one parent from the sky.   *Line* 408.

SATIRES, EPISTLES, AND ODES OF HORACE.

Lord Fanny spins a thousand such a day.
                 Satire i. *Book* ii. *Line* 6.

Satire 's my weapon, but I 'm too discreet
To run amuck, and tilt at all I meet.   *Satire* i. *Book* ii. *Line* 69.

But touch me, and no minister so sore;
Whoe'er offends, at some unlucky time
Slides into verse, and hitches in a rhyme;
Sacred to ridicule his whole life long,
And the sad burden of some merry song.
                 Satire i. *Book* ii. *Line* 76.

There St. John mingles with my friendly bowl,
The feast of reason and the flow of soul.
                 Satire i. *Book* ii. *Line* 127.

For I, who hold sage Homer's rule the best,
Welcome the coming, speed the going guest.[1]
                 Satire ii. *Book* ii. *Line* 159.

Give me again my hollow tree,
A crust of bread, and liberty.   *Satire* vi. *Book* ii. *Line* 220.

Do good by stealth, and blush to find it fame.
        Epilogue to the Satires. Dialogue i. *Line* 136.

To Berkeley every virtue under heaven.
        Epilogue to the Satires. Dialogue ii. *Line* 76.

When the brisk minor pants for twenty-one.
                 Epistle i. *Book* i. *Line* 38.

Get place and wealth; if possible, with grace;
If not, by any means get wealth and place.[2]
                 Epistle i. *Book* i. *Line* 103,

---

[1] Welcome the coming, speed the parting guest.
                 The Odyssey, Book xv. *Line* 84

[2] Get money; still get money, boy;
No matter by what means.
        Jonson, *Every Man in his Humour, Act* ii. *Sc.* 3.

EPISTLES OF HORACE—*continued.*]

Above all Greek, above all Roman fame.[1]

Epistle i. *Book* ii. *Line* 26.

The mob of gentlemen who wrote with ease.

Epistle i. *Book* ii. *Line* 108.

One simile that solitary shines
In the dry desert of a thousand lines.

Epistle i. *Book* ii. *Line* 111.

Who says in verse what others say in prose.

Epistle i. *Book* ii. *Line* 202.

Waller was smooth; but Dryden taught to join
The varying verse, the full resounding line,
The long majestic march, and energy divine.

Epistle i. *Book* ii. *Line* 267.

The last and greatest art, the art to blot.

Epistle i. *Book* ii. *Line* 281.

Who pants for glory, finds but short repose;
A breath revives him, or a breath o'erthrows.

Epistle i. *Book* ii. *Line* 300.

The many-headed monster of the pit.[2]

Epistle i. *Book* ii. *Line* 305.

" Praise undeserved is scandal in disguise."[3]

Epistle i. *Book* ii. *Line* 413.

Years following years steal something every day;
At last they steal us from ourselves away.

Epistle ii. *Book* ii. *Line* 72.

The vulgar boil, the learned roast an egg.

Epistle ii. *Book* ii. *Line* 85.

Words that wise Bacon or brave Raleigh spoke.

Epistle ii. *Book* ii. *Line* 168.

Vain was the chief's, the sage's pride !
They had no poet, and they died.   *Ode* 9. *Book* iv.

---

[1] Above any Greek or Roman name.
                    Dryden, *Upon the Death of Lord Hastings.*
[2] This many-headed monster.—Massinger, *The Roman Actor*, *Act* iii.
Sc. 2. Scott, *Lady of the Lake*, *Canto* v. *St.* 30.
    Many-headed multitude. — Sidney, *Arcadia*, *Book* ii. Shakespeare,
Coriolanus, *Act.* ii. *Sc.* 3.
[3] This line is from a poem entitled *To the Celebrated Beauties of the British
Court.* Bell's *Fugitive Poetry*, *Vol.* iii. *p.* 118.
    The following epigram is from *The Grove.* London, 1721.
            When one good line did much my wonder raise,
            In Br—st's works, I stood resolved to praise;
            And had, but that the modest author cries
            " Praise undeserved is scandal in disguise."
                        *On a Certain Line of Mr. Br——, Author of a
                        Copy of Verses called the British Beauties.*

Nature and Nature's laws lay hid in night :
God said, " Let Newton be !" and all was light.
Epitaph intended for Sir Isaac Newton.

Ye Gods ! annihilate but space and time,
And make two lovers happy.
Martinus Scriblerus on the Art of Sinking in Poetry. Ch. 11.

THE DUNCIAD.

O thou! whatever title please thine ear,
Dean, Drapier, Bickerstaff, or Gulliver!
Whether thou choose Cervantes' serious air,
Or laugh and shake in Rabelais' easy-chair.   *Book* i. *Line* 21.

Poetic Justice, with her lifted scale,
Where, in nice balance, truth with gold she weighs,
And solid pudding against empty praise.   *Book* i. *Line* 52.

Now night descending, the proud scene was o'er,
But lived in Settle's numbers one day more.   *Book* i. *Line* 89.

While pensive poets painful vigils keep,
Sleepless themselves to give their readers sleep.   *Book* i. *Line* 93.

Next o'er his books his eyes began to roll,
In pleasing memory of all he stole.   *Book* i. *Line* 127.

How index-learning turns no student pale,
Yet holds the eel of science by the tail.   *Book* i. *Line* 279.

And gentle Dulness ever loves a joke.   *Book* ii. *Line* 34.

Till Peter's keys some christen'd Jove adorn,
And Pan to Moses lends his pagan horn.   *Book* iii. *Line* 109.

All crowd, who foremost shall be damn'd to fame.
    Book iii. *Line* 158.

Silence, ye wolves! while Ralph to Cynthia howls,
And makes night hideous;[1]—answer him, ye owls.
    Book iii. *Line* 165.

A wit with dunces, and a dunce with wits.[2]   *Book* iv. *Line* 90.

The right divine of kings to govern wrong.   *Book* iv. *Line* 188.

Stuff the head
With all such reading as was never read :
For thee explain a thing till all men doubt it,
And write about it, goddess, and about it.   *Book* iv. *Line* 249.

---

[1] Making night hideous.—Shakespeare, *Hamlet, Act* i. *Sc.* 4.
[2] See Cowper, *post.*

THE DUNCIAD—*continued.*]

Led by my hand, he saunter'd Europe round,
And gather'd every vice on Christian ground. *Book* iv. *Line* 311.

Judicious drank, and greatly daring din'd.   *Book* iv. *Line* 318.

Stretch'd on the rack of a too easy chair,
And heard thy everlasting yawn confess
The pains and penalties of idleness.   *Book* iv. *Line* 342

E'en Palinurus nodded at the helm.   *Book* iv. *Line* 614.

Religion, blushing, veils her sacred fires,
And unawares Morality expires.
Nor public flame, nor private dares to shine ;
Nor human spark is left, nor glimpse divine !
Lo ! thy dread empire, Chaos, is restor'd ;
Light dies before thy uncreating word :
Thy hand, great Anarch ! lets the curtain fall ;
And universal darkness buries all.   *Book* iv. *Line* 649.

———

ELOISA TO ABELARD.

Heaven first taught letters for some wretch's aid,
Some banish'd lover, or some captive maid.   *Line* 51.

Speed the soft intercourse from soul to soul,
And waft a sigh from Indus to the Pole.   *Line* 57.

Curse on all laws but those which love has made.
Love, free as air, at sight of human ties,
Spreads his light wings, and in a moment flies.   *Line* 74.

And love th' offender, yet detest th' offence.[1]   *Line* 192.

How happy is the blameless vestal's lot !
The world forgetting, by the world forgot.   *Line* 207.

One thought of thee puts all the pomp to flight ;
Priests, tapers, temples, swim before my sight.[2]   *Line* 273.

See my lips tremble and my eyeballs roll ;
Suck my last breath, and catch my flying soul.   *Line* 323.

He best can paint them who shall feel them most.   *Line ult.*

Not chaos-like together crush'd and bruis'd,
But, as the world, harmoniously confus'd,
Where order in variety we see,
And where, though all things differ, all agree.
                            Windsor Forest. Line 13.

———

[1] She hugged the offender and forgave the offence.
                    Dryden, *Cymon and Iphigenia, Line* 107.
[2] Priests, tapers, temples, swam before my sight.
                    Edmund Smith, *Phædra and Hippolytus.*

WINDSOR FOREST—*continued.*]

A mighty hunter, and his prey was man.   *Ibid.   Line* 62.

From old Belerium to the northern main.   *Ibid.   Line* 316.

Nor Fame I slight, nor for her favours call;
She comes unlook'd for, if she comes at all.
                                    The Temple of Fame.   Line 513.

Unblemish'd let me live, or die unknown;
O grant an honest fame, or grant me none!   *Ibid.   Lin. ult.*

I am his Highness's dog at Kew;
Pray tell me, sir, whose dog are you?   *On the Collar of a Dog.*

There, take, (says Justice,) take ye each a shell;
We thrive at Westminster on fools like you;
'T was a fat oyster—live in peace—adieu.[1]
                                    Verbatim from Boileau.

Father of all! in every age,
    In every clime ador'd,
By saint, by savage, and by sage,
        Jehovah, Jove, or Lord.
                                    The Universal Prayer.   Stanza 1.

And binding nature fast in fate,
    Left free the human will.   *Stanza* 3.

And deal damnation round the land.   *Stanza* 7.

Teach me to feel another's woe,
    To hide the fault I see;
That mercy I to others show,
    That mercy show to me.[2]   *Stanza* 10.

Vital spark of heavenly flame!
Quit, O quit this mortal frame!
                                    The Dying Christian to his Soul.

Hark! they whisper; angels say,
Sister Spirit, come away!   *Ibid.*

Tell me, my soul, can this be death?   *Ibid.*

Lend, lend your wings! I mount! I fly!
O grave! where is thy victory?
O death! where is thy sting?   *Ibid.*

Thus let me live, unseen, unknown,
    Thus unlamented let me die;
Steal from the world, and not a stone
    Tell where I lie.   *Ode on Solitude*

---

[1] " Tenez vo là," dit-elle, "à chacun une écaille,
Des sottises d'autrui nous vivons au Palais;
Messieurs, l'huître étoit bonne. Adieu. Vivez en paix."
                                    Epître, ii. (*à M. L'Abbé des Roches.*)
[2] Cf. Spenser, *The Faerie Queene*, Book iv. *C.* i. *St.* 42.

What beckoning ghost along the moonlight shade
Invites my steps and points to yonder glade?[1]
> *To the Memory of an Unfortunate Lady.* **Line 1.**

By foreign hands thy dying eyes were clos'd,
By foreign hands thy decent limbs compos'd,
By foreign hands thy humble grave adorn'd,
By strangers honour'd, and by strangers mourn'd.
> *Ibid.* **Line 51.**

And bear about the mockery of woe
To midnight dances, and the public show. *Ibid.* **Line 57.**

How lov'd, how honour'd once, avails thee not,
To whom related, or by whom begot;
A heap of dust alone remains of thee;
'T is all thou art, and all the proud shall be! *Ibid.* **Line 71.**

Such were the notes thy once lov'd poet sung,
Till death untimely stopp'd his tuneful tongue.
> *Epist. to Robert, Earl of Oxford.*

Who ne'er knew joy but friendship might divide,
Or gave his father grief but when he died.
> *Epitaph on the Hon. S. Harcourt.*

The saint sustain'd it, but the woman died.
> *Epitaph on Mrs. Corbet.*

Of manners gentle, of affections mild;
In wit a man, simplicity a child.[2] *Epitaph on Gay.*

A brave man struggling in the storms of fate,
And greatly falling with a falling state.
While Cato gives his little senate laws,
What bosom beats not in his country's cause?
> *Prologue to Mr. Addison's Cato.*

The mouse that always trusts to one poor hole
Can never be a mouse of any soul.[3]
> *The Wife of Bath.* **Her Prologue. Line 298.**

Love seldom haunts the breast where learning lies,
And Venus sets ere Mercury can rise. *Ibid.* **Line 369.**

You beat your pate, and fancy wit will come;
Knock as you please, there's nobody at home.[4] *Epigram.*

---

[1] What gentle ghost, besprent with April dew,
Hails me so solemnly to yonder yew?
> Ben Jonson, *Elegy on the Lady Jane Pawlet.*
[2] Her wit was more than man, her innocence a child.
> Dryden, *Elegy on Mrs. Killegrew.*
[3] I hold a mouse's hert not worth a leek,
That hath but oon hole to sterte to.
> Chaucer, *The Prologue of The Wyfe of Bathe, V.* **572.**
[4] Cf. Cowper, *post.*

Party is the madness of many for the gain of a few.[1]
> *Thoughts on Various Subjects.*

I never knew any man in my life who could not bear another's misfortunes perfectly like a Christian. *Ibid.*

ILIAD.

Achilles' wrath, to Greece the direful spring
Of woes unnumber'd, heavenly goddess, sing ! *Book* i. *Line* 1.

The distant Trojans never injured me. *Book* i. *Line* 200.

Shakes his ambrosial curls, and gives the nod ;
The stamp of fate, and sanction of the god. *Book* i. *Line* 684.

She moves a goddess, and she looks a queen. *Book* iii. *Line* 208.

Not two strong men the enormous weight could raise ;
Such men as live in these degenerate days. *Book* v. *Line* 371.

Like leaves on trees the race of man is found,
Now green in youth, now withering on the ground :
Another race the following spring supplies ;
They fall successive, and successive rise. *Book* vi. *Line* 181.

Who dares think one thing, and another tell,
My heart detests him as the gates of hell. *Book* ix. *Line* 412.

A generous friendship no cold medium knows,
Burns with one love, with one resentment glows.
> *Book* ix. *Line* 725.

ODYSSEY.

Few sons attain the praise
Of their great sires, and most their sires disgrace.
> *Book* ii. *Line* 315.

Far from gay cities and the ways of men. *Book* xiv. *Line* 410.

Who love too much, hate in the like extreme. *Book* xv. *Line* 79.

True friendship's laws are by this rule exprest,
Welcome the coming, speed the parting guest.[2]
> *Book* xv. *Line* 83.

Whatever day
Makes man a slave takes half his worth away.
> *Book* xvii. *Line* 392.

---

[1] From Roscoe's edition of Pope, *Vol.* v. *p.* 376; originally printed in Motte's *Miscellanies*, 1727. In the edition of 1736, Pope says, " I must own that the prose part (The Thoughts on Various Subjects), at the end of the second volume, was wholly mine. January, 1734."
[2] Cf. *Satire* ii. *Book* ii. *Line* 160, *p.* 169.

ODYSSEY—*continued.*]

Yet, taught by time, my heart has learned to glow
For others' good, and melt at others' woe.   *Book* xviii. *Line* 279.

This is the Jew
That Shakespeare drew.[1]

—□—

THOMAS TICKELL. 1686—1740.

Just men, by whom impartial laws were given;
And saints who taught, and led the way to Heaven.
                    On the Death of Mr. Addison.   Line 41.

Nor e'er was to the bowers of bliss convey'd
A fairer spirit, or more welcome shade.   *Ibid.   Line* 45.

There taught us how to live; and (oh! too high
The price for knowledge) taught us how to die.[2] *Ibid.   Line* 81.

The sweetest garland to the sweetest maid.
                    To a Lady; with a Present of Flowers.

I hear a voice you cannot hear,
    Which says I must not stay,
I see a hand you cannot see,
    Which beckons me away.   *Colin and Lucy.*

—□—

DR. GEORGE SEWELL. —— —1726.

When all the blandishments of life are gone,
The coward sneaks to death, the brave live on.   *The Suicide.*

—□—

JOHN GAY. 1688—1732.

'T was when the sea was roaring
With hollow blasts of wind,
A damsel lay deploring,
All on a rock reclin'd.
                    The What D' ye call 't. Act ii. *Sc.* 8.

---

[1] On the 14th of February, 1741, Macklin established his fame as an actor, in the character of Shylock, in the "Merchant of Venice." . . . Macklin's performance of this character so forcibly struck a gentleman in the pit, that he, as it were involuntarily, exclaimed,
            " This is the Jew
            That Shakespeare drew."
It has been said that this gentleman was Mr. Pope, and that he meant his panegyric on Macklin as a satire against Lord Lansdowne.—*Biog. Dram. Vol.* i. *Pt.* ii. *p.* 469.

[2] Cf. Porteus, *Death, Line* 318.

I have taught you, my dear flock, for above thirty years how to live; and I will show you in a very short time how to die.—Sandys, *Anglorum Speculum, p.* 903.

THE WHAT D' YE CALL 'T – *continued.*]

So comes a reckoning when the banquet 's o'er,
The dreadful reckoning, and men smile no more.
Ibid. Act ii. *Sc.* 9.

'T is woman that seduces all mankind;
By her we first were taught the wheedling arts.
The Beggar's Opera. Act i. *Sc* 1.

Over the hills and far away.[1] *Ibid. Act* i. *Sc* 1.

If the heart of a man is depress'd with cares,
The mist is dispell'd when a woman appears.
Ibid. Act ii. *Sc.* 1.

The fly that sips treacle is lost in the sweets.
Ibid. Act ii. *Sc.* 2.

Brother, brother, we are both in the wrong. *Ibid. Act* ii. *Sc.* 2.

How happy could I be with either,
Were t' other dear charmer away.   *Ibid. Act* ii. *Sc.* 2.

The charge is prepar'd, the lawyers are met,
The judges all rang'd; a terrible show! *Ibid. Act* iii. *Sc.* 2.

All in the Downs the fleet was moor'd.
Sweet William's Farewell to Black-eyed Susan.

Adieu, she cried, and wav'd her lily hand. *Ibid.*

FABLES.

Long experience made him sage.
The Shepherd and the Philosopher.

Whence is thy learning? Hath thy toil
O'er books consum'd the midnight oil?[2] *Ibid.*

When yet was ever found a mother
Who 'd give her booby for another?
The Mother, the Nurse, and the Fairy.

Is there no hope? the sick man said;
The silent doctor shook his head.
The Sick Man and the Angel.

While there is life there 's hope, he cried.[3] *Ibid.*

---

[1] And 't is o'er the hills and far away.
Jockey's Lamentation. From *Wit's Mirth, Vol.* iv.
[2] 'midnight oil,' a common phrase, used by Quarles, Shenstone, Cowper, Lloyd, and others.
[3] Ἐλπίδες ἐν ζωοῖσιν, ἀνέλπιστοι δὲ θανόντες.
Theocritus, Id. iv. *Line* 42.
Ægroto, dum anima est, spes est.
Cicero, Epist. ad Att. ix. 10.

FABLES—*continued.*]

> Those who in quarrels interpose
> Must often wipe a bloody nose.   *The Mastiffs.*

> And when a lady's in the case,
> You know all other things give place.
> > *The Hare and many Friends.*

> Life is a jest, and all things show it;
> I thought so once, but now I know it.   *My own Epitaph.*

—□—

LADY MARY WORTLEY MONTAGUE. 1690—1762.

> Let this great maxim be my virtue's guide,—
> In part she is to blame that has been tried :
> He comes too near that comes to be denied.
> > *The Lady's Resolve.*[1]

> And we meet, with champagne and a chicken, at last.[2]
> > *The Lover.*

> Be plain in dress, and sober in your diet;
> In short, my deary ! kiss me, and be quiet.
> > *A Summary of Lord Lyttleton's Advice.*

> Satire should, like a polish'd razor keen,
> Wound with a touch that's scarcely felt or seen.
> > *To the Imitator of the First Satire of Horace. Book* ii.

—□—

KANE O'HARA. —— —1782.

> Pray, goody, please to moderate the rancour of your tongue;
> Why flash those sparks of fury from your eyes?
> Remember, when the judgment's weak, the prejudice is strong.
> > *Midas. Act* i. *Sc.* 4.

—□—

CHARLES MACKLIN. 1690—1797.

The law is a sort of hocus-pocus science, that smiles in yer face while it picks yer pocket; and the glorious uncertainty of it is of mair use to the professors than the justice of it.   *Love à la Mode. Act* ii. *Sc.* 1.

—□—

MATTHEW GREEN. 1696—1737.

> Fling but a stone, the giant dies.   *The Spleen. Line* 93.

---

[1] A fugitive piece, written on a window by Lady Montague, after her marriage (1713).   The last lines were taken from Overbury :—
> In part to blame is she
> Which hath without consent bin only tride :
> He comes to neere that comes to be denide.
> > *The Wife, St.* 36.

[2] What say you to such a supper with such a woman ?
> **Byron,** *Note to Letter on Bowles.*

LOUIS THEOBALD. 1691—1744.

None but himself can be his parallel.[1]   *The Double Falsehood.*

—□—

JOHN BYROM. 1691—1763.

God bless the King, I mean the faith's defender;
God bless—no harm in blessing—the pretender;
But who pretender is, or who is king,—
God bless us all,—that 's quite another thing.
To an Officer of the Army, extempore.

Take time enough: all other graces
Will soon fill up their proper places.[2]
Advice to Preach Slow.

Some say, compar'd to Bononcini,
That Mynheer Handel 's but a ninny;
Others aver that he to Handel
Is scarcely fit to hold a candle.
Strange all this difference should be
'Twixt Tweedledum and Tweedledee.
On the Feuds between Handel and Bononcini.[3]

As clear as a whistle.   *Epistle to Lloyd.*

Bone and Skin, two millers thin,
    Would starve us all, or near it;
But be it known to Skin and Bone
    That Flesh and Blood can't bear it.
Epigram on Two Monopolists.

—□—

EARL OF CHESTERFIELD. 1694—1773.

Sacrifice to the Graces.[4]   *Letter.* March 9, 1748.

---

[1] Quæris Alcidæ parem?
Nemo est nisi ipse.
Seneca, *Hercules Furens*, Act i. *Sc.* 1.
And but herself admits no parallel.
Massinger, *Duke of Milan*, Act iv. Sc. 3.

[2] Learn to read slow: all other graces
Will follow in their proper places.
Walker, *Art of Reading.*

[3] "Nourse asked me if I had seen the verses upon Handel and Bononcini, not knowing that they were mine." *Byrom's Remains* (Chetham Soc.), *Vol.* i. *p.* 173.   The last two lines have been attributed to Swift and Pope. See Scott's edition of Swift, and Dyce's edition of Pope.

[4] Literally from the Greek Θύε ταῖς Χάρισι. Diog. Laert. Lib. iv. § 6. *Xenocrates.*

"Xenocrates was always of a solemn and grave character, so that Plato was continually saying to him,—Xenocrates, sacrifice to the Graces."

Manners must adorn knowledge, and smooth its way through the world. Like a great rough diamond, it may do very well in a closet by way of curiosity, and also for its intrinsic value.   *Letter. July* 1, 1748.

Style is the dress of thoughts.   *Letter. Nov.* 24, 1749.

I assisted at the birth of that most significant word "flirtation," which dropped from the most beautiful mouth in the world. *The World. No.* 101.

> Unlike my subject now shall be my song,
> It shall be witty, and it sha'n't be long.   *Impromptu Lines.*

> The dews of the evening most carefully shun,—
> Those tears of the sky for the loss of the sun.
>   *Advice to a Lady in Autumn.*

—□—

DAVID MALLETT. 1700—1765.
> While tumbling down the turbid stream,
> Lord love us, how we apples swim!   *Tyburn.*

—□—

ROBERT BLAIR. 1699—1747.
>   The Grave, dread thing!
> Men shiver when thou 'rt nam'd : Nature, appall'd,
> Shakes off her wonted firmness.   *The Grave. Line* 9.

> The school-boy, with his satchel in his hand,
> Whistling aloud to bear his courage up.[1]   *Ibid. Line* 58.

> Friendship! mysterious cement of the soul!
> Sweet'ner of life! and solder of society!   *Ibid. Line* 88.

>   Of joys departed,
> Not to return, how painful the remembrance!   *Ibid. Line* 109.

>   The good he scorn'd
> Stalk'd off reluctant, like an ill-us'd ghost,
> Not to return; or, if it did, in visits
> Like those of angels, short and far between.[2]
>   *Ibid. Part* ii. *Line* 586.

—□—

RICHARD SAVAGE. 1698—1743.
> He lives to build, not boast, a generous race;
> No tenth transmitter of a foolish face.   *The Bastard. Line* 7.

—□—

JAMES THOMSON. 1700—1748.
> Come, gentle Spring! ethereal Mildness! come.
>   *The Seasons. Spring. Line* 1

---

[1] Whistling to keep myself from being afraid.
                    Dryden, *Amphitryon, Act* iii. *Sc.* ?.
[2] Cf. Campbell, *post.*

THE SEASONS. SPRING—*continued.*]

Base envy withers at another's joy,
And hates that excellence it cannot reach.   *Line* 283.

But who can paint
Like Nature? Can imagination boast,
Amid its gay creation, hues like hers?   *Line* 465.

Amid the roses fierce Repentance rears
Her snaky crest.   *Line* 996.

Delightful task! to rear the tender thought,
To teach the young idea how to shoot.   *Line* 1149.

An elegant sufficiency, content,
Retirement, rural quiet, friendship, books,
Ease and alternate labour, useful life,
Progressive virtue, and approving Heaven!   *Line* 1158.

The meek-ey'd Morn appears, mother of dews.
   Summer. *Line* 47.

Falsely luxurious, will not man awake?   *Line* 67.

But yonder comes the powerful King of Day
Rejoicing in the east.   *Line* 81

Ships, dim-discover'd, dropping from the clouds.   *Line* 946.

And Mecca saddens at the long delay.   *Line* 979.

Sigh'd and look'd unutterable things.   *Line* 1188.

A lucky chance, that oft decides the fate
Of mighty monarchs.   *Line* 1285.

So stands the statue that enchants the world,
So bending tries to veil the matchless boast,
The mingled beauties of exulting Greece.   *Line* 1346.

Who stemm'd the torrent of a downward age.   *Line* 1516.

Autumn nodding o'er the yellow plain.   *Autumn.* *Line* 2.

Loveliness
Needs not the foreign aid of ornament,
But is, when unadorn'd, adorn'd the most.   *Line* 204.

He saw her charming, but he saw not half
The charms her downcast modesty conceal'd.   *Line* 229.

For still the world prevail'd, and its dread laugh,
Which scarce the firm philosopher can scorn.   *Line* 233.

See, Winter comes, to rule the varied year.   *Winter.* *Line* 1.

[1] In naked beauty, more adorn'd,
More lovely, than Pandora.
   Milton, *Par. Lost, Book* iv. *Line* 713.

Cruel as death, and hungry as the grave.   *Line* 393

There studious let me sit,
And hold high converse with the mighty dead.

Line 431.

The kiss, snatch'd hasty from the sidelong maid.   *Line* 625

These as they change, Almighty Father! these
Are but the varied God.   The rolling year
Is full of Thee.   *Hymn.   Line* 1.

Shade, unperceiv'd, so softening into shade.   *Line* 25.

From seeming evil still educing good.   *Line* 114.

Come then, expressive silence, muse his praise.   *Line* 118.

A pleasing land of drowsyhed it was,
Of dreams that wave before the half-shut eye;
And of gay castles in the clouds that pass,
For ever flushing round a summer sky:
There eke the soft delights, that witchingly
Instil a wanton sweetness through the breast,
And the calm pleasures, always hover'd nigh;
But whate'er smack'd of noyance, or unrest,
Was far, far off expell'd from this delicious nest.
The Castle of Indolence.   Canto i. *Stanza* 6.

O fair undress, best dress! it checks no vein,
But every flowing limb in pleasure drowns,
And heightens ease with grace.   *Canto* i. *Stanza* 26.

Plac'd far amid the melancholy main.   *Canto* i. *Stanza* 30.

Scoundrel maxim.   *Canto* i. *Stanza* 50.

A bard here dwelt, more fat than bard beseems.

Canto i. *Stanza* 68

A little round, fat, oily man of God.   *Canto* i. *Stanza* 69

I care not, Fortune, what you me deny:
You cannot rob me of free Nature's grace;
You cannot shut the windows of the sky,
Through which Aurora shows her brightening face:
You cannot bar my constant feet to trace
The woods and lawns, by living stream, at eve:
Let health my nerves and finer fibres brace,
And I their toys to the great children leave:
Of fancy, reason, virtue, naught can me bereave.

Canto II. *Stanza* 3

For ever, Fortune, wilt thou prove
 An unrelenting foe to love;
And, when we meet a mutual heart,
 Come in between and bid us part?
       Song, For ever, Fortune.

    Whoe'er amidst the sons
Of reason, valour, liberty, and virtue,
Displays distinguish'd merit, is a noble
Of Nature's own creating. *Coriolanus.* *Act* iii. *Sc.* 3.

O Sophonisba! Sophonisba, O![1] *Sophonisba.* *Act* iii. *Sc.* 2.

When Britain first, at Heaven's command
 Arose from out the azure main,
This was the charter of her land,
 And guardian angels sung the strain:
 Rule Britannia! Britannia rules the waves!
Britons never shall be slaves. *Alfred.* *Act* ii. *Sc.* 5.

——□——

JOHN DYER. 1700—1758.

Ever charming, ever new,
When will the landscape tire the view? *Grongar Hill.* **Line** 5.

——□——

JOHN WESLEY. 1703—1791.

That execrable sum of all villanies commonly called A Slave Trade.
        Journal. *Feb.* 12, 1792.

Certainly this is a duty, not a sin. "Cleanliness is indeed next to god-liness."   *Sermon* xcii. *On Dress.*

——□——

ROBERT DODSLEY. 1703—1764.

One kind kiss before we part,
 Drop a tear, and bid adieu;
Though we sever, my fond heart
 Till we meet shall pant for you. *The Parting Kiss.*

——□——

JAMES BRAMSTON. ——1744.

But Titus said, with his uncommon sense,
When the Exclusion Bill was in suspense:
"I hear a lion in the lobby roar;
Say, Mr. Speaker, shall we shut the door
And keep him there, or shall we let him in
To try if we can turn him out again?"[2] *Art of Politics.*

---

[1] The line was altered, after the second edition, to
   "O Sophonisba! I am wholly thine."
[2] "I hope," said Col. Titus, "we shall not be wise as the frogs to whom

G

So Britain's monarch once uncover'd sat,
While Bradshaw bullied in a broad-brimm'd hat. *Man of Taste.*

—□—

DR. SAMUEL HOWARD. ——1782.

Gentle shepherd, tell me where?   *Song.*

—□—

HENRY FIELDING. 1707—1754.

All nature wears one universal grin.
                    Tom Thumb the Great.   *Act* i. *Sc.* 1.

Petition me no petitions, sir, to-day;
Let other hours be set apart for business.
To-day it is our pleasure to be drunk;
And this our queen shall be as drunk as we.   *Act* i. *Sc.* 2.

When I'm not thank'd at all, I'm thank'd enough.
I've done my duty, and I've done no more.   *Act* i. *Sc.* 3.

Thy modesty's a candle to thy merit.   *Act* i. *Sc.* 3.

To sun myself in Huncamunca's eyes.   *Act* i. *Sc.* 3.

Lo, when two dogs are fighting in the streets,
With a third dog one of the two dogs meets,
With angry teeth he bites him to the bone,
And this dog smarts for what that dog has done.[1]   *Act* i. *Sc.* 6.

Oh! the roast beef of Old England,
And oh! the old English roast beef.
                    The Roast Beef of Old England.

Jupiter gave a stork for their king. To trust expedients with such a king
on the throne would be just as wise as if there were a lion in the lobby, and
we should vote to let him in and chain him, instead of fastening the door to
keep him out."—*On the Exclusion Bill. January* 7, 1681.

Bom.   So have I heard on Afric's burning shore
          A hungry lion give a grievous roar;
          The grievous roar echoed along the shore.
Artax. So have I heard on Afric's burning shore
          Another lion give a grievous roar,
          And the first lion thought the last a bore.
                    T. B. Rhodes, *Bombastes Furioso.*

[1] Thus when a barber and a collier fight,
     The barber beats the luckless collier—white;
     The dusty collier heaves his ponderous sack,
     And, big with vengeance, beats the barber—black.
     In comes the brick-dust man, with grime o'erspread,
     And beats the collier and the barber—red;
     Black, red, and white, in various clouds are tost,
     And in the dust they raise the combatants are lost.
                    Christ. Smart, From *The Trip to Cambridge.*
                    Campbell's *Specimens, Vol.* vi. *p.* 185.

PHILIP DODDRIDGE. 1702—1751.

Live while you live, the epicure would say,
And seize the pleasures of the present day;
Live while you live, the sacred preacher cries,
And give to God each moment as it flies.
Lord, in my views let both united be;
I live in pleasure when I live to thee.

Epigram on his Family Arms.

——□——

NATHANIEL COTTON. 1707—1788.

If solid happiness we prize,
Within our breast this jewel lies;
    And they are fools who roam:
The world has nothing to bestow;
From our own selves our joys must flow,
    And that dear hut,— our home.   *The Fireside. St. 3.*

Thus hand in hand through life we'll go;
Its checker'd paths of joy and woe
    With cautious steps we'll tread.   *Ibid. St. 13.*

——□——

BENJAMIN FRANKLIN. 1706—1790.

God helps them that help themselves.[2]   *Poor Richard.*

Dost thou love life, then do not squander time, for that is the stuff life
is made of.   *Ibid.*

Plough deep while sluggards sleep.   *Ibid.*

Never leave that till to-morrow which you can do to-day.   *Ibid.*

Three removes are as bad as a fire.   *Ibid.*

    Vessels large may venture more,
    But little boats should keep near shore.   *Ibid.*

He has paid dear, very dear, for his whistle.   *The Whistle. (Nov. 1719.)*

There never was a good war or a bad peace.[3]
                    Letter to Quincy, Sept. 11, 1773.

        Here Skugg
        Lies snug,
        As a bug
        In a rug.
                From a Letter to Miss Georgiana Shipley.

---

    [1] Dum vivimus vivamus.   From Ortin's *Life of Doddridge.*
    [2] Help thyself, and God will help thee.
                        Herbert, *Jacula Prudentum.*
    [3] It hath been said that an unjust peace is to be preferred before a just
war.—S. Butler, *Speeches in the Rump Parliament.* Butler's *Remains.*

SAMUEL JOHNSON. 1709—1784.

Let observation with extensive view
Survey mankind from China to Peru.[1]

Vanity of Human Wishes. Line 1.

There mark what ills the scholar's life assail,—
Toil, envy, want, the patron, and the jail.   *Line* 159.

He left the name at which the world grew pale,
To point a moral, or adorn a tale.   *Line* 221.

Hides from himself his state, and shuns to know
That life protracted is protracted woe.   *Line* 257.

An age that melts in unperceiv'd decay,
And glides in modest innocence away.   *Line* 293.

Superfluous lags the veteran on the stage.   *Line* 308.

Fears of the brave, and follies of the wise!
From Marlborough's eyes the streams of dotage flow,
And Swift expires, a driveller and a show.   *Line* 316.

Must helpless man, in ignorance sedate,
Roll darkling down the torrent of his fate?   *Line* 345.

For patience, sovereign o'er transmuted ill.   *Line* 362.

Of all the griefs that harass the distrest,
Sure the most bitter is a scornful jest.   *London. Line* 166.

This mournful truth is everywhere confess'd,
Slow rises worth by poverty depress'd.   *Line* 176.

Each change of many-colour'd life he drew,
Exhausted worlds and then imagin'd new.

Prologue on the Opening of Drury Lane Theatre.

And panting Time toil'd after him in vain.   *Ibid.*

For we that live to please must please to live.   *Ibid.*

Catch, then, O catch the transient hour;
  Improve each moment as it flies;
Life's a short summer—man a flower—
  He dies—alas! how soon he dies!   *Winter. An Ode.*

Officious, innocent, sincere;
Of every friendless name the friend.

Verses on Robert Levet. Stanza 2.

---

[1] All human race, from China to Peru,
Pleasure, howe'er disguis'd by art, pursue.
    Rev. T. Warton, *The Universal Love of Pleasure.*

VERSES ON ROBERT LEVET—*continued.*]

> In misery's darkest cavern known,
>   His useful care was ever nigh [1]
> Where hopeless anguish pour'd his groan,
>   And lonely want retired to die.   *Stanza 5.*

> Then with no throbs of fiery pain, [2]
>   No cold gradations of decay,
> Death broke at once the vital chain,
>   And freed his soul the nearest way.   *Stanza 9.*

> Philips, whose touch harmonious could remove
> The pangs of guilty power and hapless love;
> Rest here, distrest by poverty no more,
> Here find that calm thou gav'st so oft before;
> Sleep, undisturb'd, within this peaceful shrine,
> Till angels wake thee with a note like thine !
>   *Epitaph on Claudius Philips, the Musician.*

> A Poet, Naturalist, and Historian,
> Who left scarcely any style of writing untouched,
> And touched nothing that he did not adorn. [3]
>   *Epitaph on Goldsmith.*

> How small, of all that human hearts endure,
> That part which laws or kings can cause or cure !
> Still to ourselves in every place consign'd,
> Our own felicity we make or find.
> With secret course, which no loud storms annoy
> Glides the smooth current of domestic joy.
>   *Lines added to Goldsmith's Traveller.*

> Trade's proud empire hastes to swift decay.
>   *Line added to Goldsmith's Deserted Village.*

> From thee, great God, we spring, to thee we tend,
> Path, motive, guide, original, and end.   *The Rambler.   No. 7.*

Ye who listen with credulity to the whispers of fancy, and pursue with eagerness the phantoms of hope; who expect that age will perform the promises of youth, and that the deficiencies of the present day will be supplied by the morrow; attend to the history of Rasselas, Prince of Abyssinia.   *Rasselas.   Chap.* 1.

---

[1] Var. His ready help was always nigh.
[2] Var. Then with no fiery throbbing pain.
[3] Nullum quod tetigit non ornavit.
  He adorns whatever he attempts.
      Fénelon, *Eulogy on Cicero.*
He adorned whatever subject he either spoke or wrote upon by the most splendid eloquence.—Chesterfield's *Characters : Bolingbroke.*

I am not so lost in lexicography as to forget that *words are the daughters of earth, and that things are the sons of heaven.*[1]

From *The Preface to his Dictionary.*

Words are men's daughters, but God's sons are things.[2]

From *Dr. Madden's "Boulter's Monument." Supposed to have been inserted by Dr. Johnson,* 1745.

Whoever wishes to attain an English style, familiar but not coarse, and elegant but not ostentatious, must give his days and nights to the volumes of Addison.   *Life of Addison.*

To be of no church is dangerous. Religion, of which the rewards are distant, and which is animated only by Faith and Hope, will glide by degrees out of the mind, unless it be invigorated and reimpressed by external ordinances, by stated calls to worship, and the salutary influence of example.   *Life of Milton.*

The trappings of a monarchy would set up an ordinary commonwealth.

Ibid.

His death eclipsed the gayety of nations, and impoverished the public stock of harmless pleasure.

Life of Edmund Smith (alluding to the death of Garrick).

That man is little to be envied whose patriotism would not gain force upon the plain of Marathon, or whose piety would not grow warmer among the ruins of Iona.   *Journey to the Western Islands: Inch Kenneth.*

If he does really think that there is no distinction between virtue and vice, why, Sir, when he leaves our houses let us count our spoons.

Boswell's Life of Johnson. An. 1763.

Knowledge is of two kinds. We know a subject ourselves, or we know where we can find information upon it.   *Ibid. An.* 1775.

There is nothing which has yet been contrived by man, by which so much happiness is produced as by a good tavern or inn.   *Ibid. An.* 1776.

Claret is the liquor for boys; port for men; but he who aspires to be a hero must drink brandy.   *Ibid. An.* 1779.

Who drives fat oxen should himself be fat.[3]   *Ibid. An.* 1784.

> If the man who turnips cries
> Cry not when his father dies,
> 'T is a proof that he had rather
> Have a turnip than his father.

Johnsoniana. Piozzi, 30.

---

[1] The italics and the word "forget" would seem to imply that the saying was not his own.   Sir William Jones gives a similar saying in India : " Words are the daughters of earth and deeds are the sons of heaven."

[2] Words are women, deeds are men.—Herbert, *Jacula Prudentum.* Sir Thomas Bodley, *Letter to his Librarian,* 1604.

[3] Parody on " Who rules o'er freemen should himself be free." —From Brooke's *Gustavus Vasa, First edition.*

A good hater. *Johnsoniana. Piozzi,* 39.

Books that you may carry to the fire, and hold readily in your hand, are the most useful after all. *Ibid. Hawkins,* 197.

———□———

WILLIAM PITT, EARL OF CHATHAM. 1708—1778.

The atrocious crime of being a young man. *Speech, March 6, 1741.*

Confidence is a plant of slow growth in an aged bosom.
Speech, January 14, 1766.

A long train of these practices has at length unwillingly convinced me that there is something behind the Throne greater than the King himself.[1]
Speech, March 2, 1770. (Chatham Correspondence.)

Where law ends, tyranny begins. *Speech, Jan. 9, 1770. Case of Wilkes.*

If I were an American, as I am an Englishman, while a foreign troop was landed in my country, I never would lay down my arms, never—never —never. *Speech, Nov. 18, 1777.*

Necessity is the argument of tyrants,[2] it is the creed of slaves.
Speech on the India Bill, Nov. 1783.

The poorest man may in his cottage bid defiance to all the force of the crown. It may be frail; its roof may shake; the wind may blow through it; the storms may enter, the rain may enter,—but the King of England cannot enter! all his forces dare not cross the threshold of the ruined tene-ment.[3] *Speech on the Excise Bill.*

Indemnity for the past and security for the future.[4]

The Church of England hath a Popish liturgy, a Calvinistic creed, and an Arminian clergy. *Ascribed to Pitt.*

———□———

LORD LYTTELTON. 1709—1773.

For his chaste Muse employed her heaven-taught lyre
None but the noblest passions to inspire,
Not one immoral, one corrupted thought,
One line which, dying, he could wish to blot.
Prologue to Thomson's Coriolanus.

Women, like princes, find few real friends. *Advice to a Lady.*

What is your sex's earliest, latest care,
Your heart's supreme ambition? To be fair. *Ibid.*

---

[1] Quoted by Lord Mahon, "greater than the Throne itself."—*History of England, Vol.* v. *p.* 258.
[2] Necessity, the tyrant's plea. Milton, *Par. Lost, Book* iv. *Line* 393.
[3] From Brougham's *Statesmen of George III., First Series, p.* 41.
[4] Mr. Pitt's phrase. — De Quincey, *Theol. Essays, Vol.* ii. *p.* 170. See also Russell's *Memoir of Fox, Vol.* iii. *p.* 345. *Letter to the Hon. T. Maitland.*

ADVICE TO A LADY—*continued.*]

> The lover in the husband may be lost.   *Ibid.*

> How much the wife is dearer than the bride.
> *An Irregular Ode*

> None without hope e'er loved the brightest fair,
> But love can hope where reason would despair.   *Epigram.*

> Where none admire, 't is useless to excel;
> Where none are beaux, 't is vain to be a belle.
> *Soliloquy on a Beauty in the Country.*

> Alas ! by some degree of woe
>   We every bliss must gain ;
> The heart can ne'er a transport know
>   That never feels a pain.   *Song.*

—□—

EDWARD MOORE. 1712—1757.

> Can't I another's face commend,
> And to her virtues be a friend,
> But instantly your forehead lowers,
> As if *her* merit lessened *yours?*
> *Fable* ix. *The Farmer, the Spaniel, and the Cat.*

> The maid who modestly conceals
> Her beauties, while she hides, reveals;
> Give but a glimpse, and fancy draws
> Whate'er the Grecian Venus was.
> *Fable* x. *The Spider and the Bee.*

> But from the hoop's bewitching round,
> Her very shoe has power to wound.   *Ibid.*

> Time still, as he flies, adds increase to her truth,
> And gives to her mind what he steals from her youth.
> *The Happy Marriage.*

'T is now the summer of your youth : time has not cropt the roses from your cheek, though sorrow long has washed them.
The Gamester. Act iii. *Sc.* 4.

—□—

——— DYER.

> And he that will this health deny,
> Down among the dead men let him lie.
> *Published in the early part of the reign of George I.*

—□—

LAURENCE STERNE. 1713—1768.

Go, poor devil, get thee gone; why should I hurt thee? This world surely is wide enough to hold both thee and me.
Tristram Shandy. Vol. ii. *Ch.* xii.

TRISTRAM SHANDY—*continued.*]

" Our armies swore terribly in Flanders," cried my uncle Toby, " but nothing to this." *Ibid. Vol.* iii. *Ch.* xi.

The accusing spirit, which flew up to heaven's chancery with the oath, blushed as he gave it in; and the recording angel, as he wrote it down, dropped a tear upon the word and blotted it out for ever.[1]
Ibid. Vol. vi. *Ch.* viii.

"They order," said I, "this matter better in France."
Sentimental Journey. Page 1.

I pity the man who can travel from Dan to Beersheba, and cry, 'T is all barren. *Ibid. In the Street. Calais.*

God tempers the wind to the shorn lamb.[2] *Ibid. Maria.*

" Disguise thyself as thou wilt, still, Slavery," said I, " still thou art a bitter draught." *Ibid. The Passport. The Hotel at Paris.*

——□——

WILLIAM SHENSTONE. 1714—1763.

Whoe'er has travell'd life's dull round,
　　Where'er his stages may have been,
May sigh to think he still has found
　　The warmest welcome at an inn.[3]
Written on a Window of an Inn.

So sweetly she bade me adieu,
I thought that she bade me return. *A Pastoral. Part* i.

I have found out a gift for my fair;
I have found where the wood-pigeons breed.
Ibid. Part ii. *Hope.*

For seldom shall she hear a tale
So sad, so tender, and so true. *Jemmy Dawson.*

Her cap, far whiter than the driven snow,
Emblems right meet of decency does yield.
The Schoolmistress. St. 5.

Pun-provoking thyme. *Ibid. St.* 11.

A little bench of heedless bishops here,
And there a chancellor in embryo. *Ibid. St.* 28.

---

[1] Cf. Campbell, *Pleasures of Hope,* ii. *Line* 357.
[2] Dieu mesure le froid à la brebis tondue.—Henri Estienne, *Prémices, etc., p.* 47. (1594.)
To a close-shorn sheep God gives wind by measure.—Herbert, *Jacula Prudentum.*
[3] There is nothing which has yet been contrived by man by which so much happiness is produced as by a good tavern or inn.—Johnson, *Boswell's Life,* 1766.
Archbishop Leighton often said, that if he were to choose a place to die in, it should be an inn.— *Works, Vol.* i. *p.* 76.

G*

THOMAS GRAY.   1716—1771.

Ye distant spires, ye antique towers.
    On a Distant Prospect of Eton College.   *Stanza 1.*

Ah, happy hills ! ah, pleasing shade !
   Ah, fields belov'd in vain !
Where once my careless childhood stray'd,
   A stranger yet to pain !
I feel the gales that from ye blow
   A momentary bliss bestow.   *Stanza 2.*

They hear a voice in every wind,
   And snatch a fearful joy.   *Stanza 4.*

Gay hope is theirs by fancy fed,
   Less pleasing when possest ;
The tear forgot as soon as shed,
   The sunshine of the breast.   *Stanza 5*

Alas ! regardless of their doom,
   The little victims play ;
No sense they have of ills to come,
   Nor care beyond to-day.
       .   .   .   .   .
   Ah, tell them they are men !   *Stanza 6.*

And moody madness laughing wild,
   Amid severest woe.   *Stanza 8.*

To each his sufferings ; all are men,
   Condemn'd alike to groan,—
The tender for another's pain,
   The unfeeling for his own.
Yet, ah ! why should they know their fate,
   Since sorrow never comes too late,
And happiness too swiftly flies ?
   Thought would destroy their paradise.
No more ;—where ignorance is bliss,
   'T is folly to be wise.[1]   *Stanza 10.*

Daughter of Jove, relentless power,
   Thou tamer of the human breast,
Whose iron scourge and torturing hour
   The bad affright, afflict the best !   *Hymn to Adversity*

From Helicon's harmonious springs
A thousand rills their mazy progress take.
           The Progress of Poesy. I. 1. Line 3.

---

[1] From ignorance our comfort flows.
   The only wretched are the wise.
          Prior, *To the Hon. Charles Montague.*
He that increaseth knowledge increaseth sorrow.—*Ecclesiastes* i. 18.

The Progress of Poesy—*continued.*]

Glance their many-twinkling feet.   I. 3. *Line* 11.

O'er her warm cheek, and rising bosom, move
The bloom of young Desire and purple light of Love.
     I. 3. *Line* 16.

Her track, where'er the goddess roves,
Glory pursue, and gen'rous shame,
The unconquerable mind, and freedom's holy flame.
     II. 2. *Line* 10.

Ope the sacred source of sympathetic tears.   III. 1. *Line* 12.

He pass'd the flaming bounds of place and time :
The living throne, the sapphire blaze,
Where angels tremble while they gaze,
He saw ; but, blasted with excess of light,
Closed his eyes in endless night.   III. 2. *Line* 4.

Bright-eyed Fancy, hovering o'er,
Scatters from her pictured urn
Thoughts that breathe, and words that burn.1   III. 3. *Line* 2.

Beyond the limits of a vulgar fate,
Beneath the Good how far,—but far above the Great.
     III. 3. *Line* 16.

Ruin seize thee, ruthless King !
   Confusion on thy banners wait !
Though fann'd by Conquest's crimson wing,
   They mock the air with idle state.   *The Bard.*   I. 1. *Line* 1.

Loose his beard and hoary hair
Stream'd, like a meteor, to the troubled air.2   I. 2. *Line* 5.

To high-born Hoel's harp, or soft Llewellyn's lay.
     I. 2. *Line* 14.

Dear as the light that visits these sad eyes ;
Dear as the ruddy drops that warm my heart.3
     I. 3. *Line* 12.

---

1 Words that weep and tears that speak.   Cowley, *The Prophet.*
2 An harmless flaming meteor shone for hair,
   And fell adown his shoulders with loose care.
       Cowley, *Davideis, Book* ii. *Line* 102.
   The imperial ensign, which, full high advanced,
   Shone like a meteor streaming to the wind.
       Milton, *Paradise Lost, Book* i. *Line* 536.
3 As dear to me as are the ruddy drops
   That visit my sad heart.
       Shakespeare, *Julius Cæsar, Act* ii. *Sc.* 1.
   Dear as the vital warmth that feeds my life ;
   Dear as these eyes, that weep in fondness o'er thee.
       Otway, *Venice Preserved, Act* v. *Sc.* 1.

THE BARD—*continued.*]

      Weave the warp, and weave the woof,
        The winding-sheet of Edward's race.
      Give ample room, and verge enough,[1]
        The characters of hell to trace.   II. 1. *Line* 1.

Fair laughs the morn, and soft the zephyr blows,
    While proudly riding o'er the azure realm
In gallant trim the gilded vessel goes;
    Youth on the prow, and Pleasure at the helm;
Regardless of the sweeping whirlwind's sway,
That, hush'd in grim repose, expects his ev'ning prey.
                          II. 2. *Line* 9.

Ye towers of Julius, London's lasting shame,
With many a foul and midnight murder fed.   II. 2. *Line* 11.

Visions of glory, spare my aching sight !
Ye unborn ages, crowd not on my soul !   III. 1. *Line* 11.

And truth severe, by fairy fiction drest.   III. 3. *Line* 3.

Comus, and his midnight crew.   *Ode for Music.* *Line* 2.

While bright-eyed Science watches round.   *Line* 11.

The still small voice of gratitude.   *Line* 64.

      Iron sleet of arrowy shower
      Hurtles in the darken'd air.
          The Fatal Sisters. *Line* 3

The curfew tolls the knell of parting day,
    The lowing herd winds slowly o'er the lea.[2]
The ploughman homeward plods his weary way,
    And leaves the world to darkness and to me.
        Elegy in a Country Churchyard. *Stanza* 1.

Each in his narrow cell for ever laid,
    The rude forefathers of the hamlet sleep.   *Stanza* 4.

The breezy call of incense breathing morn.   *Stanza* 5.

Nor grandeur hear with a disdainful smile
    The short and simple annals of the poor.   *Stanza* 8

The boast of heraldry, the pomp of power,
    And all that beauty, all that wealth e'er gave,
Await alike the inevitable hour.
    The paths of glory lead but to the grave.   *Stanza* 9.

---

[1] Like an ample shield,
Can take in all, and verge enough for more.
        Dryden, *Don Sebastian, Act* i. *Sc.* 1.
[2] The first edition reads,—
    "The lowing herds wind slowly o'er the lea."

ELEGY IN A COUNTRY CHURCHYARD—*continued.*]

    Where, through the long-drawn aisle and fretted vault,
      The pealing anthem swells the note of praise.   *Stanza 10.*

    Can storied urn, or animated bust,
      Back to its mansion call the fleeting breath?
    Can honour's voice provoke the silent dust,
      Or flattery soothe the dull cold ear of death?   *Stanza 11.*

    Hands that the rod of empire might have sway'd,
      Or waked to ecstasy the living lyre.   *Stanza 12.*

    But Knowledge to their eyes her ample page,
      Rich with the spoils of time, did ne'er unroll;[1]
    Chill penury repress'd their noble rage,
      And froze the genial current of the soul.   *Stanza 13.*

    Full many a gem of purest ray serene
      The dark unfathom'd caves of ocean bear :
    Full many a flower is born to blush unseen,
      And waste its sweetness on the desert air.[2]   *Stanza 14.*

    Some village Hampden, that, with dauntless breast,
      The little tyrant of his fields withstood,
    Some mute inglorious Milton here may rest,
      Some Cromwell guiltless of his country's blood.   *Stanza 15.*

    To scatter plenty o'er a smiling land,
      And read their history in a nation's eyes.   *Stanza 16.*

    Forbade to wade through slaughter to a throne,
      And shut the gates of mercy on mankind.   *Stanza 17.*

    Along the cool sequester'd vale of life,
      They kep. the noiseless tenor of their way.   *Stanza 19.*

    Implores the passing tribute of a sigh.   *Stanza 20.*

    And many a holy text around she strews,
      That teach the rustic moralist to die.   *Stanza 21.*

    For who, to dumb forgetfulness a prey,
      This pleasing anxious being e'er resign'd,
    Left the warm precincts of the cheerful day,
      Nor cast one longing ling'ring look behind?   *Stanza 22.*

---

    [1] Rich with the spoils of nature.
        Sir Thomas Browne, *Relig. Med.*, *Part* i. *Sect.* xiii.
    [2] Nor waste their sweetness in the desert air.
        Churchill, *Gotham*, *Book* ii. *Line* 20.
    And waste their music on the savage race.
        Young, *Love of Fame*, *Sat.* v. *Line* 228.

ELEGY IN A COUNTRY CHURCHYARD—*continued.*]

E'en from the tomb the voice of nature cries,
　E'en in our ashes live their wonted fires.[1]   *Stanza 23*

Brushing with hasty steps the dews away,
　To meet the sun upon the upland lawn.   *Stanza 25.*

One morn I miss'd him on the 'custom'd hill.   *Stanza 28.*

Here rests his head upon the lap of earth,
　A youth to fortune and to fame unknown :
Fair Science frown'd not on his humble birth,
　And Melancholy mark'd him for her own.   *The Epitaph.*

Large was his bounty, and his soul sincere,
　Heaven did a recompense as largely send :
He gave to misery (all he had) a tear,
　He gain'd from heaven ('t was all he wish'd) a friend.   *Ibid.*

No farther seek his merits to disclose,
　Or draw his frailties from their dread abode,
(There they alike in trembling hope repose,)
　The bosom of his Father and his God.   *Ibid.*

And weep the more, because I weep in vain.
　　　　　Sonnet.   On the Death of Mr. West.

The hues of bliss more brightly glow,
Chastis'd by sabler tints of woe.
　　Ode on the Pleasure arising from Vicissitude.   Line 45.

The meanest floweret of the vale,
The simplest note that swells the gale,
The common sun, the air, the skies,
To him are opening paradise.   *Line 53.*

And hie him home, at evening's close,
To sweet repast and calm repose.   *Line 87.*

From toil he wins his spirits light,
From busy day the peaceful night ;
Rich, from the very want of wealth,
In heaven's best treasures, peace and health.   *Line 93.*

When love could teach a monarch to be wise,
And Gospel-light first dawn'd from Bullen's eyes.[2]

Rich windows that exclude the light,
And passages that lead to nothing.   *A Long Story.*

---

[1] Yet in our ashen cold is fire yreken.
　　　　　　Chaucer, *The Reves Prologue, Line* 28.
[2] This was intended to be introduced in the poem on the "Alliance of
Education and Government."—Mason, *Vol.* iii. *p.* 114.

Too poor for a bribe, and too proud to importune ;
He had not the method of making a fortune.
On his own Character.

A favorite has no friend.[1]
On the Death of a Favorite Cat.

Now as the Paradisaical pleasures of the Mahometans consist in playing upon the flute and lying with Houris, be mine to read eternal new romances of Marivaux and Crebillon. *To Mr. West. Letter* iv. *3d Series.*

—□—

RICHARD HURD. 1720—1808.

In this awfully stupendous manner, at which Reason stands aghast, and Faith herself is half confounded, was the grace of God to man at length manifested. *Sermons. Vol.* ii. *p.* 287.

—□—

JOHN BROWN. 1715—1766.

Now let us thank the Eternal Power : convinc'd
That Heaven but tries our virtue by affliction,—
That oft the cloud which wraps the present hour
Serves but to brighten all our future days.
Barbarossa. Act v. *Sc.* 3.

And coxcombs vanquish Berkeley by a grin.
An Essay on Satire, occasioned by the Death of Mr. Pope.[2]

—□—

MARK AKENSIDE. 1721—1770.

Such and so various are the tastes of men.
Pleasures of the Imagination. Book iii. *Line* 567.

Than Timoleon's arms require,
And Tully's curule chair, and Milton's golden lyre.
Ode. On a Sermon against Glory. St. ii.

The man forget not, though in rags he lies,
And know the mortal through a crown's disguise.
Epistle to Curio.

Seeks painted trifles and fantastic toys,
And eagerly pursues imaginary joys. *The Virtuoso. St.* x.

—□—

JAMES TOWNLEY. 1715—1778.

Kitty. Shikspur? Shikspur? Who wrote it? No, I never read Shikspur.
Lady Bab. Then you have an immense pleasure to come.
High Life below Stairs. Act ii. *Sc.* 1.

From humble Port to imperial Tokay. *Ibid.*

---

[1] One of Aristotle's sayings was ᾧ φίλοι, οὐδεὶς φίλος, according to Casaubon's reading of Diog. Laertius, Lib. v. § 21, *Cui sunt amici, non est amicus.*

[2] Anderson's *British Poets*, x. 879. See note in *Contemporary Review*, Sept. 1867, *p.* 4.

DAVID GARRICK. 1716—1779.

Corrupted freemen are the worst of slaves.
                              Prologue to The Gamesters.

Their cause I plead,—plead it in heart and mind ;
A fellow-feeling makes one wondrous kind.[1]
                       Prologue on Quitting the Stage in 1776.

Let others hail the rising sun :
I bow to that whose course is run.[2]
                              On the Death of Mr. Pelham.

This scholar, rake, Christian, dupe, gamester, and poet.
                              Jupiter and Mercury.

—□—

WILLIAM COLLINS. 1720—1756.

How sleep the brave who sink to rest,
By all their country's wishes bless'd !   *Ode in* 1746.

By fairy hands their knell is rung;
By forms unseen their dirge is sung ;
There Honour comes, a pilgrim gray,
To bless the turf that wraps their clay ;
And Freedom shall awhile repair,
To dwell a weeping hermit there.   *Ibid.*

When Music, heavenly maid, was young,
While yet in early Greece she sung.   *The Passions.   Line* 1.

Filled with fury, rapt, inspir'd.   *Ibid.   Line* 10.

'T was sad by fits, by starts 't was wild.   *Ibid.   Line* 28.

In notes by distance made more sweet.   *Ibid.   Line* 60.

In hollow murmurs died away.   *Ibid.   Line* 68.

O Music ! sphere-descended maid,
Friend of pleasure, wisdom's aid !   *Ibid.   Line* 95.

Well may your hearts believe the truths I tell ;
'T is virtue makes the bliss, where'er we dwell.
                                   Eclogue 1.   *Line* 5.
Too nicely Jonson knew the critic's part ;
Nature in him was almost lost in Art.
          To Sir Thomas Hanmer on his Edition of Shakespeare.

In yonder grave a Druid lies.   *Ode on the Death of Thomson.*

---

[1] I would help others, out of a fellow-feeling.—Burton, *Anatomy of Melancholy ; Democritus to the keader.*
                  Non ignara mali, miseris succurrere disco.
                                     Virgil, *Æneid, Lib.* i. 630.
[2] Pompey . . . . bade Sylla recollect that more worshipped the risinᵣ than the setting sun.—Clough, *Dryden's Plutarch,* iv. 66, *Life of Pompey.*

JAMES MERRICK. 1720—1769.

Not what we wish, but what we want. *Hymn*

———□———

TOBIAS SMOLLETT. 1721—1771.

Thy spirit, Independence, let me share;
  Lord of the lion heart, and eagle eye,
Thy steps I follow with my bosom bare,
  Nor heed the storm that howls along the sky.
                    Ode to Independence.

Facts are stubborn things.[1]
                    Translation of Gil Blas. Book X. Ch. I.

———□———

JOHN HOME. 1724—1808.

      In the first days
Of my distracting grief, I found myself
As women wish to be who love their lords.
                    Douglas. Act i. Sc. I.

My name is Norval; on the Grampian hills
My father feeds his flocks; a frugal swain,
Whose constant cares were to increase his store,
And keep his only son, myself, at home. *Ibid. Act ii. Sc. I.*

Like Douglas conquer, or like Douglas die. *Ibid. Act v. Sc. I.*

———□———

RICHARD GIFFORD. 1725—1807.

Verse sweetens toil, however rude the sound;
  All at her work the village maiden sings,
Nor, while she turns the giddy wheel around,
  Revolves the sad vicissitudes of things. *Contemplation.*

———□———

ARTHUR MURPHY. 1727—1805.

Thus far we run before the wind. *The Apprentice. Act v. Sc. I.*

Above the vulgar flight of common souls. *Zenobia. Act v.*

———□———

OLIVER GOLDSMITH. 1728—1774.

Remote, unfriended, melancholy, slow. *The Traveller. Line I.*

Where'er I roam, whatever realms to see,
My heart untravell'd fondly turns to thee;
Still to my brother turns, with ceaseless pain,
And drags at each remove a lengthening chain. *Line 7*

---

[1] Facts are stubborn things.—Elliot, *Essay on Field Husbandry, p. 35. 1747.)*

THE TRAVELLER—*continued.*]

And learn the luxury of doing good.[1]	*Line* 22.
Some fleeting good, that mocks me with the view.	*Line* 26.
These little things are great to little man.	*Line* 42.
Creation's heir, the world, the world is mine !	*Line* 50.
Such is the patriot's boast, where'er we roam, His first, best country ever is at home.	*Line* 73.
Man seems the only growth that dwindles here.	*Line* 126.
By sports like these are all their cares beguil'd ; The sports of children satisfy the child.	*Line* 153.
But winter lingering chills the lap of May.	*Line* 172.
So the loud torrent, and the whirlwind's roar, But bind him to his native mountains more.	*Line* 217.
Alike all ages : dames of ancient days Have led their children through the mirthful maze ; And the gay grandsire, skill'd in gestic lore, Has frisk'd beneath the burden of threescore.	*Line* 251.
Embosom'd in the deep where Holland lies. Methinks her patient sons before me stand Where the broad ocean leans against the land.	*Line* 282.
Pride in their port, defiance in their eye, I see the lords of humankind pass by.[2]	*Line* 327.
The land of scholars, and the nurse of arms.	*Line* 356.
For just experience tells, in every soil, That those that think must govern those that toil.	*Line* 372.
Laws grind the poor, and rich men rule the law.	*Line* 386.
Forc'd from their homes, a melancholy train.	*Line* 409.
Vain, very vain, my weary search to find That bliss which only centres in the mind.	*Line* 423.
Sweet Auburn ! loveliest village of the plain. *The Deserted Village.*	*Line* 1.
The hawthorn bush, with seats beneath the shade, For talking age and whispering lovers made.	*Line* 13.
The bashful virgin's sidelong looks of love.	*Line* 29.

[1] For all their luxury was doing good.
Garth, *Claremont, Line* 148.
He tried the luxury of doing good.
Crabbe, *Tales of the Hall, Book* iii.
[2] Lord of humankind.—Dryden, *The Spanish Friar. Act* ii. Sc. 1.

THE DESERTED VILLAGE—*continued*.]

Ill fares the land, to hastening ills a prey,
Where wealth accumulates, and men decay.
Princes and lords may flourish, or may fade,
A breath can make them as a breath has made;[1]
But a bold peasantry, their country's pride,
When once destroy'd, can never be supplied.   *Line* 51.

His best companions, innocence and health
And his best riches, ignorance of wealth.   *Line* 61.

How blest is he who crowns, in shades like these,
A youth of labour with an age of ease !   *Line* 99.

While resignation gently slopes away,—
And, all his prospects brightening to the last,
His heaven commences ere the world be past.   *Line* 110.

The watch-dog's voice that bay'd the whispering wind,
And the loud laugh that spoke the vacant mind.   *Line* 121.

A man he was to all the country dear,
And passing rich with forty pounds a year.   *Line* 141.

Wept o'er his wounds, or, tales of sorrow done,
Shoulder'd his crutch and show'd how fields were won.
                                                            Line 157.

Careless their merits or their faults to scan,
His pity gave ere charity began.   *Line* 161.

And e'en his failings lean'd to virtue's side.   *Line* 164.

And, as a bird each fond endearment tries
To tempt its new-fledg'd offspring to the skies,
He tried each art, reprov'd each dull delay,
Allur'd to brighter worlds, and led the way.   *Line* 167.

Truth from his lips prevail'd with double sway,
And fools, who came to scoff, remain'd to pray.   *Line* 179.

And pluck'd his gown, to share the good man's smile.
                                                            Line 184.

As some tall cliff, that lifts its awful form,
Swells from the vale, and midway leaves the storm,
Though round its breast the rolling clouds are spread,
Eternal sunshine settles on its head.   *Line* 189.

---

1 C'est un verre qui luit,
Qu'un souffle peut détruire, et qu'un souffle a produit.
        De Caux (comparing the world to his hour-glass).
Who pants for glory, finds but short repose ;
A breath revives him, or a breath o'erthrows.
        Pope, *Sat. and Ep. of Horace, Book* ii. *Ep.* 1. *Line* 299.

THE DESERTED VILLAGE—*continued.*]

Well had the boding tremblers learn'd to trace
The day's disasters in his morning face;
Full well they laugh'd, with counterfeited glee,
At all his jokes, for many a joke had he;
Full well the busy whisper, circling round,
Convey'd the dismal tidings when he frown'd:
Yet was he kind, or, if severe in aught,
The love he bore to learning was in fault. *Line* 199.

In arguing, too, the parson own'd his skill,
For e'en though vanquish'd, he could argue still;
While words of learned length and thund'ring sound
Amazed the gazing rustics ranged around;
And still they gazed, and still the wonder grew
That one small head could carry all he knew. *Line* 211.

The whitewash'd wall, the nicely sanded floor,
The varnish'd clock that click'd behind the door,
The chest contriv'd a double debt to pay,
A bed by night, a chest of drawers by day. *Line* 227.

To me more dear, congenial to my heart,
One native charm, than all the gloss of art. *Line* 253.

And e'en while fashion's brightest arts decoy,
The heart, distrusting, asks if this be joy. *Line* 263.

Her modest looks the cottage might adorn,
Sweet as the primrose peeps beneath the thorn. *Line* 329.

In all the silent manliness of grief. *Line* 384.

O Luxury! thou curst by Heaven's decree. *Line* 385.

Thou source of all my bliss, and all my woe,
That found'st me poor at first, and keep'st me so. *Line* 413.

Who mix'd reason with pleasure, and wisdom with mirth.
Retaliation. Line 24.

Who, born for the universe, narrow'd his mind,
And to party gave up what was meant for mankind:
Though fraught with all learning, yet straining his throat,
To persuade Tommy Townshend to lend him a vote.
Who, too deep for his hearers, still went on refining,
And thought of convincing, while they thought of dining:
Though equal to all things, for all things unfit;
Too nice for a statesman, too proud for a wit. *Line* 31.

His conduct still right, with his argument wrong. *Line* 46.

A flattering painter, who made it his care
To draw men as they ought to be, not as they are. *Line* 63.

RETALIATION—*continued.*]

An abridgment of all that was pleasant in man.	*Line* 94.
As a wit, if not first, in the very first line.	*Line* 96.

On the stage he was natural, simple, affecting;
'T was only that when he was off he was acting.   *Line* 101.

He cast off his friends, as a huntsman his pack,
For he knew, when he pleased, he could whistle them back.
       Line 107.

Who pepper'd the highest, was surest to please.   *Line* 112.

When they talk'd of their Raphaels, Correggios, and stuff,
He shifted his trumpet, and only took snuff.   *Line* 145.

Taught by that Power that pities me,
   I learn to pity them.   *The Hermit.*   *Stanza* 6.

Man wants but little here below,
   Nor wants that little long.[1]   *Ibid.*   *Stanza* 8.

And what is friendship but a name,
   A charm that lulls to sleep,
A shade that follows wealth or fame,
   And leaves the wretch to weep?   *Ibid.*   *Stanza* 19.

The sigh that rends thy constant heart
   Shall break thy Edwin's too.   *Ibid.*   *Stanza ult.*

The naked every day he clad
   When he put on his clothes.
       Elegy on the Death of a Mad Dog.

And in that town a dog was found,
   As many dogs there be,
Both mongrel, puppy, whelp, and hound,
   And curs of low degree.   *Ibid.*

The dog, to gain his private ends,
   Went mad, and bit the man.   *Ibid.*

The man recover'd of the bite,
   The dog it was that died.   *Ibid.*

When lovely woman stoops to folly,
   And finds too late that men betray,
What charm can soothe her melancholy?
   What art can wash her guilt away?
       On Woman (*Vicar of Wakefield, Ch.* xxiv.).

The only art her guilt to cover,
   To hide her shame from every eye,
To give repentance to her lover,
   And wring his bosom, is—to die.   *Ibid.*

---

[1] Cf. Young, *Night Thoughts*, iv. *Line* 118.

> The wretch condemn'd with life to part,
>   Still, still on hope relies;
> And every pang that rends the heart
>   Bids expectation rise.   *The Captivity.* *Act* ii. *Orig. MS.*

> Hope, like the gleaming taper's light,
>   Adorns and cheers the way;
> And still, as darker grows the night,
>   Emits a brighter ray.   *Ibid.*

Measures, not men, have always been my mark.[1]
                                  The Good-Natured Man. *Act* ii.

The very pink of perfection. *She stoops to conquer.* *Act* i. *Sc.* 1.

A concatenation accordingly.   *Ibid.* *Act* i. *Sc.* 2.

Ask me no questions, and I 'll tell you no fibs. *Ibid.* *Act* iii.

> The king himself has follow'd her
>   When she has walk'd before.
>   *Elegy on Mrs. Mary Blaize.*[2]

Such dainties to them, their health it might hurt;
It 's like sending them ruffles, when wanting a shirt.[3]
                                  The Haunch of Venison.

—□—

WILLIAM MASON. 1725—1797.

The fattest hog in Epicurus' sty.   *Heroic Epistle.*

—□—

EDMUND BURKE. 1729—1797.

The writers against religion, whilst they oppose every system, are wisely careful never to set up any of their own.

  Preface to A Vindication of Natural Society.[4] *Vol.* i. *p.* 7.

"War," says Machiavel, "ought to be the only study of a prince;" and, by a prince, he means every sort of state, however constituted. "He ought," says this great political Doctor, "to consider peace only as a breathing-time, which gives him leisure to contrive, and furnishes ability to

---

[1] Of this stamp is the cant of *Not men, but measures.*—Burke, *Thoughts on the Cause of the Present Discontents.*

[2] Written in imitation of *Chanson sur le fameux La Palisse*, which is attributed to Bernard de la Monnoye.
> "On dit que dans ses amours
>   Il fut caressé des belles,
> Qui le suivirent toujours,
>   Tant qu'il marcha devant elles."

[3] To treat a poor wretch with a bottle of Burgundy and fill his snuff-box, is like giving a pair of laced ruffles to a man that has never a shirt on his back.—Tom Brown, *Laconics.*

[4] Boston Ed. 1865—1867.

execute, military plans." A meditation on the conduct of political societies made old Hobbes imagine that war was the state of nature.
> *A Vindication of Natural Society.* Vol. i. p. 15.

There is, however, a limit at which forbearance ceases to be a virtue.
> *Observations on a Late Publication on the Present State of the Nation.* Vol. i. p. 273.

Illustrious predecessor.
> *Thoughts on the Cause of the Present Discontents.* Vol. i. p. 456.

When bad men combine, the good must associate; else they will fall, one by one, an unpitied sacrifice, in a contemptible struggle.
> *Ibid.* Vol. i. p. 526.

A people who are still, as it were, but in the gristle, and not yet hardened into the bone of manhood.
> *Speech on Conciliation with America.* Vol. ii. p. 117.

A wise and salutary neglect.
> *Ibid.*

My vigour relents,—I pardon something to the spirit of liberty.
> *Ibid.* Vol. ii. p. 118.

All government, indeed every human benefit and enjoyment, every virtue and every prudent act, is founded on compromise and barter.
> *Ibid.* Vol. ii. p. 169.

The worthy gentleman who has been snatched from us at the moment of the election, and in the middle of the contest, whilst his desires were as warm, and his hopes as eager as ours, has feelingly told us what shadows we are, and what shadows we pursue.
> *Speech at Bristol on Declining the Poll.*[1] Vol ii. p. 429.

They made and recorded a sort of institute and digest of anarchy, called the Rights of Man.
> *On the Army Estimates.* Vol. iii. p. 221.

You had that action and counteraction, which, in the natural and in the political world, from the reciprocal struggle of discordant powers draws out the harmony of the universe.[2]
> *Reflections on the Revolution in France.* Vol. iii. p. 277.

It is now sixteen or seventeen years since I saw the Queen of France, then the Dauphiness, at Versailles; and surely never lighted on this orb, which she hardly seemed to touch, a more delightful vision. I saw her just above the horizon, decorating and cheering the elevated sphere she just began to move in,—glittering like the morning-star, full of life, and

---

[1] At the conclusion of one of Mr. Burke's eloquent harangues, Mr. Cruger, finding nothing to add, or perhaps, as he thought, to add with effect, exclaimed earnestly in the language of the counting-house, "I say ditto to Mr. Burke, I say ditto to Mr. Burke."— Prior's *Life of Burke, p.* 152.
[2] Mr. Breen, in his *Modern English Literature,* says : "This remarkable thought, Alison, the historian, has turned to good account; it occurs so often in his disquisitions, that he seems to have made it the staple of all wisdom and the basis of every truth."

Reflections on the Revolution in France—*continued.*]

splendour, and joy. . . Little did I dream that I should have lived to
see such disasters fallen upon her in a nation of gallant men, in a nation of
men of honour and of cavaliers.   I thought ten thousand swords must have
leaped from their scabbards to avenge even a look that threatened her with
insult.   But the age of chivalry is gone.   That of sophisters, economists,
and calculators has succeeded.   *Ibid.   Vol.* iii. *p.* 331.

The unbought grace of life, the cheap defence of nations, the nurse of
manly sentiment and heroic enterprise, is gone.   *Ibid.*

That chastity of honour which felt a stain like a wound.
Ibid.   Vol. iii. *p.* 332.

Vice itself lost half its evil, by losing all its grossness.
Ibid.   Vol. iii. *p.* 332.

Kings will be tyrants from policy, when subjects are rebels from principle.
Ibid.   Vol. iii. *p.* 334.

Learning will be cast into the mire and trodden down under the hoofs of
a swinish multitude.[1]   *Ibid.   Vol.* iii. *p.* 335.

Because half a dozen grasshoppers under a fern make the field ring with
their importunate chink, whilst thousands of great cattle, reposed beneath the shadow of the British oak, chew the cud and are silent, pray do
not imagine that those who make the noise are the only inhabitants of the
field,—that, of course, they are many in number,—or that, after all, they are
other than the little, shrivelled, meagre, hopping, though loud and troublesome insects of the hour.   *Ibid.   Vol.* iii. *p.* 344.

He that wrestles with us strengthens our nerves, and sharpens our skill.
Our antagonist is our helper.   *Ibid.   Vol.* iii. *p.* 453.

The cold neutrality of an impartial judge.
Preface to Brissot's Address.   Vol. v. *p.* 67.

And having looked to government for bread, on the very first scarcity
they will turn and bite the hand that fed them.[2]
Thoughts and Details on Scarcity.   Vol. v. *p.* 156.

All those instances to be found in history, whether real or fabulous, of a
doubtful public spirit, at which morality is perplexed, reason is staggered,
and from which affrighted Nature recoils, are their chosen and almost sole
examples for the instruction of their youth.
Letter i.   *On a Regicide Peace.   Vol.* v. *p.* 311.

Early and provident fear is the mother of safety.
Speech on the Petition of the Unitarians.   Vol. vii. *p.* 50.

---

[1] This expression was tortured to mean that he actually thought the people
no better than swine, and the phrase, *the swinish multitude,* was bruited
about in every form of speech and writing, in order to excite popular indignation.

[2] We set ourselves to bite the hand that feeds us.—*Thoughts on the Cause
of the Present Discontents.   Vol.* i. *p.* 439.

I would rather sleep in the southern corner of a little country churchyard, than in the tomb of the Capulets.[1]

Letter to Matthew Smith. Prior's Life, p. 33.

It has all the contortions of the sibyl, without the inspiration.[2]

Prior's Life of Burke.

——□——

SIR WILLIAM BLACKSTONE. 1723—1780.

The royal navy of England hath ever been its greatest defence and ornament; it is its ancient and natural strength,—the floating bulwark of our island.   *Commentaries. Vol. i. Book i. Ch. xiii. § 418.*

Time whereof the memory of man runneth not to the contrary.

Ibid. Book i. Ch. xviii. § 472.

——□——

BEILBY PORTEUS. 1731—1808.

In sober state,
Through the sequester'd vale of rural life,
The venerable patriarch guileless held
The tenor of his way.[3]   *Death. Line 108.*

One murder made a villain,
Millions a hero.   Princes were privileged
To kill, and numbers sanctified the crime.[4]   *Ibid. Line 154.*

War its thousands slays, Peace its ten thousands.
Ibid. Line 178.

Teach him how to live,
And oh! still harder lesson, how to die.[5]   *Ibid. Line 316.*

——□——

CHARLES CHURCHILL. 1731—1764.

He mouths a sentence, as curs mouth a bone.
The Rosciad. Line 322.

But, spite of all the criticising elves,
Those who would make us feel—must feel themselves.[6]
Ibid. Line 861.

---

[1] Family vault of "all the Capulets."—*Reflections on the Revolution in France. Vol.* iii. *p.* 349.

[2] When Croft's *Life of Dr. Young* was spoken of as a good imitation of Dr. Johnson's style, "No, no," said he, "it is not a good imitation of Johnson; it has all his pomp, without his force; it has all the nodosities of the oak, without its strength; it has all the contortions of the sibyl, without the inspiration."—Prior's *Life of Burke, p.* 468.

[3] Along the cool sequester'd vale of life
They kept the noiseless tenor of their way.
Gray, *Elegy, Stanza* 19.

[4] Cf. Young, p. 157.

[5] There taught us how to live; and (oh! too high
The price for knowledge) taught us how to die.
Tickell, *On the Death of Addison.*

[6] Si vis me flere, dolendum est
Primum ipsi tibi.—Horace, *Ars Poetica,* 102.

With curious art the brain, too finely wrought,
Preys on herself, and is destroyed by thought.
Epistle to William Hogarth.

Be England what she will,
With all her faults she is my country still.   *The Farewell.*

Apt alliteration's artful aid.   *Prophecy of Famine.*

Men the most infamous are fond of fame,
And those who fear not guilt yet start at shame.   *The Author.*

—□—

ISAAC BICKERSTAFF.   *Circa* 1735—1787.

Hope ! thou nurse of young desire.
Love in a Village.   Act i. Sc. 1.

There was a jolly miller once,
  Lived on the river Dee ;
He work'd and sung from morn till night :
  No lark more blithe than he.   *Ibid.*   Act i. Sc. 2.

And this the burthen of his song
  For ever used to be :—
I care for nobody, no, not I,
  If no one cares for me.[1]   *Ibid.*   Act i. Sc. 2.

Young fellows will be young fellows.   *Ibid.*   Act ii. Sc. 2.

Ay, do despise me.   I 'm the prouder for it ; I like to be despised.
The Hypocrite.   Act v. Sc. 1.

—□—

EDWARD GIBBON.   1737—1794.

History, which is, indeed, little more than the register of the crimes,
follies, and misfortunes of mankind.[2]
Decline and Fall of the Roman Empire.   Ch. iii.

A heart to resolve, a head to contrive, and a hand to execute.[3]
Ibid.   Ch. xlviii.

—□—

JAMES BEATTIE.   1735—1803.

Ah ! who can tell how hard it is to climb
The steep where Fame's proud temple shines afar ?
The Minstrel.   Book i. St. 1.

Old age comes on apace to ravage all the clime.
Ibid.   Book i. St. 25.

---

[1] If naebody care for me,
  I 'll care for naebody.
Burns, *I hae a Wife o' my Ain.*
[2] L'histoire n'est que le tableau des crimes et des malheurs.—Voltaire,
L'Ingénu, Ch. x.
[3] Heart to conceive, the understanding to direct, or the hand to execute.
—Junius, *Letter* xxxvii., *Feb.* 14, 1770.

THE MINSTREL—*continued.*]

> Mine be the breezy hill that skirts the down ;
> Where a green grassy turf is all I crave,
> With here and there a violet bestrewn,
> Fast by a brook or fountain's murmuring wave ;
> And many an evening sun shine sweetly on my grave !
>
> *Ibid. Book* ii. *St.* 17.

> At the close of the day, when the hamlet is still,
> And mortals the sweets of forgetfulness prove,
> When naught but the torrent is heard on the hill,
> And naught but the nightingale's song in the grove.
>
> *The Hermit.*

> He thought as a sage, though he felt as a man.   *Ibid.*

> But when shall spring visit the mouldering urn ?
> O, when shall it dawn on the night of the grave ?   *Ibid.*

> By the glare of false science betray'd,
> That leads to bewilder, and dazzles to blind.   *Ibid.*

> And beauty immortal awakes from the tomb.   *Ibid.*

—□—

RICHARD GRAVES. 1715—1804.

> Each curs'd his fate, that thus their project cross'd :
> How hard their lot who neither won nor lost.
>
> *An Incident in High Life.*[1]

—□—

WILLIAM COWPER. 1731—1800.

> United yet divided, twain at once.
> So sit two kings of Brentford on one throne.[2]
>
> *The Task. Book* i. *The Sofa. Line* 77.

> Nor rural sights alone, but rural sounds,
> Exhilarate the spirit, and restore
> The tone of languid Nature.   *Ibid. Line* 181.

> The earth was made so various, that the mind
> Of desultory man, studious of change,
> And pleased with novelty, might be indulged. *Ibid. Line* 506.

> God made the country, and man made the town.[3]
>
> *Ibid. Line* 749.

---

[1] From the *Festoon, A Collection of Epigrams.* London, 1767. In the *Appendix of Original Pieces*, this epigram is generally ascribed to Beattie, without reason.   It does not appear in any collection of his poems.

[2] *Two Kings of Brentford,* from Buckingham's play of *The Rehearsal.*

[3] God the first garden made, and the first city Cain.
    Cowley, *The Garden.   Essay* v.
God Almighty first planted a garden.—Bacon, *Essays.   Of Gardens.*
    Divina natura dedit agros, ars humana ædificavit urbes.
    Varro, *Res Rom.* 3, 1.

THE TASK—*continued.*]

> O for a lodge in some vast wilderness,[1]
> Some boundless contiguity of shade,
> Where rumour of oppression and deceit,
> Of unsuccessful or successful war,
> Might never reach me more.
>
> Book ii.   The Timepiece.   Line 1.

> Mountains interpos'd
> Make enemies of nations who had else,
> Like kindred drops, been mingled into one.   *Ibid.*   Line 17.

> I would not have a slave to till my ground,
> To carry me, to fan me while I sleep,
> And tremble when I wake, for all the wealth
> That sinews bought and sold have ever earn'd.   *Ibid.*   Line 29.

> Slaves cannot breathe in England; if their lungs
> Receive our air, that moment they are free;
> They touch our country and their shackles fall.[2]
>
> Ibid.   Line 40.

> England, with all thy faults I love thee still,
> My country![3]   *Ibid.*   Line 206.

> Presume to lay their hand upon the ark
> Of her magnificent and awful cause.   *Ibid.*   Line 231.

> Praise enough
> To fill the ambition of a private man,
> That Chatham's language was his mother-tongue.
>
> Ibid.   Line 235.

> There is a pleasure in poetic pains
> Which only poets know.[4]   *Ibid.*   Line 285.

> Transforms old print
> To zigzag manuscript, and cheats the eyes
> Of gallery critics by a thousand arts.   *Ibid.*   Line 364.

> Reading what they never wrote,
> Just fifteen minutes, huddle up their work,
> And with a well-bred whisper close the scene   *Ibid.*   Line 411.

> Whoe'er was edified, themselves were not.   *Ibid.*   Line 444.

---

[1] Oh that I had in the wilderness a lodging-place of wayfaring men.—
Jeremiah ix. 2.

[2] Servi peregrini, ut primum Galliæ fines penetraverint eodem momento
liberi sunt.—Bodinus, *Liber* i. *c.* 5.

[3] Be England what she will,
With all her faults she is my country still.
Churchill, The Farewell.

[4] There is a pleasure sure
In being mad which none but madmen know.
Dryden, Spanish Friar.   Act ii. Sc. 1.

THE TASK—*continued.*]

Variety's the very spice of life,
That gives it all its flavour.   *Ibid.*   *Line* 606.

        She that asks
Her dear five hundred friends.   *Ibid.*   *Line* 642.

Domestic Happiness, thou only bliss
Of Paradise that has surviv'd the fall!
      Book iii.   *The Garden.*   *Line* 41.

Great contest follows, and much learned dust. *Ibid.* *Line* 161.

From reveries so airy, from the toil
Of dropping buckets into empty wells,
And growing old in drawing nothing up.   *Ibid.*   *Line* 188.

How various his employments, whom the world
Calls idle; and who justly in return
Esteems that busy world an idler too!   *Ibid.*   *Line* 352.

Who loves a garden, loves a greenhouse too.   *Line* 566.

I burn to set the imprison'd wranglers free,
And give them voice and utterance once again.
Now stir the fire, and close the shutters fast,
Let fall the curtains, wheel the sofa round,
And while the bubbling and loud hissing urn
Throws up a steamy column, and the cups,
That cheer but not inebriate, wait on each,[1]
So let us welcome peaceful evening in.
    Book iv.   *Winter Evening.* *Line* 34.

Which not even critics criticise.   *Ibid.*   *Line* 51.

And Katerfelto, with his hair on end
At his own wonders, wondering for his bread.
'T is pleasant, through the loop-holes of retreat,
To peep at such a world,—to see the stir
Of the great Babel, and not feel the crowd. *Ibid.* *Line* 86.

While fancy, like the finger of a clock,
Runs the great circuit, and is still at home. *Ibid.* *Line* 118.

O Winter, ruler of the inverted year.   *Ibid.*   *Line* 120.

With spots quadrangular of diamond form,
Ensanguined hearts, clubs typical of strife,
And spades, the emblem of untimely graves. *Ibid.* *Line* 217.

Gloriously drunk, obey the important call. *Ibid.* *Line* 510.

---

[1] [Tar-water] is of a nature so mild and benign and proportioned to the human constitution, as to warm without heating, to cheer but not inebriate.—Bishop Berkeley, *Siris, par.* 217.

THE TASK—*continued.*]

Sidney, warbler of poetic prose.	*Ibid.*	*Line* 516.
The Frenchman's darling.[1]	*Ibid.*	*Line* 765.

But war 's a game which, were their subjects wise,
Kings would not play at.
                    Book v.   *Winter Morning Walk.*   *Line* 187.

The beggarly last doit.   *Ibid.*   *Line* 316.

As dreadful as the Manichean god,
Adored through fear, strong only to destroy.   *Ibid.*   *Line* 444.

He is the freeman whom the truth makes free.   *Ibid.*   *Line* 733.

         With filial confidence inspired,
Can lift to Heaven an unpresumptuous eye,
And smiling say, " My Father made them all !"
                                        Ibid.   *Line* 745.

There is in souls a sympathy with sounds;
And as the mind is pitch'd, the ear is pleased
With melting airs, or martial, brisk, or grave;
Some chord in unison with what we hear
Is touch'd within us, and the heart replies.
How soft the music of those village bells,
Falling at intervals upon the ear
In cadence sweet!   *Book* vi.   *Winter Walk at Noon.*   *Line* 1.

         Here the heart
May give a useful lesson to the head,
And Learning wiser grow without his books.   *Ibid.*   *Line* 85.

Knowledge is proud that he has learn'd so much ;
Wisdom is humble that he knows no more.
Books are not seldom talismans and spells.   *Ibid.*   *Line* 96.

Some to the fascination of a name
Surrender judgment hoodwink d.   *Ibid.*   *Line* 100.

I would not enter on my list of friends
(Though graced with polish'd manners and fine sense,
Yet wanting sensibility) the man
Who needlessly sets foot upon a worm.   *Ibid.*   *Line* 560.

An honest man, close-button'd to the chin,
Broadcloth without, and a warm heart within.
                                   Epistle to Joseph Hill.

Shine by the side of every path we tread
With such a lustre, he that runs may read.[2]
                              Tirocinium.   Line 79.

---

[1] It was Cowper who gave this now common name to the Mignonette.
[2] Cf. Habakkuk ii. 2.

Absence of occupation is not rest,
A mind quite vacant is a mind distress'd.
Retirement. Line 623.

An idler is a watch that wants both hands;
As useless if it goes as if it stands. *Ibid. Line* 681.

Built God a church, and laughed his word to scorn.
Ibid. Line 688.

I praise the Frenchman, his remark was shrewd,
How sweet, how passing sweet is solitude!
But grant me still a friend in my retreat,
Whom I may whisper, solitude is sweet. *Ibid. Line* 739.

Is base in kind, and born to be a slave. *Table Talk. Line* 28.

No. Freedom has a thousand charms to show,
That slaves, howe'er contented, never know. *Ibid. Line* 260.

Just knows, and knows no more, her Bible true,
A truth the brilliant Frenchman never knew. *Truth. Line* 327.

How much a dunce that has been sent to roam,
Excels a dunce that has been kept at home.
The Progress of Error. Line 415.

A kick that scarce would move a horse
   May kill a sound divine. *The Yearly Distress.*

O that those lips had language! Life has pass'd
With me but roughly since I heard thee last.
On the Receipt of my Mother's Picture.

The son of parents passed into the skies. *Ibid.*

There goes the parson, oh! illustrious spark!
And there, scarce less illustrious, goes the clerk.
On observing some Names of Little Note.

A fool must now and then be right by chance.
Conversation. Line 96.

A moral, sensible, and well-bred man
Will not affront me, and no other can. *Ibid. Line* 193.

I cannot talk with civet in the room,
A fine puss-gentleman that's all perfume. *Ibid. Line* 283.

The solemn fop; significant and budge;
A fool with judges, amongst fools a judge.[1] *Ibid. Line* 299.

---

[1] If he be not fellow with the best king, thou shalt find the best king of good fellows.—Shakespeare, *King Henry V. Act* v. *Sc.* 2.
This man (Chesterfield) I thought had been a lord among wits, but I find he is only a wit among lords.—Boswell's *Johnson, Vol.* ii. p. 13. *An.* 1754.
A wit with dunces, and a dunce with wits.—Pope, *Dunciad, Book* iv. *Line* 92.
Although too much of a soldier among sovereigns, no one could claim

His wit invites you by his looks to come,
But, when you knock, it never is at home.[1]   *Ibid.   Line* 303.

Our wasted oil unprofitably burns,
Like hidden lamps in old sepulchral urns.[2]   *Ibid.   Line* 357.

That, though on pleasure she was bent,
  She had a frugal mind.   *History of John Gilpin.*

A hat not much the worse for wear.   *Ibid.*

Now let us sing, Long live the king,
  And Gilpin long live he;
And when he next doth ride abroad,
  May I be there to see!   *Ibid.*

Toll for the brave!
  The brave that are no more!
All sunk beneath the wave,
  Fast by their native shore!
             On the Loss of the Royal George.

Misses! the tale that I relate
  This lesson seems to carry,—
Choose not alone a proper mate,
  But proper time to marry.
             Pairing Time Anticipated.

What peaceful hours I once enjoy'd!
  How sweet their memory still!
But they have left an aching void
  The world can never fill.   *Walking with God.*

And Satan trembles when he sees
The weakest saint upon his knees.   *Exhortation to Prayer.*

---

with better right to be a sovereign among soldiers.—Walter Scott, *Life of Napoleon.*

He (Steele) was a rake among scholars, and a scholar among rakes.—Macaulay, *Review of Aikin's Life of Addison.*

Temple was a man of the world amongst men of letters, a man of letters amongst men of the world.—Macaulay, *Life and Writings of Sir William Temple.*

[1] You beat your pate, and fancy wit will come;
  Knock as you please, there's nobody at home.
                Pope, *Epigram.*

[2] Love in your hearts as idly burns
  As fire in antique Roman urns.
        Butler, *Hudibras, Part* ii. *Canto* i. 309.

The story of the lamp which was supposed to have burned above 1,550 years in the sepulchre of Tullia, the daughter of Cicero, is told by Pancirollus and others.

God moves in a mysterious way
  His wonders to perform;
He plants his footsteps in the sea
    And rides upon the storm. *Light Shining out of Darkness.*

Behind a frowning providence
  He hides a shining face.   *Ibid.*

I am monarch of all I survey,
  My right there is none to dispute.
     Verses supposed to be written by Alexander Selkirk.

O Solitude! where are the charms
  That sages have seen in thy face?   *Ibid.*

But the sound of the church-going bell
  Those valleys and rocks never heard,
Ne'er sigh'd at the sound of a knell,
    Or smiled when a sabbath appeared.   *Ibid.*

How fleet is a glance of the mind!
  Compared with the speed of its flight,
The tempest itself lags behind,
    And the swift-winged arrows of light.   *Ibid.*

The path of sorrow, and that path alone,
Leads to the land where sorrow is unknown.
       To an Afflicted Protestant Lady.

'T is Providence alone secures
In every change both mine and yours.   *A Fable.*   (Moral.)

The man that hails you Tom or Jack,
And proves, by thumping on your back,[1]
  His sense of your great merit,[2]
Is such a friend, that one had need
Be very much his friend indeed
  To pardon, or to bear it.   *On Friendship.*

Beware of desperate steps. The darkest day,
Live till to-morrow, will have passed away.
      The Needless Alarm.   (Moral.)

He sees that this great roundabout,
The world, with all its motley rout,
  Church, army, physic, law,
Its customs and its businesses,
Is no concern at all of his,
  And says—what says he?—Caw.   *The Jackdaw.*

---

[1] And friend received with thumps upon the back.
          Young, *Universal Passion.*
[2] Var. "How he esteems your merit."

H

> For 't is a truth well known to most,
> That whatsoever thing is lost,
> We seek it, ere it come to light,
> In every cranny but the right.   *The Retired Cat.*

But strive still to be a man before your mother.[1]
                                   Motto of No. iii. *Connoisseur.*

—□—

ERASMUS DARWIN. 1731—1802.

> Soon shall thy arm, unconquered steam ! afar
> Drag the slow barge, or drive the rapid car ;
> Or on wide waving wings expanded bear
> The flying-chariot through the field of air.
>   *The Botanic Garden.   Part* i. *Ch.* 1. *Line* 289.

> No radiant pearl, which crested Fortune wears,
> No gem, that twinkling hangs from Beauty's ears,
> Not the bright stars, which Night's blue arch adorn,
> Nor rising suns that gild the vernal morn,
> Shine with such lustre as the tear that flows
> Down Virtue's manly cheek for others' woes.
>   *Ibid. Part* ii. *The Loves of the Plants. Canto* iii. *Line* 459.

—□—

LORD THURLOW. 1732—1806.

> The accident of an accident.
>   *Speech in Reply to the Duke of Grafton.*
>   Butler's Reminiscences, 1. 142.

When I forget my sovereign, may my God forget me.[2]
                    27 *Parl. Hist.* 680 ; *Ann. Reg.* 1789.

—□—

MRS. GREVILLE.[3] 17——17—.

> Nor peace nor ease the heart can know,
>   Which, like the needle true,
> Turns at the touch of joy or woe,
>   But, turning, trembles too.   *A Prayer for Indifference.*

---

[1] Thou wilt scarce be a man before thy mother.
               Beaumont and Fletcher, *Love's Cure, Act* ii. *Sc.* 2.
[2] Whereupon Wilkes, seated upon the foot of the throne, and who had known him long and well, is reported to have said, somewhat coarsely but not unhappily it must be allowed, "Forget you ! He 'll see you d—d first."—Brougham, *Statesmen of the Time of Geo. III. Thurlow.*
[3] The pretty Fanny Macartney.   *Walpole's Memoirs.*

W. J. MICKLE.　1734—1788.

For there 's nae luck about the house,
　There 's nae luck at a' ;
There 's little pleasure in the house
　When our gudeman 's awa'.　　　*The Mariner's Wife.*

His very foot has music in 't
　As he comes up the stairs.　　　　　　*Ibid.*

THOMAS MOSS.　*Circa* 1740—1808.

Pity the sorrows of a poor old man,
　Whose trembling limbs have borne him to your door,
Whose days are dwindled to the shortest span ;
　Oh ! give relief, and Heaven will bless your store.　*The Beggar.*

A pampered menial drove me from the door.　　　*Ibid.*

JOHN LANGHORNE.　1735—1779.

Cold on Canadian hills or Minden's plain,
Perhaps that parent mourned her soldier slain ;
Bent o'er her babe, her eye dissolved in dew ;
The big drops, mingling with the milk he drew,
Gave the sad presage of his future years,
The child of misery, baptized in tears.[1]
　　　　　　　　The Country Justice.　Part i.

JOHN WOLCOT.　1738—1819.

What rage for fame attends both great and small !
Better be d—d than mentioned not at all.
　　　　　　　　To the Royal Academicians.

Care to our coffin adds a nail, no doubt,
And every grin, so merry, draws one out.
　　　　　　　Expostulatory Odes.　Ode xv.

A fellow in a market town,
　Most musical, cried razors up and down.
　　　　　　　　Farewell Odes.　Ode iii.

---

[1] This allusion to the dead soldier and his widow, on the field of battle, was made the subject of a print by Bunbury, under which were engraved the pathetic lines of Langhorne.　Sir Walter Scott has mentioned, that the only time he saw Burns, this picture was in the room.　Burns shed tears over it ; and Scott, then a lad of fifteen, was the only person present who could tell him where the lines were to be found.—Chambers's *Cyc. of Literature, Vol.* ii. *p.* 10.

GEORGE WASHINGTON. 1732—1799.

To be prepared for war is one of the most effectual means of preserving peace.[1] *Speech to both Houses of Congress, January* 8, 1790.

——□——

JOHN ADAMS. 1735—1826.

The second day of July, 1776, will be the most memorable epocha in the history of America. I am apt to believe that it will be celebrated by succeeding generations as the great anniversary Festival. It ought to be commemorated, as the day of deliverance, by solemn acts of devotion to God Almighty. It ought to be solemnized with pomp and parade, with shows, games, sports, guns, bells, bonfires, and illuminations, from one end of this continent to the other, from this time forward for evermore.

Letter to Mrs. Adams, July 3, 1776.

——□——

PATRICK HENRY. 1736—1799.

Cæsar had his Brutus—Charles the First, his Cromwell—and George the Third—("Treason!" cried the speaker)—*may profit by their example.* If *this* be treason, make the most of it. *Speech,* 1765.

Is life so dear, or peace so sweet, as to be purchased at the price of chains and slavery? Forbid it, Almighty God! I know not what course others may take; but, as for me, give me liberty, or give me death!

Speech, March, 1775.

——□——

THOMAS PAINE. 1737—1809.

And the final event to himself (Mr. Burke) has been that, as he rose like a rocket, he fell like the stick. *Letter to the Addressers.*

These are the times that try men's souls. *The American Crisis. No.* 1.

The sublime and the ridiculous are often so nearly related, that it is difficult to class them separately. One step above the sublime makes the ridiculous, and one step above the ridiculous makes the sublime again.[2]

Age of Reason. Part ii. *ad fin. (note.)*

——□——

THOMAS JEFFERSON. 1743—1826.

The God who gave us life gave us liberty at the same time.

Summary View of the Rights of British America.

When, in the course of human events, it becomes necessary for one people to dissolve the political bands which have connected them with another, and

---

[1] Qui desiderat pacem præparet bellum.

Vegetius, *Rei Mil.* 3. *Prolog.*

[2] Probably the original of Napoleon's celebrated mot, "Du sublime au ridicule il n'y a qu'un pas."

to assume among the powers of the earth the separate and equal station to which the laws of nature and of nature's God entitle them, a decent respect to the opinions of mankind requires that they should declare the causes which impel them to the separation.

A Declaration by the Representatives of the United States of America.

We hold these truths to be self-evident: that all men are created equal; that they are endowed by their Creator with inalienable rights: that among these are life, liberty, and the pursuit of happiness.   *Ibid.*

We mutually pledge to each other our lives, our fortunes, and our sacred honour.   *Ibid.*

Error of opinion may be tolerated where reason is left free to combat it.
Inaugural Address.

Equal and exact justice to all men, of whatever state or persuasion, religious or political; peace, commerce, and honest friendship, with all nations,—entangling alliances with none; the support of the State governments in all their rights, as the most competent administrations for our domestic concerns, and the surest bulwarks against anti-republican tendencies; the preservation of the General Government in its whole constitutional vigour, as the sheet anchor of our peace at home and safety abroad; . . . . . freedom of religion; freedom of the press; freedom of person under the protection of habeas corpus; and trial by juries impartially selected,—these principles form the bright constellation which has gone before us, and guided our steps through an age of revolution and reformation.   *Ibid.*

If a due participation of office is a matter of right, how are vacancies to be obtained? Those by death are few: by resignation none.[1]
Letter to a Committee of the Merchants of New Haven, 1801.

—□—

LORD STOWELL. 1745—1836.

A dinner lubricates business.   Boswell's *Johnson*, viii. 67, *n.*

The elegant simplicity of the three per cents.
Campbell's *Chancellors, Vol.* x. *Ch.* 212.

—□—

MRS. BARBAULD. 1743—1825.

Man is the nobler growth our realms supply,
And souls are ripened in our northern sky.   *The Invitation.*

This dead of midnight is the noon of thought,
And Wisdom mounts her zenith with the stars.[2]
A Summer's Evening Meditation.

---

[1] Usually quoted, "Few die, and none resign."
[2] Often ascribed to Young.

Life ! we've been long together
Through pleasant and through cloudy weather;
  'T is hard to part when friends are dear;
  Perhaps 't will cost a sigh, a tear;
  Then steal away, give little warning,
    Choose thine own time;
Say not "Good night," but in some brighter clime
  Bid me "Good morning."   *Life.*

—□—

MRS. THRALE. 1740—1822.

The tree of deepest root is found
Least willing still to quit the ground;
'T was therefore said, by ancient sages,
  That love of life increased with years
So much, that in our latter stages,
When pains grow sharp, and sickness rages,
  The greatest love of life appears.   *Three Warnings.*

—□—

CHARLES DIBDIN. 1745—1814.

There 's a sweet little cherub that sits up aloft,
To keep watch for the life of poor Jack.   *Poor Jack.*

Did you ever hear of Captain Wattle?
He was all for love and a little for the bottle.
    Captain Wattle and Miss Roe.

—□—

HANNAH MORE. 1745—1833.

To those who know thee not, no words can paint !
And those who know thee know all words are faint !
    Sensibility.

In men this blunder still you find,
All think their little set mankind.   *Florio.   Part* i.

Small habits well pursued betimes
May reach the dignity of crimes.   *Ibid.*

—□—

SIR WILLIAM JONES. 1746—1794.

Go boldly forth, my simple lay,
Whose accents flow with artless ease,
Like orient pearls at random strung. *A Persian Song of Hafiz.*

On parent knees, a naked new-born child
Weeping thou sat'st while all around thee smiled;
So live, that, sinking in thy last long sleep,
Calm thou mayst smile, while all around thee weep.
    From the Persian.

What constitutes a state?
. . . .
> Men who their duties know,
> But know their rights, and, knowing, dare maintain.
. . . .
And sovereign law, that state's collected will,
> O'er thrones and globes elate,
Sits empress, crowning good, repressing ill.
> *Ode in Imitation of Alcæus.*

Seven hours to law, to soothing slumber seven,
Ten to the world allot, and all to heaven.[1]

—□—

JOHN LOGAN. 1748—1788.

Thou hast no sorrow in thy song,
> No winter in thy year.　　　　　*To the Cuckoo.*

—□—

CHARLES MORRIS. 1739—1832.

Solid men of Boston, make no long orations;
Solid men of Boston, banish strong potations.[2]
> *Billy Pitt and the Farmer.*

Oh give me the sweet shady side of Pall Mall.
> *Town and Country.*

—□—

JOHN TRUMBULL. 1750—1831.

But optics sharp it needs, I ween,
To see what is not to be seen.
> *McFingal.　Canto* i. *Line* 67.

But as some muskets so contrive it,
As oft to miss the mark they drive at,
And though well aimed at duck or plover,
Bear wide, and kick their owners over.　　*Canto* i. *Line* 93.

> As though there were a tie,
And obligation to posterity.
We get them, bear them, breed and nurse.
What has posterity done for us,
That we, lest they their rights should lose,
Should trust our necks to gripe of noose.
> *Canto* ii. *Line* 121.

No man e'er felt the halter draw,
With good opinion of the law.　　*Canto* iii. *Line* 489.

---

1 Six hours in sleep, in law's grave study six,
> Four spend in prayer, the rest on nature fix.
> *Translation of lines quoted by* Sir Edward Coke.
2 From Debrett's *Asylum for Fugitive Pieces, Vol.* ii. *p.* 250.

RICHARD BRINSLEY SHERIDAN. 1751—1816.

A progeny of learning.   (Mrs. Malaprop.)   *The Rivals. Act.* i. *Sc.* 2.

You are not like Cerberus, three gentlemen at once, are you?
(Mrs. Malaprop.)   Ibid. Act. iv. Sc. 2.

The quarrel is a very pretty quarrel as it stands; we should only spoil it by trying to explain it.   *Ibid. Act* iv. *Sc.* 3.

As headstrong as an allegory on the banks of the Nile.
(Mrs. Malaprop.)   Ibid. Act v. Sc. 3.

My valour is certainly going! it is sneaking off! I feel it oozing out, as it were, at the palm of my hands.   *Ibid. Act* v. *Sc.* 3.

I own the soft impeachment.   (Mrs. Malaprop.)   *Ibid. Act* v. *Sc.* 3.

Steal! to be sure they may, and, egad, serve your best thoughts as gypsies do stolen children,—disfigure them to make 'em pass for their own.[1]
The Critic. Act i. Sc. 1.

No scandal about Queen Elizabeth, I hope.   *Ibid. Act* ii. *Sc.* 1.

Where they *do* agree on the stage, their unanimity is wonderful.
The Critic. Act ii. Sc. 2.

An oyster may be crossed in love.   *Ibid. Act* iii.

You shall see a beautiful quarto page, where a neat rivulet of text shall meander through a meadow of margin.   *School for Scandal. Act* i. *Sc.* 1.

I leave my character behind me.   *Ibid. Act* ii. *Sc.* 2.

> Here 's to the maiden of bashful fifteen;
>   Here 's to the widow of fifty;
> Here 's to the flaunting, extravagant quean,
>   And here 's to the housewife that 's thrifty.
>   Let the toast pass;
>   Drink to the lass;
> I 'll warrant she 'll prove an excuse for the glass.

Ibid. Act iii. Sc. 3.

An unforgiving eye, and a damned disinheriting countenance.
Ibid. Act iv. Sc. 1.

> I ne'er could any lustre see
> In eyes that would not look on me;
> I ne'er saw nectar on a lip
> But where my own did hope to sip.   *The Duenna. Act* i. *Sc.* 2.

> Had I a heart for falsehood framed,
>   I ne'er could injure you.   *Ibid. Act* i. *Sc.* 5.

---

[1] Still pilfers wretched plans, and makes them worse;
Like gipsies, lest the stolen brat be known,
Defacing first, then claiming for his own.
Churchill, The Apology, Line 233.

THE DUENNA—*continued.*]

Conscience has no more to do with gallantry than it has with politics.
Ibid. Act ii. *Sc.* 4.

The Right Honorable gentleman is indebted to his memory for his jests
and to his imagination for his facts.[1]
Speech in Reply to Mr. Dundas. (*Sheridaniana.*)

You write with ease to show your breeding,
But easy writing 's curst hard reading.
Clio's Protest. Moore's *Life of Sheridan. Vol.* i. *p.* 155.

——□——

GEORGE CRABBE. 1754—1832.

Oh! rather give me commentators plain,
Who with no deep researches vex the brain;
Who from the dark and doubtful love to run,
And hold their glimmering tapers to the sun.[2]
The Parish Register. Pt. i. *Introduc.*

Her air, her manners, all who saw admired;
Courteous though coy, and gentle though retired;
The joy of youth and health her eyes display'd,
And ease of heart her every look convey'd. *Ibid. Pt.* ii. *Marriages.*

In this fool's paradise[3] he drank delight.
The Borough. Letter xii. *Players.*

Books cannot always please, however good;
Minds are not ever craving for their food.
Ibid. Letter xxiv. *Schools.*

In idle wishes fools supinely stay;
Be there a will, and wisdom finds a way. *The Birth of Flattery.*

——□——

ROBERT BURNS. 1759—1796.

Where sits our sulky, sullen dame,
Gathering her brows like gathering storm,
Nursing her wrath to keep it warm.   *Tam O' Shanter.*

Ah gentle dames! it gars me greet,
To think how monie counsels sweet,
How monie lengthened sage advices,
The husband frae the wife despises.   *Ibid.*

His ancient, trusty, drouthy crony;
Tam lo'ed him like a vera brither—
They had been fou for weeks thegither.   *Ibid.*

---

[1] On peut dire que son esprit brille aux dépens de sa mémoire.—Le Sage,
Gil Blas, Livre iii. *Ch.* xi.
[2] Cf. Young, *Ante, p.* 157.
[3] Cf. Milton, *Paradise Lost, Book* iii. *Line* 496.

H*

TAM O'SHANTER—*continued.*]

The landlady and Tam grew gracious
Wi' favours secret, sweet, and precious.   *Ibid.*

The landlord's laugh was ready chorus.   *ibid.*

Kings may be blest, but Tam was glorious,
O'er a' the ills o' life victorious.   *Ibid.*

But pleasures are like poppies spread,
You seize the flower, its bloom is shed;
Or, like the snow-fall in the river,
A moment white, then melts for ever.   *Ibid.*

That hour, o' night's black arch the keystane.   *Ibid.*

Inspiring, bold John Barleycorn,
What dangers thou canst make us scorn!   *Ibid.*

As Tammie gloured, amazed and curious,
The mirth and fun grew fast and furious.   *Ibid.*

Affliction's sons are brothers in distress;
A brother to relieve, how exquisite the bliss!
                                    A Winter's Night.
Then gently scan your brother man,
    Still gentler, sister woman;
Though they may gang a kennin' wrang,
    To step aside is human.   *Address to the Unco Guid.*

What 's done we partly may compute,
    But know not what 's resisted.   *Ibid.*

If there 's a hole in a' your coats,
        I rede ye tent it;
A chiel 's amang ye takin' notes,
        And, faith, he 'll prent it.
        On Captain Grose's Peregrinations through Scotland.

O wad some power the giftie gie us,
To see oursels as others see us!
It wad frae monie a blunder free us,
        And foolish notion.   *To a Louse.*

The best laid schemes o' mice and men
        Gang aft a-gley;
And leave us naught but grief and pain
        For promised joy.   *To a Mouse.*

Stern Ruin's ploughshare drives elate
    Full on thy bloom.[1]   *To a Mountain Daisy.*

---

[1] Final Ruin fiercely drives
Her ploughshare o'er creation.
            Young, *Night Thoughts*, ix. *Line* 167.

Perhaps it may turn out a sang,
 Perhaps turn out a sermon.   *Epistle to a Young Friend.*

I waive the quantum o' the sin,
 The hazard of concealing ;
But, och ! it hardens a' within,
 And petrifies the feeling !   *Ibid.*

The fear o' hell 's a hangman's whip
 To haud the wretch in order ;
But where ye feel your honour grip,
 Let that aye be your border.   *Ibid.*

An Atheist's laugh 's a poor exchange
 For Deity offended !   *Ibid.*

And may you better reck the *rede*,[1]
 Than ever did th' adviser !   *Ibid.*

In durance vile here must I wake and weep,
And all my frowzy couch in sorrow steep.[2]
      Epistle from Esopus to Maria.

His locked, lettered, braw brass collar
Shewed him the gentleman and scholar.   *The Twa Dogs.*

O Life ! how pleasant in thy morning,
Young Fancy's rays the hills adorning !
Cold-pausing Caution's lesson scorning,
     We frisk away,
Like school-boys at th' expected warning,
     To joy and play.   *Epistle to James Smith.*

O life ! thou art a galling load,
Along a rough, a weary road,
 To wretches such a I !   *Despondency.*

Should auld acquaintance be forgot,
 And never brought to min'?
Should auld acquaintance be forgot,
 And days o' lang syne ?   *Auld Lang Syne.*

Misled by fancy's meteor-ray,
   By passion driven ;
But yet the light that led astray
   Was light from heaven.   *The Vision.*

And, like a passing thought, she fled
   In light away.   *Ibid.*

---

[1] And recks not his own rede.   Shakespeare, *Hamlet*, *Act* i. *Sc.* 3.
[2] Durance vile.—W. Kenrick (1766), *Falstaff's Wedding*, *Act* i. *Sc.* 2.
It will not be amiss to take a view of the effects of this royal servitude
and vile durance, which was so deplored in the reign of the last monarch.
—Burke, *Thoughts on the Present Discontents.*

Now 's the day, and now 's the hour,
See the front o' battle lour.   *Bannockburn.*

Liberty 's in every blow !
    Let us do or die.[1]   *Ibid.*

Man's inhumanity to man
Makes countless thousands mourn.   *Man was made to mourn.*

Auld Nature swears, the lovely dears
    Her noblest work she classes, O;
Her 'prentice han' she tried on man,
    And then she made the lasses, O ![2]   *Green grow the Rashes.*

Some wee short hour ayont the twal.
                                        Death and Dr. Hornbook.

The rank is but the guinea's stamp,
    The man 's the gowd for a' that.[3]   *Is there for Honest Poverty.*

A prince can make a belted knight,[4]
    A marquis, duke, and a' that;
But an honest man 's aboon his might,
    Guid faith, he maunna fa' that.   *Ibid.*

But to see her was to love her,
Love but her, and love for ever.   *Song.   Ae Fond Kiss.*

Had we never loved sae kindly,
Had we never loved sae blindly,
Never met or never parted,
We had ne'er been broken-hearted !   *Ibid.*

To see her is to love her,
    And love but her for ever.   *Bonny Lesley*

O, my luve 's like a red, red rose,
    That 's newly sprung in June,
O, my luve 's like the melodie,
    That 's sweetly played in tune.   *Song.   A Red, Red Rose.*

It 's guid to be merry and wise,
It 's guid to be honest and true,
It 's guid to support Caledonia's cause,
And bide by the buff and the blue.
                          Here 's a health to them that 's awa.

---

[1] See Proverbs, *post.*
[2] Man was made when Nature was
      But an apprentice, but woman when she
        Was a skilful mistress of her art.   *Cupid's Whirligig.*   1607.
[3] I weigh the man, not his title; 't is not the king's stamp can make the
metal better.—Wycherley, *The Plaindealer, Act* i. Sc. I.
[4] Of the king's creation you may be; but he who makes a Count ne'er
made a man.—Southerne, *Sir Anthony Love, Act* ii. Sc. I.

'T is sweeter for thee despairing,
Than aught in the world beside,—Jessy !   *Jessy.*

Gars auld claes look amaist as weel 's the new.
The Cotter's Saturday Night.

Beneath the milk-white thorn that scents the evening gale. *Ibid.*

He wales a portion with judicious care ;
And " Let us worship God !" he says, with solemn air.   *Ibid.*

From scenes like these old Scotia's grandeur springs,
    That makes her loved at home, revered abroad :
Princes and lords are but the breath of kings,
    " An honest man 's the noblest work of God. ´   *Ibid.*

—□—

J. P. KEMBLE. 1757—1823.

I give thee all—I can no more,
    Tho' poor the offering be;
My heart and lute are all the store
    That I can bring to thee. *Lodoiska. Act* iii. *Sc.* 1.

Perhaps it was right to dissemble your love,
But—why did you kick me down stairs?
                                    The Panel.[1] *Act* i. *Sc.* 1.

—□—

GEORGE BARRINGTON. 1755——.

True patriots all; for be it understood
We left our country for our country's good.[2]
            *Prologue written for the Opening of the Play-house at
            New South Wales, Jan.* 16, 1796. *Barring-
            ton's " New South Wales," p.* 152.

—□—

WILLIAM PITT. 1759—1806.

Prostrate the beauteous ruin lies; and all
That shared its shelter, perish in its fall.
    From *The Poetry of the Anti-Jacobin. No.* xxxvi.

—□—

GEORGE COLMAN, THE YOUNGER. 1762—1836.

On their own merits modest men are dumb.
                        Epilogue to the Heir at Law.

And what 's impossible can't be,
And never, never comes to pass.   *The Maid of the Moor.*

Three stories high, long, dull, and old,
As great lords' stories often are.   *Ibid.*

· Altered from Bickerstaff's *' T is Well it's no Worse.* The lines are also
found in Debrett's *Asylum for Fugitive Pieces, Vol.* i. *p.* 15.
  2 'T was for the good of my country that I should be abroad.—Farquhar,
                        The Beaux' Stratagem, Act iii. *Sc.* 2.

Like two single gentlemen, rolled into one.
Lodgings for Single Gentlemen.

But when ill indeed,
E'en dismissing the doctor don't always succeed.   *Ibid.*

When taken
To be well shaken.
The Newcastle Apothecary.

Thank you, good sir, I owe you one.
The Poor Gentleman. Act i. *Sc.* 2.

O Miss Bailey,
Unfortunate Miss Bailey !
Love laughs at Locksmiths. Act ii. *Song.*

—□—

JAMES HURDIS. 1763—1801.

Rise with the lark, and with the lark to bed.
The Village Curate.

—□—

HENRY LEE. 1756—1816.

To the memory of the Man, first in war, first in peace, and first in the
hearts of his countrymen.
Eulogy on Washington. Delivered by Gen. Lee,
Dec. 26, 1799.[1] *Memoirs of Lee.*

—□—

DAVID EVERETT. 1769—1813.

You 'd scarce expect one of my age
To speak in public on the stage;
And if I chance to fall below
Demosthenes or Cicero,
Don't view me with a critic's eye,
But pass my imperfections by.
Large streams from little fountains flow,
Tall oaks from little acorns grow.
Lines written for a School Declamation.

—□—

MADAME ROLAND. 1754—1793.

O liberty ! liberty ! how many crimes are committed in thy name ! (1793.)

—□—

BERTRAND BARÈRE. 1755—1841.

The tree of liberty only grows when watered by the blood of tyrants.[2]
Speech in the Convention Nationale. 1792.

---

[1] To the memory of the Man, first in war, first in peace, and first in the
hearts of his fellow-citizens.—From *the Resolutions presented to the House
of Representatives, on the Death of General Washington, December,* 1799.
Marshall's Life of Washington.

[2] L'arbre de la liberté ne croît qu'arrosé par le sang des tyrans.

JOSEPH FOUCHÉ. 1763—1820.

It is more than a crime, it is a political fault;[1] words which I record because they have been repeated and attributed to others. *Memoirs of Fouché.*

———□———

THOMAS MORTON. 1764—1838.

What will Mrs. Grundy say? *Speed the Plough. Act* i. *Sc.* 1.

Push on—keep moving. *A Cure for the Heartache. Act.* ii. *Sc.* 1.

Approbation from Sir Hubert Stanley is praise indeed. *Ibid. Act* v. *Sc.* 2.

———□———

JOHN FERRIAR. 1764—1815.
ILLUSTRATIONS OF STERNE.

The princeps copy, clad in blue and gold. *Bibliomania. Line* 6.

Now cheaply bought—for thrice their weight in gold.
Ibid. Line 65.

Torn from their destined page (unworthy meed
Of knightly counsel, and heroic deed). *Ibid. Line* 121.

How pure the joy, when first my hands unfold
The small, rare volume, black with tarnish'd gold! *Ibid. Line* 137.

———□———

SIR JAMES MACKINTOSH. 1765—1832.

Diffused knowledge immortalizes itself. *Vindiciæ Gallicæ.*

The commons, faithful to their system, remained in a wise and masterly inactivity. *Ibid.*

Disciplined inaction. *Causes of the Revolution of* 1688, *ch. vii.*

The frivolous work of polished idleness.
Dissertation on Ethical Philosophy. Remarks on Thomas Brown.

———□———

ROBERT HALL. 1764—1831.

His imperial fancy has laid all nature under tribute, and has collected riches from every scene of the creation and every walk of art. (Of Burke.)
Apology for the Freedom of the Press.

He might be a very clever man by nature, for aught I know, but he laid so many books upon his head that his brains could not move. (Of Kippis.)
From Gregory's Life of Hall.

Call things by their right names. . . . . Glass of brandy and water! That is the current, but not the appropriate name; ask for a glass of liquid fire and distilled damnation. *Ibid.*

---

[1] Commonly quoted, "It is worse than a crime, it is a blunder," and attributed to Talleyrand.

KOTZEBUE. 1761—1819.

There is another and a better world.
The Stranger. Act i. Sc. 1. Trans. by A. Schink, London. 1799.

—□—

SIR SAMUEL EGERTON BRYDGES. 1762—1837.

The glory dies not, and the grief is past.
Sonnet on the Death of Sir Walter Scott.

—□—

JOHN QUINCY ADAMS. 1767—1848.

This hand, to tyrants ever sworn the foe,
For freedom only deals the deadly blow;
Then sheathes in calm repose the vengeful blade,
For gentle peace in freedom's hallowed shade.[1]
Written in an Album, 1842.

—□—

JOSIAH QUINCY. 1772—1864.

If this bill (for the admission of Orleans territory as a State) passes, it is my deliberate opinion that it is virtually a dissolution of the Union; that it will free the States from their moral obligation, and, as it will be the right of all, so it will be the duty of some, definitely to prepare for a separation, amicably if they can, violently if they must.[2]
Abridged Cong. Debates, Jan. 14, 1811. Vol. iv. p. 327.

—□—

GEORGE CANNING. 1770—1827.

Story! God bless you! I have none to tell, sir.
The Friend of Humanity and the Knife-Grinder.

I give thee sixpence! I will see thee d—d first.   *Ibid.*

So down thy hill, romantic Ashbourn, glides
The Derby dilly, carrying *Three* INSIDES.
The Loves of the Triangles. Line 178.

A sudden thought strikes me,—let us swear an eternal friendship.
Ibid. The Rovers. Act i. Sc. 1.

And finds, with keen, discriminating sight,
Black 's not so black;—nor white so *very* white.
New Morality, xxxvi.

Give me the avow'd, the erect, the manly foe,
Bold I can meet,—perhaps may turn his blow;
But of all plagues, good Heaven, thy wrath can send,
Save, save, oh! save me from the *Candid Friend!*   *Ibid.*

---

[1] Manus hæc inimica tyrannis
Ense petit placidam sub libertate quietem.
Algernon Sidney.

[2] The gentleman (Mr. Quincy) cannot have forgotten his own sentiment, uttered even on the floor of this House, "Peaceably if we can, forcibly if we must."—Henry Clay, *Speech, Jan.* 8, 1813.

I called the New World into existence to redress the balance of the old.
The King's Message. (Dec. 12, 1826.)

No, here's to the pilot that weathered the storm.
The Pilot that weathered the Storm.

—□—

SAMUEL ROGERS. 1763—1855.

A guardian angel o'er his life presiding,
Doubling his pleasures, and his cares dividing. *Human Life.*

Fireside happiness, to hours of ease
Blest with that charm, the certainty to please. *Ibid.*

The soul of music slumbers in the shell,
Till waked and kindled by the master's spell;
And feeling hearts, touch them but rightly, pour
A thousand melodies unheard before! *Ibid.*

Then, never less alone than when alone.[1] *Ibid.*

Those that he loved so long and sees no more,
Loved and still loves,—not dead, but gone before,[2]—
He gathers round him. *Ibid.*

Mine be a cot beside the hill;
  A beehive's hum shall soothe my ear;
A willowy brook, that turns a mill,
  With many a fall, shall linger near. *A Wish.*

That very law which moulds a tear
And bids it trickle from its source,
That law preserves the earth a sphere
And guides the planets in their course. *To a Tear.*

She was good as she was fair.
None—none on earth above her!
As pure in thought as angels are,
To know her was to love her.[3] *Jacqueline. St.* 1.

The good are better made by ill,
As odours crushed are sweeter still.[4] *Ibid. St.* 3.

---

[1] Numquam se minus otiosum esse, quam quum otiosus, nec minus solum, quam quum solus esset.—Cicero, *De Officiis, Lib. iii. cap.* 1.

[2] In a collection of Epitaphs published by Lackington & Co. (Vol. ii. p. 143), an epitaph is given "On Mary Angell at Stepney, who died 1693," in which this line appears, "Not lost, but gone before."—*Notes and Queries, 3d Ser.* x. *p.* 404.

[3]   To see her is to love her,
    And love but her for ever. Burns, *Bonny Lesley.*
I will, if you please, take you to the house, and introduce you to its worthy master, whom to know is to love.—Sir Humphry Davy, *Salmonia, Eighth Day.*
None knew thee but to love thee.—Halleck, *On the Death of Drake.*

[4] Virtue is like precious odours, most fragrant when they are incensed or crushed.—Bacon, *Of Adversity.*

JOHN TOBIN.   1770—1824.

The man that lays his hand upon a woman,
Save in the way of kindness, is a wretch,
Whom 't were gross flattery to name a coward.

The Honeymoon   *Act* ii. *Sc.* **1.**

She 's adorned
Amply that in her husband's eye looks lovely,—
The truest mirror that an honest wife
Can see her beauty in.

Ibid.   Act iii. *Sc.* **4.**

——□——

WILLIAM WORDSWORTH.[1]   1770—1850.

And homeless near a thousand homes I stood,
And near a thousand tables pined and wanted food.

Guilt and Sorrow.   Stanza **41.**

Action is transitory—a step, a blow,
The motion of a muscle—this way or that.

The Borderers.   Act iii.

The Child is father of the Man.[2]   *My Heart Leaps Up.*

She gave me eyes, she gave me ears;
And humble cares, and delicate fears,
A heart, the fountain of sweet tears;
And love, and thought, and joy.   *The Sparrow's Nest.*

The sweetest thing that ever grew
Beside a human door.   *Lucy Gray.   Stanza* **2.**

A simple Child,
That lightly draws its breath,
And feels its life in every limb,
What should it know of death?   *We are Seven.*

Drink, pretty creature, drink !   *The Pet Lamb.*

Until a man might travel twelve stout miles,
Or reap an acre of his neighbour's corn.   *The Brothers.*

Sweet childish days, that were as long
As twenty days are now.   *To a Butterfly.*

A noticeable Man with large gray eyes.

Stanzas written in Thomson.

---

[1] Coleridge said to Wordsworth, "Since Milton I know of no poet with so many *felicities* and unforgetable lines and stanzas as you."—*Wordsworth's Memoirs*, ii. 74.

[2] The childhood shows the man
As morning shows the day.
Milton, *Par. Regained, Book* iv. L. 220

She dwelt among the untrodden ways
   Beside the springs of Dove,
A maid whom there were none to praise
   And very few to love.   *She dwelt among the untrodden ways.*

A violet by a mossy stone
   Half hidden from the eye !
Fair as a star, when only one
   Is shining in the sky.   *Ibid.*

She lived unknown, and few could know
   When Lucy ceased to be ;
But she is in her grave, and oh !
   The difference to me !   *Ibid.*

A Briton, even in love, should be
   A subject, not a slave ! *Ere with cold beads of midnight dew.*

True beauty dwells in deep retreats,
   Whose veil is unremoved
Till heart with heart in concord beats,
   And the lover is beloved.   *To ——.*

Minds that have nothing to confer
   Find little to perceive.   *Yes ! thou art fair.*

That kill the bloom before its time ;
And blanch, without the owner's crime,
The most resplendent hair.   *Lament of Mary Queen of Scots.*

The bane of all that dread the Devil.   *The Idiot Boy.*

Something between a hindrance and a help.   *Michael.*

            Lady of the Mere,
Sole-sitting by the shores of old romance.
            A Narrow Girdle of Rough Stones.

But He is risen, a later star of dawn.   *A Morning Exercise.*

Bright gem instinct with music, vocal spark.   *Ibid.*

And he is oft the wisest man,
   Who is not wise at all.   *The Oak and the Broom.*

We meet thee, like a pleasant thought,
When such are wanted.   *To the Daisy.*

The poet's darling.   *Ibid.*

Thou unassuming Commonplace
Of Nature.   *To the same Flower.*

Oft on the dappled turf at ease
I sit, and play with similes,
Loose types of things through all degrees.   *Ibid.*

Often have I sighed to measure
By myself a lonely pleasure,
Sighed to think I read a book,
Only read, perhaps, by me.   *To the Small Celandine.*

O Cuckoo! shall I call thee Bird,
Or but a wandering voice?   *To the Cuckoo.*

One of those heavenly days that cannot die.   *Nutting.*

She was a Phantom of delight
When first she gleamed upon my sight.
                    She was a phantom of delight.

But all things else about her drawn
From May-time and the cheerful Dawn.   *Ibid.*

A Creature not too bright or good
For human nature's daily food;
For transient sorrows, simple wiles,
Praise, blame, love, kisses, tears, and smiles.   *Ibid.*

The reason firm, the temperate will,
Endurance, foresight, strength, and skill;
A perfect Woman, nobly planned,
To warn, to comfort, and command.   *Ibid.*

The stars of midnight shall be dear
To her; and she shall lean her ear
    In many a secret place
Where rivulets dance their wayward round,
And beauty born of murmuring sound
    Shall pass into her face.   *Three years she grew.*

        That inward eye
Which is the bliss of solitude.   *I wandered lonely.*

    The cattle are grazing,
    Their heads never raising;
There are forty feeding like one!   *Written in March.*

    A Youth to whom was given
So much of earth, so much of heaven.   *Ruth.*

As high as we have mounted in delight
In our dejection do we sink as low.
                    Resolution and Independence. Stanza 4.

But how can he expect that others should
Build for him, sow for him, and at his call
Love him, who for himself will take no heed at all?
                    Ibid. Stanza 6.

I thought of Chatterton, the marvellous Boy,
The sleepless Soul that perished in his pride;
Of him who walked in glory and in joy,

RESOLUTION AND INDEPENDENCE—*continued.*]
Following his plough, along the mountain-side :
By our own spirits we are deified :
We poets in our youth begin in gladness ;
But thereof come in the end despondency and madness.

Ibid. Stanza 8.

Choice word and measured phrase above the reach
Of ordinary men. *Ibid. Stanza* 14.

And mighty Poets in their misery dead. *Ibid. Stanza* 17.

"A jolly place," said he, "in times of old !
But something ails it now : the spot is cursed."

Hart-Leap Well. Part ii.

Hunt half a day for a forgotten dream. *Ibid. Part* ii.

Never to blend our pleasure, or our pride,
With sorrow of the meanest thing that feels. *Ibid.*

Sensations sweet,
Felt in the blood, and felt along the heart. *Tintern Abbey.*

That best portion of a good man's life,
His little, nameless, unremembered acts
Of kindness and of love. *Ibid.*

That blessed mood,
In which the burden of the mystery,
In which the heavy and the weary weight
Of all this unintelligible world,
Is lightened. *Ibid.*

The fretful stir
Unprofitable, and the fever of the world,
Have hung upon the beatings of my heart. *Ibid.*

The sounding cataract
Haunted me like a passion : the tall rock,
The mountain, and the deep and gloomy wood,
Their colours and their forms, were then to me
An appetite ; a feeling and a love,
That had no need of a remoter charm
By thoughts supplied, nor any interest
Unborrowed from the eye. *Ibid.*

But hearing oftentimes
The still, sad music of humanity. *Ibid.*

A sense sublime
Of something far more deeply interfused,
Whose dwelling is the light of setting suns,
And the round ocean, and the living air,

TINTERN ABBEY—*continued.*]

And the blue sky, and in the mind of man :
A motion and a spirit, that impels
All thinking things, all objects of all thought,
And rolls through all things.   *Ibid.*

Knowing that Nature never did betray
The heart that loved her.   *Ibid.*

Nor greetings where no kindness is, nor all
The dreary intercourse of daily life.   *Ibid.*

Like—but oh ! how different ! *Yes, it was the Mountain Echo.*

Type of the wise who soar, but never roam ;
True to the kindred points of Heaven and Home !
                                          To a Skylark.

            The Gods approve
The depth, and not the tumult, of the soul.   *Laodamia.*

            Mightier far
Than strength of nerve or sinew, or the sway
Of magic potent over sun and star,
Is love, though oft to agony distrest,
And though his favourite seat be feeble woman's breast.   *Ibid.*

He spake of love, such love as Spirits feel
In worlds whose course is equable and pure ;
No fears to beat away,—no strife to heal,—
The past unsighed for, and the future sure.   *Ibid.*

Of all that is most beauteous imaged there
In happier beauty ; more pellucid streams,
In ampler ether, a diviner air,
And fields invested with purpureal gleams.   *Ibid.*

Yet tears to human suffering are due ;
And mortal hopes defeated and o'erthrown
Are mourned by man, and not by man alone.   *Ibid.*

But Shapes that come not at an earthly call
Will not depart when mortal voices bid.   *Dion.*

    Shalt show us how divine a thing
    A Woman may be made.   *To a Young Lady.*

    But an old age serene and bright,
    And lovely as a Lapland night,
        Shall lead thee to thy grave.   *Ibid.*

    Alas ! how little can a moment show
    Of an eye where feeling plays
    In ten thousand dewy rays ;
    A face o er which a thousand shadows go.   *the Triad.*

The bosom-weight, your stubborn gift,
That no philosophy can lift.   *Presentiment.*

Stern Winter loves a dirge-like sound.
                              On the Power of Sound, xii.

There 's something in a flying horse,
There 's something in a huge balloon.
                         Peter Bell. Prologue. St. 1.

The common growth of Mother Earth
Suffices me,—her tears, her mirth,
Her humblest mirth and tears.   *Ibid. St.* 27.

Full twenty times was Peter feared,
For once that Peter was respected.   *Part* i. *St.* 3.

A primrose by a river's brim
A yellow primrose was to him,
And it was nothing more.   *Part* i. *St.* 12.

The soft blue sky did never melt
Into his heart; he never felt
The witchery of the soft blue sky !   *Part* i. *St.* 15.

As if the man had fixed his face,
In many a solitary place,
Against the wind and open sky !   *Part* i. *St.* 26.[1]

The holy time is quiet as a Nun
Breathless with adoration.
                      Miscellaneous Sonnets. Part i. xxx.

The world is too much with us ; late and soon,
Getting and spending, we lay waste our powers.
                              Ibid. Part i. xxxiii.

       Great God ! I 'd rather be
A Pagan suckled in a creed outworn ;
So might I, standing on this pleasant lea,
Have glimpses that would make me less forlorn ;
Have sight of Proteus rising from the sea,
Or hear old Triton blow his wreathed horn.   *Ibid.*

          To the solid ground
Of nature trusts the Mind that builds for aye.
                              Ibid. Part i. xxxiv.

---

[1] The original edition (London, 8vo, 1819) had the following as the
fourth stanza from the end of Part I., which was omitted in all subsequent
editions :—
           Is it a party in a parlour ?
       Crammed just as they on earth were crammed,—
       Some sipping punch, some sipping tea,
       But as you by their faces see,
       All silent and all damned.

MISCELLANEOUS SONNETS—*continued.*]

'T is hers to pluck the amaranthine flower
Of Faith, and round the Sufferer's temples bind
Wreaths that endure affliction's heaviest shower,
And do not shrink from sorrow's keenest wind.
Ibid.   Part i. xxxv.

Ne'er saw I, never felt, a calm so deep !
The river glideth at his own sweet will ;
Dear God ! the very houses seem asleep ;
And all that mighty heart is lying still !   *Ibid.   Part* ii. xxxvi.

And, when a damp
Fell round the path of Milton, in his hand
The Thing became a trumpet ; whence he blew
Soul-animating strains,—alas ! too few.   *Ibid.   Part* ii. i.

Soft is the music that would charm for ever ;
The flower of sweetest smell is shy and lowly.
Ibid.   Part ii. ix.

Sweet Mercy ! to the gates of Heaven
This Minstrel lead, his sins forgiven ;
The rueful conflict, the heart riven
    With vain endeavour,
And memory of Earth's bitter leaven,
    Effaced for ever.
Thoughts suggested on the Banks of Nith.

The best of what we do and are,
    Just God, forgive.
Ibid.

The foaming flood seems motionless as ice ;

.   .   .   .   .

Frozen by distance.   *Address to Kilchurn Castle.*

May no rude hand deface it,
And its forlorn *hic jacet !*
Ellen Irwin.

Some natural sorrow, loss, or pain,
That has been, and may be again.   *The Solitary Reaper.*

The music in my heart I bore,
Long after it was heard no more.
Ibid.

Because the good old rule
Sufficeth them, the simple plan,
That they should take who have the power,
    And they should keep who can.   *Rob Roy's Grave.*

The Eagle, he was lord above,
And Rob was lord below.
Ibid.

A brotherhood of venerable trees.
Sonnet.   Composed at ——— *Castle.*

Let beeves and home-bred kine partake
The sweets of Burn-mill meadow;
The swan on still St. Mary's Lake
Float double, swan and shadow !   *Yarrow Unvisited.*

O for a single hour of that Dundee
Who on that day the word of onset gave !
                        Sonnet. In the Pass of Killicranky.

A remnant of uneasy light.   *The Matron of Jedborough.*

But thou, that didst appear so fair
    To fond imagination,
Dost rival in the light of day
    Her delicate creation.   *Yarrow Visited.*

Men are we, and must grieve when even the Shade
Of that which once was great is passed away.
                        On the Extinction of the Venetian Republic.

Thou hast left behind
Powers that will work for thee; air, earth, and skies;
There 's not a breathing of the common wind
That will forget thee; thou hast great allies;
Thy friends are exultations, agonies,
And love, and man's unconquerable mind.
                        To Toussaint L' Ouverture.

Two voices are there; one is of the sea,
One of the mountains; each a mighty voice.
                Thought of a Briton on the Subjugation of Switzerland.

Plain living and high thinking are no more.
The homely beauty of the good old cause
Is gone; our peace, our fearful innocence,
And pure religion breathing household laws.
                        Written in London, September, 1802.

Thy soul was like a Star, and dwelt apart.   *London*, 1802.

So didst thou travel on life's common way,
In cheerful godliness.   *Ibid.*

We must be free or die, who speak the tongue
That Shakespeare spake; the faith and morals hold
Which Milton held.
Poems dedicated to National Independence. Part i. *Sonnet* xvi.

Every gift of noble origin
Is breathed upon by Hope's perpetual breath. *Ibid. Sonnet* xx.

A few strong instincts, and a few plain rules.
                        Ibid. Part ii.   *Sonnet* xii.

Turning, for them who pass, the common dust
Of servile opportunity to gold.   *Desultory Stanzas.*

That God's most dreaded instrument,
In working out a pure intent,
Is man—arrayed for mutual slaughter;
Yea, Carnage is his daughter.[1]
         Ode. 1815.

The sightless Milton, with his hair
Around his placid temples curled;
And Shakespeare at his side,—a freight,
If clay could think and mind were weight,
For him who bore the world !
       The Italian Itinerant.

Meek Nature's evening comment on the shows
That for oblivion take their daily birth
From all the fuming vanities of earth.
    Sky-Prospect, from the Plain of France.

The monumental pomp of age
Was with this goodly Personage ;
A stature undepressed in size,
Unbent, which rather seemed to rise,
In open victory o'er the weight
Of seventy years, to loftier height.
    The White Doe of Rylstone. Canto iii.

        Babylon,
Learned and wise, hath perished utterly,
Nor leaves her Speech one word to aid the sigh
That would lament her.
   Eccles. Sonnets. Part i. xxv.   *Missions and Travels.*

"As thou these ashes, little Brook ! wilt bear
Into the Avon, Avon to the tide
Of Severn, Severn to the narrow seas,
Into main ocean they, this deed accursed
An emblem yields to friends and enemies,
How the bold Teacher's doctrine, sanctified
By truth, shall spread, throughout the world dispersed."[2]
   Eccles. Sonnets. Part ii. xvii. *To Wickliffe.*

---

[1] Altered in later editions by omitting the last two lines, the others reading

    But Man is thy most awful instrument,
    In working out a pure intent.

[2] In obedience to the order of the Council of Constance, (1415,) the remains of Wickliffe were exhumed and burnt to ashes, and these cast into the Swift, a neighbouring brook running hard by, and "thus this brook hath conveyed his ashes into Avon; Avon into Severn, Severn into the narrow seas, they into the main ocean. And thus the ashes of Wickliffe are the emblem of his doctrine, which now is dispersed all the world over."—Fuller, *Church History, Sec.* ii. *B.* 4, *Par.* 53.

Fox says : "What Heraclitus would not laugh, or what Democritus would not weep ? . . . . For though they digged up his body, burnt

                    The feather, whence the pen
Was shaped that traced the lives of these good men,
Dropped from an Angel's wing.[1]
                 Ibid.   Part iii. v.   *Walton's Book of Lives.*

Meek Walton's heavenly memory.   *Ibid.*

But who would force the Soul, tilts with a straw
Against a Champion cased in adamant.
     Ibid.   Part iii. vii.   *Persecution of the Scottish Covenanters.*

                    Where music dwells
Lingering, and wandering on as loth to die
Like thoughts whose very sweetness yieldeth proof
That they were born for immortality.
         Ibid.   Part iii. xliii.   *Inside of King's Chapel, Cambridge.*

Myriads of daisies have shone forth in flower
Near the lark's nest, and in their natural hour
Have passed away; less happy than the one
That, by the unwilling ploughshare, died to prove
The tender charm of poetry and love.
                 Poems composed in Summer of 1833.   xxxvii.

Nor less I deem that there are Powers
Which of themselves our minds impress;
That we can feed this mind of ours
In a wise passiveness.   *Expostulation and Reply.*

Up! up! my Friend, and quit your books,
Or surely you 'll grow double :
Up! up! my Friend, and clear your looks;
Why all this toil and trouble?   *The Tables Turned.*

Come forth into the light of things,
Let Nature be your Teacher.   *Ibid.*

---

his bones, and drowned his ashes, yet the word of God and truth of his
doctrine, with the fruit and success thereof, they could not burn."
                     Book of Martyrs.   Vol. i. *p.* 606, *ed.* 1641.
  " Some prophet of that day said,
            'The Avon to the Severn runs,
               The Severn to the sea ;
            And Wickliffe's dust shall spread abroad,
               Wide as the waters be.' "
From *Address before the "Sons of New Hampshire,"* by Daniel Webster, 1849.
   These lines are similarly quoted by the Rev. John Cumming in the *Voices
of the Dead.*
       [1] The pen wherewith thou dost so heavenly sing
         Made of a quill from an Angel's wing.
                             Henry Constable, *Sonnet.*
                     Whose noble praise
         Deserves a quill pluckt from an angel's wing.
                             Dorothy Berry, *Sonnet.*

THE TABLES TURNED—*continued.*]

One impulse from a vernal wood
May teach you more of man,
Of moral evil and of good,
Than all the sages can.   *Ibid.*

In that sweet mood when pleasant thoughts
Bring sad thoughts to the mind.
                        Lines written in Early Spring.

And 't is my faith that every flower
Enjoys the air it breathes.   *Ibid.*

O Reader ! had you in your mind
Such stores as silent thought can bring,
O gentle Reader ! you would find
A tale in everything.   *Simon Lee.*

I 've heard of hearts unkind, kind deeds
With coldness still returning;
Alas ! the gratitude of men
Hath oftener left me mourning.   *Ibid.*

One that would peep and botanize
Upon his mother's grave.   *A Poet's Epitaph.* *St.* 5.

He murmurs near the running brooks
A music sweeter than their own.   *Ibid.* *St.* 10.

And you must love him, ere to you
He will seem worthy of your love.   *Ibid.* *St.* 11.

The harvest of a quiet eye,
That broods and sleeps on his own heart. *Ibid.* *St.* 13.

My eyes are dim with childish tears,
My heart is idly stirred,
For the same sound is in my ears
Which in those days I heard.   *The Fountain.*

A happy youth, and their old age
Is beautiful and free.   *Ibid.*

And often, glad no more,
We wear a face of joy, because
We have been glad of yore.   *Ibid.*

Maidens withering on the stalk.   *Personal Talk.* *St.* 1.

Dreams, books, are each a world; and books, we know,
Are a substantial world, both pure and good ;
Round these, with tendrils strong as flesh and blood,
Our pastime and our happiness will grow.

                .   .   .   .

The gentle Lady married to the Moor,
And heavenly Una with her milk-white Lamb. *Ibid.* *St.* 3.

PERSONAL TALK—*continued.*]

Blessings be with them, and eternal praise,
Who gave us nobler loves, and nobler cares,
The Poets, who on earth have made us heirs
Of truth and pure delight by heavenly lays !   *Ibid.   St. 4.*

Stern Daughter of the Voice of God !   *Ode to Duty.*

A light to guide, a rod
To check the erring, and reprove.   *Ibid.*

Give unto me, made lowly wise,
The spirit of self-sacrifice ;
The confidence of reason give ;
And in the light of truth thy Bondman let me live.   *Ibid.*

Who, doomed to go in company with Pain,
And Fear, and Bloodshed, miserable train !
Turns his necessity to glorious gain.
                    Character of the Happy Warrior.

Controls them and subdues, transmutes, bereaves
Of their bad influence, and their good receives.   *Ibid.*

But who, if he be called upon to face
Some awful moment to which Heaven has joined
Great issues, good or bad for humankind,
Is happy as a Lover.   *Ibid.*

Whom neither shape of anger can dismay,
Nor thought of tender happiness betray.   *Ibid.*

Sad fancies do we then affect,
In luxury of disrespect
To our own prodigal excess
Of too familiar happiness.   *Ode to Lycoris.*

Or, shipwrecked, kindles on the coast
False fires, that others may be lost.   *To the Lady Fleming.*

Small service is true service while it lasts :
Of humblest Friends, bright Creature ! scorn not one :
The Daisy, by the shadow that it casts,
Protects the lingering dew-drop from the Sun.
                    To a Child.   Written in her Album.

Men who can hear the Decalogue, and feel
No self-reproach.   *The Old Cumberland Beggar.*

As in the eye of Nature he has lived,
So in the eye of Nature let him die !   *Ibid.*

To be a Prodigal's Favourite,—then, worse truth,
A Miser's Pensioner,—behold our lot !   *The Small Celandine.*

The light that never was on sea or land,
The consecration, and the Poet's dream.
            Suggested by a Picture of Peele Castle in a Storm.   St. 4.

A Power is passing from the earth.
                        Lines on the Expected Dissolution of Mr. Fox.

But hushed be every thought that springs
From out the bitterness of things.   *Addressed to Sir G. H. B.*

Since every mortal power of Coleridge
Was frozen at its marvellous source ;
The rapt one, of the god-like forehead,
The heaven-eyed creature sleeps in earth :
And Lamb, the frolic and the gentle,
Has vanished from his lonely hearth.
                Extempore Effusion upon the Death of James Hogg

How fast has brother followed brother,
From sunshine to the sunless land !   *Ibid.*

            But yet I know, where'er I go,
That there hath passed away a glory from the earth.
                Ode.   Intimations of Immortality.   St. 2.

Our birth is but a sleep and a forgetting :
The soul that rises with us, our life's Star,
    Hath had elsewhere its setting,
        And cometh from afar :
    Not in entire forgetfulness,
    And not in utter darkness,
But trailing clouds of glory, do we come
    From God, who is our home :
Heaven lies about us in our infancy.

            .   .   .   .

At length the Man perceives it die away,
And fade into the light of common day.   *Ibid.   St. 5.*

The thought of our past years in me doth breed
Perpetual benediction.   *Ibid.   St. 9.*

            Those obstinate questionings
            Of sense and outward things,
            Fallings from us, vanishings ;
            Blank misgivings of a Creature
Moving about in worlds not realized,
High instincts before which our mortal Nature
Did tremble like a guilty thing surprised.   *Ibid   St. 9.*

            Truths that wake,
            To perish never.   *Ibid.*

ODE. INTIMATIONS OF IMMORTALITY—*continued.*]
>   Though inland far we be,
> Our souls have sight of that immortal sea
>   Which brought us hither.   *Ibid.*

In years that bring the philosophic mind.   *Ibid. St.* 10.

The Clouds that gather round the setting sun
Do take a sober colouring from an eye
That hath kept watch o'er man's mortality.

>   .   .   .   .   .   .

To me the meanest flower that blows can give
Thoughts that do often lie too deep for tears.   *Ibid. St.* 11.

The vision and the faculty divine;
Yet wanting the accomplishment of verse.
>   *The Excursion. Book* i.

The imperfect offices of prayer and praise.   *Ibid.*

>   That mighty orb of song,
> The divine Milton.   *Ibid.*

>   The good die first,
> And they whose hearts are dry as summer dust
> Burn to the socket.   *Ibid.*

This dull product of a scoffer's pen.   *Ibid. Book* ii.

With battlements that on their restless fronts
Bore stars.   *Ibid.*

Wisdom is ofttimes nearer when we stoop
Than when we soar.   *Ibid. Book* iii.

Wrongs unredressed, or insults unavenged.   *Ibid.*

>   Monastic brotherhood, upon rock
> Aerial.   *Ibid.*

The intellectual power, through words and things,
Went sounding on, a dim and perilous way![1]   *Ibid.*

Society became my glittering bride,
And airy hopes my children.   *Ibid.*

There is a luxury in self-dispraise;
And inward self-disparagement affords
To meditative spleen a grateful feast.   *Ibid. Book* iv.

>   Pan himself,
> The simple shepherd's awe-inspiring god !   *Ibid.*

>   I have seen
> A curious child, who dwelt upon a tract

---

[1] Three sleepless nights I passed in sounding on,
Through words and things, a dim and perilous way.
>   *The Borderers, Act* iv. *Sc.* 2.

THE EXCURSION—*continued.*]

Of inland ground, applying to his ear
The convolutions of a smooth-lipped shell ;
To which, in silence hushed, his very soul
Listened intensely ; and his countenance soon
Brightened with joy ; for from within were heard
Murmurings, whereby the monitor expressed
Mysterious union with its native sea.   *Ibid.   Book* vi.

One in whom persuasion and belief
Had ripened into faith, and faith become
A passionate intuition.   *Ibid.*

Spires whose " silent finger points to heaven."[1]   *Ibid.*

Ah ! what a warning for a thoughtless man,
Could field or grove, could any spot of earth,
Show to his eye an image of the pangs
Which it hath witnessed ; render back an echo
Of the sad steps by which it hath been trod !   *Ibid.*

And, when the stream
Which overflowed the soul was passed away,
A consciousness remained that it had left,
Deposited upon the silent shore
Of memory, images and precious thoughts
That shall not die, and cannot be destroyed.   *Ibid.   Book* vii.

Wisdom married to immortal verse.[2]   *Ibid.*

A Man he seems of cheerful yesterdays
And confident to-morrows.   *Ibid.   Book* vii.

The primal duties shine aloft, like stars ;
The charities that soothe, and heal, and bless,
Are scattered at the feet of Man, like flowers.   *Ibid.   Book* ix.

By happy chance we saw
A twofold image ; on a grassy bank
A snow-white ram, and in the crystal flood
Another and the same ![3]   *Ibid.*

---

[1] An instinctive taste teaches men to build their churches in flat countries
with spire-steeples, which, as they cannot be referred to any other object,
point as with silent finger to the sky and stars.—Coleridge, *The Friend,
No.* 14.

[2]   Lap me in soft Lydian airs,
           Married to immortal verse.—Milton, *L'Allegro.*
[3] Mounts from her funeral pyre on wings of flame,
        And soars and shines another and the same.
                              Darwin, *The Botanic Garden.*
An equivalent of the Latin phrase "alter et idem," Joseph Hall's
Mundus alter et idem, published *circa* 1600.

Another morn
Risen on mid-noon.[1]   *The Prelude.   Book* vi.

Bliss was it in that dawn to be alive,
But to be young was very Heaven !   *Ibid,   Book* xi.

The budding rose above the rose full blown.   *Ibid*

And thou art long, and lank, and brown,
As is the ribbed sea sand.

     .   .   .   .   .

And listens like a three years' child.
            Lines added to the Ancient Mariner.[2]

—□—

ROBERT SOUTHEY.   1774—1843.

How beautiful is night !
A dewy freshness fills the silent air;
No mist obscures, nor cloud, nor speck, nor stain,
  Breaks the serene of heaven :
In full-orbed glory, yonder moon divine
Rolls through the dark-blue depths.
    Beneath her steady ray
    The desert-circle spreads,
Like the round ocean, girdled with the sky.
  How beautiful is night !   *Thalaba.*

They sin who tell us Love can die :
With Life all other passions fly,
  All others are but vanity.
     The Curse of Kehama.   Canto x. *St.* 10.

    Love is indestructible :
  Its holy flame for ever burneth ;
From Heaven it came, to Heaven returneth.

     .   .   .   .

  It soweth here with toil and care,
But the harvest-time of Love is there.   *Ibid.*

  Oh ! when a Mother meets on high
    The Babe she lost in infancy,
  Hath she not then, for pains and fears,
    The day of woe, the watchful night,
    For all her sorrow, all her tears,
  An over-payment of delight ?   *Ibid.   Canto* x. *St.* 11.

Thou hast been called, O sleep ! the friend of woe;
But 't is the happy that have called thee so.
        Ibid.   Canto xv. *St.* 11.

---

[1] Verbatim from *Paradise Lost, Book* v. *Line* 310.
[2] Wordsworth, in his notes to *We are Seven,* claims to have written these
lines in the *Ancient Mariner.*

I

Blue, darkly, deeply, beautifully blue.[1]   *Madoc in Wales.* **v.**

And last of all an Admiral came,
A terrible man with a terrible name,—
A name which you all know by sight very well;
But which no one can speak, and no one can spell.
                                    The March to Moscow.   St. 8.

He passed a cottage with a double coach-house,
  A cottage of gentility;
    And he owned with a grin,
    That his favourite sin
  Is pride that apes humility.[2]   *The Devil's Walk.*

The Satanic school.
        From the Original Preface to the Vision of Judgment.

" But what good came of it at last ?"
  Quoth little Peterkin.
" Why that I cannot tell," said he;
" But 't was a famous victory."   *The Battle of Blenheim.*

  Where Washington hath left
    His awful memory
    A light for after times !
        Ode written during the War with America, **1814**

My days among the Dead are passed;
  Around me I behold,
Where'er these casual eyes are cast,
  The mighty minds of old ;
My never-failing friends are they,
  With whom I converse day by day. *Occasional Pieces.* xviii.

    The march of intellect.[3]
        *Colloquies on the Progress and Prospects of Society.
        Vol.* ii. *p.* 360.

—□—

JOSEPH HOPKINSON. 1770—1842.

Hail, Columbia ! happy land !
Hail, ye heroes ! heaven-born band !
Who fought and died in freedom's cause.   *Hail Columbia.*

—□—

WILLIAM PITT. —— —1840.

A strong nor'-wester's blowing, Bill ;
  Hark ! don't ye hear it roar now !
Lord help 'em, how I pities them
  Unhappy folks on shore now !   *The Sailor's Consolation*

---

[1] Quoted by Byron, *post.*
[2] Cf. Coleridge, *The Devil's Thoughts.*
[3] The march of the human mind is slow.—Burke, *Speech on Conciliation
with America.*

CHARLES LAMB. 1775—1834.

Gone before
To that unknown and silent shore.   *Hester. St. 7.*

I have had playmates, I have had companions,
In my days of childhood, in my joyful school-days,
All, all are gone, the old familiar faces.   *Old Familiar Faces.*

And half had stagger'd that stout Stagirite.
                                    Written at Cambridge.

Who first invented work and bound the free
And holiday-rejoicing spirit down
          .   .   .   .
To that dry drudgery at the desk's dead wood?
     .   .   .   .
Sabbathless Satan !   *Work.*

A clear fire, a clean hearth, and the rigour of the game.
                         Mrs. Battle's Opinions on Whist.

Books which are no books.   *Detached Thoughts on Books.*

——□——

THOMAS DIBDIN. 1771—1841.

O, it 's a snug little island !
A right little, tight little island ! *The Snug Little Island.*

——□——

SAMUEL TAYLOR COLERIDGE. 1772—1834.

We were the first that ever burst
Into that silent sea.   *The Ancient Mariner. Part* ii.

As idle as a painted ship
Upon a painted ocean.   *Ibid.*

Water, water, everywhere,
Nor any drop to drink.   *Ibid.*

Alone, alone, all, all alone,
Alone on a wide, wide sea.   *Ibid. Part* iv.

A spring of love gushed from my heart,
And I blessed them unaware.   *Ibid.*

O sleep ! it is a gentle thing,
Beloved from pole to pole.   *Ibid. Part* v.

A noise like of a hidden brook
In the leafy month of June,
That to the sleeping woods all night
Singeth a quiet tune.   *Ibid.*

Like one that on a lonesome road
Doth walk in fear and dread.

THE ANCIENT MARINER—*continued.*]

And, having once turned round, walks on
And turns no more his head,
Because he knows a frightful fiend
Doth close behind him tread.   *Ibid.*   Part vi.

So lonely 't was, that God himself
Scarce seemed there to be.   *Ibid.*   Part vii.

He prayeth well, who loveth well
Both man and bird and beast.   *Ibid.*

He prayeth best, who loveth best
All things, both great and small.   *Ibid.*

A sadder and a wiser man,
He rose the morrow morn.   *Ibid.*

And the Spring comes slowly up this way.   *Christabel. Part* i.

A lady so richly clad as she —
Beautiful exceedingly.   *Ibid.*

Carved with figures strange and sweet,
All made out of the carver's brain.   *Ibid.*

Her gentle limbs did she undress,
And lay down in her loveliness.   *Ibid.*

A sight to dream of, not to tell!   *Ibid.*

That saints will aid if men will call:
For the blue sky bends over all!   *Conclusion to Part* i.

Each matin bell, the Baron saith,
Knells us back to a world of death.   *Ibid.*   Part ii.

Alas! they had been friends in youth;
But whispering tongues can poison truth;
And constancy lives in realms above;
And life is thorny, and youth is vain;
And to be wroth with one we love,
Doth work like madness in the brain.   *Ibid.*

They stood aloof, the scars remaining,—
Like cliff which had been rent asunder;
A dreary sea now flows between.   *Ibid.*

Perhaps 't is pretty to force together
Thoughts so all unlike each other;
To mutter and mock a broken charm,
To dally with wrong that does no harm.   *Conclusion to Part* ii.

Yes, while I stood and gazed, my temples bare,
And shot my being through earth, sea, and air,
Possessing all things with intensest love.
O Liberty! my spirit felt thee there.   *France. An Ode.* v.

Forth from his dark and lonely hiding-place,
(Portentous sight!) the owlet Atheism,
Sailing on obscene wings athwart the noon,
Drops his blue-fringed lids, and holds them close,
And, hooting at the glorious Sun in Heaven,
Cries out, "Where is it?"   *Tears in Solitude.*

And the Devil did grin, for his darling sin
    Is pride that apes humility.[1]   *The Devil's Thoughts.*

    All thoughts, all passions, all delights,
        Whatever stirs this mortal frame,
    All are but ministers of Love,
        And feed his sacred flame.   *Love.*

Strongly it bears us along in swelling and limitless billows.
Nothing before and nothing behind but the sky and the ocean.
        The Homeric Hexameter.   Translated from Schiller.

In the hexameter rises the fountain's silvery column;
In the pentameter aye falling in melody back.
                        The Ovidian Elegiac Metre.

Blest hour! it was a luxury—to be!
            Reflections on having left a Place of Retirement.

Hast thou a charm to stay the morning star
In his steep course?   *Hymn in the Vale of Chamouni.*

Risest from forth thy silent sea of pines.   *Ibid.*

Motionless torrents! silent cataracts!   *Ibid.*

Ye living flowers that skirt the eternal frost.   *Ibid.*

Earth, with her thousand voices, praises God.   *Ibid.*

        A mother is a mother still,
            The holiest thing alive.   *The Three Graves.*

        Never, believe me,
        Appear the Immortals,
        Never alone.   *The Visit of the Gods.[2]*

        The Knight's bones are dust,
        And his good sword rust;
            His soul is with the saints, I trust.   *The Knight's Tomb.*

To know, to esteem, to love,—and then to part,
Makes up life's tale to many a feeling heart!
                    On Taking leave of ——, 1817.

---

[1] His favourite sin
    Is pride that apes humility.
                    Southey, *The Devil's Walk.*

[2] Imitated from Schiller.

In Xanadu did Kubla Khan
A stately pleasure-dome decree :
Where Alph, the sacred river, ran
Through caverns measureless to man
    Down to a sunless sea.   *Kubla Khan*

A damsel with a dulcimer
In a vision once I saw :
It was an Abyssinian maid,
And on her dulcimer she played,
Singing of Mount Abora.   *Ibid.*

For he on honey-dew hath fed,
And drunk the milk of Paradise.   *Ibid.*

Ere sin could blight or sorrow fade,
    Death came with friendly care ;
The opening bud to Heaven conveyed,
    And bade it blossom there.   *Epitaph on an Infant.*

The grand old ballad of Sir Patrick Spence.   *Dejection.* **St. 1.**

Joy is the sweet voice, Joy the luminous cloud.
    We in ourselves rejoice !
And thence flows all that charms or ear or sight,
    All melodies the echoes of that voice,
All colours a suffusion from that light.   *Ibid.* **St. 5.**

Greatness and goodness are not means, but ends !
Hath he not always treasures, always friends,
The good great man ? three treasures,—love, and light,
And calm thoughts, regular as infants' breath ;
And three firm friends, more sure than day and night,—
Himself, his Maker, and the angel Death.   *Reproof.*

    Joy rises in me, like a summer's morn.
              A Christmas Carol. **viii.**

I counted two-and-seventy stenches,
All well defined, and several stinks.   *Cologne.*

The river Rhine, it is well known,
Doth wash your city of Cologne ;
But tell me, nymphs ! what power divine
Shall henceforth wash the river Rhine ?   *Ibid.*

Flowers are lovely ; Love is flower-like ;
Friendship is a sheltering tree ;
O the Joys, that came down shower-like,
Of Friendship, Love, and Liberty,
        Ere I was old !   *Youth and Age.*

The intelligible forms of ancient poets,
The fair humanities of old religion,
The power, the beauty, and the majesty,
That had their haunts in dale, or piny mountain,
Or forest by slow stream, or pebbly spring,
Or chasms and watery depths; all these have vanished;
They live no longer in the faith of reason.
Wallenstein. Part i. *Act* ii. *Sc.* 4.

Clothing the palpable and familiar
With golden exhalations of the dawn.
The Death of Wallenstein. Act i. *Sc.* 1.

Often do the spirits
Of great events stride on before the events,
And in to-day already walks to-morrow. *Ibid. Act* v. *Sc.* 1.

I have heard of reasons manifold
Why Love must needs be blind,
But this the best of all I hold,—
His eyes are in his mind.
To a Lady, offended by a Sportive Observation.

What outward form and feature are
He guesseth but in part;
But what within is good and fair
He seeth with the heart. *Ibid.*

My eyes make pictures, when they are shut. *A Day-Dream.*

Be that blind bard, who on the Chian strand,
By those deep sounds possessed with inward light,
Beheld the Iliad and the Odyssey,
Rise to the swelling of the voiceful sea. *Fancy in Nubibus.*

Our myriad-minded Shakespeare. *Biog. Lit. Ch.* xv.

A dwarf sees farther than the giant when he has the giant's shoulder
to mount on.[1] *The Friend. Sec.* i. *Essay* 8.

——□——

JAMES MONTGOMERY. 1771—1854.

When the good man yields his breath
(For the good man never dies).[2]
The Wanderer of Switzerland. Part v.

Friend after friend departs,—
Who hath not lost a friend?
There is no union here of hearts,
That finds not here an end. *Friends.*

---

[1] A dwarf on a giant's shoulders sees further of the two.—Herbert, *Jacula Prudentum.*
Grant them but dwarfs, yet stand they on giants' shoulders, and may see the further.—Fuller, *The Holy State, Ch.* vi. 8.
[2] Θνήσκειν μὴ λέγε τοὺς ἀγαθούς.—Callim, *Ep.* x.

Once, in the flight of ages past,
There lived a man.   *The Common Lot.*

'T is not the whole of life to live :
    Nor all of death to die.   *The Issues of Life and Death.*

If God hath made this world so fair,
Where sin and death abound,
How beautiful beyond compare
Will paradise be found !
       The Earth full of God's Goodness.

Here in the body pent,
Absent from Him I roam ;
Yet nightly pitch my moving tent
A day's march nearer home.   *At Home in Heaven.*

Gashed with honourable scars,
    Low in Glory's lap they lie ;
Though they fell, they fell like stars,
    Streaming splendour through the sky.
       The Battle of Alexandria.

Prayer is the soul's sincere desire,
    Uttered or unexpressed,
The motion of a hidden fire
    That trembles in the breast.
       Original Hymns.   *What is Prayer ?*

—□—

WILLIAM ROBERT SPENCER. 1770—1834.

Too late I stayed,—forgive the crime,—
    Unheeded flew the hours ;
How noiseless falls the foot of time,[1]
    That only treads on flowers. *Lines to Lady A. Hamilton.*

—□—

THOMAS CAMPBELL. 1777—1844.

'T is distance lends enchantment to the view,
And robes the mountain in its azure hue.
       Pleasures of Hope.   *Part* i. *Line* **7.**

But hope, the charmer, lingered still behind.   *Line* **40.**

O Heaven ! he cried, my bleeding country save.   *Line* **359.**

Hope, for a season, bade the world farewell,
And Freedom shriek'd—as Kosciusko fell !   *Line* **381.**

On Prague's proud arch the fires of ruin glow,
His blood-dyed waters murmuring far below.   *Line* **385.**

And rival all but Shakespeare's name below.   *Line* **472.**

---

[1] Noiseless foot of time.—Shakespeare, *All 's Well that Ends Well,*
Act v. *Sc.* 3.

PLEASURES OF HOPE—*continued.*]

Who hath not owned, with rapture-smitten frame,
The power of grace, the magic of a name?   *Part* ii. *Line* 5.

Without the smile from partial beauty won,
O what were man?—a world without a sun.   *Line* 21.

The world was sad,—the garden was a wild;
And Man, the hermit, sighed—till Woman smil'd.   *Line* 37.

While Memory watches o'er the sad review
Of joys that faded like the morning dew.   *Line* 45.

There shall be love, when genial morn appears,
Like pensive Beauty smiling in her tears.   *Part* ii. *Line* 95.

And Muse on Nature with a poet's eye.   *Line* 98.

That gems the starry girdle of the year.   *Line* 194.

Melt, and dispel, ye spectre-doubts, that roll
Cimmerian darkness o'er the parting soul!   *Line* 263.

O Star-eyed Science! hast thou wandered there,
To waft us home the message of despair?   *Line* 325.

But, sad as angels for the good man's sin,
Weep to record, and blush to give it in.[1]   *Line* 357.

Cease, every joy, to glimmer on my mind,
But leave—oh! leave the light of Hope behind!
What though my winged hours of bliss have been,
Like angel-visits, few and far between.[2]   *Line* 375.

The hunter and the deer a shade.[3] *O'Conner's Child. St.* 5.

Another's sword has laid him low,
    Another's and another's;
And every hand that dealt the blow,
    Ah me! it was a brother's!   *Ibid.   St.* 10.

'T is the sunset of life gives me mystical lore,
And coming events cast their shadows before.[4]
                    Lochiel's Warning.

With his back to the field, and his feet to the foe.   *Ibid.*

I.
Ye mariners of England!
    That guard our native seas:
Whose flag has braved a thousand years,
    The battle and the breeze!   *Ye Mariners of England.*

[1] Cf. Sterne, p. 191.
[2] Cf. Norris, p. 141, and Blair, p. 180.
[3] Verbatim from Freneau's *Indian Burying-Ground.*
[4] Poets are the hierophants of an unapprehended inspiration; the mirrors of the gigantic shadows which futurity casts upon the present.—Shelley, *A Defence of Poetry.*

YE MARINERS OF ENGLAND—*continued.*]

III.

Britannia needs no bulwarks,
  No towers along the steep;
Her march is o'er the mountain-waves,
  Her home is on the deep.

IV.

The meteor flag of England
  Shall yet terrific burn;
Till danger's troubled night depart,
  And the star of peace return.

The combat deepens. On, ye brave,
Who rush to glory, or the grave!   *Hohenlinden.*

There came to the beach a poor exile of Erin;
  The dew on his thin robe was heavy and chill!
For his country he sighed, when at twilight repairing,
  To wander alone by the wind-beaten hill. *The Exile of Erin.*

To bear is to conquer our fate.
            On visiting a Scene in Argyleshire.

The sentinel stars set their watch in the sky.[1]
            The Soldier's Dream.

In life's morning march, when my bosom was young.   *Ibid.*

But sorrow returned with the dawning of morn,
And the voice in my dreaming ear melted away.   *Ibid.*

There was silence deep as death;
And the boldest held his breath,
For a time.   *Battle of the Baltic.*

Triumphal arch, that fill'st the sky,
  When storms prepare to part;
I ask not proud Philosophy
  To teach me what thou art.   *To the Rainbow.*

A stoic of the woods,—a man without a tear.
           Gertrude. Part i. *St.* 23.

O Love! in such a wilderness as this.   *Ibid. Part* iii. *St.* 1.

The torrent's smoothness, ere it dash below!
           Ibid. Part iii. *St.* 5.

Drink ye to her that each loves best,
  And if you nurse a flame
That's told but to her mutual breast,
  We will not ask her name.   *Drink ye to her.*

To live in hearts we leave behind,
Is not to die.   *Hallowed Ground.*

---

[1] The starres, bright centinels of the skies.
  Habington, *Castara, Dialogue between Night and Araphil.*

JONATHAN M. SEWALL. 1748—1808.

No pent-up Utica contracts your powers,
But the whole boundless continent is yours.
$\qquad$ *Epilogue to Cato.*[1]

——□——

ROBERT EMMET. 1780—1803.

Let there be no inscription upon my tomb; let no man write my epitaph:
no man can write my epitaph.
$\qquad$ *Speech on his Trial and Conviction for High Treason,*
September, 1803.

——□——

WALTER SCOTT. 1771—1832.

Such is the custom of Branksome Hall.
$\qquad$ *The Lay of the Last Minstrel.*   *Canto* i. *St.* vii.

If thou wouldst view fair Melrose aright,
Go visit it by the pale moonlight.
$\qquad$ *Canto* ii. *St.* 1.

O fading honours of the dead !
O high ambition, lowly laid !
$\qquad$ *Canto* ii. *St.* 10.

I was not always a man of woe.
$\qquad$ *Canto* ii. *St.* 12.

I cannot tell how the truth may be;
I say the tale as 't was said to me.
$\qquad$ *Canto* ii. *St.* 22.

In peace, Love tunes the shepherd's reed;
In war, he mounts the warrior's steed;
In halls, in gay attire is seen;
In hamlets, dances on the green.
Love rules the court, the camp, the grove,
And men below, and saints above;
For love is heaven, and heaven is love.
$\qquad$ *Canto* iii. *St.* 1.

Her blue eyes sought the west afar,
For lovers love the western star.
$\qquad$ *Canto* iii. *St.* 24.

Along thy wild and willowed shore.
$\qquad$ *Canto* iv. *St.* 1.

$\qquad\qquad$ Ne'er
Was flattery lost on Poet's ear :
A simple race ! they waste their toil
For the vain tribute of a smile.
$\qquad$ *Canto* iv. *St.* 35.

Call it not vain;—they do not err
Who say, that, when the Poet dies,
Mute Nature mourns her worshipper,
And celebrates his obsequies.
$\qquad$ *Canto* v. *St.* 1.

[1] Written for the Bow Street Theatre, Portsmouth, New Hampshire.

THE LAY OF THE LAST MINSTREL—*continued.*]

    True love 's the gift which God has given
    To man alone beneath the heaven :
      It is not fantasy's hot fire,
        Whose wishes, soon as granted, fly ;
      It liveth not in fierce desire,
        With dead desire it doth not die ;
    It is the secret sympathy,
    The silver link, the silken tie,
    Which heart to heart, and mind to mind,
    In body and in soul can bind.   *Canto* v. *St.* 13.

    Breathes there the man, with soul so dead,
    Who never to himself hath said,
      This is my own, my native land !
    Whose heart hath ne'er within him burned,
    As home his footsteps he hath turned
      From wandering on a foreign strand ?
    If such there breathe, go, mark him well ;
    For him no Minstrel raptures swell ;
    High though his titles, proud his name,
    Boundless his wealth as wish can claim ;
    Despite those titles, power, and pelf,
    The wretch, concentred all in self,
    Living, shall forfeit fair renown,
    And, doubly dying, shall go down
    To the vile dust, from whence he sprung,
    Unwept, unhonour'd, and unsung.   *Canto* vi. *St.* 1.

    O Caledonia ! stern and wild,
    Meet nurse for a poetic child !
    Land of brown heath and shaggy wood ;
    Land of the mountain and the flood.   *Canto* vi. *St.* 2.

Profaned the God-given strength, and marred the lofty line.
                Marmion.   *Introduc. to Canto* 1.

Just at the age 'twixt boy and youth,
When thought is speech, and speech is truth.
                    Introduc. to Canto ii.

When, musing on companions gone,
We doubly feel ourselves alone.   *Ibid.*

 'T is an old tale and often told ;
    But did my fate and wish agree,
 Ne'er had been read, in story old,
 Of maiden true betrayed for gold,
    That loved, or was avenged, like me.   *Canto* ii. *St.* 27.

MARMION—*continued*.]

> In the lost battle,
>> Borne down by the flying,
> Where mingles war's rattle
>> With groans of the dying.   *Canto* iii. *St.* 10.

Where's the coward that would not dare
  To fight for such a land?   *Canto* iv. *St.* 30.

Lightly from fair to fair he flew,
And loved to plead, lament, and sue;
Suit lightly won, and short-lived pain,
For monarchs seldom sigh in vain.   *Canto* v. *St.* 9.

With a smile on her lips, and a tear in her eye.   *Canto* v. *St.* 12.

But woe awaits a country when
She sees the tears of bearded men.   *Canto* v. *St.* 16.

> And dar'st thou then
To beard the lion in his den,
  The Douglas in his hall?   *Canto* vi. *St.* 14.

O, what a tangled web we weave,
When first we practise to deceive!   *Canto* vi. *St.* 17.

O woman! in our hours of ease,
Uncertain, coy, and hard to please,
And variable as the shade
By the light quivering aspen made;
When pain and anguish wring the brow,
A ministering angel thou!   *Canto* vi. *St.* 30.

"Charge, Chester, charge! on, Stanley, on!"
Were the last words of Marmion.   *Canto* vi. *St.* 32.

O for a blast of that dread horn [1]
On Fontarabian echoes borne.   *Canto* vi. *St.* 33.

To all, to each, a fair good night,
And pleasing dreams, and slumbers light!
            Ibid.   L'Envoy.   To the Reader.

In listening mood, she seemed to stand,
The guardian Naiad of the strand.
        The Lady of the Lake.   Canto i. *St.* 17.

And ne'er did Grecian chisel trace
A Nymph, a Naiad, or a Grace,
Of finer form, or lovelier face.   *Canto* i. *St.* 18.

A foot more light, a step more true,
Ne'er from the heath-flower dashed the dew.   *Ibid.*

---

[1] O for the voice of that wild horn.—*Rob Roy, Ch.* 2.

THE LADY OF THE LAKE—*continued.*]

On his bold visage middle age
Had slightly pressed its signet sage,
Yet had not quenched the open truth
And fiery vehemence of youth :
Forward and frolic glee was there,
The will to do, the soul to dare.   *Canto* i. *St.* 21.

Sleep the sleep that knows not breaking,
Morn of toil, nor night of waking.   *Canto* i. *St.* 31.

Hail to the Chief who in triumph advances !   *Canto* ii. *St.* 19.

Some feelings are to mortals given,
With less of earth in them than heaven.   *Canto* ii. *St.* 22.

Time rolls his ceaseless course.   *Canto* iii. *St.* 1.

Like the dew on the mountain,
  Like the foam on the river,
Like the bubble on the fountain,
  Thou art gone, and for ever !   *Canto* iii. *St.* 16.

The rose is fairest when 't is budding new,
  And hope is brightest when it dawns from fears.
The rose is sweetest washed with morning dew,
  And love is loveliest when embalmed in tears.   *Canto* iv. *St.* 1.

Art thou a friend to Roderick ?   *Canto* iv. *St.* 30.

Come one, come all ! this rock shall fly
From its firm base as soon as I.   *Canto* v. *St.* 10.

And the stern joy which warriors feel
In foemen worthy of their steel.   *Ibid.*

Who o'er the herd would wish to reign,
Fantastic, fickle, fierce, and vain !—
Vain as the leaf upon the stream,
And fickle as a changeful dream ;
Fantastic as a woman's mood,
And fierce as Frenzy's fevered blood.
Thou many-headed monster thing,
O, who would wish to be thy king !   *Canto* v. *St.* 30.

  Where, where was Roderick then ?
One blast upon his bugle horn
  Were worth a thousand men.   *Canto* vi. *St.* 18.

Come as the winds come, when
  Forests are rended ;
Come as the waves come, when
  Navies are stranded.   *Pibroch of Donald Dhu.*

In man's most dark extremity
  Oft succour dawns from Heaven.
                        The Lord of the Isles.   *Canto* i. *St.* 20.

Spangling the wave with lights as vain
As pleasures in the vale of pain,
    That dazzle as they fade.   *Canto* i. *St.* 23.

O, many a shaft, at random sent,
Finds mark the archer little meant !
And many a word, at random spoken,
May soothe, or wound, a heart that 's broken ! *Canto* v. *St.* 18.

Where lives the man that has not tried
How mirth can into folly glide,
        And folly into sin ! *The Bridal of Triermain. Canto* i. *St.* 21.

When Israel, of the Lord beloved,
    Out from the land of bondage came,
Her fathers' God before her moved,
    An awful guide in smoke and flame.   *Ivanhoe.*   *Ch.* xl.

Sea of upturned faces.   *Rob Roy.*   *Ch.* xx.

There 's a gude time coming.   *Ibid.*   *Ch.* xxxii.

My foot is on my native heath, and my name is MacGregor.
                                     Ibid.   *Ch.* xxxiv.

Sound, sound the clarion, fill the fife !
    To all the sensual world proclaim,
One crowded hour of glorious life
    Is worth an age without a name.
                        Old Mortality.   *Ch.* xxxiv. *p.* 451.

    Within that awful volume lies
    The mystery of mysteries !   *The Monastery.*   *Ch.* xii.

And better had they ne'er been born,
Who read to doubt, or read to scorn.   *Ibid.*

Widowed wife and wedded maid.   *The Betrothed.*   *Ch.* xv.

But with the morning cool reflection came.[1]
                        Highland Widow.   Introduction.

What can they see in the longest kingly line in Europe, save that it runs
back to a successful soldier ?[2]   *Woodstock.*   *Vol.* ii. *Ch.* xxxvii.

---

[1] At length the morn, and cold indifference, came.
                        Rowe, *The Fair Penitent, Act* i. *Sc.* 1.
[2] Un soldat tel que moi peut justement prétendre
    À gouverner l'état, quand il l'a su défendre.
    Le premier qui fut roi, fut un soldat heureux :
    Qui sert bien son pays, n'a pas besoin d'aïeux.
                        Voltaire, *Merope, Act* i. *Sc.* 3.

SAMUEL WOODWORTH. 1785—1842.

The old oaken bucket, the iron-bound bucket,
The moss-covered bucket, which hung in the well.   *The Bucket.*

——□——

THOMAS MOORE. 1779—1852.

This narrow isthmus 'twixt two boundless seas,
The past, the future, two eternities !
                    Lalla Rookh.   The Veiled Prophet of Khorassan.

There 's a bower of roses by Bendemeer's stream.   *Ibid.*

Like the stained web that whitens in the sun,
Grow pure by being purely shone upon.   *Ibid.*

            One morn a Peri at the gate
            Of Eden stood disconsolate.   *Paradise and the Peri.*

But the trail of the serpent is over them all.   *Ibid.*

O, ever thus, from childhood's hour,
    I 've seen my fondest hopes decay ;
I never loved a tree or flower,
    But 't was the first to fade away.
I never nursed a dear gazelle,
    To glad me with its soft black eye,
But when it came to know me well,
    And love me, it was sure to die.   *The Fire Worshippers.*

Beholding heaven, and feeling hell.   *Ibid.*

As sunshine, broken in the rill,
Though turned astray, is sunshine still.   *Ibid.*

Farewell, farewell to thee, Araby's daughter.   *Ibid.*

Alas ! how light a cause may move
Dissension between hearts that love !
Hearts that the world in vain had tried,
And sorrow but more closely tied ;
That stood the storm, when waves were rough,
Yet in a sunny hour fall off,
Like ships that have gone down at sea,
When heaven was all tranquillity.   *The Light of the Harem.*

And, oh ! if there be an Elysium on earth,
            It is this, it is this.   *Ibid.*

Love on through all ills, and love on till they die   *Ibid.*

How shall we rank thee upon glory's page ?
Thou more than soldier and just less than sage.
                    Poems relating to America.   To Thomas Hume.

Go where glory waits thee;
But, while fame elates thee,
Oh! still remember me.
Irish Melodies.   Go where glory waits.

The harp that once through Tara's halls
　The soul of music shed,
Now hangs as mute on Tara's walls,
　As if that soul were fled.
So sleeps the pride of former days,
　So glory's thrill is o'er,
And hearts that once beat high for praise,
　Now feel that pulse no more.　　*The Harp that once.*

Fly not yet, 't is just the hour
When pleasure, like the midnight flower
That scorns the eye of vulgar light,
Begins to bloom for sons of night,
　And maids who love the moon.　　　*Fly not yet.*

　　Oh stay!—Oh stay!—
Joy so seldom weaves a chain
Like this to-night, that, oh! 't is pain
　To break its links so soon.　　　　*Ibid.*

And the heart that is soonest awake to the flowers
　Is always the first to be touch'd by the thorns.
　　　　　　O think not my spirits.

Rich and rare were the gems she wore,
And a bright gold ring on her wand she bore.　*Rich and rare.*

There is not in the wide world a valley so sweet
As that vale in whose bosom the bright waters meet.
　　　　　　The Meeting of the Waters.

Shall I ask the brave soldier, who fights by my side
In the cause of mankind, if our creeds agree?
　　　　　　Come send round the wine.

　　The moon looks
　　On many brooks,
"The brook can see no moon but this." [1]
　　　　　While gazing on the moon's light.

No, the heart that has truly lov'd never forgets,
　But as truly loves on to the close!
As the sunflower turns on her god, when he sets,
　The same look which she turn'd when he rose.
　　　　　Believe me, if all those endearing.

---

[1] This image was suggested by the following thought, which occurs somewhere in Sir William Jones's Works: "The moon looks upon many night-flowers, the night-flower sees but one moon."

And when once the young heart of a maiden is stolen,
The maiden herself will steal after it soon.   *Ill Omens.*

But there 's nothing half so sweet in life
As love's young dream.   *Love's Young Dream.*

To live with them is far less sweet
Than to remember thee ! [1]   *I saw thy form.*

'T is the last rose of summer,
Left blooming alone.   *Last Rose of Summer.*

When true hearts lie wither'd
And fond ones are flown,
Oh ! who would inhabit
This bleak world alone ?   *Ibid.*

You may break, you may shatter the vase, if you will,
But the scent of the roses will hang round it still.
          Farewell ! But whenever you welcome the hour.

Thus, when the lamp that lighted
The traveller at first goes out,
He feels awhile benighted,
And looks around in fear and doubt.
But soon, the prospect clearing,
By cloudless starlight on he treads,
And thinks no lamp so cheering
As that light which Heaven sheds. *I 'd mourn the hopes.*

No eye to watch, and no tongue to wound us,
All earth forgot, and all heaven around us.   *Come o'er the sea.*

The light that lies
In woman's eyes.   *The time I 've lost.*

My only books
Were woman's looks,
And folly 's all they 've taught me.   *Ibid.*

I know not, I ask not, if guilt 's in that heart,
I but know that I love thee, whatever thou art.
          Come, rest in this bosom.

Wert thou all that I wish thee, great, glorious, and free,
First flower of the earth, and first gem of the sea.
          Remember thee.

All that 's bright must fade,—
The brightest still the fleetest ;
All that 's sweet was made
But to be lost when sweetest !
          National Airs. All that 's bright must fade.

[1] In imitation of Shenstone's inscription, "Heu ! quanto minus est cum reliquis versari quam tui meminisse."

Those evening bells ! those evening bells !
How many a tale their music tells !
Of youth, and home, and that sweet time
When last I heard their soothing chime.   *Those Evening Bells.*

Oft, in the stilly night
 Ere Slumber's chain has bound me,
Fond Memory brings the light
 Of other days around me ;
  The smiles, the tears,
  Of boyhood's years,
The words of love then spoken ;
  The eyes that shone
  Now dimm'd and gone,
The cheerful hearts now broken !   *Oft in the stilly night.*

  I feel like one
  Who treads alone
Some banquet-hall deserted,
  Whose lights are fled,
  Whose garlands dead,
And all but he departed !   ·   *Ibid.*

As half in shade and half in sun
 This world along its path advances,
May that side the sun 's upon
 Be all that e'er shall meet thy glances !
    Peace be around thee.

If I speak to thee in Friendship's name,
 Thou think'st I speak too coldly ;
If I mention Love's devoted flame,
 Thou say'st I speak too boldly.   *How shall I woo ?*

To sigh, yet feel no pain,
 To weep, yet scarce know why ;
To sport an hour with Beauty's chain,
 Then throw it idly by.   *The Blue Stocking.*

This world is all a fleeting show,
 For man's illusion given ;
The smiles of joy, the tears of woe,
 Deceitful shine, deceitful flow,—
There 's nothing true but Heaven !
  Sacred Songs.   The world is all a fleeting show.

Sound the loud timbrel o'er Egypt's dark sea !
Jehovah has triumph'd—his people are free.
  Ibid.   Sound the loud timbrel.

Here bring your wounded hearts, here tell your anguish—
Earth has no sorrow that Heaven cannot heal.
  Ibid.   Come, ye Disconsolate.

I knew, by the smoke that so gracefully curled
  Above the green elms, that a cottage was near,
And I said, " If there 's peace to be found in the world,
  A heart that was humble might hope for it here."
Poems relating to America. Ballad Stanzas.

To Greece we give our shining blades.   *Evenings in Greece.*

Ay, down to the dust with them, slaves as they are !
  From this hour let the blood in their dastardly veins,
That shrunk at the first touch of Liberty's war,
  Be wasted for tyrants, or stagnate in chains.
On the Entry of the Austrians into Naples, 1821.

A Persian's Heaven is eas'ly made,
  'T is but black eyes and lemonade.
Intercepted Letters.   Letter vi.

Who ran
Through each mode of the lyre, and was master of all.
On the Death of Sheridan.

Whose wit, in the combat, as gentle as bright,
Ne'er carried a heart-stain away on its blade.   *Ibid.*

Weep on ; and, as thy sorrows flow,
  I 'll taste the luxury of woe.   *Anacreontic.*

The minds of some of our statesmen, like the pupil of the human eye,
contract themselves the more, the stronger light there is shed upon them.
Preface to Corruption and Intolerance.

—◻—

ALLAN CUNNINGHAM.   1785—1842.

A wet sheet and a flowing sea,
  A wind that follows fast,
And fills the white and rustling sail,
  And bends the gallant mast.
A Wet Sheet and a Flowing Sea.

While the hollow oak our palace is,
  Our heritage the sea.   *Ibid.*

—◻—

REGINALD HEBER.   1783—1826.

Failed the bright promise of your early day !   *Palestine.*

No hammers fell, no ponderous axes rung ; [1]
Like some tall palm the mystic fabric sprung.
Majestic silence !   *Ibid.*

---

[1] Altered in later editions to
    No workman steel, no ponderous axes rung,
    Like some tall palm the noiseless fabric sprung.

Silently as a dream the fabric rose,
No sound of hammer or of saw was there.
  Cowper, *The Task, Book* v.   *The Winter Morning Walk.*

Brightest and best of the sons of the morning!
Dawn on our darkness, and lend us thine aid.   *Epiphany.*

By cool Siloam's shady rill
    How sweet the lily grows.
                    First Sunday after Epiphany. No. ii.

When spring unlocks the flowers to paint the laughing soil.
                    Seventh Sunday after Trinity.

Death rides on every passing breeze,
    He lurks in every flower.   *At a Funeral.*

Thou art gone to the grave! but we will not deplore thee,
Though sorrows and darkness encompass the tomb.
                    Ibid.   No. ii.

Thus heavenly hope is all serene,
    But earthly hope, how bright soe'er,
Still fluctuates o'er this changing scene,
    As false and fleeting as 't is fair.
                    On Heavenly Hope and Earthly Hope.

From Greenland's icy mountains,
    From India's coral strand,
Where Afric's sunny fountains
    Roll down their golden sand.   *Missionary Hymn.*

Though every prospect pleases,
    And only man is vile.   *Ibid.*

I see them on their winding way,
Above their ranks the moonbeams play.
                    Lines written to a March.

—□—

JOSEPH STORY. 1779--1845.

Here shall the Press the People's right maintain,
Unawed by influence and unbribed by gain;
Here patriot Truth her glorious precepts draw,
Pledged to Religion, Liberty, and Law.
    Motto of the Salem Register.   Life of Story, Vol. i. *p.* 127.

—□—

STEPHEN DECATUR. 1779—1820.

Our country! In her intercourse with foreign nations, may she always
be in the right; but our country, right or wrong.
                    Toast given at Norfolk.   April, 1816.

—□—

DANIEL WEBSTER. 1782—1852.

When my eyes shall be turned to behold for the last time the sun in
heaven, may I not see him shining on the broken and dishonoured frag-

ments of a once glorious Union; on States dissevered, discordant, belligerent; on a land rent with civil feuds, or drenched, it may be, in fraternal blood.   *Second Speech on Foot's Resolution.*

Liberty and Union, now and for ever, one and inseparable.   *Ibid.*

We wish that this column, rising towards heaven among the pointed spires of so many temples dedicated to God, may contribute also to produce, in all minds, a pious feeling of dependence and gratitude. We wish, finally, that the last object to the sight of him who leaves his native shore, and the first to gladden his who revisits it, may be something which shall remind him of the liberty and the glory of his country. Let it rise! let it rise, till it meet the sun in his coming; let the earliest light of the morning gild it, and the parting day linger and play on its summit.

Address on Laying the Corner-Stone of the Bunker Hill Monument, 1825.

He smote the rock of the national resources, and abundant streams of revenue gushed forth. He touched the dead corpse of Public Credit, and it sprung upon its feet.[1]   *Speech on Hamilton, March* 10, 1831.

On this question of principle, while actual suffering was yet afar off, they (the Colonies) raised their flag against a power, to which, for purposes of foreign conquest and subjugation, Rome, in the height of her glory, is not to be compared,—a power which has dotted over the surface of the whole globe with her possessions and military posts, whose morning-drum beat, following the sun, and keeping company with the hours, circles the earth with one continuous and unbroken strain of the martial airs of England.[2]

Speech, May 7, 1834.

Sea of upturned faces.[3]   *Speech, September* 30, 1842.

---

[1] He it was that first gave to the law the air of a science. He found it a skeleton, and clothed it with life, colour, and complexion; he embraced the cold statue, and by his touch it grew into youth, health, and beauty.— Barry Yelverton (Lord Avonmore) *on Blackstone.*

[2] Why should the brave Spanish soldier brag the sun never sets in the Spanish dominions, but ever shineth on one part or other we have conquered for our king?—Capt. John Smith, *Advertisements for the Unexperienced, &c., Coll. Mass. Hist. Soc.,* 3d. Ser. Vol. iii. *p.* 49.

I am called
The richest monarch in the Christian world;
The sun in my dominions never sets.

Ich heisse
Der reichste Mann in der getauften Welt;
Die Sonne geht in meinem Staat nicht unter.

Schiller, *Don Karlos, Act* i. Sc. 6.

The stake I play for is immense,—I will continue in my own dynasty the family system of the Bourbons, and unite Spain for ever to the destinies of France. Remember that the sun never sets on the immense empire of Charles V. (Napoleon, February, 1807).—Walter Scott, *Life of Napoleon.*

[3] This phrase, commonly supposed to have originated with Mr. Webster, occurs in *Rob Roy.* Vol. i. Ch. 20.

CHARLES MINER. 1780—1865.

When I see a merchant over-polite to his customers, begging them to taste a little brandy and throwing half his goods on the counter, thinks I, that man has an axe to grind.   *Who'll turn Grindstones.*[1]

———□———

WASHINGTON IRVING. 1783—1859.

Free-livers on a small scale, who are prodigal within the compass of a guinea.   *The Stout Gentleman.*

The Almighty Dollar, that great object of universal devotion throughout our land, seems to have no genuine devotees in these peculiar villages.
The Creole Village.

———□———

SIR W. F. P. NAPIER. 1785—1860.

Napoleon's troops fought in bright fields, where every helmet caught some beams of glory, but the British soldier conquered under the cool shade of aristocracy; no honours awaited his daring, no despatch gave his name to the applauses of his countrymen; his life of danger and hardship was uncheered by hope, his death unnoticed.
Peninsular War.   Vol. ii. Book xi. Ch. 3.   1810.

———□———

LORD BYRON. 1788—1824.

Farewell! if ever fondest prayer
  For other's weal avail'd on high,
Mine will not all be lost in air,
  But waft thy name beyond the sky.   *Farewell! if ever.*

I only know we loved in vain—
  I only feel—Farewell!—Farewell!   *Ibid.*

    When we two parted
      In silence and tears,
    Half broken-hearted
      To sever for years.   *When we two parted.*

Fools are my theme, let satire be my song.
English Bards and Scotch Reviewers.   Line 6.

'T is pleasant, sure, to see one's name in print;
A book's a book, although there's nothing in 't.   *Line 51.*

With just enough of learning to misquote.   *Line 66.*

            As soon
Seek roses in December,—ice in June;
  Hope constancy in wind, or corn in chaff,
Believe a woman, or an epitaph,
  Or any other thing that's false, before
You trust in critics.   *Line 75.*

---

[1] From *Essays from the Desk of Poor Robert the Scribe. Doylestown, Pa.,* 1815.   It first appeared in the *Wilkesbarre Gleaner.*   1811.

ENGLISH BARDS AND SCOTCH REVIEWERS—*continued.*]

Perverts the Prophets and purloins the Psalms.   *Line* 326.

O Amos Cottle !   Phœbus ! what a name !   *Line* 399.

So the struck eagle, stretched upon the plain,
No more through rolling clouds to soar again,
Viewed his own feather on the fatal dart,
And winged the shaft that quivered in his heart.[1]   *Line* 826.

Yet truth will sometimes lend her noblest fires,
And decorate the verse herself inspires :
This fact, in Virtue's name, let Crabbe attest :
Though Nature's sternest painter, yet the best.   *Line* 839.

Maid of Athens, ere we part,
Give, oh, give me back my heart !   *Maid of Athens.*

Had sighed to many though he loved but one.
                    Childe Harold's Pilgrimage.   Canto i. *St.* 5.

If ancient tales say true, nor wrong these holy men.
                                          Canto i. *St.* 7.

Maidens, like moths, are ever caught by glare,
And Mammon wins his way where Seraphs might despair.
                                          Canto i. *St.* 9.

Might shake the saintship of an anchorite.   Canto i. *St.* 11.

Adieu, adieu ! my native shore
Fades o'er the waters blue.   Canto i. *St.* 13.

My native land—good night !   Canto i. *St.* 13.

O Christ ! it is a goodly sight to see
What Heaven hath done for this delicious land.   Canto i. *St.* 15.

In hope to merit Heaven by making earth a Hell.
                                          Canto i. *St.* 20.

By Heaven ! it is a splendid sight to see
For one who hath no friend, no brother there.   Canto i. *St.* 40

Still from the fount of Joy's delicious springs
Some bitter o'er the flowers its bubbling venom flings.[2]
                                          Canto i. *St.* 82.

---

[1] That eagle's fate and mine are one,
      Which on the shaft that made him die
   Espied a feather of his own,
      Wherewith he wont to soar so high.
          Waller, *To a Lady singing a Song of his Composing.*

Like a young eagle, who has lent his plume
To fledge the shaft by which he meets his doom;
See their own feathers pluck'd, to wing the dart
Which rank corruption destines for their heart.
                            T. Moore, *Corruption.*

[2] Medio de fonte leporum
Surgit amari aliquid quo[i] in ipsis floribus angat.
                    Lucretius.   iv. l. 1133.

CHILDE HAROLD'S PILGRIMAGE—*continued.*]

War, war is still the cry,—"war even to the knife!"[1]

Canto i. *St.* 86.

Gone, glimmering through the dream of things that were.

Canto ii. *St.* 2.

A school-boy's tale, the wonder of an hour!　　*Canto* ii. *St.* 2.

Dim with the mist of years, gray flits the shade of power.

Canto ii. *St.* 2.

The dome of Thought, the palace of the Soul.[2]

Canto ii. *St.* 6.

Ah! happy years! once more who would not be a boy?

Canto ii. *St.* 23.

None are so desolate but something dear,
Dearer than self, possesses or possess'd.　　*Canto* ii. *St.* 24.

But midst the crowd, the hum, the shock of men,
To hear, to see, to feel, and to possess,
And roam along, the world's tired denizen,
With none who bless us, none whom we can bless.

Canto ii. *St.* 26.

Cooped in their winged sea-girt citadel.　　*Canto* ii. *St.* 28.

Fair Greece! sad relic of departed worth!
Immortal, though no more; though fallen, great!

Canto ii. *St.* 73.

Hereditary bondsmen! know ye not,
Who would be free, themselves must strike the blow?

Canto ii. *St.* 76.

A thousand years scarce serve to form a state;
An hour may lay it in the dust.　　*Canto* ii. *St.* 84.

Land of lost gods and godlike men.　　*Canto* ii. *St.* 85.

Where'er we tread, 't is haunted, holy ground.　　*Canto* ii. *St.* 88.

Age shakes Athena's tower, but spares gray Marathon.

Canto ii. *St.* 88.

Ada! sole daughter of my house and heart.　　*Canto* iii. *St.* 1.

Once more upon the waters! yet once more!
And the waves bound beneath me as a steed
That knows his rider.　Welcome to the roar!　　*Canto* iii. *St.* 2.

I am as a weed,
Flung from the rock, on Ocean's foam, to sail
Where'er the surge may sweep, the tempest's breath prevail.

Canto iii. *St.* 2.

---

[1] "War even to the knife," was the reply of Palafox, the governor of Saragoza, when summoned to surrender by the French, who besieged that city in 1808.

[2] And keeps that palace of the soul.—Waller, *Of Tea.*

CHILDE HAROLD'S PILGRIMAGE—*continued.*]

Years steal

Fire from the mind as vigour from the limb;
And life's enchanted cup but sparkles near the brim.

Canto iii.   *St.* 8.

There was a sound of revelry by night,
And Belgium's Capital had gathered then
Her Beauty and her Chivalry, and bright
The lamps shone o'er fair women and brave men;
A thousand hearts beat happily; and when
Music arose with its voluptuous swell,
Soft eyes looked love to eyes which spake again,
And all went merry as a marriage-bell.   *Canto* iii. *St.* 21.

On with the dance! let joy be unconfined.   *Canto* iii. *St.* 22.

And there was mounting in hot haste.   *Canto* iii. *St.* 25.

Or whispering, with white lips—"The foe! They come! They come!"

Canto iii. *St* 25.

Grieving, if aught inanimate e'er grieves,
Over the unreturning brave.   *Canto* iii. *St.* 27.

Battle's magnificently-stern array.   *Canto* iii. *St.* 28.

And thus the heart will break, yet brokenly live on.

Canto iii. *St.* 32.

But quiet to quick bosoms is a hell.   *Canto* iii. *St.* 42.

He who surpasses or subdues mankind,
Must look down on the hate of those below.   *Canto* iii. *St.* 45.

All tenantless, save to the crannying wind.   *Canto* iii. *St.* 47.

The castled crag of Drachenfels
Frowns o'er the wide and winding Rhine.   *Canto* iii. *St.* 55.

He had kept

The whiteness of his soul, and thus men o'er him wept.

Canto iii. *St.* 57.

But there are wanderers o'er Eternity
Whose bark drives on and on, and anchor'd ne'er shall be.

Canto iii. *St.* 70.

By the blue rushing of the arrowy Rhone.   *Canto* iii. *St.* 71.

To me

High mountains are a feeling, but the hum
Of human cities torture.   *Canto* iii. *St.* 72.

This quiet sail is as a noiseless wing
To waft me from distraction.   *Canto* iii. *St.* 85.

On the ear

Drops the light drip of the suspended oar.   *Canto* iii. *St.* 86.

CHILDE HAROLD'S PILGRIMAGE—*continued.*]

All is concentred in a life intense,	
Where not a beam, nor air, nor leaf is lost,	
But hath a part of being.	*Canto* iii. *St.* 89.
In solitude, where we are *least* alone.	*Canto* iii. *St.* 90.

The sky is changed ! and such a change ! O night,
And storm, and darkness ! ye are wondrous strong,
Yet lovely in your strength, as is the light
Of a dark eye in woman ! Far along,
From peak to peak, the rattling crags among
Leaps the live thunder. *Canto* iii. *St.* 92.

Sapping a solemn creed with solemn sneer. *Canto* iii. *St.* 107.

I have not loved the world, nor the world me.
Canto iii. *St.* 113.

I stood
Among them, but not of them. *Canto* iii. *St.* 113.

I stood in Venice, on the Bridge of Sighs;
A palace and a prison on each hand. *Canto* iv. *St.* 1.

Where Venice sate in state, throned on her hundred isles.
Canto iv. *St.* 1.

Striking the electric chain wherewith we are darkly bound.
Canto iv. *St.* 23.

The cold—the changed—perchance the dead—anew,
The mourn'd, the loved, the lost—too many !—yet how few !
Canto iv. *St.* 24.

Parting day
Dies like the dolphin, whom each pang imbues
With a new colour as it gasps away,
The last still loveliest, till—'t is gone—and all is gray.
Canto iv. *St.* 29.

The Ariosto of the North. *Canto* iv. *St* 40.

Italia ! Oh Italia ! thou who hast
The fatal gift of beauty.[1] *Canto* iv. *St.* 42.

Fills
The air around with beauty. *Canto* iv. *St.* 49.

Let these describe the undescribable. *Canto* iv. *St.* 53.

The starry Galileo with his woes. *Canto* iv. *St.* 54.

The poetry of speech. *Canto* iv. *St.* 58.

The hell of waters ! where they howl and hiss. *Canto* iv. *St.* 69.

---

[1] A translation of the famous sonnet of Filicaja :—*Italia, Italia, o tu cui feo la sorte !*

CHILDE HAROLD'S PILGRIMAGE—*continued.*]

The Niobe of nations! there she stands.   *Canto* iv. *St.* 79.

Yet, Freedom! yet thy banner, torn, but flying,
Streams like the thunder-storm *against* the wind.
                                                 Canto iv. *St.* 98.

Heaven gives its favourites—early death.[1]   *Canto* iv. *St.* 102.

                    Man!
Thou pendulum betwixt a smile and tear.   *Canto* iv. *St.* 109.

Egeria! sweet creation of some heart
Which found no mortal resting-place so fair
As thine ideal breast.   *Canto* iv. *St.* 115.

The nympholepsy of some fond despair.   *Canto* iv. *St.* 115.

Thou wert a beautiful thought, and softly bodied forth.
                                                 Canto iv. *St.* 115.

Alas! our young affections run to waste,
Or water but the desert.   *Canto* iv. *St.* 120.

I see before me the Gladiator lie.   *Canto* iv. *St.* 140.

There were his young barbarians all at play,
There was their Dacian mother,—he, their sire,
Butcher'd to make a Roman holiday.   *Canto* iv. *St.* 141.

"While stands the Coliseum, Rome shall stand;
When falls the Coliseum, Rome shall fall;
And when Rome falls,—the World."[2]   *Canto* iv. *St.* 145.

Scion of chiefs and monarchs, where art thou?
Fond hope of many nations, art thou dead?
Could not the grave forget thee, and lay low
Some less majestic, less beloved head?   *Canto* iv. *St.* 168.

Oh! that the desert were my dwelling-place,
With one fair Spirit for my minister,
That I might all forget the human race,
And, hating no one, love but only her!   *Canto* iv. *St.* 177.

There is a pleasure in the pathless woods,
There is a rapture on the lonely shore,
There is society, where none intrudes,
By the deep Sea, and music in its roar:
I love not Man the less, but Nature more.
                                                 Canto iv. *St.* 178.

---

[1] Cf. *Don Juan*, *Canto* iv. *St.* 12.
[2] Literally, the exclamation of the pilgrims in the eighth century, as recorded by the Venerable Bede.
   Cf. Gibbon, *Decline and Fall*, *Ch.* 71.

CHILDE HAROLD'S PILGRIMAGE—*continued.*]

Roll on, thou deep and dark blue Ocean—roll !
Ten thousand fleets sweep over thee in vain ;
Man marks the earth with ruin—his control
Stops with the shore.   *Canto* iv. *St.* 179.

He sinks into thy depths with bubbling groan,
Without a grave, unknell'd, uncoffin'd, and unknown.
      Canto iv. *St.* 179.

Time writes no wrinkle on thine azure brow—[1]
Such as creation's dawn beheld, thou rollest now.
      Canto iv. *St.* 182.

Thou glorious mirror, where the Almighty's form
Glasses itself in tempests.   *Canto* iv. *St.* 183.

And I have loved thee, Ocean ! and my joy
Of youthful sports was on thy breast to be
Borne, like thy bubbles, onward : from a boy
I wanton'd with thy breakers,

.   .   .   .   .   .

And trusted to thy billows far and near,
And laid my hand upon thy mane—as I do here.[2]
      Canto iv. *St.* 184.

And what is writ, is writ,—
Would it were worthier !   *Canto* iv. *St.* 185.

Farewell ! a word that must be, and hath been—
A sound which makes us linger ;—yet—farewell.
      Canto iv. *St.* 186.

Hands promiscuously applied,
Round the slight waist, or down the glowing side.   *The Waltz.*

He who hath bent him o'er the dead
Ere the first day of death is fled,
The first dark day of nothingness,
The last of danger and distress,
Before Decay's effacing fingers
Have swept the lines where beauty lingers.
      The Giaour. Line 68.

Such is the aspect of this shore ;
'T is Greece, but living Greece no more !
So coldly sweet, so deadly fair,
We start, for soul is wanting there.   *Line* 90.

Shrine of the mighty ! can it be
That this is all remains of thee ?   *Line* 106.

---

[1] And thou vast ocean, on whose awful face
Time's iron feet can print no ruin-trace.
     Robert Montgomery, *The Omnipresence of the Deity.*
[2] See Pollok, p. 288.

THE GIAOUR—*continued.*]

> For freedom's battle, once begun,
> Bequeath'd by bleeding sire to son,
> Though baffled oft, is ever won.   *Line* 123.

> And lovelier things have mercy shown
> To every failing but their own;
> And every woe a tear can claim,
> Except an erring sister's shame.   *Line* 418.

> The keenest pangs the wretched find
>   Are rapture to the dreary void,
> The leafless desert of the mind,
>   The waste of feelings unemploy'd.   *Line* 957.

> Better to sink beneath the shock
> Than moulder piecemeal on the rock !   *Line* 969.

> The cold in clime are cold in blood,
>   Their love can scarce deserve the name.   *Line* 1099.

> I die—but first I have possess'd,
> And come what may, I *have been* blest.   *Line* 1114.

> She was a form of life and light,
> That, seen, became a part of sight;
> And rose, where'er I turned mine eye·
> The Morning-star of Memory !
> Yes, Love indeed is light from heaven,
>   A spark of that immortal fire
> With Angels shared, by Alla given,
>   To lift from earth our low desi .   *Line* 1127.

> Know ye the land where the cypress and myrtle
>   Are emblems of deeds that are done in their clime;
> Where the rage of the vulture, the love of the turtle,
>   Now melt into sorrow, now madden to crime?[1]
>   *The Bride of Abydos.*   *Canto* i. *St.* 1.

> Where the virgins are soft as the roses they twine,
> And all, save the spirit of man, is divine?   *Canto* i. *St.* 1.

> Who hath not proved how feebly words essay
> To fix one spark of Beauty's heavenly ray ?
> Who doth not feel, until his failing sight
> Faints into dimness with its own delight,
> His changing cheek, his sinking heart confess
> The might—the majesty of Loveliness?   *Canto* i. *St.* 6.

---

[1] Know'st thou the land where the lemon-trees bloom,
Where the gold orange glows in the deep thicket's gloom,
Where a wind ever soft from the blue heaven blows,
And the groves are of laurel, and myrtle, and rose ?
                          Goethe, *Wilhelm Meister.*

THE BRIDE OF ABYDOS—*continued.*]

The light of love, the purity of grace,
The mind, the music breathing from her face,[1]
The heart whose softness harmonized the whole,
And oh ! that eye was in itself a Soul.   *Canto* i. *St.* 6.

The blind old man of Scio's rocky isle.   *Canto* ii. *St.* 2.

Be thou the rainbow to the storms of life !
The evening beam that smiles the clouds away,
And tints to-morrow with prophetic ray !   *Canto* ii. *St.* 20.

He makes a solitude, and calls it—peace.[2]   *Canto* ii. *St.* 20.

Hark ! to the hurried question of Despair :
" Where is my child ?"—an Echo answers—" Where?"[3]

O'er the glad waters of the dark blue sea,
Our thoughts as boundless, and our souls as free,
Far as the breeze can bear, the billows foam,
Survey our empire, and behold our home.
                                The Corsair. Canto i. *St.* 1.

She walks the waters like a thing of life,
And seems to dare the elements to strife.   *Canto* i. *St.* 3.

The power of Thought,—the magic of the Mind.   *Canto* i. *St.* 8.

The many still must labour for the one !   *Canto* i. *St.* 8.

There was a laughing Devil in his sneer.   *Canto* i. *St.* 9.

Hope withering fled, and Mercy sighed Farewell !   *Canto* i. *St.* 9.

                        Farewell !
For in that word, —that fatal word,—howe'er
We promise—hope—believe,—there breathes despair.
                                Canto i. *St.* 15,

No words suffice the secret soul to show,
For truth denies all eloquence to woe.   *Canto* iii. *St.* 22.

He left a Corsair's name to other times,
Linked with one virtue and a thousand crimes.[4]   *Canto* iii. *St.* 24.

Lord of himself,—that heritage of woe !
                                Lara. Canto i. *St.* 2.

---

[1] Cf. Lovelace, p. 96, and Browne's *Religio Medici. Part* ii. *Sec.* 9.
[2] Solitudinem faciunt,—pacem appellant.—Tacitus, *Agricola, Cap.* 30.
[3] I came to the place of my birth, and cried, " The friends of my Youth, where are they ?" And an Echo answered, " Where are they ?"—From *An Arabic MS.*
[4] Hannibal, as he had mighty virtues, so had he many vices ; *unam virtutem mille vitia comitantur :* as Machiavel said of Cosmo de Medici, he had two distinct persons in him.—Burton, *Anat. of Mel. Democritus to the Reader.*

> She walks in beauty, like the night
>   Of cloudless climes and starry skies;
> And all that's best of dark and bright
>   Meet in her aspect and her eyes;
> Thus mellow'd to that tender light
>   Which Heaven to gaudy day denies.
>   *Hebrew Melodies.   She walks in beauty.*

> The Assyrian came down like the wolf on the fold,
> And his cohorts were gleaming in purple and gold.
>   *Ibid.   The Destruction of Sennacherib.*

> It is the hour when from the boughs
>   The nightingale's high note is heard;
> It is the hour when lovers' vows
>   Seem sweet in every whisper'd word.   *Parisina.   St. 1.*

> Fare thee well! and if for ever,
>   Still for ever, fare *thee well.*   *Fare thee well.*

> Born in the garret, in the kitchen bred.   *A Sketch.*

> In the desert a fountain is springing,
>   In the wide waste there still is a tree,
> And a bird in the solitude singing,
>   Which speaks to my spirit of *thee.*   *Stanzas to Augusta.*

> When all of Genius which can perish dies.
>   *Monody on the Death of Sheridan.   Line* 22.

> Folly loves the martyrdom of Fame.   *Line* 68.

> Who track the steps of Glory to the grave.   *Line* 74.

> Sighing that Nature formed but one such man,
> And broke the die—in moulding Sheridan.[1]   *Line* 117.

> Oh, God! it is a fearful thing
> To see the human soul take wing
> In any shape, in any mood.   *Prisoner of Chillon*, viii.

> And both were young, and one was beautiful. *The Dream. St.* 2.

>   And to his eye
> There was but one beloved face on earth,
> And that was shining on him.   *St.* 2.

>   She was his life,
> The ocean to the river of his thoughts,[2]
> Which terminated all.   *St.* 2.

---

[1] Natura il fece, e poi ruppe la stampa.
                    Ariosto, *Orlando Furioso, Canto* x. *St.* 80.
The idea that *Nature lost the perfect mould* has been a favourite one with all song writers and poets, and is found in the literature of all European nations.—*Book of English Songs, p.* 28.
    [2] She floats upon the river of his thoughts.
                    Longfellow, *The Spanish Student.   Act* ii. *Sc.* 3.
                Si che chiaro
Per essa scenda della mente il fiume.—Dante, *Purg. Canto* 13. 89.

The Dream—*continued.*]

A change came o'er the spirit of my dream.   *St.* 3.

And they were canopied by the blue sky,
So cloudless, clear, and purely beautiful,
That God alone was to be seen in Heaven.   *St.* 4.

There's not a joy the world can give like that it takes away.
                          Stanzas for Music.   There's not a joy.

I had a dream which was not all a dream.   *Darkness.*

My boat is on the shore,
    And my bark is on the sea.   *To Thomas Moore.*

Here's a sigh to those who love me,
    And a smile to those who hate;
And, whatever sky's above me,
    Here's a heart for every fate.   *Ibid.*

Were't the last drop in the well,
    As I gasp'd upon the brink,
Ere my fainting spirit fell,
    'T is to thee that I would drink.   *Ibid.*

So we'll go no more a roving
    So late into the night.   *So we'll go.*

Mont Blanc is the monarch of mountains;
    They crown'd him long ago
On a throne of rocks, in a robe of clouds,
    With a diadem of snow.   *Manfred. Act* i. *Sc.* 1.

                    The heart ran o'er
With silent worship of the great of old !—
The dead, but sceptred sovereigns, who still rule
Our spirits from their urns.   *Ibid. Act* iii. *Sc.* 4.

For most men (till by losing rendered sager)
Will back their own opinions by a wager.   *Beppo. St.* 27.

Soprano, basso, even the contra-alto
Wished him five fathom under the Rialto.   *St.* 32.

His heart was one of those which most enamour us,
Wax to receive, and marble to retain.[1]   *St.* 34.

Besides, they always smell of bread and butter.   *St.* 39.

                    That soft bastard Latin
Which melts like kisses from a female mouth.   *St.* 44.

Heart on her lips, and soul within her eyes,
Soft as her clime, and sunny as her skies.   *St.* 45.

---

[1] For her my heart is wax to be moulded as she pleases, but enduring as marble to retain whatever impression she shall make upon it.—Cervantes, *La Gitanilla.*

K

BEPPO—*continued.*]

Oh, Mirth and Innocence ! Oh, Milk and Water !
Ye happy mixtures of more happy days !   *St.* 80.

And if we do but watch the hour,
There never yet was human power
Which could evade, if unforgiven,
The patient search and vigil long
Of him who treasures up a wrong.   *Mazeppa.*   x.

They never fail who die
In a great cause.   *Marino Faliero.*   *Act* ii. *Sc.* 2.

Whose game was empires, and whose stakes were thrones,
Whose table earth—whose dice were human bones.
                                The Age of Bronze.   *St.* 3.

I loved my country, and I hated him.
                        The Vision of Judgment.   lxxxiii.

Sublime tobacco ! which from east to west
Cheers the tar's labour or the Turkman's rest.
                        The Island.   *Canto* ii. *St.* 19.

Divine in hookas, glorious in a pipe,
When tipp'd with amber, mellow, rich, and ripe ;
Like other charmers, wooing the caress
More dazzlingly when daring in full dress ;
Yet thy true lovers more admire by far
Thy naked beauties—Give me a cigar !   *Canto* ii. *St.* 19.

My days are in the yellow leaf ;
    The flowers and fruits of love are gone ;
The worm, the canker, and the grief
    Are mine alone !   *On my Thirty-sixth Year.*

In virtues nothing earthly could surpass her,
Save thine " incomparable oil," Macassar !
                        Don Juan.   *Canto* i. *St.* 17.

But—oh ! ye lords of ladies intellectual !
Inform us truly, have they not hen-pecked you all ?
                                    Canto i. *St.* 22.

The languages, especially the dead,
    The sciences, and most of all the abstruse,
The arts, at least all such as could be said
    To be the most remote from common use.   *Canto* i. *St.* 40.

Her stature tall—I hate a dumpy woman.   *Canto* i. *St.* 61.

Christians have burnt each other, quite persuaded
That all the Apostles would have done as they did.
                                    Canto i. *St.* 83.

And whispering " I will ne'er consent,"—consented.
                                    Canto i. *St.* 117.

Don Juan—*continued.*]

    'T is sweet to hear the watch-dog's honest bark
      Bay deep-mouthed welcome as we draw near home;
    'T is sweet to know there is an eye will mark
      Our coming, and look brighter when we come.
                            Canto i. *St.* 123.

Sweet is revenge—especially to women.   *Canto* i. *St.* 124.

And truant husband should return, and say,
  "My dear, I was the first who came away."   *Canto* i. *St.* 141.

Man's love is of man's life a thing apart,
'T is woman's whole existence.   *Canto* i. *St.* 194.

In my hot youth,—when George the Third was King.
                            Canto i. *St.* 212.

So for a good old-gentlemanly vice,
I think I must take up with avarice.   *Canto* i. *St.* 216.

What is the end of Fame? 't is but to fill
  A certain portion of uncertain paper.   *Canto* i. *St.* 218.

At leaving even the most unpleasant people
And places, one keeps looking at the steeple. *Canto* ii. *St.* 14.

There 's naught, no doubt, so much the spirit calms
As rum and true religion.   *Canto* ii. *St.* 34.

A solitary shriek, the bubbling cry
Of some strong swimmer in his agony.   *Canto* ii. *St.* 53.

             All who joy would win
Must share it,—Happiness was born a twin. *Canto* ii. *St.* 172.

A long, long kiss, a kiss of youth and love.   *Canto* ii. *St.* 168.

Alas ! the love of women ! it is known
  To be a lovely and a fearful thing.   *Canto* ii. *St.* 199.

In her first passion, woman loves her lover :
  In all the others, all she loves is love.[1]   *Canto* iii. *St.* 3.

        He was the mildest manner'd man
That ever scuttled ship or cut a throat.   *Canto* iii. *St.* 41.

The isles of Greece, the isles of Greece !
  Where burning Sappho loved and sung. *Canto* iii. *St.* 86. 1.

Eternal summer gilds them yet,
But all, except their sun, is set.   *Canto* iii. *St.* 86. 1.

The mountains look on Marathon—
  And Marathon looks on the sea ;
And musing there an hour alone,
  I dreamed that Greece might still be free. *Canto* iii. *St.* 86. 3.

[1] Dans les premières passions les femmes aiment l'amant, et dans les autres elles aiment l'amour.—La Rochefoucauld. *Maxim* 497.

DON JUAN—*continued.*]

> You have the Pyrrhic dance as yet,
>   Where is the Pyrrhic phalanx gone?
> Of two such lessons, why forget
>   The nobler and the manlier one?
> You have the letters Cadmus gave—
> Think ye he meant them for a slave?   *Canto* iii. *St.* 86. 10.

> Place me on Sunium's marbled steep,
>   Where nothing, save the waves and I,
> May hear our mutual murmurs sweep;
>   There, swan-like, let me sing and die.   *Canto* iii. *St.* 86. 16.

> But words are things, and a small drop of ink,
>   Falling, like dew, upon a thought, produces
> That which makes thousands, perhaps millions, think.
>   *Canto* iii. *St.* 88.

> And if I laugh at any mortal thing,
> 'T is that I may not weep.   *Canto* iv. *St.* 4.

> The precious porcelain of human clay.[1]   *Canto* iv. *St.* 11.

> "Whom the gods love die young," was said of yore.[2]
>   *Canto* iv. *St.* 12.

> These two hated with a hate
>   Found only on the stage.   *Canto* iv. *St.* 93.

> "Arcades ambo," *id est*—blackguards both.   *Canto* iv. *St.* 93.

> Oh! "darkly, deeply, beautifully blue,"[3]
>   As some one somewhere sings about the sky.
>   *Canto* iv. *St.* 110.

> I 've stood upon Achilles' tomb,
> And heard Troy doubted : time will doubt of Rome.
>   *Canto* iv. *St.* 101.

> That all-softening, overpowering knell,
> The tocsin of the soul—the dinner bell.   *Canto* v. *St.* 49.

> The women pardoned all except her face.   *Canto* v. *St.* 113.

> Heroic, stoic Cato, the sententious,
> Who lent his lady to his friend Hortensius.   *Canto* vi. *St.* 7.

> A "strange coincidence," to use a phrase
> By which such things are settled now-a-days. *Canto* vi. *St.* 78.

---

[1] Cf. Dryden, *Don Sebastian*, Act i. Sc. 1.
[2] Quem Di diligunt
   Adolescens moritur.— Plautus, *Bacch.*, Act iv. Sc. 6.
   Ὃν οἱ θεοὶ φιλοῦσιν ἀποθνήσκει νέος.—Menander, *apud Stob. Flor.* cxx. 8.
[3] Quoted from Southey,

>   "Though in blue ocean seen
>   Blue, darkly, deeply, beautifully blue."
>   *Madoc in Wales*, v.

Don Juan—*continued.*]

The drying up a single tear has more
Of honest fame, than shedding seas of gore.   *Canto* viii. *St.* 3.

Thrice happy he whose name has been well spelt
In the despatch : I knew a man whose loss
Was printed *Grove*, although his name was Grose.
                                        Canto viii. *St.* 18.

And wrinkles, the d—d democrats, won't flatter.
                                        Canto x. *St.* 24.

Oh for a *forty parson power*.   *Canto* x. *St.* 34.

When Bishop Berkeley said " there was no matter,"
   And proved it—'t was no matter what he said.
                                        Canto xi. *St.* 1.

And, after all, what is a lie? 'T is but
   The truth in masquerade.   *Canto* xi. *St.* 37.

'T is strange the mind, that very fiery particle,
Should let itself be snuff'd out by an article.   *Canto* xi. *St.* 59.

Of all tales 't is the saddest—and more sad,
Because it makes us smile.   *Canto* xiii. *St.* 9.

Cervantes smiled Spain's chivalry away.   *Canto* xiii. *St.* 11.

Society is now one polished horde,
Formed of two mighty tribes, the *Bores* and *Bored*.
                                        Canto xiii. *St.* 95.

'T is strange—but true; for truth is always strange;
Stranger than fiction.   *Canto* xiv. *St.* 101.

The Devil hath not, in all his quiver's choice,
An arrow for the heart like a sweet voice.   *Canto* xv. *St.* 13.

I awoke one morning and found myself famous.
                 Memoranda from his Life, by Moore, ch. xiv.

The best of Prophets of the future is the Past.
                           Letter, January 28, 1821.

—☐—

LEIGH HUNT. 1784—1859.

Abou Ben Adhem (may his tribe increase)
Awoke one night from a deep dream of peace.
                                        Abou Ben Adhem.

And lo! Ben Adhem's name led all the rest.   *Ibid.*

O for a seat in some poetic nook,
Just hid with trees and sparkling with a brook.
                                        Politics and Poetics.

With spots of sunny openings, and with nooks
To lie and read in, sloping into brooks.   *The Story of Rimini.*

JOHN PIERPONT.   1785—1866.

A weapon that comes down as still
   As snow-flakes fall upon the sod;
But executes a freeman's will,
   As lightning does the will of God;
And from its force, nor doors nor locks
Can shield you;—'t is the ballot-box.
                                    A Word from a Petitioner.

——□——

WILLIAM L. MARCY.   1786–1857.

They see nothing wrong in the rule that to the victors belong the spoils
of the enemy.   *Speech in the United States Senate, January,* 1832.

——□——

PERCY BYSSHE SHELLEY.   1792—1822.

How wonderful is Death!
Death and his brother Sleep.   *Queen Mab.*   i.

Power, like a desolating pestilence,
Pollutes whate'er it touches; and obedience,
Bane of all genius, virtue, freedom, truth,
Makes slaves of men, and of the human frame
A mechanized automaton.   *Ibid.*   iii.

        Heaven's ebon vault,
Studded with stars unutterably bright,
Thro' which the moon's unclouded grandeur rolls,
Seems like a canopy which love has spread
To curtain her sleeping world.   *Ibid.*   iv.

            Then black despair,
The shadow of a starless night, was thrown
Over the world in which I moved alone.
            The Revolt of Islam.   Dedication.   St. vi.

With hue like that when some great painter dips
His pencil in the gloom of earthquake and eclipse.
                        Ibid.   Canto v. *St.* xxiii.

Kings are like stars—they rise and set—they have
The worship of the world, but no repose.[1]   *Hellas.*

    All love is sweet,
Given or returned.   Common as light is love,
And its familiar voice wearies not ever.

    .   .   .   .   .   .

They who inspire it most are fortunate,
As I am now; but those who feel it most
Are happier still.[2]   *Prometheus Unbound.   Act* ii. *Sc.* 5.

---

[1] Princes are like to heavenly bodies, which cause good or evil times, and
which have much veneration, but no rest.—Bacon, *Essay* xx. *Empire.*

[2] The pleasure of love is in loving.   We are happier in the passion we
feel than in that we excite.—Rochefoucauld, *Maxim* 78.

Those who inflict must suffer, for they see
The work of their own hearts, and that must be
Our chastisement or recompense. *Julian ana Maddala.*

Most wretched men
Are cradled into poetry by wrong;
They learn in suffering what they teach in song. *Ibid.*

I could lie down like a tired child,
   And weep away the life of care
Which I have borne, and yet must bear.
Stanzas, written in Dejection, near Naples.

That orbed maiden, with white fire laden,
   Whom mortals call the moon. *The Cloud.* iv.

A pard-like spirit, beautiful and swift. *Adonais.* xxxii.

Life, like a dome of many-coloured glass,
Stains the white radiance of eternity. *Ibid.* lii.

Music, when soft voices die,
   Vibrates in the memory—
Odours, when sweet violets sicken,
   Live within the sense they quicken.
Poems written in 1821. *To* ——

The desire of the moth for the star,
   Of the night for the morrow,
The devotion to something afar
   From the sphere of our sorrow!
Poems written in 1821. *To* ——.

—□—

EATON STANNARD BARRETT. 1785—1820.

Not she with trait'rous kiss her Saviour stung,
Not she denied him with unholy tongue;
She, while apostles shrank, could danger brave,
Last at his cross, and earliest at his grave.
Woman. Part i. Ed. 1828

—□—

MISS FANNY STEERS.

The last link is broken
   That bound me to thee,
And the words thou hast spoken
   Have rendered me free. *Song.*

Not she with trait'rous kiss her Master stung,
Not she denied him with unfaithful tongue;
She, when apostles fled, could danger brave,
Last at his cross, and earliest at his grave.
From the original edition of 1818

FELICIA HEMANS. 1794—1835.

Leaves have their time to fall,
And flowers to wither at the North-wind's breath,
    And stars to set ;—but all,
Thou hast all seasons for thine own, O Death !

The Hour of Death.

Alas ! for love, if thou art all,
    And naught beyond, O Earth !   *The Graves of a Household.*

The breaking waves dash'd high
    On a stern and rock-bound coast ;
And the woods, against a stormy sky,
    Their giant branches toss'd.

The Landing of the Pilgrim Fathers in New England.

Ay, call it holy ground,
    The soil where first they trod,
They have left unstain'd what there they found,—
    Freedom to worship God.   *Ibid.*

The boy stood on the burning deck,
    Whence all but him had fled ;
The flame that lit the battle's wreck
    Shone round him o'er the dead.   *Casabianca.*

——□——

MISS —— WROTHER.

Hope tells a flattering tale,[1]
    Delusive, vain, and hollow,
Ah let not Hope prevail,
    Lest disappointment follow.

From *The Universal Songster.   Vol.* ii. *p.* 86.

——□——

JOHN KEATS. 1796—1821.

A thing of beauty is a joy for ever ;
Its loveliness increases ; it will never
Pass into nothingness.   *Endymion.   Line* 1.

Philosophy will clip an angel's wings.   *Lamia.   Part* ii.

    Music's golden tongue
Flatter'd to tears this aged man and poor.

The Eve of St. Agnes.   St. 3.

---

[1] Hope told a flattering tale,
        That Joy would soon return ;
    Ah, naught my sighs avail,
        For love is doomed to mourn.   *Anon.   Vol.* i. *p.* 320.[2]
[2] Air by Giovanni Paisiello (1741—1816).

THE EVE OF ST. AGNES—*continued*.]

As though a rose should shut, and be a bud again. *Ibid. St.* 27.

And lucent sirups, tinct with cinnamon. *Ibid. St.* 30.

That large utterance of the early gods! *Hyperion. Book* i.

Those green-robed senators of mighty woods,
Tall oaks, branch-charmed by the earnest stars,
Dream, and so dream all night without a stir. *Ibid.*

Thou foster-child of Silence and slow Time.
Ode on a Grecian Urn.

Heard melodies are sweet, but those unheard
Are sweeter; therefore, ye soft pipes, play on;
Not to the sensual ear, but, more endear'd,
Pipe to the spirit ditties of no tone. *Ibid.*

Beauty is truth, truth beauty,—that is all
Ye know on earth, and all ye need to know. *Ibid.*

Hear ye not the hum
Of mighty workings? *Addressed to Haydon.*

Then felt I like some watcher of the skies
When a new planet swims into his ken;
Or like stout Cortez when with eagle eyes
He stared at the Pacific—and all his men
Look'd at each other with a wild surmise—
Silent, upon a peak in Darien.
On first looking into Chapman's Homer.

The poetry of earth is never dead.
On the Grasshopper and Cricket.

——□——

CHARLES WOLFE. 1791—1823.

Not a drum was heard, not a funeral note,
As his corse to the rampart we hurried.
The Burial of Sir John Moore.

But he lay like a warrior taking his rest,
With his martial cloak around him. *Ibid.*

We carved not a line, and we raised not a stone,
But we left him alone with his glory! *Ibid.*

——□——

HENRY HART MILMAN.

And the cold marble leapt to life a god. *The Belvidere Apollo.*

Too fair to worship, too divine to love. *Ibid.*

K*

RICHARD MONCKTON MILNES.

But on and up, where Nature's heart
  Beats strong amid the hills.
               Tragedy of the Lac de Gaube. St. **2.**

Great thoughts, great feelings came to them,
  Like instincts, unawares.   *The Men of Old.*

A man's best things are nearest him,
  Lie close about his feet.   *Ibid.*

The beating of my own heart
  Was all the sound I heard.   *I wandered by the Brookside.*

—□—

J. HOWARD PAYNE. 1792—1852.

Mid pleasures and palaces though we may roam,
Be it ever so humble there's no place like home.[1]
                     Home, Sweet Home.[2]

—□—

JOHN LOUIS UHLAND. 1787—1862.

  Take, O boatman, thrice thy fee;
  Take,—I give it willingly;
  For, invisible to thee,
  Spirits twain have cross'd with me.   *The Passage.*

—□—

THOMAS NOON TALFOURD. 1795—1854.

          So his life has flowed
From its mysterious urn a sacred stream,
In whose calm depth the beautiful and pure
Alone are mirror d; which, though shapes of ill
May hover round its surface, glides in light,
And takes no shadow from them.   *Ion.* *Act* i. *Sc.* 1.

          'T is a little thing
To give a cup of water; yet its draught
Of cool refreshment, drain'd by fever'd lips,
May give a shock of pleasure to the frame
More exquisite than when Nectarean juice
Renews the life of joy in happiest hours.   *Act* i. *Sc.* 2.

—□—

ROBERT POLLOK. 1799—1827.

He laid his hand upon "the Ocean's mane"
And played familiar with his hoary locks.[3]
          The Course of Time. *Book* iv. *Line* 389.

---

[1] "Home is home though it be never so homely" is a proverb, and is found in the collections of the seventeenth century.
[2] From *The Opera of Clari—the Maid of Milan.*
[3] Cf. Byron, *Childe Harold, Canto* iv. *St.* 184.

THE COURSE OF TIME—*continued.*]

> He was a man
> Who stole the livery of the court of Heaven
> To serve the Devil in.   *Book* viii. *Line* 616.

> With one hand he put
> A penny in the urn of poverty,
> And with the other took a shilling out.   *Book* viii. *Line* 632.

—□—

THOMAS HAYNES BAYLY. 1797—1839.

> I 'd be a Butterfly; living a rover,
> Dying when fair things are fading away.
>   *I'd be a Butterfly.*

> Oh! no! we never mention her,
> Her name is never heard;
> My lips are now forbid to speak
> That once familiar word. *Oh! no! we never mention her.*

> We met—'t was in a crowd.   *We met.*

> Why don't the men propose, mamma,
> Why don't the men propose? *Why don't the men propose?*

> She wore a wreath of roses,
> The night that first we met.   *She wore a wreath.*

> Tell me the tales that to me were so dear,
> Long, long ago, long, long ago.   *Long, long ago.*

> The rose that all are praising
> Is not the rose for me.   *The rose that all are praising.*

> O pilot! 't is a fearful night,
> There 's danger on the deep.   *The Pilot.*

> Absence makes the heart grow fonder;
> Isle of Beauty, fare thee well!   *Isle of Beauty.*

> Gayly the Troubadour
> Touched his guitar.   *Welcome me home.*

—□—

JOHN KEBLE. 1796—1821.

> Why should we faint and fear to live alone,
> Since all alone, so Heaven has willed, we die,
> Nor even the tenderest heart, and next our own,
> Knows half the reasons why we smile and sigh.
>   *The Christian Year. Twenty-fourth Sunday after Trinity.*

> 'T is sweet, as year by year we lose
> Friends out of sight, in faith to muse
> How grows in Paradise our store.   *Burial of the Dead.*

THE CHRISTIAN YEAR—*continued.*]

> Abide with me from morn till eve,
> For without Thee I cannot live ;
> Abide with me when night is nigh,
> For without Thee I dare not die.   *Evening.*

—□—

BRYAN W. PROCTER.

> The sea ! the sea ! the open sea !
> The blue, the fresh, the ever free !   *The Sea.*

> I 'm on the sea ! I 'm on the sea !
> I am where I would ever be,
> With the blue above and the blue below,
> And silence wheresoe'er I go.   *Ibid.*

> I never was on the dull, tame shore,
> But I loved the great sea more and more.   *Ibid.*

—□—

LORD BROUGHAM.

Let the soldier be abroad if he will, he can do nothing in this age. There is another personage, a personage less imposing in the eyes of some, perhaps insignificant. The schoolmaster is abroad, and I trust to him, armed with his primer, against the soldier in full military array.

Speech, January 29, 1828.

In my mind, he was guilty of no error, he was chargeable with no exaggeration, he was betrayed by his fancy into no metaphor, who once said, that all we see about us, Kings, Lords, and Commons, the whole machinery of the state, all the apparatus of the system, and its varied workings, end in simply bringing twelve good men into a box.

Present State of the Law, Feb. 7, 1828.

Pursuit of knowledge under difficulties.[1]

—□—

MICHAEL J. BARRY.

> But whether on the scaffold high,
>   Or in the battle's van,
> The fittest place where man can die
> Is where he dies for man !
> From *The Dublin Nation, Sept.* 28, 1844.   *Vol.* ii. *p.* 809.

—□—

EDWARD BULWER LYTTON.

> Beneath the rule of men entirely great
> The pen is mightier than the sword.   *Richelieu. Act* ii. *Sc.* 2.

---

[1] The title given by Lord Brougham to a book published in 1830, under the superintendence of the Society for the Diffusion of Useful Knowledge.

RICHELIEU—*continued.*]

Take away the sword;
States can be saved without it; bring the pen !   *Ibid.*

In the lexicon of youth, which fate reserves
For a bright manhood, there is no such word
As—*fail.*   *Ibid.   Act* ii. *Sc.* 2.

Alone !—that worn-out word,
So idly spoken, and so coldly heard;
Yet all that poets sing, and grief hath known,
Of hopes laid waste, knells in that word—ALONE !
                                    The New Timon.   Part ii. 7.

——□——

WILLIAM MOTHERWELL. 1797—1835.

I 've wandered east, I 've wandered west,
    Through many a weary way;
But never, never can forget
    The love of life's young day.   *Jeannie Morison.*

And we, with Nature's heart in tune,
    Concerted harmonies.   *Ibid.*

——□——

THOMAS HOOD. 1798—1845.

We watched her breathing through the night,
    Her breathing soft and low,
As in her breast the wave of life
    Kept heaving to and fro.   *The Death-Bed.*

Our very hopes belied our fears,
    Our fears our hopes belied;
We thought her dying when she slept,
    And sleeping when she died.   *Ibid.*

One more Unfortunate
Weary of breath,
Rashly importunate,
Gone to her death.   *The Bridge of Sighs.*

Take her up tenderly,
Lift her with care;
Fashioned so slenderly,
Young, and so fair !   *Ibid.*

Alas for the rarity
Of Christian charity
Under the sun !   *Ibid.*

Even God's providence
Seeming estranged.   *Ibid.*

Boughs are daily rifled
By the gusty thieves,
And the book of Nature
Getteth short of leaves.   *The Seasons.*

When he is forsaken,
Withered and shaken,
What can an old man do but die?   *Ballad.*

It is not linen you 're wearing out,
    But human creatures' lives.[1]   *Song of the Shirt.*

My tears must stop, for every drop,
    Hinders needle and thread.   *Ibid.*

But evil is wrought by want of thought
    As well as want of heart.   *The Lady's Dream.*

And there is even a happiness
That makes the heart afraid.   *Ode to Melancholy.*

There 's not a string attuned to mirth,
But has its chord in Melancholy.   *Ibid.*

I remember, I remember
The fir-trees dark and high;
I used to think their slender tops
Were close against the sky;
It was a childish ignorance,
But now 't is little joy
To know I 'm further off from heaven
Than when I was a boy.   *I remember, I remember.*

Seemed washing his hands with invisible soap
    In imperceptible water.   *Miss Kilmansegg.*

Gold! Gold! Gold! Gold!
Bright and yellow, hard and cold.   *Ibid. Her Moral.*

Spurned by the young, but hugged by the old
To the very verge of the churchyard mould.   *Ibid.*

How widely its agencies vary—
To save—to ruin—to curse—to bless—
As even its minted coins express,
Now stamped with the image of Good Queen Bess,
And now of a Bloody Mary.   *Ibid.*

Oh! would I were dead now,
Or up in my bed now,
To cover my head now
And have a good cry!   *A Table of Errata.*

---

[1] It 's no fish ye 're buying, it 's men's lives.—Scott, *The Antiquary,*
Ch. xi.

RUFUS CHOATE. 1799—1859.

There was a State without King or nobles; there was a church without a Bishop; there was a people governed by grave magistrates which it had selected, and equal laws which it had framed.

Speech before the New England Society,
New York, December 22, 1843.

We join ourselves to no party that does not carry the flag and keep step to the music of the Union.   *Letter to the Whig Convention.*

Its constitution the glittering and sounding generalities of natural right which make up the Declaration of Independence.

Letter to the Maine Whig Committee.

— ◻ —

THOMAS K. HERVEY. 1799—1859.

The tomb of him who would have made
    The world too glad and free.   *The Devil's Progress.*

He stood beside a cottage lone,
    And listened to a lute,
One summer's eve, when the breeze was gone,
    And the nightingale was mute.   *Ibid.*

A love that took an early root
    And had an early doom.   *Ibid.*

Like ships, that sailed for sunny isles,
    But never came to shore !   *Ibid.*

A Hebrew knelt in the dying light,
    His eye was dim and cold,
The hairs on his brow were silver-white,
    And his blood was thin and old.   *Ibid.*

— ◻ —

W. M. PRAED. 1802—1839.

Twelve years ago I was a boy,
    A happy boy, at Drury's.   *School and School-fellows.*

Some lie beneath the churchyard stone,
    And some before the speaker.   *Ibid.*

I remember, I remember
    How my childhood fleeted by,—
The mirth of its December,
    And the warmth of its July.   *I remember, I remember.*

— ◻ —

THOMAS B. MACAULAY. 1800—1859.

She (the Roman Catholic Church) may still exist in undiminished vigour, when some traveller from New Zealand shall, in the midst of a vast soli-

tude, take his stand on a broken arch of London Bridge to sketch the
ruins of St. Paul's.[1]   *Review of Ranke's History of the Popes.*

The Puritans hated bearbaiting, not because it gave pain to the bear, but
because it gave pleasure to the spectators.[2]

History of England.   Vol. i. *Ch.* 2.

> To every man upon this earth
>   Death cometh soon or late,
> And how can man die better
>   Than facing fearful odds,
> For the ashes of his fathers
>   And the temples of his gods?

Lays of Ancient Rome.   Horatius, xxvii.

> How well Horatius kept the bridge
>   In the brave days of old.

Ibid. lxx.

——□——

JOHN K. INGRAM.

> Who fears to speak of Ninety-eight?
>   Who blushes at the name?
> When cowards mock the patriot's fate,
>   Who hangs his head for shame?

From *The Dublin Nation, April* 1, 1843. *Vol.* i. *p.* 339.

---

[1] The same image was employed by Macaulay in 1824, in the concluding
paragraph of a review of Mitford's *Greece,* and he repeated it in his review
of Mill's *Essay on Government,* in 1829.

Who knows but that hereafter some traveller like myself will sit down
upon the banks of the Seine, the Thames, or the Zuyder Zee, where
now, in the tumult of enjoyment, the heart and the eyes are too slow to
take in the multitude of sensations? Who knows but he will sit down
solitary amid silent ruins, and weep a people inurned and their greatness
changed into an empty name?—Volney's *Ruins, Ch.* 2.

At last some curious traveller from Lima will visit England, and give
a description of the ruins of St. Paul's, like the editions of Baalbec and
Palmyra.—Horace Walpole, *Letter to Mason, Nov.* 24, 1774.

Where now is Britain?
  .   .   .   .   .

> Even as the savage sits upon the stone
> That marks where stood her capitols, and hears
> The bittern booming in the weeds, he shrinks
> From the dismaying solitude.   Henry Kirke White, *Time.*

In the firm expectation, that when London shall be an habitation of
bitterns, when St. Paul and Westminster Abbey shall stand, shapeless and
nameless ruins in the midst of an unpeopled marsh; when the piers of
Waterloo Bridge shall become the nuclei of islets of reeds and osiers, and
cast the jagged shadows of their broken arches on the solitary stream, some
Transatlantic commentator will be weighing in the scales of some new and
now unimagined system of criticism the respective merits of the Bells and
the Fudges, and their historians.—Shelley, *Dedication to Peter Bell.*

[2] Even bearbaiting was esteemed heathenish and unchristian; the sport
of it, not the inhumanity, gave offence.—Hume, *History of England,
Vol.* i. *Ch.* 62.

GEORGE P. MORRIS. 1802—1864.

Woodman, spare that tree !
   Touch not a single bough !
In youth it sheltered me,
   And I 'll protect it now.   *Woodman, spare that Tree.*

A song for our banner? The watchword recall
  Which gave the Republic her station :
"United we stand—divided we fall !"
  It made and preserves us a nation !
The union of lakes—the union of lands—
  The union of States none can sever—
The union of hearts—the union of hands—
  And the Flag of our Union for ever ! *The Flag of our Union.*

Near the lake where drooped the willow,
   Long time ago !   *Near the Lake.*

——□——

JAMES ALDRICH. 1810—1856.

Her suffering ended with the day,
   Yet lived she at its close,
And breathed the long, long night away,
   In statue-like repose.   *A Death-Bed.*

But when the sun, in all his state,
   Illumed the eastern skies,
She passed through Glory's morning gate,
   And walked in Paradise.   *Ibid.*

——□——

WILLIAM CULLEN BRYANT.

To him who in the love of Nature holds
Communion with her visible forms, she speaks
A various language.   *Thanatopsis.*

Go forth under the open sky, and list
To Nature's teachings.   *Ibid.*

Old Ocean's gray and melancholy waste,—
Are but the solemn decorations all
Of the great tomb of man.   *Ibid.*

           All that tread
The globe are but a handful to the tribes
That slumber in its bosom.   *Ibid.*

So live that when thy summons comes to join
The innumerable caravan which moves
To that mysterious realm where each shall take
His chamber in the silent halls of death,

THANATOPSIS—*continued.*]

> Thou go not, like the quarry-slave at night,
> Scourged to his dungeon, but, sustained and soothed
> By an unfaltering trust, approach thy grave,
> Like one that wraps the drapery of his couch
> About him, and lies down to pleasant dreams.   *Ibid.*

> The stormy March has come at last,
>   With wind and clouds and changing skies;
> I hear the rushing of the blast
>   That through the snowy valley flies.   *March.*

> But 'neath yon crimson tree,
> Lover to listening maid might breathe his flame,
> Nor mark, within its roseate canopy,
>   Her blush of maiden shame.   *Autumn Woods.*

> The groves were God's first temples.   *Forest Hymn.*

The melancholy days are come, the saddest of the year,
Of wailing winds, and naked woods, and meadows brown and sear.
                                        The Death of the Flowers.

And sighs to find them in the wood and by the stream no more.   *Ibid.*

> Loveliest of lovely things are they,
>   On earth that soonest pass away.
> The rose that lives its little hour
> Is prized beyond the sculptured flower.
>   *A Scene on the Banks of the Hudson.*

> Truth crushed to earth shall rise again :
>   The eternal years of God are hers;
> But Error, wounded, writhes with pain,
>   And dies among his worshippers.   *The Battle-field.*

——□——

HENRY TAYLOR.

The world knows nothing of its greatest men.
            Philip Van Artevelde.   Part i.   *Act* 1. *Sc.* 5.

He that lacks time to mourn, lacks time to mend.
Eternity mourns that.   'T is an ill cure
For life's worst ills, to have no time to feel them.
Where sorrow's held intrusive and turned out,
There wisdom will not enter, nor true power,
Nor aught that dignifies humanity.   *Ibid.*

            We figure to ourselves
The thing we like, and then we build it up
As chance will have it, on the rock or sand :
For thought is tired of wandering o'er the world,
And homebound Fancy runs her bark ashore.   *Ibid.*

PHILIP VAN ARTEVELDE—*continued.*]

                              Such souls,
Whose sudden visitations daze the world,
Vanish like lightning, but they leave behind
A voice that in the distance far away
Wakens the slumbering ages.   *Act* i. *Sc.* 7.

—□—

WILLIAM H. SEWARD.

There is a higher law than the Constitution.   *Speech, March* 11, 1850.

It is an irrepressible conflict between opposing and enduring forces.
                              Speech, Oct. 25, 1858.

—□—

PHILIP JAMES BAILEY.

We live in deeds, not years; in thoughts, not breaths; [1]
In feelings, not in figures on a dial.
We should count time by heart-throbs. He most lives
Who thinks most, feels the noblest, acts the best.   *Festus.*

Life 's but a means unto an end, that end,
Beginning, mean, and end to all things—God.   *Ibid.*

Poets are all who love, who feel great truths,
And tell them : and the truth of truths is love.   *Ibid.*

—□—

ALFRED TENNYSON.

Broad based upon her people's will,
And compassed by the inviolate sea.   *To the Queen.*

For it was in the golden prime
Of good Haroun Alraschid.
                    Recollections of the Arabian Nights.

Across the walnuts and the wine.   *The Miller's Daughter.*

O Love, O fire! once he drew
With one long kiss my whole soul through
My lips, as sunlight drinketh dew.   *Fatima. St.* 3.

I built my soul a lordly pleasure-house,
Wherein at ease for aye to dwell.   *The Palace of Art.*

From yon blue heaven above us bent,
The grand old gardener and his wife
Smile at the claims of long descent.
                    Lady Clara Vere de Vere.

---

[1] A life spent worthily should be measured by a nobler line,—by deeds,
not years.—Sheridan, *Pizarro, Act* iv. *Sc.* 1.

LADY CLARA VERE DE VERE—*continued.:*

> Howe'er it be, it seems to me,
> 'T is only noble to be good.[1]
> Kind hearts are more than coronets,
>   And simple faith than Norman blood.   *Ibid.*

You must wake and call me early, call me early, mother dear:
To-morrow 'll be the happiest time of all the glad New Year;
Of all the glad New Year, mother, the maddest, merriest day;
For I 'm to be Queen o' the May, mother, I 'm to be Queen o' the May.
                                           The May Queen.

I am a part of all that I have met.[2]   *Ulysses.*

In the spring a livelier iris changes on the burnish'd dove;
In the spring a young man's fancy lightly turns to thoughts of love.
                                           Locksley Hall.

Love took up the harp of Life, and smote on all the chords with might;
Smote the chord of Self, that, trembling, passed in music out of sight. *Ibid.*

He will hold thee, when his passion shall have spent its novel force,
Something better than his dog, a little dearer than his horse.   *Ibid.*

Like a dog, he hunts in dreams.   *Ibid.*

With a little hoard of maxims preaching down a daughter's heart. *Ibid.*

>   This is truth the poet sings,
> That a sorrow's crown of sorrow is remembering happier things.[3] *Ibid.*

But the jingling of the guinea helps the hurt that Honour feels. *Ibid.*

Men, my brothers, men the workers, ever reaping something new. *Ibid.*

Yet I doubt not through the ages one increasing purpose runs,
And the thoughts of men are widened with the process of the suns. *Ibid.*

I will take some savage woman, she shall rear my dusky race.   *Ibid.*

I the heir of all the ages, in the foremost files of time.   *Ibid.*

---

[1] Nobilitas sola est atque unica virtus.
                              Juvenal, *Sat.* viii. *Line* 20.
    To be noble, we 'll be good.   *Winefreda.*
[2] I live not in myself, but I become
    Portion of that around me.
                    Byron, *Childe Harold, Canto* iii. *St.* 72.
        [3] Nessum maggior dolore
    Che ricordarsi del tempo felice
    Nella miseria.   Dante, *Inferno, Book* v. *St.* 121.
    For of fortunes sharpe adversite,
    The worst kind of infortune is this,
    A man that has been in prosperite,
    And it remember, whan it passed is.
            Chaucer, *Troilus and Creseide, Book* iii. *Line* 1625.
 In omni adversitate fortunæ, infelicissimum genus est infortunii fuisse
felicem.   Boethius, *De Consol. Phil., Lib.* ii.

Locksley Hall—*continued.*]

Let the great world spin for ever down the ringing grooves of change. *Ibid.*

Better fifty years of Europe than a cycle of Cathay. *Ibid.*

> But O! for the touch of a vanish'd hand,
> And the sound of a voice that is still! *Break, break, break.*

> But the tender grace of a day that is dead
> Will never come back to me. *Ibid.*

We are ancients of the earth,
And in the morning of the times. *The Day-Dream. L'Envoi.*

With prudes for proctors, dowagers for deans,
And sweet girl-graduates in their golden hair.
The Princess. Prologue.

A rosebud set with little wilful thorns,
And sweet as English air could make her, she. *Ibid.*

> Jewels five-words long,
> That on the stretched forefinger of all time
> Sparkle for ever. *Ibid. Canto* ii.

Blow, bugle, blow, set the wild echoes flying,
Blow, bugle; answer echoes, dying, dying, dying.
Ibid. Canto iii.

> O love, they die in yon rich sky,
> They faint on hill or field or river:
> Our echoes roll from soul to soul,
> And grow for ever and for ever.
> Blow, bugle, blow, set the wild echoes flying,
> And answer, echoes, answer, dying, dying, dying.
> *Ibid. Canto* iii.

> Tears, idle tears, I know not what they mean,
> Tears from the depth of some divine despair
> Rise in the heart, and gather to the eyes,
> In looking on the happy Autumn fields,
> And thinking of the days that are no more. *Ibid. Canto* iv.

> Unto dying eyes
> The casement slowly grows a glimmering square.
> *Ibid. Canto* iv.

> Dear as remembered kisses after death,
> And sweet as those by hopeless fancy feigned
> On lips that are for others; deep as love,
> Deep as first love, and wild with all regret;
> O Death in Life! the days that are no more. *Ibid. Canto* iv.

> Sweet is every sound,
> Sweeter thy voice, but every sound is sweet;
> Myriads of rivulets hurrying through the lawn,
> The moan of doves in immemorial elms,
> And murmuring of innumerable bees. *Ibid. Canto* vii.

THE PRINCESS—*continued.*]

Happy he
With such a mother! faith in womankind
Beats with his blood, and trust in all things high
Comes easy to him, and though he trip and fall,
He shall not blind his soul with clay.   *Ibid.   Canto* vii.

Never morning wore
To evening, but some heart did break.   *In Memoriam.*   vi.

And topples round the dreary west
A looming bastion fringed with fire.   *Ibid.* xv.

And from his ashes may be made
The violet of his native land.[1]   *Ibid.* xviii.

I do but sing because I must,
And pipe but as the linnets sing.   *Ibid.* xxi.

The shadow cloak'd from head to foot,
Who keeps the keys of all the creeds.   *Ibid.* xxiii.

And Thought leapt out to wed with Thought
Ere Thought could wed itself with Speech.   *Ibid.* xxiii.

'T is better to have loved and lost,
Than never to have loved at all.   *Ibid.* xxvii.

Her eyes are homes of silent prayer.   *Ibid.* xxxii.

Whose faith has centre everywhere,
Nor cares to fix itself to form.   *Ibid.* xxxiii.

Short swallow-flights of song, that dip
Their wings . . . . and skim away.   *Ibid.* xlvii.

Hold thou the good : define it well :
For fear divine Philosophy
Should push beyond her mark, and be
Procuress to the Lords of Hell.   *Ibid.* lii.

O yet we trust that somehow good
Will be the final goal of ill.   *Ibid.* liii.

But what am I ?
An infant crying in the night :
An infant crying for the light :
And with no language but a cry.   *Ibid.* liii.

So careful of the type she seems,
So careless of the single life.   *Ibid.* liv.

The great world's altar-stairs,
That slope through darkness up to God.   *Ibid.* liv.

Who battled for the true, the just.   *Ibid.* lv.

---

[1] Cf. Shakespeare, *Hamlet, Act* v. *Sc.* i.

IN MEMORIAM—*continued.*]

And grasps the skirts of happy chance,
And breasts the blows of circumstance.   *Ibid.* lxiii.

And lives to clutch the golden keys,
To mould a mighty state's decrees,
And shape the whisper of the throne.   *Ibid.* lxiii.

So many worlds, so much to do,
So little done, such things to be.   *Ibid.* lxxii.

Thy leaf has perished in the green.   *Ibid.* lxxiv.

There lives more faith in honest doubt,
Believe me, than in half the creeds.   *Ibid.* xcv.

Ring out wild bells to the wild sky.   *Ibid.* cv.

Ring out, ring out my mournful rhymes,
But ring the fuller minstrel in.   *Ibid.*

Ring out old shapes of foul disease,
Ring out the narrowing lust of gold;
Ring out the thousand wars of old,
Ring in the thousand years of peace.

Ring in the valiant man and free,
The eager heart, the kindlier hand;
Ring out the darkness of the land,
Ring in the Christ that is to be.   *Ibid.*

And thus he bore without abuse
The grand old name of gentleman,
Defamed by every charlatan,
And soil'd with all ignoble use.   *Ibid.* cx

One God, one law, one element,
And one far-off divine event,
To which the whole creation moves.   *Ibid. Conclusion.*

—□—

FRANCES ANNE KEMBLE.

A sacred burden is this life ye bear,
Look on it, lift it, bear it solemnly,
Stand up and walk beneath it steadfastly.
Fail not for sorrow, falter not for sin,
But onward, upward, till the goal ye win.
          Lines addressed to the Young Gentlemen leaving the
          Lenox Academy, Mass.

—□—

JOHN G. WHITTIER.

The hope of all who suffer,
The dread of all who wrong.
          The Mantle of St. John De Matha.

Making their lives a prayer.
                              On receiving a Basket of Sea Mosses.

For of all sad words of tongue or pen,
The saddest are these : " It might have been ! " *Maud Muller.*

——□——

EDGAR A. POE. 1811—1849.

Perched upon a bust of Pallas, just above my chamber door,—
    Perched, and sat, and nothing more.   *The Raven.*

Take thy beak from out my heart, and take thy form from off my door !
    Quoth the Raven : " Nevermore."   *Ibid.*

——□——

A. H. LAYARD.

I have always believed that success would be the inevitable result if the
two services, the army and the navy, had fair play, and if we sent the right
man to fill the right place.

        Speech, January, 15, 1855.   Hansard, *Parl. Debates, Third Series,*
            Vol. 138, *p.* 2077.

——□——

CHARLES SPRAGUE.

Lo, where the stage, the poor, degraded stage,
Holds its warped mirror to a gaping age.   *Curiosity.*

Through life's dark road his sordid way he wends,
An incarnation of fat dividends.   *Ibid.*

Behold ! in Liberty's unclouded blaze
We lift our heads, a race of other days. *Centennial Ode. St.* 22.

Yes, social friend, I love thee well,
    In learned doctors' spite ;
Thy clouds all other clouds dispel,
    And lap me in delight.   *To my Cigar.*

——□——

ALBERT G. GREENE. 1802—1867.

Old Grimes is dead,—that good old man,—
    We ne'er shall see him more :
He used to wear a long black coat,
    All buttoned down before.   *Old Grimes.*

——□——

CHRISTOPHER P. CRANCH.

Thought is deeper than all speech ;
    Feeling deeper than all thought ;
Souls to souls can never teach
    What unto themselves was taught.   *Stanzas.*

RALPH WALDO EMERSON.

Not from a vain or shallow thought
His awful Jove young Phidias brought.   *The Problem.*

But from the heart of Nature rolled
The burdens of the Bible old.   *Ibid.*

The hand that rounded Peter's dome,
And groined the aisles of Christian Rome,
Wrought in a sad sincerity;
Himself from God he could not free;
He builded better than he knew;—
The conscious stone to beauty grew.   *Ibid.*

Earth proudly wears the Parthenon
As the best gem upon her zone.   *Ibid.*

Good-bye, proud world! I 'm going home:
Thou art not my friend, and I 'm not thine.   *Good-Bye.*

What are they all in their high conceit,
When man in the bush with God may meet?   *Ibid.*

               If eyes were made for seeing,
Then Beauty is its own excuse for being.   *The Rhodora.*

The silent organ loudest chants
    The master's requiem.   *Dirge.*

Here once the embattled farmers stood,
And fired the shot heard round the world.
    Hymn, sung at the Completion of the Concord Monument.

——□——

FITZ-GREENE HALLECK.

Strike—for your altars and your fires;
Strike—for the green graves of your sires;
    God, and your native land!   *Marco Bozzaris.*

Come to the bridal chamber, Death!
    Come to the mother's, when she feels,
For the first time, her first-born's breath;
    Come when the blessed seals
That close the pestilence are broke,
And crowded cities wail its stroke;
Come in consumption's ghastly form,
The earthquake shock, the ocean storm;
Come when the heart beats high and warm,
    With banquet song, and dance, and wine;
And thou art terrible,—the tear,
The groan, the knell, the pall, the bier,
And all we know, or dream, or fear
    Of agony are thine.   *Ibid.*

MARCO BOZZARIS—*continued.*]

But to the hero, when his sword
  Has won the battle for the free,
Thy voice sounds like a prophet's word;
  And in its hollow tones are heard
    The thanks of millions yet to be.   *Ibid.*

One of the few, the immortal names,
  That were not born to die.   *Ibid.*

Green be the turf above thee,
  Friend of my better days;
None knew thee but to love thee,[1]
  Nor named thee but to praise.
                    On the Death of Joseph Rodman Drake.

Such graves as his are pilgrim-shrines,
  Shrines to no code or creed confined,—
The Delphian vales, the Palestines,
  The Meccas of the mind.   *Burns.*

They love their land, because it is their own,
  And scorn to give aught other reason why;
Would shake hands with a king upon his throne,
  And think it kindness to his majesty.   *Connecticut.*

—□—

ALEXANDER SMITH. 1830—1867.

Like a pale martyr in his shirt of fire.
                    A Life Drama. Sc. ii.

In winter when the dismal rain
  Came down in slanting lines,
And Wind, that grand old harper, smote
  His thunder-harp of pines.   *Ibid.*

A poem round and perfect as a star.   *Ibid.*

—□—

HENRY W. LONGFELLOW.

Look, then, into thine heart, and write!
                    Voices of the Night Prelude.

Tell me not, in mournful numbers,
  "Life is but an empty dream!"
For the soul is dead that slumbers,
  And things are not what they seem.   *A Psalm of Life.*

Art is long, and Time is fleeting,[2]
  And our hearts, though stout and brave,
Still, like muffled drums, are beating
  Funeral marches to the grave.   *Ibid.*

---

[1] Cf. Rogers, *Jacqueline.*
[2] Ars longa, vita brevis.—Hippocrates, *Aphorism* i.

A PSALM OF LIFE—*continued.*]

Trust no future, howe'er pleasant !
Let the dead Past bury its dead !   *Ibid.*

Lives of great men all remind us
We can make our lives sublime,
And, departing, leave behind us
Footprints on the sands of time.   *Ibid.*

Still achieving, still pursuing,
Learn to labour, and to wait.   *Ibid.*

There is a Reaper, whose name is **Death,**
And, with his sickle keen,
He reaps the bearded grain at a breath,
And the flowers that grow between.
The Reaper and the Flowers.

The star of the unconquered will.   *The Light of Stars.*

O, fear not in a world like this,
And thou shalt know ere long,—
Know how sublime a thing it is
To suffer and be strong.   *Ibid.*

Spake full well, in language quaint and olden,
One who dwelleth by the castled Rhine,
When he called the flowers, so blue and golden,
Stars, that in earth's firmament do shine.   *Flowers.*

The hooded clouds, like friars,
Tell their beads in drops of rain.   *Midnight Mass.*

No tears
Dim the sweet look that Nature wears.
Sunrise on the Hills.

No one is so accursed by fate,
No one so utterly desolate,
But some heart, though unknown,
Responds unto his own.   *Endymion.*

For Time will teach thee soon the truth,
There are no birds in last year's nest !
It is not always May.

This is the place.   Stand still, my steed,
Let me review the scene,
And summon from the shadowy Past
The forms that once have been.   *A Gleam of Sunshine.*

Standing, with reluctant feet,
Where the brook and river meet,
Womanhood and childhood fleet !   *Maidenhood.*

O thou child of many prayers !
Life hath quicksands,—life hath snares !   *Ibid.*

The day is done, and the darkness
　　Falls from the wings of Night,
As a feather is wafted downward
　　From an eagle in his flight.　　　*The Day is Done.*

A feeling of sadness and longing,
　　That is not akin to pain,
And resembles sorrow only
　　As the mist resembles the rain.　　　　　*Ibid.*

And the night shall be filled with music,
　　And the cares that infest the day
Shall fold their tents like the Arabs,
　　And as silently steal away.　　　　　　*Ibid.*

This is the forest primeval.　　　　　*Evangeline.　Part* I.

When she had passed, it seemed like the ceasing of exquisite music.
　　　　　　　　　　　　　　Ibid.　Part I, i.

Blossomed the lovely stars, the forget-me-nots of the angels.
　　　　　　　　　　　　　　Ibid.　Part I, iii.

Into a world unknown,—the corner-stone of a nation ¹
　　　　　　　　　The Courtship of Miles Standish.

O suffering, sad humanity !
O ye afflicted ones, who lie
Steeped to the lips in misery,
Longing, and yet afraid to die,
　　Patient, though sorely tried !　　　*The Goblet of Life.*

　　　Sail on, O Ship of State !
Sail on, O UNION, strong and great !
Humanity with all its fears,
With all the hopes of future years,
Is hanging breathless on thy fate !
　　　　　　　　　The Building of the Ship.

Our hearts, our hopes, are all with thee,
Our hearts, our hopes, our prayers, our tears,
Our faith triumphant o'er our fears,
Are all with thee,—are all with thee !　　　　*Ibid.*

There is no flock, however watched and tended,
　　But one dead lamb is there !
There is no fireside, howsoe'er defended,
　　But has one vacant chair.　　　　　*Resignation.*

The air is full of farewells to the dying,
　　And mournings for the dead.　　　　　*Ibid.*

There is no Death ! What seems so is transition;
　　This life of mortal breath
Is but a suburb of the life elysian,
　　Whose portal we call Death.　　　　　*Ibid.*

¹ Plymouth Rock.

In the elder days of Art,
    Builders wrought with greatest care
Each minute and unseen part;
    For the gods see everywhere.   *The Builders.*

                    Time has laid his hand
Upon my heart, gently, not smiting it,
But as a harper lays his open palm
Upon his harp, to deaden its vibrations. *The Golden Legend.*

The leaves of memory seemed to make
    A mournful rustling in the dark.   *The Fire of Drift-wood.*

Who ne'er his bread in sorrow ate,
    Who ne'er the mournful midnight hours
Weeping upon his bed has sate,
    He knows you not, ye Heavenly Powers.
From Goethe's Wilhelm Meister. Motto, Hyperion. Book i.

Something the heart must have to cherish,
    Must love, and joy, and sorrow learn;
Something with passion clasp or perish,
    And in itself to ashes burn.   *Motto, Hyperion. Book* ii.

Though the mills of God grind slowly, yet they grind exceeding small; [1]
Though with patience He stands waiting, with exactness grinds He all.
        Retribution. From the Sinngedichte of Friedrich von Logau.

——□——

OLIVER WENDELL HOLMES.

The freeman casting with unpurchased hand
The vote that shakes the turrets of the land.
                        Poetry, a Metrical Essay.

    Ay, tear her tattered ensign down!
        Long has it waved on high,
    And many an eye has danced to see
        That banner in the sky.   *Ibid.*

    Nail to the mast her holy flag,
        Set every threadbare sail,
    And give her to the God of storms,
        The lightning and the gale.   *Ibid.*

When the last reader reads no more.   *The Last Reader.*

The mossy marbles rest
On the lips that he has prest
        In their bloom;
And the names he loved to hear
Have been carved for many a year
        On the tomb.   *The Last Leaf.*

[1] Ὀψὲ θεοῦ μῦλοι ἀλέουσι τὸ λεπτὸν ἄλευρον.—*Oracula Sibyllina, Lib.* viii.
L. 14.

THE LAST LEAF—*continued.*]

    I know it is a sin
    For me to sit and grin
      At him here;
    But the old three-cornered hat,
    And the breeches, and all that,
      Are so queer!
                    Ibid.

Thou say'st an undisputed thing
  In such a solemn way.
               To an Insect.

Thine eye was on the censer,
  And not the hand that bore it.
               Lines by a Clerk.

Where go the poet's lines?
  Answer, ye evening tapers!
Ye auburn locks, ye golden curls,
  Speak from your folded papers!
               The Poet's Lot.

Their discords sting through Burns and Moore
  Like hedgehogs dressed in lace. *The Music-Grinders.*

You think they are crusaders, sent
  From some infernal clime,
To pluck the eyes of Sentiment,
  And dock the tail of Rhyme,
To crack the voice of Melody,
  And break the legs of Time.
               Ibid.

And, since, I never dare to write
  As funny as I can. *The Height of the Ridiculous.*

Yes, child of suffering, thou mayst well be sure,
He who ordained the Sabbath loves the poor!
               Urania.

And, when you stick on conversation's burrs,
Don't strew your pathway with those dreadful *urs.*
               Ibid.

You hear that boy laughing?—you think he's all fun;
But the angels laugh, too, at the good he has done;
The children laugh loud as they troop to his call,
And the poor man that knows him laughs loudest of all!
               The Boys.

—□—

SARAH FLOWER ADAMS.

    Nearer, my God, to Thee,
      Nearer to Thee!
    E'en though it be a cross
      That raiseth me;
    Still all my song shall be,
    Nearer, my God, to Thee,
      Nearer to Thee!

ELIZA COOK.

I love it—I love it, and who shall dare
To chide me for loving that old arm-chair !
The Old Arm-Chair.

——□——

CHARLES DICKENS.

In a Pickwickian sense. *Pickwick. Ch. i.*

Oh, a dainty plant is the Ivy green,
    That creepeth o'er ruins old !
Of right choice food are his meals, I ween,
    In his cell so lone and cold.
Creeping where no life is seen,
    A rare old plant is the Ivy green. *Ibid. Ch. vi.*

He 's tough, ma'am, tough is J. B.   Tough and de-vilish sly.
Dombey and Son. Ch. vii.

When found, make a note of. *Ibid. Ch. xv.*

The bearings of this observation lays in the application on it.
Ibid. Ch. xxiii.

A demd, damp, moist, unpleasant body ! *Nicholas Nickleby. Ch. xxxiv.*

My Life is one demd horrid grind. *Ibid. Ch. lxiv.*

Barkis is willin'. *David Copperfield. Ch. v.*

Whatever was required to be done, the Circumlocution Office was before-
hand with all the public departments in the art of perceiving HOW NOT TO
DO IT. *Little Dorrit. Ch. x.*

In came Mrs. Fezziwig, one vast substantial smile.
Christmas Carol. Stave two.

——□——

JAMES RUSSELL LOWELL.

'T is heaven alone that is given away,
    'T is only God may be had for the asking.
The Vision of Sir Launfal.

And what is so rare as a day in June ?
    Then, if ever, come perfect days ;
Then Heaven tries the earth if it be in tune,
    And over it softly her warm ear lays. *Ibid.*

This child is not mine as the first was,
    I cannot sing it to rest,
I cannot lift it up fatherly
    And bless it upon my breast ;

Yet it lies in my little one's cradle,
    And sits in my little one's chair,
And the light of the heaven she 's gone to
    Transfigures its golden hair. *The Changeling.*

To win the secret of a weed's plain heart.   *Sonnet* xxv.

Earth's noblest thing, a woman perfected.   *Irenè.*

Truth for ever on the scaffold, Wrong for ever on the throne.
        The Present Crisis.

Before man made us citizens, great Nature made us men.   *The Capture.*

—▫—

OLD TESTAMENT.

It is not good that the man should be alone.   *Genesis* ii. 18.

In the sweat of thy face shalt thou eat bread. . . . . For dust thou art,
and unto dust shalt thou return.   *Gen.* iii. 19.

The mother of all living.   *Gen.* iii. 20.

Am I my brother's keeper?   *Gen.* iv. 9.

My punishment is greater than I can bear.   *Gen.* iv. 13.

There were giants in the earth in those days.   *Gen.* vi. 4.

But the dove found no rest for the sole of her foot.   *Gen.* viii. 9.

Whoso sheddeth man's blood, by man shall his blood be shed.
        Gen. ix. 6.

In a good old age.   *Gen.* xv. 15.

His hand will be against every man, and every man's hand against him.
        Gen. xvi. 12.

Bring down my gray hairs with sorrow to the grave.   *Gen.* xlii. 38.

Unstable as water, thou shalt not excel.   *Gen.* xlix. 4.

I have been a stranger in a strange land.   *Exodus* ii. 22.

Unto a land flowing with milk and honey.   *Ex.* iii. 8.   *Jer.* xxxii. 22.

Darkness which may be felt.   *Ex.* x. 21.

The Lord went before them by day in a pillar of a cloud, to lead them
the way; and by night in a pillar of fire.   *Ex.* xiii. 21.

Man doth not live by bread only.   *Deuteronomy* viii. 3.

The wife of thy bosom.   *Deut.* xiii. 6.

Eye for eye, tooth for tooth, hand for hand, foot for foot.   *Deut.* xix. 21.

The secret things belong unto the Lord our God.   *Deut.* xxix. 29.

He kept him as the apple of his eye.   *Deut.* xxxii. 10.

As thy days, so shall thy strength be.   *Deut.* xxxiii. 25.

I am going the way of all the earth.   *Joshua* xxiii. 14.

I arose a mother in Israel.   *Judges* v. 7.

She brought forth butter in a lordly dish. *Judges* v. 25.

The Philistines be upon thee, Samson. *Judges* xvi. 9.

For whither thou goest, I will go; and where thou lodgest, I will lodge: thy people shall be my people, and thy God my God. *Ruth* i. 16.

Quit yourselves like men. 1 *Samuel* iv. 9.

Is Saul also among the prophets? 1 *Sam.* x. 11.

A man after his own heart. 1 *Sam.* xiii. 14.

Tell it not in Gath; publish it not in the streets of Askelon. 2 *Sam.* i. 20.

Saul and Jonathan were lovely and pleasant in their lives, and in their death they were not divided. 2 *Sam.* i. 23.

How are the mighty fallen in the midst of the battle! 2 *Sam.* i. 25.

Very pleasant hast thou been unto me: thy love to me was wonderful, passing the love of women. 2 *Sam.* i. 26.

Tarry at Jericho until your beards be grown. 2 *Sam.* x. 5.

And Nathan said to David, Thou art the man. 2 *Sam.* xii. 7.

And are as water spilt on the ground, which cannot be gathered up again. 2 *Sam.* xiv. 14.

A proverb and a by-word among all people. 1 *Kings* ix. 7.

How long halt ye between two opinions? 1 *Kings* xviii. 21.

Behold, there ariseth a little cloud out of the sea, like a man's hand. 1 *Kings* xviii. 44.

A still, small voice. 1 *Kings* xix. 12.

Let not him that girdeth on his harness boast himself as he that putteth it off. 1 *Kings* xx. 11.

There is death in the pot. 2 *Kings* iv. 40.

Is thy servant a dog, that he should do this great thing? 2 *Kings* viii. 13.

And the driving is like the driving of Jehu, the son of Nimshi: for he driveth furiously. 2 *Kings* ix. 20.

One that feared God and eschewed evil. *Job* i. 1.

And Satan came also. *Job* i. 6.

Naked came I out of my mother's womb, and naked shall I return thither: the Lord gave, and the Lord hath taken away; blessed be the name of the Lord. *Job* i. 21.

Skin for skin, yea, all that a man hath, will he give for his life. *Job.* ii. 4.

There the wicked cease from troubling, and there the weary be at rest. *Job* iii. 17.

L

In thoughts from the visions of the night, when deep sleep falleth on men
Job iv. 13; xxxiii. 15

Yet man is born unto trouble, as the sparks fly upward.   *Job* v. 7.

He taketh the wise in their own craftiness.   *Job* v. 13.

Thou shalt come to thy grave in a full age, like as a shock of corn cometh
in in his season.   *Job* v. 26.

How forcible are right words !   *Job* vi. 25.

My days are swifter than a weaver's shuttle.   *Job* vii. 6.

He shall return no more to his house, neither shall his place know him
any more.[1]   *Job* vii. 10. Cf. xvi. 22.

I would not live alway.   *Job* vii. 16.

Before I go whence I shall not return, even to the land of darkness and
the shadow of death.   *Job* x. 21.

Ye are the people, and wisdom shall die with you.   *Job* xii. 2.

Man that is born of a woman is of few days, and full of trouble.
Job xiv. 1.

Miserable comforters are ye all.   *Job* xvi. 2.

The King of terrors.   *Job* xviii. 14.

I am escaped with the skin of my teeth.   *Job* xix. 20.

Seeing the root of the matter is found in me.   *Job* xix. 28.

The price of wisdom is above rubies.   *Job* xxviii. 18.

When the ear heard me, then it blessed me ; and when the eye saw me,
it gave witness to me.   *Job* xxix. 11.

I caused the widow's heart to sing for joy.   *Job* xxix. 13.

I was eyes to the blind, and feet was I to the lame.   *Job* xxix. 15.

The house appointed for all living.   *Job* xxx. 23.

Oh . . . . that mine adversary had written a book !   *Job* xxxi. 25.

He multiplieth words without knowledge.   *Job* xxxv. 16.

Who is this that darkeneth counsel by words without knowledge ?
Job xxxviii. 2.

When the morning stars sang together, and all the sons of God shouted
for joy.   *Job* xxxviii. 7.

Hitherto shalt thou come, but no further; and here shall thy proud
waves be stayed.   *Job* xxxviii. 11.

---

[1] For the wind passeth over it, and it is gone; and the place thereof shall
know it no more.—*Psalm* ciii. 16.
  Usually quoted, "The place that has known him shall know him no
more."

Canst thou bind the sweet influences of Pleiades, or loose the bands of Orion?   *Job* xxxviii. 31.

He saith among the trumpets, Ha, ha; and he smelleth the battle afar off, the thunder of the captains and the shouting.   *Job* xxxix. 25.

Canst thou draw out leviathan with an hook?   *Job* xli. 1.

His heart is as firm as a stone; yea, as hard as a piece of the nether millstone.   *Job* xli. 24.

He maketh the deep to boil like a pot.   *Job* xli. 31.

I have heard of thee by the hearing of the ear: but now mine eye seeth thee.   *Job* xlii. 5.

His leaf also shall not wither.   *Psalm* i. 3.

Out of the mouths of babes and sucklings.   *Ps* viii. 2.

Thou hast made him a little lower than the angels.   *Ps.* viii. 5.

The fool hath said in his heart, There is no God.   *Ps.* xiv. 1; liii. 1.

He that sweareth to his own hurt, and changeth not.   *Ps.* xv. 4.

The lines are fallen unto me in pleasant places.   *Ps.* xvi. 6.

Keep me as the apple of the eye, hide me under the shadow of thy wings.
                                                               Ps. xvii. 8.

The sorrows of death compassed me.   *Ps.* xviii. 4.

Yea, he did fly upon the wings of the wind.   *Ps.* xviii. 10.

The heavens declare the glory of God; and the firmament sheweth his handywork.   *Ps.* xix. 1.

Day unto day uttereth speech, and night unto night sheweth knowledge.
                                                               Ps. xix. 2.

I may tell all my bones.   *Ps.* xxii. 17.

He maketh me to lie down in green pastures: he leadeth me beside the still waters.   *Ps.* xxiii. 2.

Thy rod and thy staff they comfort me.   *Ps.* xxiii. 4.

From the strife of tongues.   *Ps.* xxxi. 20.

He fashioneth their hearts alike.   *Ps.* xxxiii. 15.

I have been young, and now am old; yet have I not seen the righteous forsaken, nor his seed begging bread.   *Ps.* xxxvii. 25.

Spreading himself like a green bay-tree.   *Ps.* xxxvii. 35.

Mark the perfect man, and behold the upright.   *Ps.* xxxvii. 37.

While I was musing the fire burned.   *Ps.* xxxix. 3.

Lord, make me to know mine end, and the measure of my days, what it is; that I may know how frail I am.   *Ps.* xxxix. 4.

Verily every man at his best state is altogether vanity.   *Psalm* xxxix. 5.

He heapeth up riches, and knoweth not who shall gather them.
Ps. xxxix. 6

Blessed is he that considereth the poor.   *Ps.* xli. 1.

As the hart panteth after the water brooks.   *Ps.* xlii. 1.

Deep calleth unto deep.   *Ps.* xlii. 7.

My tongue is the pen of a ready writer.   *Ps.* xlv. 1.

Beautiful for situation, the joy of the whole earth, is Mount Zion, ...
the city of the great King.   *Ps.* xlviii. 2

Man being in honour abideth not; he is like the beasts that perish.
Ps. xlix. 12, 20.

The cattle upon a thousand hills.   *Ps.* l. 10.

Oh that I had wings like a dove !   *Ps.* lv. 6.

We took sweet counsel together.   *Ps.* lv. 14.

The words of his mouth were smoother than butter, but war was in his
heart.   *Ps.* lv. 21.

They are like the deaf adder that stoppeth her ear; which will not
hearken to the voice of charmers, charming never so wisely.   *Ps.* lviii. 4, 5.

Vain is the help of man.   *Ps.* lx. 11 ; cviii. 12.

He shall come down like rain upon the mown grass.   *Ps.* lxxii. 6.

His enemies shall lick the dust.   *Ps.* lxxii. 9.

As a dream when one awaketh.   *Ps.* lxxiii. 20.

For promotion cometh neither from the east, nor from the west, nor from
the south.   *Ps.* lxxv. 6.

He putteth down one and setteth up another.   *Ps.* lxxv. 7.

They go from strength to strength.   *Ps.* lxxxiv. 7.

For a day in thy courts is better than a thousand.   I had rather be a door-
keeper in the house of my God, than to dwell in the tents of wickedness.
Ps. lxxxiv. 10.

Mercy and truth are met together : righteousness and peace have kissed
each other.   *Ps.* lxxxv. 10.

For a thousand years in thy sight are but as yesterday when it is past.
Ps. xc. 4.

We spend our years as a tale that is told.   *Ps.* xc. 9.

The days of our years are threescore years and ten ; and if by reason of
strength they be fourscore years, yet is their strength labour and sorrow :
for it is soon cut off, and we fly away.   *Ps.* xc. 10.

So teach us to number our days, that we may apply our hearts unto wisdom.
Psalm xc. 12.

Nor for the pestilence that walketh in darkness; nor for the destruction that wasteth at noonday.
Ps. xci. 6.

As for man his days are as grass; as a flower of the field so he flourisheth.
Ps. ciii. 15.

For the wind passeth over it, and it is gone; and the place thereof shall know it no more.
Ps. ciii. 16.

Wine that maketh glad the heart of man.
Ps. civ. 15.

Man goeth forth unto his work and to his labour until the evening.
Ps. civ. 23.

They that go down to the sea in ships, that do business in great waters.
Ps. cvii. 23.

They reel to and fro, and stagger like a drunken man, and are at their wit's end.
Ps. cvii. 27.

I said in my haste, All men are liars.
Ps. cxvi. 11.

Precious in the sight of the Lord is the death of his saints.
Ps. cxvi. 15.

The stone which the builders refused is become the head stone of the corner.
Ps. cxviii. 22.

A lamp unto my feet and a light unto my path.
Ps. cxix. 105.

The sun shall not smite thee by day, nor the moon by night.
Ps. cxxi. 6.

Peace be within thy walls and prosperity within thy palaces.
Ps. cxxii. 7.

He giveth his beloved sleep.
Ps. cxxvii. 2.

Happy is the man that hath his quiver full of them.
Ps. cxxvii. 5.

Thy children like olive-plants round about thy table.
Ps. cxxviii. 3.

I will not give sleep to mine eyes, or slumber to mine eyelids.
Ps. cxxxii. 4. *Prov.* vi. 4.

Behold how good and how pleasant it is for brethren to dwell together in unity.
Fs. cxxxiii. 1.

We hanged our harps upon the willows.
Ps. cxxxvii. 2.

If I forget thee, O Jerusalem, let my right hand forget her cunning.
Ps. cxxxvii. 5.

If I take the wings of the morning, and dwell in the uttermost parts of the sea.
Ps. cxxxix. 9.

For I am fearfully and wonderfully made.
Ps. cxxxix. 14.

Put not your trust in princes.
Ps. cxlvi. 3.

Wisdom crieth without; she uttereth her voice in the street.
Proverbs i. 20.

Her ways are ways of pleasantness, and all her paths are peace.
Proverbs iii. 17.

Wisdom is the principal thing; therefore get wisdom; and with all thy getting get understanding.   *Prov.* iv. 7.

The path of the just is as the shining light, that shineth more and more unto the perfect day.   *Prov.* iv. 18.

Go to the ant, thou sluggard; consider her ways, and be wise.
Prov. vi. 6.

Yet a little sleep, a little slumber, a little folding of the hands to sleep.
Prov. vi. 10; xxiv. 33.

So shall thy poverty come as one that travelleth, and thy want as an armed man.   *Prov.* vi. 11.

As an ox goeth to the slaughter.   *Prov.* vii. 22.   *Jer.* xi. 19.

Wisdom is better than rubies.   *Prov.* viii. 11.

Stolen waters are sweet, and bread eaten in secret is pleasant.
Prov. ix. 17.

He knoweth not that the dead are there; and that her guests are in the depths of hell.   *Prov.* ix. 18.

A wise son maketh a glad father.   *Prov.* x. 1.

The memory of the just is blessed.   *Prov.* x. 7.

In the multitude of counsellors there is safety.   *Prov.* xi. 14; xxiv. 6.

He that is surety for a stranger shall smart for it.   *Prov.* xi. 15.

A righteous man regardeth the life of his beast; but the tender mercies of the wicked are cruel.   *Prov.* xii. 10.

Hope deferred maketh the heart sick.   *Prov.* xiii. 12.

The way of transgressors is hard.   *Prov.* xiii. 15.

He that spareth his rod hateth his son.   *Prov.* xiii. 24.

Fools make a mock at sin.   *Prov.* xiv. 9.

The heart knoweth his own bitterness; and a stranger doth not inter-meddle with his joy.   *Prov.* xiv. 10.

The prudent man looketh well to his going.   *Prov.* xiv. 15.

Righteousness exalteth a nation.   *Prov.* xiv. 34.

A soft answer turneth away wrath.   *Prov.* xv. 1.

A merry heart maketh a cheerful countenance.   *Prov.* xv. 13.

Better is a dinner of herbs where love is, than a stalled ox and hatred therewith.   *Prov.* xv. 17.

A word spoken in due season, how good is it!   *Prov.* xv. 23.

A man's heart deviseth his way; but the Lord directeth his steps.
Proverbs xvi. 9.

Pride goeth before destruction, and an haughty spirit before a fall.
Prov. xvi. 18.

The hoary head is a crown of glory. *Prov.* xvi. 31.

A gift is as a precious stone in the eyes of him that hath it. *Prov.* xvii. 8.

He that repeateth a matter separateth very friends. *Prov.* xvii. 9.

He that hath knowledge spareth his words. *Prov.* xvii. 27

Even a fool, when he holdeth his peace, is counted wise. *Prov.* xvii. 28.

A wounded spirit who can bear? *Prov.* xviii. 14.

A man that hath friends must shew himself friendly; and there is a friend that sticketh closer than a brother. *Prov.* xviii. 24.

He that hath pity upon the poor lendeth unto the Lord. *Prov.* xix. 17.

Wine is a mocker, strong drink is raging. *Prov.* xx. 1.

Every fool will be meddling. *Prov.* xx. 3.

The hearing ear and the seeing eye. *Prov.* xx. 12.

It is better to dwell in a corner of the house-top, than with a brawling woman in a wide house. *Prov.* xxi. 9.

A good name is rather to be chosen than great riches. *Prov.* xxii. 1.

Train up a child in the way he should go; and when he is old, he will not depart from it. *Prov.* xxii. 6.

The borrower is servant to the lender. *Prov.* xxii. 7.

Remove not the ancient landmark. *Prov.* xxii. 28; xxiii. 10.

Seest thou a man diligent in his business? he shall stand before kings; he shall not stand before mean men. *Prov.* xxii. 29.

For riches certainly make themselves wings. *Prov.* xxiii. 5.

As he thinketh in his heart, so is he. *Prov.* xxiii. 7.

Drowsiness shall clothe a man with rags. *Prov.* xxiii. 21.

Look not thou upon the wine, when it is red; when it giveth his colour in the cup; . . . . at the last it biteth like a serpent and stingeth like an adder. *Prov.* xxiii. 31, 32.

If thou faint in the day of adversity, thy strength is small. *Prov.* xxiv. 10.

A word fitly spoken is like apples of gold in pictures of silver.
Prov. xxv. 11.

For thou shalt heap coals of fire upon his head. *Prov.* xxv. 22.

As cold waters to a thirsty soul, so is good news from a far country.
Prov. xxv. 25.

Answer a fool according to his folly.   *Proverbs* xxvi. 5.

Seest thou a man wise in his own conceit? there is more hope of a fool than of him.   *Prov.* xxvi. 12.

There is a lion in the way; a lion is in the streets.   *Prov.* xxvi. 13.

Wiser in his own conceit than seven men that can render a reason.
Prov. xxvi. 16.

Whoso diggeth a pit shall fall therein.   *Prov.* xxvi. 27.

Boast not thyself of to-morrow; for thou knowest not what a day may bring forth.   *Prov.* xxvii. 1.

Open rebuke is better than secret love.   *Prov.* xxvii. 5.

Faithful are the wounds of a friend.   *Prov.* xxvii. 6.

A continual dropping in a very rainy day and a contentious woman are alike.   *Prov.* xxvii. 15.

Iron sharpeneth iron, so a man sharpeneth the countenance of his friend.
Prov. xxvii. 17.

Though thou shouldest bray a fool in a mortar among wheat, with a pestle, yet will not his foolishness depart from him.   *Prov.* xxvii. 22.

The wicked flee when no man pursueth: but the righteous are bold as a lion.   *Prov.* xxviii. 1.

He that maketh haste to be rich shall not be innocent. *Prov.* xxviii. 20.

Remove far from me vanity and lies; give me neither poverty nor riches; feed me with food convenient for me.   *Prov.* xxx. 8.

The horse-leech hath two daughters, crying, Give, give. *Prov.* xxx. 15.

Her children arise up and call her blessed.   *Prov.* xxxi. 28.

Vanity of vanities, ... all is vanity.   *Ecclesiastes* i. 2; xii. 8.

One generation passeth away and another generation cometh.
Eccles. i. 4.

The eye is not satisfied with seeing.   *Eccles.* i. 8.

There is no new thing under the sun.   *Eccles.* i. 9.

All is vanity and vexation of spirit.   *Eccles.* i. 14.

He that increaseth knowledge increaseth sorrow.   *Eccles.* i. 18.

One event happeneth to them all.   *Eccles.* ii. 14.

To everything there is a season, and a time to every purpose under the heaven.   *Eccles.* iii. 1.

A threefold cord is not quickly broken.   *Eccles.* iv. 12.

God is in heaven, and thou upon earth; therefore let thy words be few.
Eccles. v. 2

Better is it that thou shouldest not vow, than that thou shouldest vow and not pay.   *Eccles.* v. 5.

The sleep of a labouring man is sweet. *Ecclesiastes* v. 12.

A good name is better than precious ointment. *Eccles.* vii. 1.

It is better to go to the house of mourning than to go to the house of feasting. *Eccles.* vii. 2.

As the crackling of thorns under a pot, so is the laughter of a fool. *Eccles.* vii. 6.

In the day of prosperity be joyful, but in the day of adversity consider. *Eccles.* vii. 14.

Be not righteous overmuch. *Eccles.* vii. 16.

God hath made man upright; but they have sought out many inventions. *Eccles.* vii. 29.

There is no discharge in that war. *Eccles.* viii. 8.

To eat and to drink and to be merry. *Eccles.* viii. 15. *Luke* xii. 19.

For a living dog is better than a dead lion. *Eccles.* ix. 4.

Whatsoever thy hand findeth to do, do it with thy might; for there is no work, nor device, nor knowledge, nor wisdom, in the grave. *Eccles.* ix. 10.

The race is not to the swift, nor the battle to the strong. But time and chance happeneth to them all. *Eccles.* ix. 11.

Dead flies cause the ointment of the apothecary to send forth a stinking savour. *Eccles.* x. 1.

For a bird of the air shall carry the voice, and that which hath wings shall tell the matter. *Eccles.* x. 20.

Cast thy bread upon the waters, for thou shalt find it after many days. *Eccles.* xi. 1.

In the place where the tree falleth, there it shall be. *Eccles.* xi. 3.

He that observeth the wind shall not sow; and he that regardeth the clouds shall not reap. *Eccles.* xi. 4.

In the morning sow thy seed, and in the evening withhold not thine hand. *Eccles.* xi. 6.

Truly the light is sweet, and a pleasant thing it is for the eyes to behold the sun. *Eccles.* xi. 7.

Rejoice, O young man, in thy youth. *Eccles.* xi. 9.

Remember now thy Creator in the days of thy youth. *Eccles.* xii. 1.

And the grinders cease because they are few, and those that look out of the windows be darkened. *Eccles.* xii. 3.

And the grasshopper shall be a burden, and desire shall fail; because man goeth to his long home, and the mourners go about the streets. *Eccles.* xii. 5.

L*

Or ever the silver cord be loosed, or the golden bowl be broken, or the pitcher be broken at the fountain, or the wheel broken at the cistern.

Ecclesiastes xii. 6.

Then shall the dust return to the earth as it was; and the spirit shall return unto God who gave it.

Eccles. xii. 7.

The words of the wise are as goads, and as nails fastened by the masters of assemblies.

Eccles. xii. 11.

Of making many books there is no end; and much study is a weariness of the flesh.

Eccles. xii. 12.

Let us hear the conclusion of the whole matter : Fear God and keep his commandments; for this is the whole duty of man.

Eccles. xii. 13.

For lo, the winter is past, the rain is over and gone; the flowers appear on the earth; the time of the singing of birds is come, and the voice of the turtle is heard in our land.

The Song of Solomon ii. 11, 12.

The little foxes, that spoil the vines.

The Song of Solomon ii. 15.

Terrible as an army with banners.

The Song of Solomon vi. 4, 10.

Like the best wine, ... that goeth down sweetly, causing the lips of those that are asleep to speak.

The Song of Solomon vii. 9.

Love is strong as death; jealousy is cruel as the grave.

The Song of Solomon viii. 6.

Many waters cannot quench love.

The Song of Solomon viii. 7.

The ox knoweth his owner, and the ass his master's crib.

Isaiah i. 3.

The whole head is sick, and the whole heart faint.

Is. i. 5.

They shall beat their swords into ploughshares, and their spears into pruning-hooks; nation shall not lift up sword against nation, neither shall they learn war any more.

Is. ii. 4. *Mic.* iv. 3.

In that day a man shall cast his idols . . . . to the moles and to the bats.

Is. ii. 20.

Cease ye from man, whose breath is in his nostrils.

Is. ii. 22.

Grind the faces of the poor.

Is. iii. 15.

In that day seven women shall take hold of one man.

Is. iv. 1.

Woe unto them that call evil good, and good evil !

Is. v. 20.

I am a man of unclean lips.

Is. vi. 5.

Wizards that peep and that mutter.

Is. viii. 19.

To the law and to the testimony.

Is. viii. 20.

The wolf also shall dwell with the lamb, and the leopard shall lie down with the kid.

Is. xi. 6.

Hell from beneath is moved for thee to meet thee at thy coming.

Is. xiv. 9.

How art thou fallen from heaven, O Lucifer, son of the morning !
Isaiah xiv. 12.

Babylon is fallen, is fallen. *Is.* xxi. 9.

Let us eat and drink; for to-morrow we shall die. *Is.* xxii. 13.

Fasten him as a nail in a sure place. *. xxii. 23.

Whose merchants are princes. *Is.* xxiii. 8.

A feast of fat things. *Is.* xxv. 6.

For precept must be upon precept, precept upon precept; line upon line, line upon line; here a little, and there a little. *Is.* xxviii. 10.

We have made a covenant with death, and with hell are we at agreement. *Is.* xxviii. 15.

The desert shall rejoice, and blossom as the rose. *Is.* xxxv. 1.

Thou trustest in the staff of this broken reed. *Is.* xxxvi. 6.

Set thine house in order. *Is.* xxxviii. 1.

All flesh is grass. *Is.* xl. 6.

Behold, the nations are as a drop of a bucket, and are counted as the small dust of the balance. *Is.* xl. 15.

A bruised reed shall he not break, and the smoking flax shall he not quench. *Is.* xlii. 3.

There is no peace, saith the Lord, unto the wicked. *Is.* xlviii. 22.

He is brought as a lamb to the slaughter. *Is.* liii. 7.

Let the wicked forsake his way, and the unrighteous man his thoughts. *Is.* lv. 7.

A little one shall become a thousand, and a small one a strong nation. *Is.* lx. 22.

To give unto them beauty for ashes, the oil of joy for mourning, the garment of praise for the spirit of heaviness. *Is.* lxi. 3.

I have trodden the wine-press alone. *Is.* lxiii. 3.

We all do fade as a leaf. *Is.* lxiv. 6.

Peace, peace; when there is no peace. *Jeremiah* vi. 14; viii. 11.

Amend your ways and your doings. *Jer.* vii. 3; xxvi. 13.

Is there no balm in Gilead? is there no physician there ? *Jer.* viii. 22.

Oh that I had in the wilderness a lodging-place of wayfaring men ! *Jer.* ix. 2.

Can the Ethiopian change his skin, or the leopard his spots? *Jer.* xiii. 23.

As if a wheel had been in the midst of a wheel. *Ezekiel* x. 10.

The fathers have eaten sour grapes, and the children's teeth are set on edge. *Ez.* xviii. 2. *Jer.* xxxi. 29.

Thou art weighed in the balances, and art found wanting. *Daniel* v. 27.

The thing is true, according to the law of the Medes and Persians, which altereth not.

Dan. vi. 12.

For they have sown the wind, and they shall reap the whirlwind.

Hosea viii. 7.

I have multiplied visions, and used similitudes.   *Hos.* xii. 10.

Your old men shall dream dreams, your young men shall see visions.

Joel ii. 28.

Multitudes, multitudes in the valley of decision.   *Joel* iii. 14.

But they shall sit every man under his vine and under his fig-tree.

Micah iv. 4.

Write the vision, and make it plain upon tables, that he may run that readeth it.   *Habakkuk* ii. 2.

I was wounded in the house of my friends.   *Zechariah* xiii. 6.

But unto you that fear my name shall the Sun of righteousness arise with healing in his wings.   *Malachi* iv. 2.

Miss not the discourse of the elders.   *Ecclesiasticus* viii. 9.

He that toucheth pitch shall be defiled therewith.   *Ecclus.* xiii. 1.

He will laugh thee to scorn.   *Ecclus.* xiii. 7.

Whose talk is of bullocks.   *Ecclus.* xxxviii. 25.

These were honourable men in their generations.   *Ecclus.* xliv. 7.

Great is truth, and mighty above all things.   *Esdras* iv. 51.

Let us crown ourselves with rosebuds, before they be withered.

Wisdom of Solomon ii. 8.

And Nicanor lay dead in his harness.   1 *Maccabees* xv. 28.

—□—

NEW TESTAMENT.

Rachel weeping for her children, and would not be comforted, because they are not.   *Matthew* ii. 18.   *Jer.* xxxi. 15.

Man shall not live by bread alone.   *Matt.* iv. 4.   *Deut.* viii. 3.

Ye are the salt of the earth : but if the salt have lost his savour, wherewith shall it be salted ?   *Matt.* v. 13.

Ye are the light of the world. A city that is set on an hill cannot be hid.

Matt. v. 14.

But when thou doest alms, let not thy left hand know what thy right hand doeth.   *Matt.* vi. 3.

Where your treasure is, there will your heart be also.   *Matt.* vi. 21.

Ye cannot serve God and Mammon. *Matthew* vi. 24.

Consider the lilies of the field, how they grow; they toil not, neither do they spin. *Matt.* vi. 28.

Take therefore no thought for the morrow; for the morrow shall take thought for the things of itself. Sufficient unto the day is the evil thereof. *Matt.* vi. 34.

Neither cast ye your pearls before swine. *Matt.* vii. 6.

Ask, and it shall be given you; seek, and ye shall find; knock, and it shall be opened unto you. *Matt.* vii. 7.

The foxes have holes, and the birds of the air have nests; but the Son of man hath not where to lay his head. *Matt.* viii. 20.

The harvest truly is plenteous, but the labourers are few. *Matt.* ix. 37.

Be ye therefore wise as serpents, and harmless as doves. *Matt.* x. 16.

But the very hairs of your head are all numbered. *Matt.* x. 30.

But Wisdom is justified of her children. *Matt.* xi. 19. *Luke* vii. 35.

The tree is known by his fruit. *Matt.* xii. 33.

Out of the abundance of the heart the mouth speaketh. *Matt.* xii. 34.

Pearl of great price. *Matt.* xiii. 46.

A prophet is not without honour, save in his own country and in his own house. *Matt.* xiii. 57.

Be of good cheer: it is I; be not afraid. *Matt.* xiv. 27.

And if the blind lead the blind, both shall fall into the ditch. *Matt.* xv. 14.

Yet the dogs eat of the crumbs which fall from their masters' table. *Matt.* xv. 27.

Get thee behind me, Satan. *Matt.* xvi. 23.

For what is a man profited, if he shall gain the whole world, and lose his own soul? *Matt.* xvi. 26.

It is good for us to be here. *Matt.* xvii. 4.

What therefore God hath joined together, let not man put asunder. *Matt.* xix. 6.

It is easier for a camel to go through the eye of a needle, than for a rich man to enter into the kingdom of God. *Matt.* xix. 24.

Which have borne the burden and heat of the day. *Matt.* xx. 12.

Is it not lawful for me to do what I will with mine own? *Matt.* xx. 15.

For many are called, but few are chosen. *Matt.* xxii. 14.

Render therefore unto Cæsar the things which are Cæsar's, and unto God the things that are God's. *Matt.* xxii. 21.

Woe unto you, . . . for ye pay tithe of mint and anise and cummin.

Matthew xxiii. 23.

Ye blind guides, which strain at a gnat and swallow a camel.

Matt. xxiii. 24.

For ye are like unto whited sepulchres, which indeed appear beautiful outward, but are within full of dead men's bones. *Matt.* xxiii. 27.

As a hen gathereth her chickens under her wings.   *Matt.* xxiii. 37.

For wheresoever the carcase is, there will the eagles be gathered together.

Matt. xxiv. 28.

Unto every one that hath shall be given, and he shall have abundance : but from him that hath not shall be taken away even that which he hath.

Matt. xxv. 29.

Watch and pray, that ye enter not into temptation : the spirit indeed is willing, but the flesh is weak.   *Matt.* xxvi. 41.

The sabbath was made for man, and not man for the sabbath.

Mark ii. 27.

If a house be divided against itself, that house cannot stand.

Mark iii. 25.

He that hath ears to hear, let him hear.   *Mark* iv. 9.

My name is Legion.   *Mark* v. 9.

Where their worm dieth not, and the fire is not quenched. *Mark* ix. 44.

Glory to God in the highest, and on earth peace, good will toward men.

Luke ii. 14.

And now also the axe is laid unto the root of the trees.   *Luke* iii. 9.

Physician, heal thyself.   *Luke* iv. 23.

The labourer is worthy of his hire.   *Luke* x. 7.   1 *Tim.* v. 18.

Go, and do thou likewise.   *Luke* x. 37.

But one thing is needful : and Mary hath chosen that good part, which shall not be taken away from her.

Luke x. 42.

He that is not with me is against me.   *Luke* xi. 23.

And I will say to my soul, Soul, thou hast much goods laid up for many years; take thine ease, eat, drink, and be merry.   *Luke* xii. 19.

Let your loins be girded about, and your lights burning.   *Luke* xii. 35.

For the children of this world are in their generation wiser than the children of light.

Luke xvi. 8.

It were better for him that a mill-stone were hanged about his neck, and he cast into the sea.

Luke xvii. 2.

Remember Lot's wife.   *Luke* xvii. 32.

Out of thine own mouth will I judge thee.   *Luke* xix. 22.

For if they do these things in a green tree, what shall be done in the dry?
Luke xxiii. 31.

Can there any good thing come out of Nazareth? *John* i. 46.

The wind bloweth where it listeth. *John* iii. 8.

He was a burning and a shining light. *John* v. 35.

Gather up the fragments that remain, that nothing be lost. *John* vi. 12.

Judge not according to the appearance. *John* vii. 24.

The Truth shall make you free. *John* viii. 32.

For the poor always ye have with you. *John* xii. 8.

Walk while ye have the light, lest darkness come upon you.
John xii. 35.

Let not your heart be troubled. *John* xiv. 1.

In my Father's house are many mansions. *John* xiv. 2.

Greater love hath no man than this, that a man lay down his life for his friends. *John* xv. 13.

It is hard for thee to kick against the pricks. *Acts* ix. 5.

Lewd fellows of the baser sort. *Acts* xvii. 5.

The law is open. *Acts* xix. 38.

It is more blessed to give than to receive. *Acts* xx. 35.

Speak forth the words of truth and soberness. *Acts* xxvi. 25.

For there is no respect of persons with God. *Romans* ii. 11.

As some affirm that we say, Let us do evil that good may come.
Rom. iii. 8.

Fear of God before their eyes. *Rom.* iii. 18.

Who against hope believed in hope. *Rom.* iv. 18.

For the wages of sin is death. *Rom.* vi. 23.

And we know that all things work together for good to them that love God. *Rom.* viii. 28.

A zeal of God, but not according to knowledge. *Rom.* x. 2.

Be not wise in your own conceits. *Rom.* xii. 16.

Therefore if thine enemy hunger, feed him; if he thirst, give him drink: for in so doing thou shalt heap coals of fire on his head. *Rom.* xii. 20.

Be not overcome of evil, but overcome evil with good. *Rom.* xii. 21.

The powers that be are ordained of God. *Rom.* xiii. 1.

Render therefore to all their dues. *Rom.* xiii. 7.

Owe no man anything, but to love one another. *Rom.* xiii. 8.

Love is the fulfilling of the law. *Romans* xiii. 10.

Let every man be fully persuaded in his own mind. *Rom.* xiv. 5.

I have planted, Apollos watered; but God gave the increase.

1 Corinthians iii. 6

Every man's work shall be made manifest. *1 Cor.* iii. 13.

Not to think of men above that which is written.[1] *1 Cor.* iv. 6.

Absent in body, but present in spirit. *1 Cor.* v. 3.

Know ye not that a little leaven leaveneth the whole lump? *1 Cor.* v. 6.

For the fashion of this world passeth away. *1 Cor.* vii. 31.

I am made all things to all men. *1 Cor.* ix. 22.

Wherefore let him that thinketh he standeth take heed lest he fall.

1 Cor. x. 12.

As sounding brass, or a tinkling cymbal. *1 Cor.* xiii. 1.

When I was a child, I spake as a child. *1 Cor.* xiii. 11.

For now we see through a glass, darkly. *1 Cor.* xiii. 12.

Let all things be done decently and in order. *1 Cor.* xiv. 40.

Be not deceived : evil communications corrupt good manners.[2]

1 Cor. xv. 33.

The first man is of the earth, earthy. *1 Cor.* xv. 47.

In the twinkling of an eye. *1 Cor.* xv. 52.

O death, where is thy sting? O grave, where is thy victory?

1 Cor. xv. 55.

Not of the letter, but of the spirit; for the letter killeth, but the spirit giveth life.

2 Cor. iii. 6.

We walk by faith, not by sight. *2 Cor.* v. 7.

Behold, now is the accepted time. *2 Cor.* vi. 2.

By evil report and good report. *2 Cor.* vi. 8.

The right hands of fellowship. *Galatians* ii. 9.

For every man shall bear his own burden. *Gal.* vi. 5

Whatsoever a man soweth, that shall he also reap. *Gal.* vi. 7.

Be ye angry, and sin not : let not the sun go down upon your wrath.

Ephesians iv. 26.

For to me to live is Christ, and to die is gain. *Philippians* i. 21.

Whose God is their belly, and whose glory is in their shame.

Phil. iii. 19.

---

[1] Usually quoted, " to be *wise* above that which is written."

[2] Φθείρουσιν ἤθη χρήσθ' ὁμιλίαι κακαί.—Menander.

Dübner's edition of his *Fragments*, appended to Aristophanes in Didot's *Bibliotheca Græca, p.* 102, *l.* 101.

Whatsoever things are true, whatsoever things are honest, whatsoever things are just, whatsoever things are pure, whatsoever things are lovely, whatsoever things are of good report; if there be any virtue, and if there be any praise, think on these things. *Philippians* iv. 8.

Touch not; taste not; handle not. *Colossians* ii. 21.

Let your speech be always with grace, seasoned with salt. *Col.* iv. 6.

Remembering without ceasing your work of faith and labour of love.
1 *Thessalonians* i. 3.

Study to be quiet. 1 *Thess.* iv. 11.

Prove all things; hold fast that which is good. 1 *Thess.* v. 21.

The law is good, if a man use it lawfully. 1 *Timothy* i. 8.

Not greedy of filthy lucre. 1 *Tim.* iii. 3.

Busy-bodies, speaking things which they ought not. 1 *Tim.* v. 13.

Drink no longer water, but use a little wine for thy stomach's sake.
1 *Tim.* v. 23.

For the love of money is the root of all evil. 1 *Tim.* vi. 10.

Fight the good fight. 1 *Tim.* vi. 12.

Rich in good works. 1 *Tim.* vi. 18.

Science falsely so called. 1 *Tim.* vi. 20.

I have fought a good fight, I have finished my course, I have kept the faith. 2 *Tim.* iv. 7.

Unto the pure all things are pure. *Titus* i. 15.

Now faith is the substance of things hoped for, the evidence of things not seen. *Hebrews* xi. 1.

Of whom the world was not worthy. *Heb.* xi. 38.

A cloud of witnesses. *Heb.* xii. 1.

For whom the Lord loveth he chasteneth. *Heb.* xii. 6.

The spirits of just men made perfect. *Heb.* xii. 23.

Be not forgetful to entertain strangers, for thereby some have entertained angels unawares. *Heb.* xiii. 2.

Blessed is the man that endureth temptation; for when he is tried, he shall receive the crown of life. *James* i. 12.

Behold, how great a matter a little fire kindleth ! *James* iii. 5.

The tongue can no man tame; it is an unruly evil.[1] *James* iii. 8.

Resist the devil, and he will flee from you. *James* iv. 7.

Hope to the end. 1 *Peter* i. 13.

---

[1] Usually quoted, "The tongue is an unruly member."

Fear God.   Honour the king.   1 *Peter* ii. 17.

Ornament of a meek and quiet spirit.   1 *Peter* iii. 4.

Giving honour unto the wife as unto the weaker vessel.   1 *Peter* iii. 7.

Be ye all of one mind.   1 *Peter* iii. 8.

Charity shall cover the multitude of sins.   1 *Peter* iv. 8.

Be sober, be vigilant; because your adversary, the devil, as a roaring lion,
walketh about, seeking whom he may devour.   1 *Peter* v. 8.

The dog is turned to his own vomit again.   2 *Peter* ii. 22.

Bowels of compassion.   1 *John* iii. 17.

There is no fear in love; but perfect love casteth out fear.   1 *John* iv. 18.

Be thou faithful unto death.   *Revelation* ii. 10.

He shall rule them with a rod of iron.   *Rev.* ii. 27.

I am Alpha and Omega, the beginning and the end, the first and the last.
                                                                      Rev. xxii. 13.

—□—

BOOK OF COMMON PRAYER.

We have left undone those things which we ought to have done; and we
have done those things which we ought not to have done.

Morning Prayer.

The noble army of martyrs.   *Ibid.*

Afflicted, or distressed, in mind, body, or estate.

Prayer for all Conditions of Men.

Have mercy upon us miserable sinners.   *The Litany.*

From envy, hatred, and malice, and all uncharitableness.   *Ibid.*

The world, the flesh, and the devil.   *Ibid.*

The kindly fruits of the earth.   *Ibid.*

Read, mark, learn, and inwardly digest.

Collect for the Second Sunday in Advent.

Renounce the devil and all his works.   *Baptism of Infants.*

The pomps and vanity of this wicked world.   *Catechism.*

To keep my hands from picking and stealing.   *Ibid.*

To do my duty in that state of life unto which it shall please God to call
me.
                                                                      Ibid.

An outward and visible sign of an inward and spiritual grace.   *Ibid.*

Let him now speak, or else hereafter for ever hold his peace.

Solemnization of Matrimony.

To have and to hold from this day forward, for better for worse, for
richer for poorer, in sickness and in health, to love and to cherish, till death
us do part.
                                                                      Ibid.

SOLEMNIZATION OF MATRIMONY—*continued.*]
   To love, cherish, and to obey.   *Ibid.*

   With this ring I thee wed, with my body I thee worship, and with all my worldly goods I thee endow.   *Ibid.*

   In the midst of life we are in death.[1]   *The Burial Service.*

   Earth to earth, ashes to ashes, dust to dust, in sure and certain hope of the Resurrection.   *Ibid.*

   But it was even thou, my companion, my guide, and mine own familiar friend.   *The Psalter. Ps.* lv. 14.

   The iron entered into his soul.   *Ps.* cv. 18.

—□—

TATE AND BRADY.

And though he promise to his loss,
He makes his promise good.   *Ps.* xv. 5.

The sweet remembrance of the just
Shall flourish when he sleeps in dust.   *Ps.* xci. 4.

[1] This is derived from a Latin antiphon, said to have been composed by Notker, a monk of St. Gall, in 911, while watching some workmen building a bridge at Martinsbrücke, in peril of their lives. It forms the groundwork of Luther's antiphon *De Morte.*

APPENDIX

A Cadmean victory.   *Greek Proverb.*

Συμμισγόντων δὲ τῇ ναυμαχίῃ, Καδμείη τις νίκη τοῖσι Φωκαιεῦσι ἐγένετο

                                                      Herod. i. 166.

A Cadmean victory was one in which the victors suffered as much as their enemies.

The half is more than the whole.

Νήπιοι· οὐδὲ ἴσασιν ὅσῳ πλέον ἥμισυ παντός.

                                      Hesiod, *Works and Days*, v. 40.

To leave no stone unturned.

Πάντα κινῆσαι πέτρον.—Euripides, *Heraclid.* 1002.

This may be traced to a response of the Delphic Oracle, given to Polycrates, as the best means of finding a treasure buried by Xerxes' general, Mardonius, on the field of Platæa. The Oracle replied, Πάντα λίθον κίνει, *Turn every stone.*

                                 Corp. Parœmiogr. Græc. i. *p.* 146.

The blood of the Martyrs is the seed of the Church.

Plures efficimur, quoties metimur a vobis ; semen est sanguis Christianorum.
                                      Tertullian, *Apologet., c. 50.*

Man is a two-legged animal without feathers.

Plato having defined man to be a two-legged animal without feathers, he (Diogenes) plucked a cock, and, bringing him into the school, said "Here is Plato's man." From which there was added to the definition, "with broad, flat nails."

                   Diogenes Laertius, *Lib.* vi. *c.* ii. *Vit. Diog. Ch.* vi. § 40.

I believe it, because it is impossible.

                        Credo, quia impossibile.
This is a misquotation of Tertullian, whose words are,

                        Certum est, quia impossibile est. *De Carne Christi, c. 5.*

Every man is the architect of his own fortune.

Sed res docuit id verum esse quod in carminibus Appius ait, "Fabrum esse suæ quemque fortunæ."

                               Pseudo-Sallust. Epist. de Rep. Ordin. ii. 1.

Cæsar's wife should be above suspicion.

> Cæsar was asked why he had divorced his wife. " Because," said he, " I would have the chastity of my wife clear even of suspicion."
>
> Plutarch, *Life of Cæsar. Ch.* 10.

Strike, but hear.

> Eurybiades lifting up his staff as if he was going to strike, Themistocles said " Strike if you will, but hear."
>
> Plutarch, *Life of Themistocles.*

Where the shoe pinches.

> In the Life of Æmilius Paulus, Plutarch relates the story of a Roman being divorced from his wife. " This person being highly blamed by his friends, who demanded,—was she not chaste? was she not fair?— holding out his shoe asked them whether it was not new, and well made. Yet, added he, none of you can tell where it pinches me."

To smell of the lamp. Plutarch, *Life of Demosthenes. Ch.* 8.

Appeal from Philip drunk to Philip sober.

> Inserit se tantis viris mulier alienigeni sanguinis : quæ a Philippo rege temulento immerenter damnata, Provocarem ad Philippum, inquit, sed sobrium. *Val. Maximus. Lib.* vi. *cap.* 2.

To call a spade a spade. Plutarch, *Reg. et Imp. Apoph. Philip.* xv.

> Τὰ σῦκα σῦκα, τὴν σκάφην δὲ σκάφην ὀνομάζων·
>
> Aristophanes, as quoted in Lucian, *Quom. Hist. sit conscrib.* 41.

Begging the question.

> This is a common logical fallacy, *petitio principii ;* and the first explanation of the phrase is to be found in Aristotle's Topica, viii. 13, where the five ways of begging the question are set forth. The earliest English work in which the expression is found is " *The Arte of Logike plainlie set forth in our English Tongue, &c.* 1584."

The sinews of war.

> Æschines (*Adv. Ctesiph.* ch. 53) ascribes to Demosthenes the expression ὑποτέτμηται τὰ νεῦρα τῶν πραγμάτων, " the sinews of affairs are cut." Diogenes Laertius, in his Life of Bion (lib. iv. c. 7, § 3), represents that philosopher as saying τὸν πλοῦτον εἶναι νεῦρα πραγμάτων, " that riches were the sinews of business," or, as the phrase may mean, " of the state." Referring, perhaps, to this maxim of Bion, Plutarch says in his Life of Cleomenes (c. 27), " He who first called money the sinews of the state seems to have said this with special reference to *war.*" Accordingly we find money called expressly τά νεῦρα τοῦ πολέμου, " the sinews of war," in Libanius, *Orat.* xlvi. (vol. ii. p. 477, ed. Reiske), and by the Scholiast on Pindar, Olymp. i. 4 (comp. Photius, *Lex.* s. v. Μεγάνορος πλούτου). So Cicero Philipp. v. 2, " nervos belli infinitam pecuniam."

Adding insult to injury.

    A fly bit the bare pate of a bald man; who, endeavouring to crush it, gave himself a heavy blow. Then said the fly, jeeringly : "You wanted to revenge the sting of a tiny insect with death; what will you do to yourself, who have added insult to injury?"

> Quid facies tibi,
> Injuriæ qui addideris contumeliam?

    Phædrus, *The Bald Man and the Fly. Book* v. *Fable* 3.

When at Rome, do as the Romans do.

    St. Augustine was in the habit of dining upon Saturday as upon Sunday; but, being puzzled with the different practices then prevailing (for they had begun to fast at Rome on Saturday), consulted St. Ambrose on the subject. Now at Milan they did not fast on Saturday, and the answer of the Milan saint was this :—

    "When I am here, I do not fast on Saturday; when at Rome, I do fast on Saturday."

    "Quando hic sum, non jejuno Sabbato : quando Romæ sum, jejuno Sabbato."   St. Augustine, *Epistle* xxxvi. *to Casulanus.*

    When they are at Rome, they do there as they see done.

    Burton, *Anatomy of Melancholy, Part* iii. *Sec.* 4, *Mem.* 2, *Subs.* 1.

> I see the right, and I approve it too,
> Condemn the wrong, and yet the wrong pursue.

> Video meliora proboque;
> Deteriora sequor.

    Ovid, *Metamorphosis, Book* vii. *Line* 29. *Translated by Tate and Stonestreet,* ed. *Garth.*

The Art preservative of all arts.

    From the inscription upon the façade of the house at Harlem, formerly occupied by Laurent Koster or Coster, who is charged, among others, with the invention of printing. Mention is first made of this inscription about 1628.

> MEMORIÆ SACRUM
> TYPOGRAPHIA
> ARS ARTIUM OMNIUM
> CONSERVATRIX.
> HIC PRIMUM INVENTA
> CIRCA ANNUM MCCCCXL.

> That same man, that runnith awaie,
> Maie again fight an other daie.

    Erasmus, *Apothegms, Trans. by* Udall, 1542.

> For those that fly may fight again,
> Which he can never do that's slain.

    Butler, *Hudibras. Part* iii. *Canto* 3.

He that fights and runs away
May turn and fight another day;
But he that is in battle slain
Will never rise to fight again.
> Ray's *History of the Rebellion, p.* 48.   Bristol, 1752.

For he who fights and runs away
May live to fight another day;
But he who is in battle slain
Can never rise and fight again.
> *The Art of Poetry on a New Plan.   Edited by* Oliver
> Goldsmith (?)   *Vol.* ii. *p.* 147.   London, 1761.

Sed omissis quidem divinis exhortationibus illum magis Græcum ver-
siculum secularis sententiæ sibi adhibent.   *Qui fugiebat, rursus præ-
liabitur :* ut et rursus forsitan fugiat.
> Tertullian, *De Fuga in Persecutione, c.* 10.

The corresponding Greek,
> Ἀνὴρ ὁ φευγων καὶ πάλιν μαχήσεται,

is ascribed to Menander in Dübner's edition of his *Fragments*
(appended to Aristophanes in Didot's *Bibliotheca Græca*), p. 91.

Qui fuit, peut revenir aussi;
Qui meurt, il n'en est pas ainsi.   Scarron (1610—1660).

Souvent celuy qui demeure
Est cause de son meschef;
Celuy qui fuit de bonne heure
Peut combattre derechef.
> From the *Satyre Menippée,* 1594.

Junius, Aprilis, Septémq; Nouemq; tricenos,
Vnum plus reliqui, Februs tenet octo vicenos,
At si bissextus fuerit superadditur vnus.
> Harrison's *Description of Britaine,* prefixed to
> Holinshed's *Chronicles,* 1577.

Thirty dayes hath Nouember,
Aprill, June, and September,
February hath xxviii alone,
And all the rest have xxxi.
> Grafton's *Chronicles of England,* 1590.

Thirty days hath September,
April, June, and November,
February eight-and-twenty all alone,
And all the rest have thirty-one;
Unless that leap year doth combine,
And give to February twenty-nine.
> *The Return from Parnassus.*   London, 1606.

Thirty days hath September,
April, June, and November,
All the rest have thirty-one
Excepting February alone :
Which hath but twenty-eight, in fine,
Till leap year gives it twenty-nine.

> Common in the New England States.

Fourth, eleventh, ninth, and sixth,
Thirty days to each affix ;
Every other thirty-one
Except the second month alone.

> Common in Chester County, Pa. among the Friends.

It is unseasonable and unwholesome in all months that have not **an**
R in their name to eat an oyster.   Butler, *Dyet's Dry Dinner.* 1599.

Old wood to burn ! Old wine to drink ! Old friends to trust ! Old authors
to read !

Alonso of Aragon was wont to say, in commendation of age, that
age appeared to be best in these four things.

> Melchior, *Floresta Española de Apothegmas o sentencias, &c.*, ii.
> 1. 20. Bacon, *Apothegms*, 97.

Is not old wine wholesomest, old pippins toothsomest, old wood
burns brightest, old linen wash whitest ? Old soldiers, sweetheart, are
surest, and old lovers are soundest.

> John Webster, *Westward Ho. Act* ii. *Sc.* 2.

What find you better or more honourable than age ? Take the pre-
heminence of it in everything : in an old friend, in old wine, in an old
pedigree.   Shakerly Marmion, *The Antiquary. Act* ii. *Sc.* 1.

I love everything that 's old. Old friends, old times, old manners,
old books, old wine.—Goldsmith, *She Stoops to Conquer. Act* i. *Sc.* 1.

Nose, nose, nose, nose,
And who gave thee that jolly red nose?

Sinament and Ginger, Nutmegs and Cloves,
And that gave me my jolly red nose.[1]

> Ravenscroft's *Deuteromela, Song No. 7.* 1609.

Begone, dull Care, I prithee begone from me ;
Begone, dull Care, thou and I shall never agree.

> Playford's *Musical Companion.* 1687.

Fiat Justitia ruat Cœlum.

This phrase, used by Lord Mansfield in the case of King *vs.* Wilkes,
Burrow's Reports, *vol.* iv., 2562 (A.D.) 1770, is found in Ward's *Simple
Cobbler of Aggawam in America.* (First printed in 1645.)

---

[1] Cf. Beaumont and Fletcher, *The Knight of the Burning Pestle, Act* i.
Sc. 3.

God always favours the heaviest battalions.

> Deos fortioribus adesse.   'Tacitus, *Hist.* *Book* iv. xvii.

> Dieu est d'ordinaire pour les gros escadrons contre les petits.
>   Bussy Rabutin, *Lettres,* iv. 91. *Oct.* 18, 1677.

> Le nombre des sages sera toujours petit. Il est vrai qu'il est augmenté; mais ce n'est rien en comparaison des sots, et par malheur on dit que Dieu est toujours pour les gros bataillons.
>   Voltaire *to M. Le Riche, February* 6, 1770

> When Adam dolve, and Eve span,
> Who was then the gentleman?
> > Lines used by John Ball, to encourage the Rebels in Wat Tyler's Rebellion. Hume's *History of England. Vol.* i. *Ch.* 17, *Note* 8.

> Now bething the, gentilman,
> How Adam dalf and Eve span.
> > From *a MS. of the* 15*th Century in the British Museum. Songs and Carols.*

The same proverb existed in German. Agricola (*Prov. No.* 264).

> So Adam reutte, und Eva span;
> Wer was da ein eddelman.

Die in the last ditch.

> To William of Orange may be ascribed this saying. When Buckingham urged the inevitable destruction which hung over the United Provinces, and asked him whether he did not see that the Commonwealth was ruined, "There is one certain means," replied the prince, "by which I can be sure never to see my country's ruin,—*I will die in the last ditch."*   Hume, *History of England.* 1672.

A Rowland for an Oliver.

> These were two of the most famous in the list of Charlemagne's twelve peers; and their exploits are rendered so ridiculously and equally extravagant by the old romancers, that from thence arose that saying, amongst our plain and sensible ancestors, of giving one a "Rowland for his Oliver," to signify the matching one incredible lie with another.   Thomas Warburton.

All is lost save honour.

> It was from the imperial camp near Pavia, that Francis the First, before leaving for Pizzighettone, wrote to his mother the memorable letter which, thanks to tradition, has become altered to the form of this sublime laconism : "Madame, tout est perdu fors l'honneur."
> The true expression is, "Madame, pour vous faire savoir comme se

porte le reste de mon infortune, de toutes choses ne m'est demeuré
que l'honneur et la vie qui est sauvé."

Martin, Histoire de France. Tom. viii.

Hobson's choice.

Tobias Hobson was the first man in England that let out hackney
horses. When a man came for a horse, he was led into the stable,
where there was a great choice, but he obliged him to take the horse
which stood next to the stable door ; so that every customer was alike
well served according to his chance, from whence it became a proverb,
when what ought to be your election was forced upon you, to say
" Hobson's choice."

Spectator. No. 509.

Put your trust in God, my boys, and keep your powder dry.

Colonel Blacker, Oliver's Advice. 1834.

There is a well-authenticated anecdote of Cromwell. On a certain
occasion, when his troops were about crossing a river to attack the
enemy, he concluded an address, couched in the usual fanatic terms in
use among them, with these words : " Put your trust in God; but
mind to keep your powder dry."

Hayes's Ballads of Ireland. Vol. i. p. 191.

Am I not a man and a brother ?

From a medallion by Wedgwood (1768), representing a negro in
chains, with one knee on the ground, and both hands lifted up to
heaven. This was adopted as a characteristic seal by the Anti-slavery
Society of London.

> For angling-rod, he took a sturdy oak;
> For line a cable, that in storm ne'er broke;
> . . . .
> His hook was baited with a dragon's tail,
> And then on rock he stood to bob for whale.

From The Mock Romance, a rhapsody attached to The
Loves of Hero and Leander</i>, published in London in
the years 1653 and 1677. Chambers's <i>Book of Days,
Vol.</i> i. <i>p.</i> 173.</div>

In Chalmers's *British Poets* the following is ascribed to William
King (1663—1712).

> His angle-rod made of a sturdy oak;
> His line a cable which in storms ne'er broke;
> His hook he baited with a dragon's tail,
> And sat upon a rock, and bobbed for whale.

Upon a Giant's Angling.

As good as a play.

An exclamation of Charles II. when in Parliament attending the
discussion of Lord Ross's Divorce Bill.

The king remained in the House of Peers while his speech was taken into consideration, — a common practice with him; for the debates amused his sated mind, and were sometimes, he used to say, as good as a comedy.

Macaulay, *Review of the Life and Writings of Sir William Temple.*

When in doubt, win the trick.

Hoyle, *Twenty-four Rules for Learners. Rule 12.*

Rebellion to tyrants is obedience to God.

From an inscription on the cannon near which the ashes of President John Bradshaw were lodged, on the top of a high hill near Martha Bay in Jamaica.

Stiles's *History of the Three Judges of King Charles I.*

This supposititious epitaph was found among the papers of Mr. Jefferson, and in his handwriting. It was supposed to be one of Dr. Franklin's spirit-stirring inspirations.

Randall's *Life of Jefferson. Vol.* iii. *p.* 585.

Nation of shopkeepers.

From an oration purporting to have been delivered by Samuel Adams at the State House in Philadelphia, August 1, 1776. *Philadelphia, printed, London, reprinted for E. Johnson, No.* 4, *Ludgate Hill.* MDCCLXXVI.'

To found a great empire for the sole purpose of raising up a people of customers may at first sight appear a project fit only for a nation of shopkeepers.—Adam Smith, *Wealth of Nations. Vol.* ii. *Book* iv. *Ch.* vii. *Part* 3. 1775.

And what is true of a shopkeeper is true of a shopkeeping nation.

Tucker, *Dean of Gloucester. Tract.* 1766.

Speech was given to man to conceal his thoughts.

Ils n'employent les paroles que pour déguiser leurs pensées.

Voltaire, *Dialogue* xiv. *Le Chapon et la Poularde.*

When Harel wished to put a joke or witticism into circulation, he was in the habit of connecting it with some celebrated name, on the chance of reclaiming it if it took. Thus he assigned to Talleyrand in the *Nain Jaune* the phrase, "Speech was given to man to disguise his thoughts." Fournier, *L'Esprit dans l'Histoire.*

Where Nature's end of language is declined,
And men talk only to conceal the mind.

Young, *Love of Fame. Satire* ii. *Line* 207.

The germ of this saying is to be found in Jeremy Taylor; South, Butler, Young, Lloyd, and Goldsmith have repeated it after him.

---

[1] No such American edition has ever been seen, but at least four copies are known of the London issue. A German translation of this oration was printed in 1778, perhaps at Berne; the place of publication is not given.— Wells's *Life of Adams.*

Beginning of the end.

Mr. Fournier asserts, on the written authority of Talleyrand's brother, that the only breviary used by the ex-bishop was *L'Improvitateur Franaçis*, a compilation of anecdotes and *bons-mots*, in twenty-one duodecimo volumes.

Whenever a good thing was wandering about in search of a parent, he adopted it; amongst others, " C'est le commencement de la fin."

> To shew our simple skill,
> That is the true beginning of our end.
>> Shakespeare, *Midsummer Night's Dream.   Act* v. *Sc.* 1.

Defend me from my friends.

The French Ana assign to Maréchal Villars taking leave of Louis XIV. this aphorism, " Defend me from my friends; I can defend my-self from my enemies."

> But of all plagues, good Heaven, thy wrath can send,
> Save, save, oh save me from the candid friend !
>> Canning, *The New Morality.*

Orthodoxy is my doxy, Heterodoxy is another man's doxy.

" I have heard frequent use," said the late Lord Sandwich, in a debate on the Test Laws, " of the words 'orthodoxy' and 'hetero-doxy'; but I confess myself at a loss to know precisely what they mean." "Orthodoxy, my Lord," said Bishop Warburton, in a whisper,— " orthodoxy is my doxy,—heterodoxy is another man's doxy."

>> Priestley's *Memoirs.   Vol.* i. *p.* 372.

No one is a hero to his valet.

This phrase is commonly attributed to Madame de Sévigné, but, on the authority of Madame Aisse, belongs to Madame Cornuel.

>> *Lettres, édit. J. Ravenal.*   1853.

Few men are admired by their servants.

>> Montaigne, *Essais.   Book* iii. *Ch.* 11.

When Hermodotus in his poems described Antigonus as the son of Helios (the sun), " My valet-de-chambre," said he, " is not aware of this."   Plutarch, *De Iside et Osiride.   Ch.* xxiv.

Greatest happiness of the greatest number.

Priestley was the first (unless it was Beccaria) [1] who taught my lips to pronounce this sacred truth,—that the greatest happiness of the greatest number is the foundation of morals and legislation.

>> Bentham's *Works.   Vol.* x. *p.* 142.

---

[1] The expression is used by Beccaria in the introduction to his *Essay on Crimes and Punishments.*

Ridicule the test of truth.-

How comes it to pass, then, that we appear such cowards in reasoning, and are so afraid to stand the test of ridicule?

> Shaftesbury, *Characteristicks. A Letter concerning
> Enthusiasm. Sec. 2.*

Truth, 't is supposed, may bear all lights; and one of those principal
lights or natural mediums by which things are to be viewed, in order
to a thorough recognition, is ridicule itself.

> *Ibid. Essay on the Freedom of Wit and Humour. Sec. 1.*

'T was the saying of an ancient sage,[2] that humour was the only test
of gravity; and gravity, of humour. For a subject which would not
bear raillery was suspicious; and a jest which would not bear a serious
examination was certainly false wit. *Ibid. Sec. v.*

> Even such is Time, that takes on trust
> Our youth, our joyes, our all we have,
> And pays us but with age and dust;
> Who in the dark and silent grave,
> When we have wandered all our ways,
> Shuts up the story of our days;
> But from this earth, this grave, this dust,
> My God shall raise me up, I trust.
>> *Verses written by Sir Walter Raleigh the night before
>> his death.* According to Oldys, they were found
>> in his Bible.

> Go, Soul, the body's guest,
> Upon a thankless arrant;
> Fear not to touch the best,
> The truth shall be thy warrant;
> Go, since I needs must die,
> And give the world the lie. *The Lie.*

This poem is traced in manuscript to the year 1593. It first appeared
in print in Davison's *Poetical Rhapsody*, second edition, 1608. It has
been assigned to various authors, but on Raleigh's side there is good
evidence, besides the internal testimony, which appears to us irre-
sistible. Two answers to it, written in Raleigh's lifetime, ascribe it to
him; and two manuscript copies of the period of Elizabeth bear the
title of "Sir Walter Rawleigh his Lie."

> Chambers's *Cyclopædia. Vol.* i. *p.* 120.

---

[1] We have, oftener than once, endeavoured to attach some meaning to that
aphorism, vulgarly imputed to Shaftesbury, which, however, we can find
nowhere in his works, that *ridicule is the test of truth.*—Carlyle, *Miscellanies. Voltaire.*

[2] Gorgias Leontinus, *apud Arist. Rhetor, lib.* 3, *cap.* 18

Carpet knights.

As much valour is to be found in feasting as in fighting; and some of
our city captains and carpet knights will make this good, and prove it.

Burton, *Anatomy of Melancholy. Pt.* i. *Sec.* 2, *Mem.* 2, *Subs.* 2

From Percy's Reliques.

My mind to me a kingdom is;[1]
Such perfect joy therein I find,
As far exceeds all earthly bliss,
That God and Nature hath assigned.
Though much I want that most would have,
Yet still my mind forbids to crave.

My mind to me a kingdom is. From Byrd's
Psalmes, Sonnets, &c., 1588.

He that had neyther been kithe nor kin
Might have seen a full fayre sight. *Guy of Gisborne.*

L ite, late yestreen I saw the new moone,
Wi' the auld moon in hir arme. *Sir Patrick Spens.*[2]

Weep no more, lady, weep no more,
Thy sorrow is in vain;
For violets plucked the sweetest showers
Will ne'er make grow again.

The Friar of Orders Gray.

Every white will have its black,
And every sweet its sour. *Sir Carline.*

We 'll shine in more substantial honours,
And to be noble we 'll be good. *Winifreda* (1726).

And when with envy Time, transported,
Shall think to rob us of our joys,
You 'll in your girls again be courted,
And I 'll go wooing in my boys. *Ibid.*

He that wold not when he might,
He shall not when he wolda.[3] *The Baffled Knight.*

---

[1] Mens regnum bona possidet.
Seneca, *Thyestes, Act* ii. *Line* 380.
My mind to me an empire is
While grace affordeth health.
Robert Southwell (1560—1595). *Look Home.*
[2] I saw the new moon, late yestreen,
Wi' the auld moon in her arm.
From *The Minstrelsy of the Scottish Border.*
[3] He that will not when he may,
When he will, he shall have nay.
Burton, *Anat. of Mel. p.* iii. *Sec.* 2, *Mem.* 5, *Subs.* 5.

The Guard dies, but never surrenders.

This phrase, attributed to Cambronne, who was made prisoner at Waterloo, was vehemently denied by him. It was invented by Rougemont, a prolific author of *mots*, two days after the battle, in the *Indépendant.* Fournier, *L'Esprit dans l'Histoire.*

I do not give you to posterity as a pattern to imitate, but an example to deter. Junius, *Letter* xii. *To the Duke of Grafton.*

The heart to conceive, the understanding to direct, or the hand to execute.[1] *Letter* xxxvii. *City Address and the King's Answer.*

Private credit is wealth, public honour is security; the feather that adorns the royal bird supports its flight; strip him of his plumage, and you fix him to the earth. *Letter* xlii. *Affair of the Falkland Islands.*

From the New England Primer.

> In Adam's fall,
> We sinned all.
>
> My Book and Heart
> Must never part.
>
> Young Obadias,
> David, Josias,—
> All were pious.
>
> Peter deny'd
> His Lord, and cry'd.
>
> Young Timothy
> Learnt sin to fly.
>
> Xerxes did die,
> And so must I.
>
> Zaccheus he
> Did climb the tree
> Our Lord to see.

Our days begin with trouble here,
    Our life is but a span,
And cruel death is always near,
    So frail a thing is man.

Now I lay me down to take my sleep,
I pray the Lord my soul to keep;
If I should die before I wake,
I pray the Lord my soul to take.

His wife, with nine small children and one at the breast, following him to the stake.—*Martyrdom of Mr. John Rogers. Burnt at Smithfield, Feb.* 14, 1554.

---

[1] Cf. Gibbon, p. 208.

The wisdom of many and the wit of one.

A definition of a proverb which Lord John Russell gave one morning at breakfast, at Mardock's,—"One man's wit, and all men's wisdom."
Memoirs of Mackintosh. Vol. ii. *p.* 473.

Count that day lost whose low descending sun
Views from thy hand no worthy action done.
Staniford's *Art of Reading. Third Edition, p.* 27. *Boston,* 1803.

In the Preface to Mr. Nichol's work on *Autographs,* among other albums noticed by him as being in the British Museum is that of David Krieg with Jacob Bobart's autograph, and the following verses.[1]

"*Virtus sua gloria.*"

Think that day lost whose [low] descending sun
Views from thy hand no noble action done.

Bobart died about 1726. He was a son of the celebrated botanist of that name.

Order reigns in Warsaw.

General Sebastian announced the fall of Warsaw in the Chamber of Deputies, Sept. 16, 1834 : Des lettres que je reçois de Pologne m'annoncent que la tranquillité règne à Varsovie.
Dumas, *Memoires,* 2*nd Series. Vol.* iv. *Ch.* 3.

A foreign nation is a contemporaneous posterity.

Byron's European fame is the best earnest of his immortality, for a foreign nation is a kind of contemporaneous posterity.
Stanley, or The Recollections of a Man of the World. Vol. ii. *p.* 89.

Young men think old men fools, and old men know young men to be so.

Quoted by Camden as a saying of one Dr. Metcalf. It is now in many people's mouths, and likely to pass into a proverb.
Ray's *Proverbs, p.* 145, *ed. Bohn.*

—□—

PROVERBIAL EXPRESSIONS,

FROM ENGLISH WRITERS, WHICH ARE OF COMMON ORIGIN.

All that glisters is not gold.
Shakespeare, *Merchant of Venice, Act* ii. *Sc.* 7.

All is not gold that glisteneth.   Middleton, *A Fair Quarrel, Act* v. *Sc.* 1.

All thing, which that shineth as the gold
Ne is no gold, as I have herd it told.
Chaucer, *The Chanones Yemannes Tale, Line* 243.

---

[1] *Notes and Queries,* 1*st Series, Vol.* vii. *p.* 159.

All is not golde that outward shewith bright.

> Lydgate, *On the Mutability of Human Affairs.*

Gold all is not that doth golden seem.

> Spenser, *Faerie Queene, Book* ii. *Canto* 8, *St.* 14.

All is not gold that glisters.   Herbert, *Jacula Prudentum.*

All, as they say, that glitters is not gold.   Dryden, *Hind and Panther.*

Another, yet the same.

> Pope, *Dunciad, Book* iii. Tickell, *From a Lady in England.* Johnson, *Life of Dryden.* Darwin, *Botanic Garden, Pt.* i. *Canto* 4, *l.* 380. Wordsworth, *The Excursion, Book* ix. Scott, *The Abbot, Ch.* 1.

Aliusque et idem.   Horace, *Carm. Sec. l.* 10.

At sixes and sevens.   Middleton, *The Widow. Act* i. *Sc.* 2.

Better late than never.

> Tusser, *Five Hundred Points of Good Husbandry.* Bunyan, *Pilgrim's Progress, Pt.* 1. Murphy, *The School for Guardians, Act* 1.

By hook or crook.

> Spenser, *Faerie Queene, Book* iii. *Canto* 1, *St.* 17. Beaumont and Fletcher, *Women Pleased, Act* i. *Sc.* 3.

Castles in the air.

> Stirling, *Sonnets, S.* 6. Burton, *Anatomy of Melancholy, The Author's Abstract.* Sidney, *Defence of Poesy.* Sir Thomas Browne, *Letter to a Friend.* Giles Fletcher, *Christ's History, Pt.* ii. Swift, *Duke Grafton's Answer.* Broome, *Poverty and Poetry.* Fielding, *Epistle to Walpole.* Cibber, *Non Juror, Act* ii. Churchill, *Epistle to Lloyd.* Shenstone, *On Taste, Pt.* ii. Lloyd, *Epistle to Colman.*

Compare great things with small.

> Virgil, *Georgics, Book* iv. *l.* 176. Milton, *Par. Lost, Book* ii. *l.* 921. Cowley, *The Motto.* Dryden, *Ovid's Met., Book* i. *l.* 727. Tickell, *Poem on Hunting.* Pope, *Windsor Forest.*

Comparisons are odious.

> Burton, *Anat. of Mel., Pt.* iii. *Sec.* 3, *Mem.* 1, *Subs.* 2. Heywood, *A Woman killed with Kindness, Act* i. *Sc.* 1. Donne, *El.* 8. Herbert, *Jacula Prudentum.*

Comparisons are odorous.

> Shakespeare, *Much Ado about Nothing, Act* iii. *Sc.* 5.

Comparisons are offensive.   *Don Quixote, Pt.* ii. *Ch.* 1.

Dark as pitch.   Ray's *Proverbs.* Bunyan, *Pilgrim's Progress. Pt.* 1.

Deeds, not words.

> Beaumont and Fletcher, *The Lover's Progress, Act* iii. *Sc.* 1. Butler, *Hudibras, Pt.* i. *C.* 1, *l.* 867.

M

Devil take the hindmost.
>Beaumont and Fletcher, *Bonduca*, *Act* iv. *Sc.* 3.   Butler, *Hudibras*,
>*Pt.* i. *Canto* 2, *l.* 633.   Prior, *Ode on Taking Nemur.*   Pope,
>*Dunciad*, *Book* ii. *l.* 60.   Burns, *To a Haggis.*

Diamonds cut diamonds.   Ford, *The Lover's Melancholy*, *Act* i. *Sc.* 1.

Discretion the best part of valour.
>Beaumont and Fletcher, *A King, and no King*, *Act* iv. *Sc.* 3.

The better part of valour is discretion.
>Shakespeare, *Henry IV.*, *Pt.* i. *Act* v. *Sc.* 4.   Churchill, *The Ghost*,
>*Book* i. *l.* 232.

Eat thy cake and have it too.
>Herbert, *The Size.*   Bickerstaff, *Thomas and Sally.*

Enough is good as a feast.
>Ray's *Proverbs.*   Bickerstaff, *Love in a Village*, *Act* iii. *Sc.* 1.

Every tub must stand upon its own bottom.
>Ray's *Proverbs.*   Bunyan, *Pilgrim's Progress*, Macklin, *The Man of
>the World*, *Act* i. *Sc.* 2.

Every why hath a wherefore.
>Shakespeare, *Comedy of Errors*, *Act* ii. *Sc.* 2.   Butler, *Hudibras*, *Pt.* i.
>*Canto* 1, *l.* 132.

Facts are stubborn things.
>Smollett, *Trans. Gil Blas*, *Book* x. *Ch.* 1.   Elliot, *Essay on Field
>Husbandry*, *p.* 35, *n.* (1747).

Faint heart ne'er won fair lady.
>Britain's *Ida*, *Canto* v. *St.* 1.   King, *Orpheus and Eurydice.*   Burns,
>*To Dr. Blacklock.*   Colman, *Love Laughs at Locksmiths*, *Act* i.

Fast and loose.   Shakespeare, *Love's Labour's Lost*, *Act* i. *Sc.* 1.

Give an inch he'll take an ell.
>John Webster, *Sir Thomas Wyatt.*   Hobbes, *Liberty and Necessity*,
>*No.* iii.

Give ruffles to a man who wants a shirt.
>Sorbière (1610—1670), from *The French Anas.*   Tom Brown, *La-
>conics.*   Goldsmith, *The Haunch of Venison.*

God sends meat, and the Devil sends cooks.
>Ray's *Proverbs.*   Garrick, *Epigram on Goldsmith's Retaliation.*

Golden mean.
>Horace, *Book* 2, *Ode* x. 5.   *My mind to me a Kingdom is.*   Massinger,
>*The Great Duke of Florence*, *Act* i. *Sc.* 1.   Pope, *Moral Essays*,
>*Epistle* iii. *l.* 246.

Great wits will jump.

> Sterne, *Tristram Shandy.*   Byrom, *The Nimmers.*

Good wits will jump.

> Cougham, *Camden Soc. Pub. p.* 20.   Duke of Buckingham, *The Chances,* Act v. Sc. 1.

Gray mare will prove the better horse.

> *The Marriage of True Wit and Science.*   Butler, *Hudibras, Pt.* ii. Canto 2, *l.* 698.   Fielding, *The Grub Street Opera,* Act ii. Sc. 4. Prior, *Epilogue to Lucius.*
>
> [Mr. Macaulay thinks that this proverb originated in the preference generally given to the gray mares of Flanders over the finest coach-horses of England.—*History of England, Vol.* i. Ch. 3.]

Hail, fellow, well met.

> Tom Brown, *Amusement,* viii.   Swift, *My Lady's Lamentation.*

He knew what's what.

> Skelton, *Why come ye not to Courte? l.* 1106.   Butler, *Hudibras, Pt.* i. Canto 1, *l.* 149.

He must go that the Devil drives.

> Peele, *Edward I.*   Shakespeare, *All's Well that Ends Well,* Act i. Sc. 3.

He must have a long spoon, that must eat with the Devil.

> Chaucer, *The Squiere's Tale, Pt.* ii. *l.* 256.   Marlowe, *The Jew of Malta,* Act iii. Sc. 5.   Shakespeare, *Two Gentlemen of Verona,* Act iv. Sc. 3.   *Apius and Virginia.*

Honesty is the best policy.

> *Don Quixote, Pt.* ii. Ch. 33.   Byrom, *The Nimmers.*

Ill wind turns none to good.   Tusser, *Moral Reflections on the Wind.*

Ill blows the wind that profits nobody.

> Shakespeare, *Henry VI., Pt.* iii. Act ii. Sc. 5.

Not the ill wind which blows no man good.

> Shakespeare, *Henry IV., Pt.* ii. Act v. Sc. 3.

In spite of my [thy] teeth.

> Middleton, *A Trick to catch the Old One,* Act i. Sc. 2.   Southerne, *Sir Anthony Love,* Act iii. Sc. 1.   Fielding, *Eurydice Hissed.*   Garrick, *The Country Girl,* Act iv. Sc. 3.

It was no chylden's game.   Pilkington, *Tournament of Tottenham,* 1631.

Let the world slide.

> Shakespeare, *The Taming of the Shrew,* Induc. 1.   John Heywood, *Be merry, Friends.*

Let us do or die.

> Beaumont and Fletcher, *The Island Princess,* Act ii. Sc. 4.   Burns, *Bannockburn.*   Campbell, *Gertrude.*

[Scott says "this expression is a kind of common property, being the motto, we believe, of a Scottish family."—*Review of Gertrude, Scott's Misc. Vol.* i. *p.* 153.]

Look a gift horse in the mouth.
>   Rabelais, *Book* i. *Ch.* xi. Butler, *Hudibras, Pt.* i. *Canto* 1, *l.* 490. *Also quoted by* St. Jerome.

Look ere thou leap, see ere thou go.
>   Tusser, *Five Hundred Points of Good Husbandry, Ch.* 57.

Look before you ere you leap.   Butler, *Hudibras, Pt.* ii. *Canto* 2, *l.* 502.

Love me little, love me long.   Marlowe, *Jew of Malta, Act* iv. Herrick.

Lucid interval.
>   Bacon, *Henry VII.* Fuller, *A Pisgah Sight of Palestine, Book* iv. *Ch.* 2. South, *Sermon, Vol.* viii. *p.* 403. Dryden, *MacFlecknoe.* Johnson, *Life of Lyttelton.* Burke, *On the French Revolution.*

Nisi suadeat intervallis.
>   Bracton, *fol.* 1243, *and fol.* 420, *b.*   *Register Original,* 267 *a,* 1270.

Main chance.
>   Shakespeare, *Henry VI., Pt.* ii. *Act* i. *Sc.* 1. Butler, *Hudibras, Pt.* ii. *Canto* 2. Dryden, *Persius, Sat.* vi.

Midnight oil.
>   Gay, *Shepherd and Philosopher.* Shenstone, *Elegy* xi. Cowper, *Retirement.* Lloyd, *On Rhyme.*

Moon is made of green cheese.
>   *Jack Jugler, p.* 46. Rabelais, *Book* i. *Ch.* xi. Butler, *Hudibras, Pt.* ii. *Canto* 3, *l.* 263.

Mother-wit.
>   Spenser, *Faerie Queene, Book* iv. *Canto* x. *St.* 21. Marlowe, *Prol Tamberlaine the Great, Pt.* i. Shakespeare, *Taming of the Shrew, Act* ii. *Sc.* 1.

More the merrier.
>   Title of a *Book of Epigrams,* 1608. Beaumont and Fletcher, *The Scornful Lady, Act* i. *Sc.* 1.   *The Sea Voyage, Act* i. *Sc.* 2.

Neither fish nor flesh, nor good red herring.
>   Sir H. Sheers, *Satyr on the Sea Officers.* Tom Brown, *Æneus Sylvius's Letter.* Dryden, *Epilogue to the Duke of Guise.*

Nine days' wonder.
>   Beaumont and Fletcher, *The Noble Gentleman, Act* iii. *Sc.* 4. Quarles, *Emblems, Book* i. viii.

No better than you should be.
>Beaumont and Fletcher, *The Coxcomb*, Act iv. Sc. 3. Fielding, *The Temple Beau, Sc.* 3.

No love lost between us.
>Goldsmith, *She Stoops to Conquer*, Act iv. Garrick, *Correspondence*, 1759. Fielding, *The Grub Street Opera*, Act i. Sc. 4.

Of two evils the less is always to be chosen.
>Thomas à Kempis, *Imitation of Christ, Book* ii. *Ch.* 12. Hooker's *Polity, Book* v. *Ch.* lxxxi.

Of two evils ⁎ have chose the least. Prior, *Imitation of Horace.*

E duobus malis minimum eligendum.
>Erasmus, *Adages.* Cicero, *De Officiis.*

Of harmes two the lesse is for to cheese.
>Chaucer, *Troilus and Creseide, Book* ii. *l.* 470.

Paradise of fools. Fools' paradise.
>Shakespeare, *Romeo and Juliet*, Act ii. Sc. 4. Milton, *Par. Lost, Book* iii. *l.* 496. Pope, *Dunciad, Book* iii. Fielding, *The Modern Husband*, Act i. Sc. 9. Crabbe, *The Borough, Letter* xii. Quevedo, *Visions*, iv. L'Estrange's *Trans.* Murphy, *All in the Wrong*, Act i.

Picked up his crumbs. Murphy, *The Upholsterer*, Act i.

Plain as a pike-staff.
>Terence in English, 1641. Duke of Buckingham, *Speech in the House of Lords*, 1675. Smollett, *Trans. Gil Blas, Book* xii. *Ch.* 8.

Rhyme nor reason.
>*Pierre Patelin*, quoted by Tyndale (1530). Spenser, *On his Promised Pension.* Peele, *Edward I.* Shakespeare, *As You Like It*, Act iii. Sc. 2. *Merry Wives of Windsor*, Act v. Sc. 5. *Comedy of Errors*, Act ii. Sc. 2.

>[Sir Thomas More advised an author who had sent him his manuscript to read, "to put it in rhyme." Which being done, Sir Thomas said, "Yea, marry, now it is somewhat, for now it is rhyme; before it was neither rhyme nor reason."]

Remedy worse than the disease.
>Bacon, *Of Seditions and Troubles.* Beaumont and Fletcher, *Love's Cure*, Act iii. Sc. 2. Suckling's *Letters, A Dissuasion from Love.* Dryden's *Juvenal, Sat.* xvi. *l.* 32.

Smell a rat.
>Ben Jonson, *Tale of a Tub*, Act iv. Sc. 3. Butler, *Hudibras, Pt.* i. Canto 1, *l.* 281. Farquhar, *Love and a Bottle.*

Spare the rod, and spoil the child.

> Ray's *Proverbs.* Butler, *Hudibras, 1 t.* ii. *Canto* 1, *i.* 844.

Speech is silver, silence is gold.   *A German Proverb.*

Speech is like cloth of Arras, opened and put abroad, whereby the imagery doth appear in figure ; whereas in thoughts they lie but as in packs.

> Plutarch, *Life of Themistocles.* From Bacon's *Essays, On Friendship.*

Spick and span new.

> Ford, *The Lover's Melancholy,* Act i. Sc. 1. Farquhar, *Preface to his Works.*

Set my ten commandments in your face.

> Shakespeare, *Henry VI., Pt.* ii. *Act* i. *Sc.* 3. *Selimus, Emperor of the Turks,* 1594. *Westward Hoe,* 1607. Erasmus, *Apophthegms.*

Strike while the iron is hot.

> John Webster, *Westward Hoe, Act* ii. *Sc.* 1. Farquhar, *The Beaux' Stratagem, Act* iv. *Sc.* 1.

Tell truth, and shame the devil.

> Shakespeare, *Henry IV., Pt.* i. *Act* iii. *Sc.* 1. Swift, *Mary the Cook-maid's Letter.*

The lion is not so fierce as they paint him.

> Herbert, *Jacula Prudentum.* Fuller, *On Expecting Preferment.*

Though I say it that should not say it.

> Beaumont and Fletcher, *Wit at Several Weapons, Act* ii. *Sc.* 2. Fielding, *The Miser, Act* iii. *Sc.* 2. Cibber, *The Rival Fools, Act* ii. *The Fall of British Tyranny, Act* iv. *Sc.* 2.

Through thick and thin.

> Spenser, *Faerie Queene, Book* iii. *Canto* 1, *St.* 17. Middleton, *The Roaring Girl, Act* iv. *Sc.* 2. Kemp, *Nine Days' Wonder.* Butler, *Hudibras, Pt.* i. *Canto* ii. *l.* 369. Dryden, *Absalom and Achitophel, Pt.* ii. *l.* 414. Pope, *Dunciad, Book* ii. Cowper, *John Gilpin.*

To make a virtue of necessity.

> Rabelais, *Book* i. *Ch.* xi. Chaucer, *Knight's Tale, l.* 3044. Shakespeare, *Two Gentlemen of Verona, Act* iv. *Sc.* 2. Dryden, *Palamon and Arcite.*
>
> [In the additions of Hadrianus Junius to the Adages of Erasmus, he remarks (under the head of *Necessitatem edere*), that a very familiar proverb was current among his countrymen, viz. *Necessitatem in virtutem commutare.*]

To see and to be seen.

> Chaucer, *The Prologe of the Wyfe of Bathe, l.* 552. Ben Jonson, *Epithalamion, St.* 3, *l.* 4. Dryden, *Ovid's Art of Love, Book* i. *l.* 109. Goldsmith, *Citizen of the World, Letter* 71.

Turn over a new leaf.
> Middleton, *Anything for a Quiet Life, Act* iii. *Sc.* 3.

Two of a trade seldom agree.
> Ray's *Proverbs.* Gay, *The Old Hen and the Cock.* Murphy, *The Apprentice, Act* iii.

Two strings to his bow.
> Hooker's *Polity, Book* v. *Ch.* lxxx. Butler, *Hudibras, Pt.* iii. *Canto* 1. *l.* 1. Churchill, *The Ghost, Book* iv. Fielding, *Love in Several Masques, Sc.* xiii.

Virtue is her own reward.
> Dryden, *Tyrannic Love, Act* iii. *Sc.* 1.

Virtue is its own reward.
> Prior, *Im. of Horace, Book* iii. *Ode* 2. Gray, *Epistle to Methuen.* Home, *Douglas, Act* iii. *Sc.* 1.

Virtue is to herself the best reward.
> Henry More, *Cupid's Conflict.*

Ipsa quidem Virtus sibimet pulcherrima merces.
> Silius Italicus, *Punica, Lib.* xiii. *l.* 663.

> Wherever God erects a house of prayer,
> The devil always builds a chapel there.
>> De Foe, *The True-Born Englishman, Pt.* i. *l.* 1.

> God never had a church but there, men say,
> The devil a chapel hath raised by some wyles.
> I doubted of this saw, till on a day
> I westward spied great Edinburgh's Saint Gyles.
>> Drummond, *Posthumous Poems.*

No sooner is a temple built to God, but the Devil builds a chapel hard by.
> George Herbert, *Jacula Prudentum.*

Where God hath a temple, the Devil will have a chapel.
> Burton, *Anatomy of Melancholy, Pt.* iii. *Sc.* iv. *M.* 1, *Subs.* 1.

Wrong sow by the ear.
> Ben Jonson, *Every Man in his Humour, Act* ii. *Sc.* 1. Butler, *Hudibras, Pt.* ii. *Canto* 3, *l.* 580. Colman, *Heir-at-Law, Act* i. *Sc.* 1.

Word and a blow.
> Shakespeare, *Romeo and Juliet, Act* iii. *Sc.* 1. Dryden, *Amphitryon. Act* i. *Sc.* 1. Bunyan, *Pilgrim's Progress, Pt.* i.

Parish me no parishes.
> Peele, *The Old Wive's Tale.*

Grace me no grace, nor uncle me no uncle.
> Shakespeare, *Richard II., Act* ii. *Sc.* 3.

Thank me no thanks, and proud me no prouds.
> Shakespeare, *Romeo and Juliet, Act* iii. *Sc.* 5.

Vow me no vows.
> Beaumont and Fletcher, *Wit without Money, Act* iv. *Sc.* 4.

Plot me no plots.
> Beaumont and Fletcher, *The Knight of the Burning Pestle, Act* ii. *Sc.* 5.

O me no O's.   Ben Jonson, *The Case is Altered, Act* v. *Sc.* 1.

Cause me no causes.
> Massinger, *A new Way to pay Old Debts, Act* i. *Sc.* 3.

Virgin me no virgins.   *Ibid. Act* iii. *Sc.* 2

End me no ends.   *Ibid. Act* v. *Sc.* 1

Front me no fronts.   Ford, *The Lady's Trial, Act* ii. *Sc.* 1.

Midas me no Midas.   Dryden, *The Wild Gallant, Act* ii. *Sc.* 1.

Madam me no Madam.   *Ibid. Act* ii. *Sc.* 2.

Petition me no petitions.   Fielding, *Tom Thumb, Act* i. *Sc.* 2

Map me no maps.   Fielding, *Rape upon Rape. Act* i. *Sc.* 5.

But me no buts.
> *Ibid. Act* ii. *Sc.* 2.   Aaron Hill, *Snake in the Grass, Sc.* 1.

Play me no plays.   Foote, *The Knight, Act* ii.

Clerk me no clerks.   Scott, *Ivanhoe, Ch.* 20.

Diamond me no diamonds ! prize me no prizes.
> Tennyson, *Idyls of the King, Elaine.*

INDEX

AARON's serpent, 160.
Abashed the devil stood, 110.
Abdiel, the seraph, 111.
Abide with me, 290.
Abodes, blessed, 159.
Abou Ben Adhem, 283.
Abound, sin and death, 254.
Above all Greek, 170.
    all Roman fame, 170.
    any Greek, 134.
    that which is written, 326.
    the reach, 235.
    the smoke and stir, 116.
    the vulgar flight, 199.
Abra was ready, 142.
Abraham's bosom, 41.
Abridgment of all that is pleasant in
    man, 203.
Abroad, schoolmaster is, 290.
Absence makes the heart grow fonder,
    289.
Absent from him I roam, 254.
    in body, 326.
Absolute rule, 109.
    sway, 141.
    the knave is, 69.
Abstracts and brief chronicles, 64.
Abundance of the heart, 323.
Abuse, stumbling on, 47.
Abusing the king's English, 12.
Abyss, into this wild, 107.
Abyssinian maid, 252.
Academe, grove of, 115.
Academes that nourish all the world,
    18.
Accept a miracle, 157.
Accepted time, 326.
Accident of an accident, 216.
Accidents by flood and field, 73.
Accommodated, excellent to be, 36.
Accomplishment of verse, 245.
According to the appearance, 325.
    to knowledge, 325.
Account, beggarly, 48.
    sent to my, 63.
Accoutred as I was, 49.

Accuse not nature, **113.**
Achilles' tomb, 282.
    wrath, 175.
Aching void, 214.
Acorns, oaks from little, 228.
Acquaintance, auld, 225.
    upon better, 12.
Acre of his neighbour's corn, 232.
Acres, over whose, walked, 32.
Act and know, does both, 130.
    to the swelling, 52.
    well your part, 161.
Acting of a dreadful thing, 49.
    when off the stage, 203.
Action and counteraction, 205.
    faithful in, 164.
    how like an angel in, 64.
    in the tented field, 73.
    is transitory, 232.
    lose the name of, 66.
    makes fine the, 92.
    no noble, done, 342.
    of the tiger, 37.
    pious, 65.
    suit the, to the word, 66.
    vice dignified by, 47.
Actions, of my living, 44.
    of the just, 95.
    of the last age, 98.
    virtuous, 137.
Actor, condemn not the, 14.
    well-graced, 32.
Actors, these our, 11.
Acts being seven ages, 25.
    illustrious, 101.
    little nameless, 235.
    nobly, does well, 154.
    our angels are, 87.
    the best who thinks most, 297.
    those graceful, 113.
    unremembered, 235.
Ada! sole daughter, 271.
Adage, cat i' the, 54.
Adam dolve, and Eve span, 335.
    the goodliest man, 109.
    the offending, 37.

M*

Behold now is the accepted time, 326.
  our home, 277.
  the child, 160.
  the upright, 313.
Beholding heaven, 262.
Being, God a necessary, 138.
Being's end and aim, 161.
Belated peasant, 104.
Belerium, old, 173.
Belgium's capital, 272.
Belial, sons of, 103.
Belief, prospect of, 52.
Bell, as a sullen, 36.
  church-going, 215.
  each matin, 250.
  silence that dreadful, 74.
  strikes one, 154.
Belle, 't is vain to be a, 190.
Bellman, fatal, 55.
Bells jangled out of tune, 66.
  ring out wild, 301.
  those evening, 265.
  those village, 212.
Belly, God send thee good ale, 6.
  whose God is their, 326.
  with good capon lin'd, 25.
Belongings, thy, 13.
Beloved face on earth, 278.
  from pole to pole, 249.
Bemus'd in beer, 167.
Ben Adhem's name led, 283.
Bench of heedless bishops, 191.
Bend a knotted oak, 151.
Bendemeer's stream, 262.
Bends the gallant mast, 266.
Beneath the churchyard stone, 293.
  the good how far, 193.
  the milk-white thorn, 227.
  the rule of men, 290.
Benedick the married man, 16.
Benediction, perpetual, 244.
Benighted, feels awhile, 264.
  walks, 117.
Bent him o'er the dead, 275.
  o'er her babe, 217.
  top of my, 67.
Bequeathed by bleeding sire, 276.
Bereaves of their bad influence, 243.
Berkeley, coxcombs vanquish, 197.
  every virtue under heaven to, 169.
  said there was no matter, 283.
Bermoothes, still vexed, 10.

Berries harsh and crude, 119.
  two lovely, 20.
Berth was of the wombe of morning dew, 7.
Beside a human door, 23e.
  the springs of Dove, 233.
  the still waters, 313.
Besier seemed than he was, 1.
Besotted base ingratitude, 118.
Besprent with April dew, 174.
Best administered, is best, 161.
  are but shadows, 20.
  can paint them, 172.
  companions, 201.
  days, 41.
  good man, 139.
  laid schemes, 224.
  men moulded out of faults, 15.
  of prophets, 283.
  of what we do, 238.
  portion of a good man's life, 235.
  riches, 201.
Best state, man at his, 314.
  who does the, 154.
Bestial, what remains is, 75.
Bestride the narrow world, 49.
Beteem the winds of heaven, 60.
Betray, nature never did, 236.
Betrayed for gold, 258.
Better be d—d, 217.
  be with the dead, 56.
  bettered expectation, 16.
  days, have seen, 48.
  fifty years of Europe, 299.
  for worse, 328.
  grace, does it with a, 28.
  had they ne'er been born, 261.
  horse, gray mare the, 345.
  is a dinner of herbs, 316.
  late than never, 4, 343.
  part of valour, 35.
  reck the rede, 225.
  spared a better man, 35.
  than his dog, 298.
  than one of the wicked, 32.
  than you should be, 347.
  thou shouldest not vow, 318.
  to be lowly born, 42.
  to have loved and lost, 300.
  to hunt in fields, 133.
  to reign in hell, 102.
  to sink beneath the shock, 27(
Better-half, 9.
Bettering of my mind, 10.

Can imagination boast, 181.
it be that this is all, 275.
such things be, 56.
this be death, 173.
Candid friend, 230.
where we can, be, 158.
Candied tongue, 66.
Candle, hold a, 179.
match with the, 157.
not worth the, 93.
out, out, brief, 58.
throws his beams, 23.
to the sun, 157.
to thy merit, 184.
Candles are all out, 54.
night's, are burnt out, 47.
Cane, clouded, 167.
Canker and the grief are mine, 280.
galls the infants, 61.
Cankers of a calm world, 35.
Cannon by our sides, 70.
Cannon's mouth, in the, 25.
Cannot come to good, 60.
tell how the truth may be, 257.
Canon 'gainst self-slaughter, 60.
Canonized bones, 62.
Canopied by the blue sky, 279.
Canopy, most excellent, 64.
under the, 44.
Cap of youth, 69.
whiter than the driven snow, 191.
Capability and godlike reason, 69.
Capitol, betrayed the, 140
drizzled blood upon the, 50.
Captain, a choleric word, in the, 14.
Christ, 32.
ill, attending, 79.
jewels in the carcanet, 79.
Captive, all ears took, 27.
good, attending, 79.
Capulets, tomb of the, 207.
Carcanet, jewels in the, 79.
Carcase is, eagles will gather, 324.
of Robinson Crusoe, 198.
Card, reason the, 160.
speak by the, 69.
Cards, old age of, 163.
Care adds a nail, 217.
beyond to-day, 192.
fig for, 83.
for nobody, 208.
his useful, was ever nigh, 187.
in heaven, is there, 6.

Care is an enemy to life, 28.
keeps his watch, 47.
life of, 285.
o' the main chance, 128.
ravelled sleave of, 55.
that buy it with much, 21.
will kill a cat, 90.
wrinkled, 120.
Cared not to be at all, 104.
Career of his humour, 16.
Careless childhood, 192.
of the single life, 300.
shoe-string, 95.
their merits, 201.
Cares beguiled by sports, 200.
dividing, 231.
eating, 120.
fret thy soul with, 7.
heart of a man is depress'd with, 177.
nobler loves and, 243.
that infest the day, 306.
Caress, wooing the, 280.
Carnage is his daughter, 240.
Carnegie, John, lais heer, 143.
Carpet knights, 340.
Carrying three insides, 230.
Cart, ballads from a, 135.
Carved not a line, 287.
with figures strange, 250.
Carver's brain, 250.
Casca, the envious, 51.
Case, lady is in the, 178.
reason of the, 138.
Cassius, help me, 49.
lean and hungry, 49.
Cast bread upon the waters, 319.
of thought, 66.
off his friends, 203.
set my life upon a, 42.
Casting a dim religious light, 121.
with unpurchased hand, 307.
Castle, a man's house is his, 5.
hath a pleasant seat, 53.
Castled crag of Drachenfels, 272.
Rhine, 305.
Castles in the air, 343.
in the clouds, 182.
Casuists doubt, 163.
Cat, care will kill a, 90.
endow a college or a, 164.
i' the adage, 54.
monstrous tail our, has, 144.
will mew, 70.
Catalogue, go for men in the, 55.

N

Death, way to dusty, 58.
　　what should it know of? 232.
　　what we fear of, 15.
　　where is thy sting? 173, 326.
　　which nature never made, 155.
　　whose portal we call, 306.
　　wonderful is, 284.
Death-bed is a detector, 155.
Death-beds, ask, 154.
Death's pale flag, 48.
Debt, a double, to pay, 202.
　　to nature, 92.
Debtor to his profession, 81.
Debts, he that dies pays all, 11.
Decalogue, men who can hear the, 243.
Decay, gradations of, 187.
　　muddy vesture of, 23.
　　unperceiv'd, 186.
Decays and glimmerings, 125.
Decay's effacing fingers, 275.
Deceit in gorgeous palace, 47.
Deceitful shine, 265.
　　woman, 140.
Deceivers, men were, ever, 16.
December, roses in, 269.
　　when men wed, 26.
Decencies, content to dwell in, 163.
　　that daily flow, 113.
Decency, right meet of, 191.
Decent limbs composed, 174.
Decently and in order, 326.
Decide, who shall, 163.
Decider of dusty titles, 89.
Decision, valley of, 322.
Declined into the vale of years, 76.
Dedes, gentil, 2.
Dedicate his beauty, 45.
Dedicated to closeness, 10.
Deed, attempt, and not the, 55.
　　dignified by the doer, 27.
　　go with it, unless the, 57.
　　of dreadful note, 56.
　　so shines a good, 23.
　　without a name, 57.
Deeds are men, 188.
　　are the sons of heaven, 188.
　　blessings wait on virtuous, 151.
　　devilish, excused, 109.
　　foul, will rise, 61.
　　live in, 297.
　　means to do ill, 31.
　　not words, 343.
Deep and gloomy wood, 235.
　　as a well, 47.

Deep as first love, 299.
　　bottom of the, 33.
　　calleth unto deep, 314.
　　damnation of his taking-off, 54.
　　danger on the, 289.
　　embosom'd in the, 200.
　　for his hearers, 202.
　　home is on the, 256.
　　in the lowest, 108.
　　malice to conceal, 108.
　　on his front engraven, 105.
　　sleep falleth on men, 312.
　　spirits from the vasty, 34.
　　tipple in the, 96.
　　versed in books, 115.
　　yet clear, 98.
Deeper than all speech, 302.
　　than plummet, 11.
Deep-mouthed welcome, 281.
Deer a shade, 255.
　　let the strucken, 67.
　　mice and such small, 71.
Defamed by every charlatan, 301.
Defect, cause of this, 64.
　　fine by, 163.
Defective comes by cause, 64.
Defence, admit of no, 137.
　　against injury, 5.
Defend me from my friends, 338.
　　your departed friend, 134.
Defer, madness to, 154.
　　till to-morrow, 151.
Defiance in their eye, 200.
Deficiencies of the present day, 187.
Deformed, unfinished, 40.
Degenerate days, 175.
Degree, all in the, 160.
　　ours of low, 203.
　　of woe, bliss must gain by, 190.
Degrees, fine by, 143.
　　grows up by, 88.
　　ill habits gather by, 135.
　　of kin, 129.
　　scorning the base, 49.
Deified by our own spirits, 235.
Deity offended, 225.
Dejection do we sink as low, 234.
Delay, amorous, 109.
　　each dull, 201.
　　law's, 65.
Delays are dangerous, 136.
　　have dangerous ends, 136.
Deliberates, woman that, 148.
Deliberation sat, 105.
Delicate creatures, call these, ours, 76.

O

Play with similes, 233.
Played at bo-peep, 94.
 familiar with his hoary locks, 288.
Player, life 's a poor, 58.
Players, men and women merely, 25.
Playmates, I have had, 249.
Plays round the head, 161.
 such fantastic tricks, 14.
Plaything, some livelier, 160.
Plea so tainted, 22.
Plead lament and sue, 259.
 like angels, 54.
Pleasant hast thou been, 311.
 in their lives, 311.
 in thy morning, 225.
 sure to see one's name in print, 269.
 thought, we meet thee like a, 233.
 to severe, 134.
 to think on, 94.
 vices, 72.
Pleasantness, ways of, 316.
Please, certainty to, 231.
 surest to, 203.
 to live, 186.
Pleased, I would do what I, 5.
 not the million, 64.
 to the last, 158.
 with a rattle, 160.
 with novelty, 209.
 with this bauble, 160.
Pleasing anxious being, 195.
 dreadful thought, 148.
 dreams and slumbers, 259.
 memory of all he stole, 171.
 shade, 192.
Pleasure after pain, sweet is, 120
 all hope, 136.
 at the helm, 194.
 ease, content, 161.
 frown at, 156.
 howe'er disguised, 186.
 in poetic pains, 210.
 in the pathless woods, 274.
 little, in the house, 217.
 man of, is a man of pains, 156.
 mixed reason with, 202.
 never to blend our, 235.
 no, where no profit grows, 26.
 of being cheated, 129.
 of love is in loving, 285.
 of the game, 143.
 praise all his, 152.

Pleasure, reason's whole, 161.
 she was bent, on, 214.
 shock of, 288.
 sure in being mad, 136.
 take, some to, 163.
 to be drunk, 184.
 to the spectators, 294.
 treads upon the heels of, 151.
Pleasure-dome, stately, 252.
Pleasures and palaces, 288.
 are like poppies, 224.
 doubling his, 231.
 in the vale of pain, 261.
 of the present day, 185.
 pretty, might me move, 8.
 prove, all the, 9.
Pledge our sacred honours, 219.
Pledged to religion, 267.
Pleiades, sweet influences of, 313.
Plentiful lack of wit, 64.
Plenty as blackberries, 34.
 o'er a smiling land, 195.
Plighted clouds, 117.
Plodders, continual, 17.
Plot me no plots, 350.
 this blessed, this earth, 31.
Plough deep, 185.
 following his, 235.
Ploughman homeward plods, 194.
Ploughshare o'er creation, 156.
 stern Ruin's, 224.
Ploughshares, swords into, 320.
Pluck bright honour, 33.
 from the memory, 58.
 out the heart, 67.
 up drowned honour, 33.
 your berries, 119.
Plucked his gown, 201.
Plume, of amber snuff-box, 167.
Plummet, deeper than a, 11.
Plump Jack, banish, 34.
Plunged in, accoutred as I was, 49.
Plurisy of people, 89.
Pocket, pick a, 141.
Poem, himself to be a true, 123.
 round and perfect, 304.
Poet, and the lover, 20.
 naturalist, and historian, 187.
 once lov'd, 174.
 soaring in the high reason of his fancies, 123.
 they had no, 176.
Poet's brain, 84.
 darling, 233.
 eye in frenzy rolling, 20.

Smoothing the raven down, 117.
Smooth-lipped shell, 246.
Smoothness, torrent's, 256.
Smote the chord of Self, 298.
Snail, creeping like, 25.
Snails, feet like, 94.
Snake, scotch'd the, 56.
   wounded, 165.
Snapper-up of trifles, 29.
Snatch a fearful joy, 192.
   a grace, 164.
Sneer, laughing Devil in his, 277.
   solemn, 273.
   teach the rest to, 168.
Snore upon the flint, 78.
Snow, December, 31.
   fall in the river, 224.
   mockery king of, 32.
   pure as, 66.
   rosebuds fill'd with, 82.
Snow-flakes fall, 284.
Snow-white ram, 246.
Snuff, only took, 203.
Snuff'd out by an article, 283.
Snug, as a bug, 185.
   little Island, 249.
So much to do, 301.
Soap, invisible, 292.
Soar, wont to, 201.
Sober certainty, 117.
   go to bed, 87.
   in your diet, 178.
   second thoughts, 138.
Soberness, truth and, 325.
Society became my glittering bride, 245.
   one polished horde, 283.
   solitude is best, 113.
   where none intrudes, 274.
Socrates whom well inspir'd, 115.
Soft answer, 316.
   as her clime, 279.
   as young, 155.
   black eye, with its, 262.
   eyes looked love, 272.
   impeachment, 222.
   is the music, 238.
   is the strain, 166.
   the zephyr blows, 194.
   voices die, 285.
Softening into shade, 182.
Softly bodied forth, 274.
Soil, grows on mortal, 119.
   not in this, 118.
   thus leave thee, native, 114.

Soil where first they trod, 286.
Soiled with all ignoble use, 301.
Soils, rich, are often to be weeded, 81.
Solar walk or milky way, 158.
Sold him a bargain, 18.
   to slavery, 73.
Soldat heureux, 261.
Solder of society, 180.
Soldier among sovereigns, 213.
   and afeard, 57.
   armed with resolution, 146.
   ask the brave, 263.
   be abroad, 290.
   blasphemy in the, 13.
   full of strange oaths, 25.
   himself have been a, 32.
   more than, 262.
   successful, 261.
Soldier's pole is fallen, 10.
   virtue, 77.
Soldiers bore dead bodies, 33.
   substance of ten thousand, 42.
Sole judge of truth, 160.
   of her foot, 310.
Solemn acts of devotion, 218.
   creed, sapping a, 273.
   fop, 213.
   sneer, 273.
   temples, 11.
Sole-sitting by the shores, 233.
Solid flesh would melt, 60.
   ground of nature, 238.
   happiness we prize, 185.
   men of Boston, 221.
   pudding, 171.
Solitary shriek, 281.
Solitude, bird in the, 278.
   bliss of, 234.
   he makes a, 277.
   how passing sweet is, 213.
   is sweet, 213.
   least alone in, 273.
   sometimes is best society, 113
   where are the charms, 215.
Some are born great, 48.
   asked me where, 94.
   natural tears, 114.
   said, John, print it, 137.
   say no evil thing, 117.
   sipping punch, 237.
   three ages since, 18.
Something after death, 65.
   better than his dog, 298.
   dangerous in me, 70.
   in a flying horse, 237.

Take any shape but that, 56.
  away the sword, 291.
  each man's censure, 61.
  heed lest he fall, 326.
  her up tenderly, 291.
  him for all in all, 60.
  mine ease in mine inn, 34.
  my walks abroad, 149.
  no note of time, 154.
  O boatman, thrice thy fee, 288.
  O, take those lips away, 15.
  physic, pomp, 71.
  some savage woman, 298.
  the good the gods provide thee, 131.
  the prison'd soul, 117.
  time enough, 179.
  ye each a shell, 173.
Takin' notes, chiel's amang ye, 224.
Taking, what a, was he in, 13.
Tale, a plain, shall put you down, 34.
  adorn a, 186.
  an honest, speeds best, 41.
  as 't was said to me, 257.
  every, condemns me, 42.
  every shepherd tells his, 120.
  hope tells a flattering, 286.
  in every thing, 242.
  't is an old, 258.
  of Troy divine, 121.
  round unvarnish'd, 73.
  school-boy's, 271.
  so sad, so tender, 191.
  tellen his, untrewe, 2.
  that I relate, 214.
  that is told, 314.
  thereby hangs a, 24, 27,
  told by an idiot, 58.
  told his soft, 146.
  twice-told, tedious as a, 30.
  unfold, I could a, 62.
  which holdeth children, 8.
  who shall telle a, 2.
Tales, ancient, say true, 270.
  play truant at his, 18.
  that to me were so dear, 289.
Talk, greatly wise to, 154.
  how he will, 140.
  is of bullocks, 322.
  of dreams, 46.
  spent an hour's, withal, 8.
  to conceal the mind, 157.
  too much, 132.
  who never think, 143.
Talking age, for, 200.

Talking, he will be, 16.
Talks as familiarly of roaring lions, 30.
Tall oaks from little acorns, 228.
  so, to reach the pole, 150.
Tally, score and, 39.
Tam was glorious, 224.
Tame villatic fowl, 116.
Tamer of the human breast, 192.
Tangled web we weave, 259.
Tangles of Neæra's hair, 119.
Tapers swim before my sight, 172.
  to the sun, 223.
Tara's halls, harp through, 263.
Tarnished gold, black with, 229.
Tarry at Jericho, 311.
Task is smoothly done, 118.
Task-master's eye, 122.
Taste, little more, 146.
  never, who always drink, 143.
  not ; handle not, 327.
  of death but once, 50.
  of sweetness, 34.
  of your quality, 64.
  whose mortal, 101.
Tastes of men, 197.
Tatter'd clothes, through, 72.
  ensign down, tear her, 307.
Tatters, tear a passion to, 66.
Taught by that power, 203.
  by time, 176.
  her dazzling fence, 118.
  highly fed and lowly, 27.
  men must be, 166.
  the wheedling arts, 177.
  us how to die, 176.
  us how to live, 176.
Tax for being eminent, 146.
  not you, you elements, 71.
Tea, sometimes take, 167.
Teach him how to live, 207.
  in song, what they, 285.
  me to feel another's woe, 173.
  souls to souls can never, 302.
  the rest to sneer, 168.
  the young idea, 181.
  thee safety, 30.
  you more of man, 242.
Teaching by examples, 152.
Team of little atomies, 45.
Tear a passion to tatters, 106.
  betwixt a smile and, 274.
  drying up a single, 283.
  each other's eyes, 150.
  every woe can claim, 276.

R

R*

Whirlwind, rides in the, 148.
Whirlwind's roar, 200.
   sway, sweeping, 194.
Whisper, full well the busy, 202.
   hark! they, 173.
   of the throne, 301.
   well-bred, 210.
Whispered it to the woods, 112.
Whispering I will ne'er consent, consented, 280.
   lovers made, 200.
   tongues can poison truth, 250.
   wind, bay'd the, 201.
   with white lips, 272.
Whispers of each other's watch, 38.
   of fancy, 187.
   the o'erfraught heart, 57.
Whist, the wild waves, 10.
Whistle, blackbird to, 126.
   clear as a, 179.
   her off, 75.
   paid dear for his, 185.
   them back, 203.
   wel ywette, 2.
Whistled for want of thought, 132.
Whistles, pipes and, 25.
Whistling aloud, 180.
   of a name, 162.
White as heaven, 88.
   black and gray, 108.
   fire laden, 285.
   radiance, 285.
   so very white, 230.
   wench's black eye, 47.
   whose red and, 28.
   will have its black, 340.
Whited sepulchres, 324.
White-handed Hope, 117.
Whiteness of his soul, 272.
Whitens in the sun, 262.
Whiter than driven snow, 199.
Whitewash'd wall, 202.
Whither thou goest I will go, 311.
Who a sermon flies, 92.
   as they sung, 117.
   breaks a butterfly, 168.
   breathes must suffer, 142.
   builds a church to God, 164.
   but must laugh, 168.
   can hold a fire, 31.
   dares do more, 53.
   does the best, 154.
   fears to speak, 294.
   love too much, 175.
   loves a garden, 211.

Who ne'er knew joy, 174.
   never mentions hell, 164.
   o'er the herd, 260.
   overcomes by force, 103.
   shall decide, 163.
   shall telle, 2.
   steals my purse, 75.
   sweeps a room, 92.
   think not God at all, 115.
   think too little, 132.
   would not be a boy, 271.
   would not weep, 168.
Whoe'er she be, 97.
   was edified, 210.
Whole duty of man, 320.
   head is sick, 320.
   heart is faint, 320.
   of life to live, 254.
   world kin, makes the, 44.
Wholesome, nights are, 59.
Whom begot, by, 174.
   the gods love, 282.
Whooping, out of all, 25.
Whores were burnt alive, 143.
Whose dog are you, 173.
Why a wherefore, every, 126.
   all this toil, 241.
   and wherefore, 38.
   did you kick me, 227.
   don't the men propose, 289.
   is plain as way to parish church, 24.
   man of morals, 99.
   should every creature drink, 99.
   so pale and wan, 93.
Wicked cease from troubling, 31.
   flee when no man pursueth, 318.
   forsake his way, 321.
   little better than one of the, 32.
   no peace unto the, 321.
   or charitable, intents, 62.
   something, this way comes, 57.
Wickedness, method in, 88.
   tents of, 314.
Wickliffe's dust shall spread abroad, 240.
Wide as a church door, 47.
   was his parish, 2.
Widow of fifty, 222.
   some undone, 87.
Widow's heart to sing, 312.
Widowed wife, 261.
Wielded at will, 115.
Wife and children impediments to great enterprises, 80.